MW01223127

Air Force Roles and Missions:
A History

Warren A. Trest

AIR FORCE HISTORY AND MUSEUMS PROGRAM
Washington, D.C.
1998

Library of Congress Cataloging in Publication Data

Trest, Warren A.
　　Air Force Roles and Missions: A History/ Warren A. Trest.
　　　　p.　　cm.

　　Includes bibliographical references.

　　　　1. United States. Air Force—History. I. Title.
　　　　UG633 .T74 1998
　　　　358.4'00973—ddc21

　　　　　　　　　　　　　　　　　　98-44142
　　　　　　　　　　　　　　　　　　CIP

For sale by the U.S. Government Printing Office
Superintendent of Documents, Mail Stop: SSOP, Washington, DC 20402-9328
ISBN 0-16-049778-7

ACKNOWLEDGEMENTS

This book is a progeny of kindred minds. Its central themes were handed down from the men and women who made air power history via those who wrote it. To friends and colleagues sharing both the burden and the birthright, I am forever grateful.

I must acknowledge above all others the support, guidance, and encouragement given to me by Herman S. Wolk, Senior Historian of the Air Force History Support Office. As true friend and "book doctor," he had the leading role in shepharding this volume through the minefields of bureaucratic review to its final objective. I owe a special tribute to the late Col. John F. Shiner, former Deputy Chief, Office of Air Force History (AFCHO), whose loyalty and devotion to Air Force history nurtured my enthusiasm for doing this study. Mrs. Tammy Rodriguez, Editorial Assistant at the Air Force Historical Research Agency (AFHRA), Maxwell AFB, Alabama, deserves much of the credit for timely completion of the manuscript.

I am indebted to Dr. Richard P. Hallion, the Air Force Historian, for the vision he brought to the Air Force historical program. I also wish to thank two former Chiefs of Air Force History, Dr. Richard H. Kohn and Maj. Gen. John W. Huston, for their friendship and support. Other key supporters were Col. Richard S. Rauschkolb, Commander of the AFHRA; Col. John Schlight, formerly Deputy Chief AFCHO; Col. Elliott Converse, formerly Commander AFHRA; and Mr. Lloyd H. Cornett, Jr., formerly AFHRA Director.

Other colleagues in the Office of Air Force History who helped with planning, researching, or writing the volume include Jacob Neufeld, Bernie Nalty, Dan Mortensen, Wayne Thompson, George Watson, William C. Heimdahl, Walton Moody, and Richard I. Wolf.

Within AFHRA, I am indebted to the late Richard B. Morse and his successor, Lynn Gamma, for the superb research assistance provided by the Archives Branch. I wish to thank in particular Joseph Caver, Archie Difante, Essie G. Roberts, Ann D. Webb, and Sandi Smith for their archival support. Hugh Ahmann, Faye Davis, and Pauline Tubbs of the Oral History Program and James S. Howard also assisted. Edward Russell, Edward Cummings, Peggy Selman, and TSgt. Douglas Bagley helped in countless ways. Two former editorial assistants, Lois Wagner and Yolanda Alston, gave unstintingly of their time and expertise.

A special salute is due to Gen. Jacob E. Smart (USAF Ret.); Brig. Gen. Edwin H. Simmons, Director of Marine Corps History; I. B. Holley, Jr.; Robert F. Futrell; Edward J. Marolda; Col. Phillip S. Meilinger; Col. Dennis M. Drew; David MacIsaac; and James Titus for their support.

FOREWORD

The twentieth century witnessed the emergence of three-dimensionality in war: surface forces now became prey for attackers operating above and below the earth and its oceans. The aerial weapon, prophesied for centuries, became a reality, as did air power projection forces. This insightful book by Warren A. Trest traces the doctrinal underpinnings of the modern United States Air Force, the world's only global air force. We—the men and women who serve in the Air Force, but also our fellow airmen in America's other military services—are the heirs and beneficiaries of a long heritage of doctrinal development and military thought.

Our predecessors pursued a vision of airborne global reach and power that often put them at odds with those who could not break free of the confines of conventional thought and lock-step traditionalism. Fortunately, they had the courage of their convictions and the faith in their vision to continue to pursue the goal of global air power despite such resistance. Today, America is a genuine aerospace power, and that pioneering vision dating to the days of the Wright brothers, has expanded to encompass operations in space and between the mediums of air and space. As we approach the new millenium, it is well to ponder the lessons and the history of how a small group of truly gifted airmen transformed their nation's military establishment, and, in so doing, the world around them.

Dr. Richard P. Hallion
The Air Force Historian

CONTENTS

PREFACE

When this volume was conceived, no official definition of roles and missions existed. As the volume progressed, however, intense scrutiny of the subject emanating from the Goldwater-Nichols Reorganization Act of 1986 and the winding down of the Cold War stimulated an active interest in formal terminology. The search for formal definition added to the roles and missions lore, but it did not affect this work. The popular military usage and meaning of roles and missions long ago became commonplace in official documents and military literature.

Accepted usage dating from the post-World War II period established the synonymity of the phrase roles and missions with the legally framed functions of the armed forces, as set forth by executive order pursuant to the National Security Act of 1947. Approved by President Harry S. Truman on July 28, 1947, that landmark legislation created the United States Air Force and unified the armed forces under the National Military Establishment and later the Department of Defense (DOD). The Act failed, however, to end bitter interservice feuding over roles and missions which began with the birth of military aviation in 1907 and intensified over the intervening years.

The phrase roles and missions actually predates the National Security Act of 1947-appearing often in unification debates which preceded the law's enactment. Documents from this period show military officers using the phrase frequently when expressing their views on the functions of the armed forces. While defending the Army Air Forces before congressional hearings in March 1947, Gen. Carl A. Spaatz challenged a Navy proposal to delineate the services' functions in pending legislation-arguing persuasively that the President "prescribes the roles and missions of the Army, Navy, and Air Forces." When Dwight D. Eisenhower and other top Army generals agreed, Spaatz's argument prevailed.[1]

President Truman issued Executive Order 9877 prescribing the functions of the armed forces on the same day he approved the National Security Act of 1947. While Truman's order and subsequent DOD directives do not use the phrase roles and missions, frequent reference to it was made in meetings at Key West, Florida, and Newport, Rhode Island, in 1948 to clarify the functions of the Army, Navy, and Air Force. The following year, the expression arose frequently during the controversial B–36 hearings. The issue of roles and missions monopolized impassioned debates over close air support and other air power concerns during the Korean War.

By the time President Eisenhower signed the Defense Reorganization Act of 1958, roles and missions replaced the term "functions" in current military literature. In the April 1956 issue of *The Air Power Historian*, a retired Air Force general described an unsatisfactory "roles and missions garden" in which military aviation had grown between the wars.[2] The next year, a book celebrating the

Roles and Missions

Golden Anniversary of Air Force history (1907-1957) devoted a chapter to roles and missions.[3] Although still formally undefined, the phrase was a familiar part of the military vocabulary.

Five years later, the authors of a compact study entitled *A History of Marine Corps Roles and Missions, 1776-1962*, predicted a problem in analyzing historical issues without a formal point of reference. The authors traced the roots of contemporary roles and missions terminology to the wording of the National Security Act of 1947 and Executive Order 9877. Breaking down the phrase into "roles" and "missions", they acknowledged general acceptance of the terms as "substitutes for the official language" found in the 1947 documents. They concluded that Marine Corps "roles" and "missions" were synonymous with "duties" and "responsibilities," as derived from the parent documents and as defined in the *Unified Action Armed Forces, the Dictionary of United States Terms for Joint Usage*, and related Marine Corps manuals.[4]

Through American involvement in the Vietnam War and for nearly two decades afterward, roles and missions remained the preferred terminology to describe the functions of the armed forces. A 1987 collection of basic documents on roles and missions compiled by the Office of Air Force History bears this out. This study broadened the accepted meaning to include the "primary functions and responsibilities" of the three services. It drew a parallel between roles and functions as broad areas of authority, and between missions and responsibilities as more specific categories of tasking, when it stated:

> Roles and missions is a term which encompasses the broad range of service activities and specified tasks within several categories. Within the overall role of air operations, the Army Air Forces (AAF) after World War II possessed four main missions: strategic bombardment, support of ground operations, air defense, and air transport.[5]

As seen in the cited historical studies, military scholars seeking formal definitions have generally viewed roles and missions as separate terms rather than as a phrase. Moreover, recent studies found that roles, missions, and functions were often used interchangeably to "refer to a single concept." This is supported by a paper presented at an April 1990 Air Force doctrine conference at Maxwell AFB, Alabama, and by an article titled "Roles, Missions, and Functions: Terms of Debate" in the summer 1994 issue of *Joint Forces Quarterly*.[6]

An Air Staff officer who briefed at the 1990 doctrine conference announced that the phrase roles and missions was "inappropriate" and had been replaced in joint usage by "roles and functions." The officer referenced formal definitions from a "Report on Roles and Functions of the Armed Forces" by outgoing Chairman of the Joint Chiefs of Staff (JCS), Adm. William J. Crowe, Jr., in September 1989. The Crowe report was required by Title 10, United States Code,

as amended by the Goldwater-Nichols Reorganization Act of 1986, which directed that the JCS Chairman report periodically to the Secretary of Defense on recommended changes to the assigned functions of the armed forces to achieve
maximum effectiveness. The law required reports every three years or upon
request of the President or the Secretary of Defense.[7]

In an appended list of definitions, the Crowe report defined roles as "The
broad and enduring purposes for which a Service was established." Missions
were "Those tasks assigned to a Unified or Specified command by the President
or the Secretary of Defense." Functions were "Those more specific responsibilities assigned to a Service through executive action which permit it to successfully fulfill its legally established role." The document further defined primary
and collateral functions:

> a. Primary Function. Those principal responsibilities assigned
> to a Service within its role for which it may allocate fiscal
> resources and generate force structure. More than one Service
> can be assigned a primary function for each mode of warfare.
>
> b. Collateral function. Those responsibilities assigned to a
> Service to support another Service or Defense Agency's pri-
> mary function. A Service may not generate force structure
> based solely upon a collateral function. More than one Service
> can be assigned a collateral function.[8]

General Colin L. Powell (Crowe's successor as JCS Chairman) filed another report in February 1993. Although the title of Powell's report, "Roles,
Missions, and Functions of the Armed Forces of the United States," was different from Crowe's, the terminology was essentially the same. General Powell
agreed that "roles, missions, and functions" were often used interchangeably, but
he sought to clarify "the important distinctions" between them. "Simply stated,"
he said, "the primary function of the Service is to provide forces organized,
trained and equipped to perform a role-to be employed by a CINC [a combatant
commander] in the accomplishment of a mission."[9] The authors of the 1994 *Joint
Forces Quarterly* article amplified this in their explanation of roles: "Essentially,
roles established each service's primacy in its respective form or arena of war:
land, sea, or air."[10]

All of the sources cited trace the roots of modern roles and missions to the
postwar unification debates and the National Security Act of 1947. Primed by
the stormy rise of American air power between the wars, however, the taproot of
the roles and missions debate goes much deeper. "Before the appearance of air
power, there was no reason to debate roles and missions," an Air Force scholar
recently wrote. The water's edge provided a natural boundary for fixing lines of
responsibility between land and sea warfare. The advent of air power, which

Roles and Missions

"overlapped both the land and the sea," blurred these lines and altered the roles and missions landscape forevermore. Thus, the air power odyssey that leads to modern roles and missions of the armed forces began with the birth of military aviation in 1907.[11] There the story begins.

Orville and Wilbur Wright's efforts to sell their airplane to the U.S. government were initially ignored.

CHAPTER I

ORIGINS: EMERGING MILITARY AVIATION ROLES

Prior to World War I, the potential military roles of the airplane aroused interest in few Americans. The nation did not have a large standing army, and annual appropriations could not support large expenditures for unproven weapons or equipment. From 1902-1912, the Regular Army had an average troop strength of about 75,000 officers and enlisted men while annual appropriations averaged $93.6 million. The Army dealt with insurrection in the Philippines and minor hemispheric problems close to home at the turn of the century, but no major threats to U.S. security portended a need for increases in troop levels or substantially larger defense appropriations.[1] While the U.S. economy enjoyed moderate prosperity, the American public did not condone unbridled government spending. The War Department learned this in 1903 when Congress and the public criticized the Signal Corps for secretly spending $50,000 to finance the unsuccessful flying experiments of Samuel P. Langley, noted scientist and Secretary of the Smithsonian Institution.[2]

The conservative mood of the nation and the Army's reluctance to appear wasteful may explain the government's failure to capitalize on the military potential of the Wright airplane until almost four years after the epic flight at Kitty Hawk, North Carolina, on December 17, 1903. Foreign governments sent representatives to negotiate with the Wrights in 1904 and 1905, but Orville and Wilbur preferred to give their own government first claim on their invention. Twice in 1905, the brothers offered their airplane to the U.S. government for "scouting and carrying messages in time of war." On both occasions, the Board of Ordnance and Fortifications, the office responsible for approving new military weaponry, was indifferent to the Wright brothers' proposal. On the other hand, British, French, and German governments expressed avid interest in the military potential of the airplane. Experimental flying activity in other industrialized countries after the success at Kitty Hawk forced the Wrights to negotiate abroad to keep up with looming international competition.[3] In February 1907, the brothers informed Lt. Thomas E. Selfridge that they did not intend to sell sole use of their invention to any foreign government and were concerned about the advantages it offered to other countries. "A lead gained is easily retained; but a stern chase is a long one," the Wrights wrote. "It is this lead that we propose to sell."[4] By the time the United States took a serious interest in the military role of the airplane, European powers had a head start in experimenting with military aeronautics that endured beyond World War I.

The military roles of American aviation would have been even further behind had President Theodore Roosevelt not interceded in the spring of 1907. Roosevelt directed his Secretary of War, William H. Taft, to reopen negotiations with the Wright brothers after prominent members of the Aero Club of America

Roles and Missions

Brigadier General James Allen served as Chief Signal Officer and Air Chief for the U.S. Army from 1906 to 1913. *(NASM photo)*

informed him of the War Department's rebuff. After ordering the Board of Ordnance and Fortification to resume negotiations with the Wright Company in March 1907, the Secretary of War told the Signal Corps to investigate possible military uses of the airplane. On August 1, 1907, the Chief Signal Officer of the Army, Brig. Gen. James Allen, established an Aeronautical Division in his organization. He placed Capt. Charles DeF. Chandler in charge of "all matters pertaining to military ballooning, air machines, and all kindred subjects." This measured official response (the Division consisted of Chandler and two enlisted men) heralded the beginning of Army aviation in the United States. The Board of Ordnance and Fortification completed a contract with the Wrights in February 1908, and the Signal Corps accepted its first Wright Flyer on August 2, 1909.[5]

Experimenting With New Roles

In his annual report on the Signal Corps for fiscal year 1910, General Allen suggested another explanation for the United States' failure to jump into military aviation. "It is frequently said that the United States, due to its isolated position, is not likely to become involved in war," Allen wrote, "and therefore the most economical procedure in aerial navigation is to wait until other nations have determined upon the types best suited to military purposes, thus shifting the expense of experiment and development to other nations." The fallacy of this argument was that it gave other industrialized powers an edge in experience and technology, not a prudent position if the United States were to go to war against them. The Army had been unprepared for war with Spain in 1898, Allen recalled, and the result was "great confusion, expense, and unnecessary loss of life." It would be even more difficult to create an effective aviation capability after war was declared than other specialties, the General said, because "the demands of this new service will undoubtedly require higher qualities of training, judgement and courage than any other branch of military service."[6]

The tenor of the Chief Signal Officer's 1910 report reflected the difference that three years had made in the War Department's outlook toward the military potential of the airplane. In October 1907, after establishing the Aeronautical Division, General Allen told the Board of Ordnance and Fortification that he did not think the Wrights' flying machine was suitable for military purposes. He recommended against its purchase. Allen suggested that the only possible military aviation roles would be for "observation and reconnaissance, or as an offensive weapon to drop explosives." He thought dirigible balloons were better suited for these roles.[7] Two months later, he reversed his position and agreed to purchase the airplane after interviewing Wilbur Wright and being briefed on aviation progress abroad by Maj. George O. Squier, who had recently toured foreign air centers.[8]

In July 1909, Orville Wright piloted his airplane to Alexandria, Virginia, to convince U.S. military leaders of the viability of his creation. *(NASM photo)*

Reporting to Congress in December 1910, Secretary of War J.M. Dickinson recounted his observation of air activity in Berlin and Paris and echoed the Chief Signal Officer's concern for the lag in Army aviation. He cited the report of an American officer's observation of French Army maneuvers of 1910:

> The most striking thing was the aeroplane. The biplanes and monoplanes were everywhere. They traveled with great speed and must have seen everything except where the troops could be concealed in the woods. An efficient aeroplane corps is certainly indispensable to an Army.[9]

Roles and Missions

While the Secretary of War did not request specific air appropriations, he did ask Congress to provide the Signal Corps "a reasonable number of the better type of machines for instruction purposes and for field work."[10] In March 1911, Congress passed the first appropriations bill authorizing funds specifically for Army aeronautics. Money for the first Wright flyer came from a special fund. The small amount the Signal Corps spent on flying operations came out of its general maintenance funds. The 1911 appropriations authorized $125,000, with $50,000 paid immediately. The Signal Corps ordered five new planes at about $5,000 each. In October, the Army retired its first and only airplane as a museum piece.[11]

The 1911 appropriations enabled the Signal Corps to build a flying school at College Park, Maryland, and expand flying training to other parts of the country, Hawaii, and the Philippines. This heightened activity encouraged modest advances in military aviation and created more opportunities for innovative officers to experiment with aviation roles. Army field service regulations in 1910 stated that balloons or flying machines would be used for reconnaissance, but early pilots were eager to try other purposes for the airplane. Among the experiments were primitive attempts at bombing and firing machine guns from airplanes. Signal Corps members attempted visual and telegraphic communications from the air.[12]

Hangars were filled with airplanes at the flying school at College Park, Maryland, in 1911. *(NASM photo)*

The prospect of dropping explosives from the air appealed to imaginative minds even before balloons were used during the Civil War for aerial observation and to direct cannon fire. While armies of industrialized Europe had experimented with aerial bombing, American officers were not idle. At the San Francisco air meet in January 1911, Lt. Myron S. Crissy, Army Coast Artillery, performed the first recorded live bombing from an American plane. Crissy reported that "everyone seemed afraid of the live bombs." He told the *San Francisco Examiner* that he hoped the experiment would encourage the War

Department to explore aerial bombing as an adjunct to coastal artillery. One observer expressed his belief that the danger was greater from the airplane falling on one's head than from the bombs.[13] In October 1911, Lt. Thomas DeWitt Milling tested the experimental Scott bombsight at College Park, but the tests were inconclusive and overshadowed by news of the first airplane bombing mission flown in war. In November, during fighting between Italian and Turkish armies in Libya, Italian Army Lt. Guilio Gavott flew the historic mission, dropping four small projectiles on Turkish adversaries in the Libyan desert.[14]

Most of the Army's early practice and experimental work in airplanes was concentrated at College Park, Maryland, except when the planes flew south for the winter. Instructors at College Park primarily trained pilots, but they found time to experiment with new equipment and participate in maneuvers with ground troops in 1912. In June, Captain Chandler, commander of the school, fired the Lewis machine gun from an airplane for the first time. The Lewis gun, invented by Col. Isaac N. Lewis, became standard armament on Allied planes during World War I. The College Park instructors also conducted successful tests with wireless radios and aerial photography. Lieutenants Henry H. Arnold and Milling and others successfully adjusted artillery fire from airplanes in tests at Fort Riley, Kansas, in November. By the end of 1912, College Park had 14 flying officers, 39 enlisted men, and 9 airplanes.[15] Progress was being made, but times were still hard for the Army. In 1912, when the Signal Corps sought a larger appropriation for aviation, Army Chief of Staff Maj. Gen. Leonard Wood lowered the estimate to $100,000 with a penciled remark that what the Army needed was "rifles and cannon, not airplanes."[16]

Despite his early experience with aircraft, Lt. Benjamin Foulois, shown here piloting a Wright Flyer in 1911, argued against the creation of a separate air arm. *(NASM photo)*

Roles and Missions

Emergence of Naval Aviation and Joint Policy

The Navy's early development of aviation roles paralleled the Army's. As an official Navy observer at the first demonstration of the Army's Wright flyer at Fort Myer, Virginia, in September 1908, Lt. George C. Sweet reported on the advantages of operating airplanes from naval vessels for scouting and observation missions. His report, which reached the Secretary of the Navy in December, recommended purchasing a few flying machines so the Navy could develop special features for naval uses. The acting Secretary of the Navy disapproved a subsequent request by the Bureau of Equipment for two airplanes. In November 1909, Lieutenant Sweet became the first Navy officer to fly when he was taken aloft by Army Lt. Frank P. Lahm at College Park. Sweet and other Navy enthusiasts continued to argue for planes for fleet reconnaissance.[17]

Experimental flights by two civilian aviators stimulated official interest in naval aviation. In November 1910, Curtiss exhibition pilot Eugene Ely launched his airplane from a platform on the bow of the anchored USS *Birmingham* in the first successful takeoff from a naval vessel. Two months later, Ely landed atop a platform on the armored cruiser USS *Pennsylvania* at anchor in San Francisco Bay, then took off and returned to nearby Selfridge Field. In January 1911, Glenn H. Curtiss made the first successful seaplane flight at San Diego. The following month, assisted by Lt. T.G. Ellyson, the first naval officer to undergo flight training, Curtiss flew the seaplane to San Diego from North Island, taxied alongside the USS *Pennsylvania*, and was hoisted aboard by a crane. Curtiss also trained a few Army officers, and this joint training activity eventually led to both services establishing facilities at North Island. In May 1912, the Navy ordered the first Marine Corps officer to flight training, marking the birth of Marine Corps aviation. Navy and Marine Corps pilots experimented with new roles after their training. As with the Army, the primary purpose of naval aviation before World War I was observation and reconnaissance.[18]

During this early period, the Navy had less money than the Army to develop military aviation. In 1911, when appropriations gave Army aeronautics its initial $125,000, the Navy Bureau of Navigation received only $25,000 to develop its flying program. The disparity widened over the next three years, as appropriations for Army flying grew to $500,000, while the Navy received only $50,000. Both services' air appropriations surged dramatically after the outbreak of hostilities in Europe in 1914, especially after the United States declared war in April 1917. For fiscal years 1916 through 1918, the Army's air appropriations soared to $71 million while the Navy's portion was $66 million. America's expenditures on military aviation before 1914 were insignificant compared to other industrialized countries such as France, Germany, and Russia, which had spent millions.[19]

With both services adapting military aeronautics to their own needs, the War and Navy Departments saw advantages in establishing formal channels to cooperate in areas of mutual interest. In November 1916, the Secretaries of War and

Navy agreed to appoint a joint board to develop policy for a lighter than air service. Before the officers completed this initial tasking, the secretaries sent War College studies on defense against air attack to the joint board with instructions to examine "the whole subject of local cooperation of naval and military forces in time of war and preparation for war."[20]

The Board's report, submitted for approval in March 1917, observed that the services should develop plans and regulations for the joint development, organization, and operation of their aeronautical services, rather than develop each air service separately "within delimited exact areas of responsibility." This report made the first formal statement of roles and missions responsibilities between the two air arms. "While the operations of the aeronautical service of the Navy will be principally over the water, and those of the Army principally over the land," the officers reported, "it may be said that a war with a first class power will find the two services constantly operating together." For coastal defense, the coastline and adjacent waters formed a theater of joint operations in which naval aviation had precedence prior to an invasion, and Army aviation had precedence after the invaders came ashore. In either event, the services had supplemental responsibilities in support of each other.[21]

The Army's primary air defense role was to defend harbors, cities, and other vital targets ashore. This included the general defense of naval installations, although the Navy was responsible for local defense with antiaircraft guns. Additionally, the Army was responsible for aircraft operating in conjunction with the mobile Army and providing fire control for coastal defenses. Navy aircraft operated primarily in support of the fleet. Those operating from shore bases under the commandants of Naval Districts or advanced bases flew scouting missions and reported movements of enemy forces at sea, attacked enemy forces at sea, and assisted the Army when enemy operations were in the immediate vicinity of the coast. The Board recommended close cooperation in developing aircraft for both services and in formulating joint plans to use air forces. Significantly, decisions governing the employment of air forces were to be based on "the general military situation rather than the special situations of either the Army or Navy." Supplemental forces came under the control of the service which had primary responsibility.[22]

This report, submitted on the eve of America's entry into World War I, served as joint policy until after the armistice in November 1918. The joint board continued to meet intermittently to consider questions involving the use of airfields, a plan for aerial coastal defense, the sale of aeronautical equipment abroad, and the Army and Navy policy relating to aircraft. Army and Navy officers also served as members of the National Advisory Committee for Aeronautics (NACA) after Congress formed this independent committee in 1915 to oversee the scientific study of manned flight.

Other temporary boards and committees sprang up during the war. The Aircraft Production Board was in charge of reviewing aircraft requirements and contracting for aircraft and air materiel production. The Joint Army-Navy Technical Board was established to standardize the types and designs of planes to be procured. Both boards were at the center of the raging controversy over the government's failure to meet its extravagant promises for aircraft production during the war.[23]

Army Air Roles on the Eve of War

The outbreak of World War I was pivotal in the development of roles and missions by belligerent national air forces. Official U.S. views on aviation, however, progressed slowly until after the United States entered the war in April 1917. Army field regulations issued in 1914 made minor revisions to the assigned roles of aircraft, specifying that military aircraft were to be employed at the direction of the commander to whose forces they were assigned. There were also provisions for the aero squadron commander to exercise immediate control over assigned aircraft. While reconnaissance remained the primary function of the Army's planes, the regulations broadened the definition to include "strategic and tactical reconnaissance and the observation of artillery fire." Other changes reflected the success of experiments with weapons and communications devices. The regulations stated that airplanes were "used to prevent hostile aerial reconnaissance" and that reconnoiterers would report results via "radiotelegraphy, signals, and the dropping of messages."[24]

Congressional concern over the status of military aviation rose slightly before America's entry into the war. In February 1913, Democratic Representative James Hay of West Virginia sponsored a bill to separate Army air activities from the Signal Corps. Hay wanted to replace the Aeronautical Division with an Army organization equal to other branches, directly under the Chief of Staff. Nearly unanimous opposition killed the Hay bill. Even ardent supporters of military aviation thought Hay's proposal was radical for the time. Lieutenant Benjamin D. Foulois, one of the Army's first air pioneers, said it was too early for a separate air arm. Lieutenant Arnold was among the trained pilots who opposed the bill. Captain William L. Mitchell, who had not yet learned to fly, said he thought Hay's proposal was premature, but he predicted that the fledgling air arm would someday outgrow its parent organization.

The only Signal Corps officer who testified in favor of the Hay Bill was Capt. Paul Beck, who had participated in early flying experiments. Beck cited four military purposes of the airplane (reconnaissance, fire control for artillery, aggressive action, and occasional transportation) and thought existing arrangements under the Signal Corps stifled growth in each of these roles. Faced with overwhelming opposing testimony, the Hay Bill died without leaving the House Committee on Military Affairs.[25]

A substitute bill drafted by the same committee became law on July 18, 1914. It retained some features of the defeated legislation, including statutory recognition for Army aviation and provisions for more pilots and extra pay. The new law created an Aviation Section in the Signal Corps and charged it with operating or supervising the operation of all military aircraft and with training officers and enlisted men in military aviation. The Aviation Section was authorized 60 officers and 260 enlisted men. Acknowledging that other pressing needs of the service had limited the development of an adequate air fleet and training of personnel, Secretary of War Lindley M. Garrison said the new statute placed the War Department "in a position to push the development of this most important branch of the military establishment."[26]

The limited improvements accruing from the new legislation proved inadequate in light of dawning events. Amid growing awareness of the U.S. lag in aeronautics, the lame performance of the 1st Aero Squadron during the punitive expedition into Mexico in 1916 exposed Army aviation's shortcomings to greater scrutiny. This same year, the aerial exploits of the Lafayette Escadrille and other combatant squadrons were front-page news. From the spring into the winter of 1915, when revolutionary activity in Mexico raised tensions along the Texas border, planes from the 1st Aero Squadron flew scouting missions out of Brownsville, Texas. Mechanical problems marred their effectiveness.

Problems with the few operational airplanes became more critical in March 1916, when the Squadron, commanded by Capt. Benjamin D. Foulois, took eight planes to Columbus, New Mexico, to support Gen. John J. Pershing's incursion into Mexico. President Woodrow Wilson ordered Pershing and a force of 15,000 to pursue Pancho Villa after he raided Columbus and killed several citizens. The rugged mountains and extreme weather of northern Mexico took their toll on Foulois' battered planes. By April 20, he was left with only two of the eight planes the Squadron had flown into Mexico. Compounding problems, these aircraft were declared "unsafe for further field conditions." When the press reported the pilots' concerns with the unsafe planes and flying conditions, the War Department investigated the complainers rather than the complaints. Foulois and his officers denied the statements attributed to them.[27]

Discontent among Army aviators over Signal Corps' administration of aviation was spreading. Only one officer spoke in favor of a separate corps during the 1913 congressional hearings. Secretary of War Newton D. Baker's testimony in similar hearings in the spring of 1916 revealed widespread dissatisfaction among flying officers. Baker acknowledged some "tall talk" among younger officers about the need for a separate service for aviation, but he admitted administrative problems had created impatience among the "young and eager" flyers. He said he intended to correct these problems.

Rather than create a separate corps, the Secretary said he planned a shake-up in the Aviation Section which included assigning a new leader, "a man of mature yet severe judgment and trained disciplinary ideas to restrain the exuberance of youth." The War Department censured Brig. Gen. George Scriven, who had replaced Allen as Chief Signal Officer in 1913, then removed Col. Samuel

Roles and Missions

Reber as Chief of the Aviation Section, reprimanding him for poor judgment and administration. Captain William Mitchell temporarily headed the section until Lt. Col. George O. Squier returned from overseas-where he was serving as a military attache in London and official observer of the war front-to replace Reber. As Squier's deputy, Mitchell began pilot training in his off-duty time in the fall of 1916.[28]

In August 1916, Congress provided more than $13 million in emergency funding to help overcome the deficit in military aeronautics. More importantly, Congress passed the National Defense Act of 1916 to strengthen the capabilities of the Army to cope with a possible national emergency. President Wilson had been successful in keeping the United States out of the war in Europe, but Germany's unrestrained submarine warfare made the oceans unsafe for American vessels and increased the danger of widening the conflict. Called "the most comprehensive legislation the American Congress had yet passed,"[29] the 1916 act authorized a peacetime regular army of 175,000, organized into 65 regiments of infantry, 25 of cavalry, 21 of artillery, and more.

For the air arm, the act enlarged the Aviation Section of the Signal Corps and authorized eight aero squadrons. The reserve corps of officers and enlisted men bolstered the regular forces. The Army had only begun to build toward these authorized force levels when the United States declared war against Germany in the spring of 1917.[30] As the United States entered the war, the air arm had increased to only 65 officers, of whom 35 were pilots; 1,087 enlisted men; and 55 trainer airplanes.[31]

The increased authorizations had no immediate effect on the roles of the air arm, but aerial warfare in Europe made the War Department aware that military aviation roles were changing. Secretary of War Baker said in 1916 that the war in Europe had shown that the air arm could no longer be regarded merely as "an auxiliary service for scouting, carrying messages, and to a limited extent in controlling gunfire." The war demonstrated that airplanes could serve as offensive weapons, and Baker said that the United States would probably add armed planes and other fighting capabilities to its air fleet. He implied that the Army would create a new organization to command the fighting air arm, but the Air Service was not established until after the United States declared war.[32]

Air Service Roles in World War I

Because of their late entry into World War I, American airmen did not contribute much to the development of the air weapon's roles in combat. Neither the Army nor the Navy possessed combat aircraft, and both services relied on the Allies for planes to equip their front-line units. The Allies helped train American pilots and provided an orientation to aerial warfare. Some U.S. pilots flew with Allied squadrons, but logistical and training delays kept Air Service squadrons from deploying in support of the American Expeditionary Force (AEF) until

April 1918. By that time, after nearly four years of hostilities, Allied airmen had proved the airplane to be a useful weapon in roles beyond reconnaissance and observation.[33] The belligerents introduced many new roles for air warfare before U.S. squadrons reached the front. They flew missions definable as close air support of ground troops, interdiction, bombardment, counterair operations, artillery fire control or adjustment, observation, and reconnaissance.[34]

After four years, a rudimentary doctrine for the employment of air forces emerged. The basic principles of an air campaign were identified to include air superiority, unity of command, concentration of force, economy of force, surprise, mobility, and exploitation. These principles mirrored land and sea warfare doctrine. American airmen learned that control of the air was a prerequisite for successful air campaigns and that a sustained offensive in the air and on the ground was the best means to achieve victory. Air-to-air combat evolved from the defense of observation and reconnaissance airplanes, which had supported the land battle since 1914 when the first aerial photographs were taken of enemy positions.[35] Antiaircraft weapons appeared early in the war to defend against air attacks. Suppression of these weapons became part of the air campaign.[36]

During the course of the war, airmen witnessed the mercurial nature of air superiority when the victor was unable to exploit his advantage, giving opposing forces time to recover with new aircraft and tactics. From the appearance of Fokker pursuit airplanes, which gained temporary mastery for the Germans in 1915, the battle for air superiority seesawed as each side introduced higher performance aircraft and experimented with new tactics. By concentrating their pursuit forces at the front, the Central Powers controlled the skies for a few days at Verdun. The Allies countered, all but denying use of the air in the battle of the Somme. Through a vigorous rebuilding program, the Central Powers retook the air initiative in 1917, only to lose it again when U.S. airmen joined the Allies.[37]

No appreciable close air support missions were flown before the battles at Verdun and the Somme, when large formations of DH–4s and Nieuports flew bombing and strafing raids to support troops in battle. Thereafter, air superiority operations focused on preventing or facilitating tactical strike operations as well as on reconnaissance. The first assault airplanes designed specifically for attacks against troops and equipment did not appear at the front until 1917 when the Germans introduced the armored Junkers aircraft. Other European powers responded with their own versions, and both sides flew support missions through the rest of the war.[38]

Airmen found ground commanders' attitudes toward aviation generally favorable when missions were flown in direct, visible support of the battlefield, but they were skeptical when air campaigns occurred behind enemy lines. Relatively little interdiction was flown because Marshal Ferdinand Foch, the Allied Commander in Chief, and Gen. Douglas Haig, Commander of the British Army in France, insisted on using every available plane in immediate support of their armies. General John J. Pershing, AEF Commander, shared this view when

Roles and Missions

U.S. forces entered the war. When air operations were concentrated behind enemy lines, frontline troops complained they did not receive adequate support, not understanding the valuable assistance the air arm provided by keeping enemy supplies and reinforcements from reaching the frontlines.[39]

The Germans introduced rudimentary strategic bombardment in early 1915 when they sent Zeppelins on long-range night bombing missions over Paris and London. The French and British flew limited short distance bombing missions in the first months of the war against targets close to the front lines. More disruptive than damaging, the German raids provoked counter long-range bombardment by Great Britain's Royal Naval Air Service, which temporarily extended its air defense responsibilities to include attacking enemy Zeppelin bases from forward air fields in France. In mid-1917, Germany's long-range operations grew to include large-scale Gotha bomber raids against London. While the bombers did not inflict heavy damage, they often completed their missions despite numerically superior British defense forces. The Gotha raids prompted the British to divert a large number of guns and planes from the front lines in defense. Although this weakened the front, it forced the British to concentrate their fighter squadrons and maximize their defense effort, making it more costly and difficult for German bombers to get through. With time, the British planned and executed a counter air strategy. In the fall of 1917, the British decided on an offensive air policy. In 1918, they created the Royal Air Force (RAF) to execute the policy. While the offensive air policy never got under way, it influenced the thinking of American airmen about the future role of independent air forces.[40]

Among Allied officers consulted on the employment of combat air forces, Maj. Gen. Hugh M. Trenchard, the Commander of Great Britain's Royal Flying Corps in France, was a primary influence on Air Service thinking. As an aeronautical observer in the spring of 1917, Maj. William Mitchell visited Trenchard, observed his operations, and listened to his views on air combat. One of the leading airpower thinkers of his time, Trenchard was among the first to embrace the principles of unified command and offensive air warfare. His views centered on battlefield dynamics and were oriented toward tactical employment of air forces more than strategic bombardment. Trenchard taught that air resources should not be fragmented by spreading them among ground organizations but that they should be unified under a single commander who could concentrate them when and where they were needed to support tactical objectives. This guiding principle, which used the inherent flexibility of airpower to its best advantage, helped shape Air Service thinking on the command and employment of air forces after the war.[41]

In the early summer of 1917, Mitchell was the senior aviator in France. He became General Pershing's chief aviation officer when the AEF Commander arrived in Paris in June. Mitchell urged the AEF to adopt a dual program of tactical operations to support ground forces and independent strategic operations. Mitchell's proposal called for tactical units to be attached directly to field armies

William (Billy) Mitchell, rapidly promoted to the rank of Brigadier General, stands before his plane. *(NASM photo)*

for observation, artillery fire control, air defense, and ground attack. Strategical groups of bomber and pursuit formations would be organized separately to wage an offensive campaign "against enemy aircraft and enemy material, at a distance from the actual line." According to Mitchell, the strategic mission was analogous to the one "the independent cavalry used to have, as distinguished from divisional cavalry." He believed that no decision could be reached on the ground before a decision was won in the air.

Support for Mitchell's study came from a number of AEF flying officers, including Maj. Raynal C. Bolling who led a special mission to Europe in the summer of 1917 to gather technical information from the Allies. Impressed by the emphasis that the French, British, and Italians placed on strategic bombardment, Bolling suggested that sustained, large-scale bombardment might deter-

Major Raynal Bolling became an early supporter of Billy Mitchell's plan to split air power resources into strategic and tactical forces in World War I. *(NASM photo)*

mine the war's outcome. Although not convinced of the necessity to implement Mitchell's proposals, General Pershing appointed both Mitchell and Bolling to a board of officers charged with examining Mitchell's proposals and recommending a course for Army aviation in the conflict. The board endorsed Mitchell's proposed organization and concept of operations, including separate strategic air forces.[42]

Unmoved by the board's endorsement, General Pershing remained dubious of the need for a separate strategical air program. He was aware of the political appeal that strategic bombardment against Germany had for the Allies, but his primary concern was that his ground forces have adequate aerial support. In July 1917, he approved an AEF organization to provide aviation units to support only ground forces. Undaunted, Mitchell resubmitted his proposal in August asking for both tactical and strategical programs for the AEF. His persistence was rewarded when the AEF finally adopted his ideas in October 1917.[43]

While Pershing needed Mitchell to prepare the air forces for combat, he wanted more mature leadership at higher headquarters. In September, he appointed Brig. Gen. William L. Kenly as Chief of Air Service, AEF. Kenly was a field artillery officer who expressed his interest in flying by taking the aviation course at San Diego before shipping overseas. Mitchell thought well of Kenly, whose appointment freed him to concentrate on preparing Air Service units for the front. In October, Mitchell became Commander of the Air Service in the Zone of the Advance and began "all arrangements for putting our troops on the line." Among other activities, Mitchell and his staff prepared manuals "describing the duties of pursuit, observation, and bombardment aviation."[44]

Mitchell also drew up general principles for the employment of aviation which were later described as "probably the Air Service's first formal statement of doctrine."[45] He introduced the principles with a declaration that the Air Service was an offensive arm of the Army, and, as such, its function was to help other arms in their appointed mission. "Alone it cannot bring about a decision," he wrote. Reflecting his earlier ideas on the organization of military aviation, Mitchell divided air employment into two general classes, tactical and strategical. Tactical aviation included observation, pursuit, and tactical bombardment formations to assist troops in combat. Mitchell delineated between tactical bombardment and strategical missions. Tactical bombardment was carried out within 25,000 yards of the front lines, basically the outer limits of long-range artillery. Strategical missions were flown at greater than 25,000 yards from friendly forces.

The mission of strategical aviation was independent, and its role entirely offensive. Strategical forces included pursuit squadrons to fight enemy aircraft, day bombardment squadrons, and night bombardment squadrons. The objective of day bombing was to force hostile aircraft to rise and fight by striking aerodromes, conduct long-distance reconnaissance, and attack personnel and material. Night bombardment squadrons destroyed enemy elements and lines of communication.[46]

The compatible team of Kenly-Mitchell faced its demise with the arrival of Brig. Gen. Benjamin Foulois to take over the Air Service in November. Pershing put Foulois in command, but he was not pleased by Washington's interference. A career aviator, Foulois was more reserved than Mitchell. His inadequate support of Pershing's Mexican border campaign against Pancho Villa did not commend him to the General. Relations between Foulois and Mitchell began badly and worsened daily. Feuding between the two officers so angered Pershing that he nearly fired both. Instead, shortly after Air Service squadrons entered combat on the western front in May 1918, Pershing replaced Foulois with Brig. Gen. Mason Patrick, a distinguished officer and classmate of Pershing's who confessed to having "never before seen an airplane, save casually." Foulois became second in command under Patrick. Mitchell remained in command of air combat at the front.[47]

General Pershing confided to General Trenchard that he put this regular army officer in command of the Air Service because Army aviators had "a visionary faith in three-dimensional warfare" that did not conform to reality or "the teachings of West Point." Trenchard considered Pershing "too Army-minded."[48] Particularly irksome to Pershing was the emphasis Foulois and his staff gave to strategic bombardment. When he became Air Service Chief in November, Foulois approved a plan by Lt. Col. Edgar S. Gorrell for an independent AEF bombardment program, including "round the clock bombing." Foulois then appointed Gorrell to head strategic aviation in the AEF's Zone of Advance, a position he held for only a few weeks, probably because of friction with Mitchell. While there, however, Gorrell coordinated the AEF's strategic planning with General Trenchard whose government ordered him to establish an independent bombardment force near Nancy to bomb German industrial centers. It was unclear whether American and French units would join Trenchard's strategic bombardment offensive planned for the spring of 1919, but Trenchard later said

Roles and Missions

Mitchell probably would have commanded the Allied Independent Air Force had the war lasted a few months longer. Meanwhile, in the summer of 1918, partly because of strong feelings against the independence associated with it, the name of strategical aviation in the AEF was changed to "GHQ Air Service Reserve."[49]

Upon deploying to the front in the spring of 1918, most Air Service squadrons were under Mitchell's command in the Toul sector-one of the quiet frontal areas. The squadrons flew in support of I Corps forces commanded by Maj. Gen. Hunter Liggett, a seasoned field commander whom Mitchell praised as "one of the ablest soldiers" he had ever met.[50] That Liggett shared his "views on the importance of air power" added flavor to the relationship. "Liggett and Mitchell made a perfect ground-air-team," a biographer wrote, "a model of co-operation for a later war."[51] With insufficient U.S. divisions in France in the spring of 1918 to form an American army, pressure built for Pershing to disperse fresh American troops among the depleted ranks of Allied units. Pershing resisted merging his troops with the Allied armies, proposing instead to field an American army to fight beside the French and the British as soon as the U.S. buildup permitted. The deteriorating Allied situation in late 1917 and early 1918, however, required that some AEF divisions join the fighting before enough trained Americans were on hand to form a national army.[52]

Hoping to defeat the forces aligned against them before the American army was ready, the Central Powers took the offensive on all fronts. In the east, Russian armies collapsed before the German onslaught in the fall of 1917, followed closely by the Austrian rout of the Italians to the south. British and French armies drew from their waning resources to aid the Italians, and the collapse of Russia released additional German divisions for the Western Front. Thus reinforced, Gen. Erich Ludendorff began his offensive in March 1918, driving deep into France toward Amiens. General Pershing had no recourse but to volunteer American units to strengthen critical seams in the front lines to help stem Ludendorff's advance.[53]

To repair the loose operational coordination among Allied armies, the coalition governments appointed Marshal Ferdinand Foch as Supreme Allied Commander in Chief in April 1918. In his new role, Foch wielded unified command over the various national armies fighting on the Western Front. In July, Foch gave Pershing tactical control of a sector in the Chateau-Thierry region, with only one division assigned. Eight U.S. divisions remaining in the French Corps area joined in counteroffensives against the Marne and Ameins salients in July and August. In the battle at Chateau-Thierry in July, air squadrons flying support for the American division learned a costly lesson. Air units were decimated when employed piecemeal against numerically superior German forces flying the latest Fokker D–7 pursuit planes. Although Mitchell was not at Chateau-Thierry, he saw Trenchard's views on the need to concentrate air forces to achieve aerial superiority confirmed. The losses helped Mitchell convince Pershing and Allied commanders of the need to mass air power offensively during the American advance at St. Mihiel.[54]

General Foch approved the organization of the American First Army, to be formed in August and assigned to a sector extending north of St. Mihiel. He also approved plans for an American offensive against the St. Mihiel salient, a bastion projecting from the Hindenburg Line. This area was of great value to the Germans and was resistant to serious assaults earlier in the war. Reducing the salient would prevent the enemy from interrupting traffic on the Paris-Nancy railroad and would free the railroad north through St. Mihiel to Verdun. The Allies needed to gain control of the salient between the Meuse and the Argonne forest before they could initiate a successful offensive against the enemy's communications. The Allies planned to use the combined armies in a converging action extending battle lines eastward to the Meuse. Supported by the French offensive to his left, Pershing directed the First Army in the historic assault at St. Mihiel.[55]

Assigned as Chief of Air Service, First Army, Colonel Mitchell was responsibile for the air phase of the battle. Borrowing air units from the British, French, and Italians, Mitchell amassed the largest combat air force yet assembled-a multinational force of nearly 1,500 pursuit, bomber, assault, and observation aircraft. To plan and direct the air offensive, Mitchell gathered a staff from the participating air forces. The pursuit squadrons quickly gained control of the air space over the advancing American soldiers, while the bombers and assault planes kept the enemy on the defensive by sustained strikes against vital rear areas. As a result, friendly warplanes operated almost unopposed over the battle area as American ground forces completed their objective with few losses in just four days, from September 12 to 16. Pershing praised Mitchell's "organization and control of the tremendous concentration of air forces" which enabled the First Army to reduce the salient, free from interference by hostile air forces.[56] Mitchell's example of unified direction of combined air forces by a single commander set a precedent for future wars.

After the victory at St. Mihiel, the U.S. Army regrouped for an extended campaign against a vital line extending from the Argonne forest to the Meuse. While still supporting troops fighting in the St. Mihiel salient, friendly air units played an important role in supporting the American buildup in the new assault area. General Pershing recalled that "the movement of the immense number of troops and the amount of supplies involved in the Meuse-Argonne battle, over the few roads available, and confined entirely to the hours of darkness, was one of the most delicate and difficult problems of the war."[57] The situation was made more difficult by the large number of enemy air forces drawn to the area by the attack on St. Mihiel. Air Service squadrons had to shield the massive troop movement from these enemy forces. "To assure the essential secrecy was a serious problem for the Air Service," General Patrick explained. "The troop movements had to be screened from enemy aerial observation, yet it was desired that no great increase in our own aerial activity should give to the enemy an indication of our battle plans."[58]

Roles and Missions

The Meuse-Argonne offensive, which lasted from September 26 until the Armistice on November 11, was waged on a much wider front against fixed enemy positions-requiring that Pershing divide his forces into two armies to tighten the span of control over frontal units and strategic reserves. Supporting air forces were divided accordingly, but they remained under the central direction of Mitchell, who rose from the St. Mihiel victory to the rank of brigadier general. The French withdrawal of three-quarters of the planes they had put at Mitchell's disposal at St. Mihiel left him with a smaller force for the Meuse-Argonne offensive. Still, Mitchell applied the same successful principles of air warfare.[59]

As their experience grew, Mitchell and his flyers became adept at countering the tactics of opposing forces and reduced their own losses while increasing those of the enemy. The principles of mass and tactical surprise were inherent to the tactics that Mitchell employed to carry out successful day bombardment missions. Heavy losses from daylight raids forced both the Allies and the Central Powers toward night bombardment. Knowing that bombardment missions drew enemy pursuit airplanes to the area—either rising to engage the bombers or swooping down from the clouds—Mitchell massed his bombers, with strict formation discipline, protecting them with flights of pursuit aircraft. The echelons of bombardment and escort aircraft consistently trapped and outgunned enemy planes.[60]

In his final report on the Air Service, AEF, General Patrick summarized the status of the air units and the roles they performed during the war. There were 45 U.S. squadrons equipped with 740 airplanes assigned to frontline armies when hostilities ceased. Twelve of the squadrons had American-built airplanes and Liberty engines. Reporting that Air Service pilots shot down 781 (confirmed) enemy airplanes and 73 (confirmed) enemy balloons while losing 289 airplanes and 48 balloons to enemy fire, Patrick cited other mission performance:

> Our squadrons, in round number, took part in 150 bombing raids, during which they dropped over 275,000 pounds of explosives on the enemy. They flew 35,000 hours over the lines and took 18,000 photographs of enemy positions, from which 585,000 prints were made by the Photographic Sections attached to observation groups. On innumerable occasions they regulated the fire of our Artillery, flew in contact with Infantry during attacks, and from a height of only a few yards from the ground they machine-gunned and bombed enemy batteries, convoys and troops on the march.[61]

Neither General Patrick's nor General Pershing's report addressed the question of strategic bombardment or mentioned plans for the Air Service to participate in a future independent Allied strategic air offensive. In his final report,

Maj. Gen. Mason M. Patrick, Chief of the Air Service in World War I, offered an early analysis of the effectiveness of air combat operations. *(NASM photo)*

Pershing commended the Air Services' "courageous deeds" as an auxiliary of the Army, but he made no assessment of its combat roles. The only issue Pershing raised concerning aviation was the "slowness in production" at home, which made it difficult to obtain planes and equipment at the front.[62]

General Patrick cited a more basic problem with the relationship between ground and air commanders and their staffs. Because of the newness of the air arm, ground commanders lacked sufficient understanding of the Air Service's combat roles and capabilities. Young air officers were inexperienced in working with other Army branches. "There was throughout our experience a marked tendency on the part of commanders of the larger ground units and their staffs to regard the air force as a staff service rather than a combat arm," Patrick wrote. "There was lack of knowledge of the best ways in which to use this new arm, and too little regard was paid to the local tactical situation and to the necessity for the combined employment of the air force and all other combatant arms." Patrick complained that division, corps, and army commanders often failed to exercise full command of the tactical air forces assigned to them because they were unaware of aviation's roles and capabilities.[63]

The Air Service at Home and Postwar Roles

At home, the War Department called America's poor record of aircraft production "one of the greatest problems of the war." When the United States declared war in 1917, Premier Alexandre Ribot of France cabled President Wilson asking for a powerful enough American air force by 1918 to enable the Allies "to win supremacy of the air." The War Department ordered Foulois to Washington to oversee drafting the ambitious aircraft program while Congress authorized production of 22,625 planes, 45,000 aircraft engines, and training of 6,210 pilots.

The clouds of American planes the Allies hoped would darken the skies over Europe never materialized. The United States produced 30,000 aviation engines by war's end, but only 1,200 American-made DH–4s were shipped to the forward area. American manufacturers built British de Havilland biplanes because there were no suitable U.S. combat designs. After American-made DH–4s began arriving in the summer of 1918, United States pilots still flew Nieuports and other airplanes furnished by the Allies.[64]

Congress and the public bitterly criticized government oversight and coordination of the aircraft program. Following an extensive Senate investigation, Congress passed the Overman Act of May 20, 1918, giving the president authority to regulate and coordinate wartime production. Upon signing the act, President Wilson issued Executive Order 2862 removing Army aviation from the jurisdiction of the Signal Corps and reorganizing the air arm into two bureaus. In anticipation of the presidential order, the Secretary of War established a new Division of Military Aeronautics to take over training and operations of the air arm in April 1918. Major General William Kenly assumed command of the division. A Bureau of Aircraft Production was created to oversee production of aircraft, engines, and equipment. This arrangement continued until August 1918 when the Bureau's Director, Dr. John D. Ryan became dual-hatted as Director of the Air Service and Second Assistant Secretary of War for air, combining administration of aviation personnel and equipment. "Although this appeared to be a move in the direction of separate cabinet representation for the air arm," a legislative historian noted, "it turned out to be only a wartime innovation."[65]

Ryan resigned two weeks after the Armistice, admitting to having never "taken over the actual direction of Military Aeronautics" and to making no "real change in its operations."[66] General Kenly testified that appointments to the Air Service were not made based on experience, but they "may be due to favoritism or due to relationship, but it affects the morale of the department." Kenly advised that the air arm "be put into the hands of a man conversant with the work and thoroughly in earnest about it."[67] Major General Charles T. Menoher became chief of the Air Service in December 1918 shortly after returning from field artillery and infantry command in France.[68] William Mitchell reported as Menoher's assistant in March.

Having remained in France after the Armistice to help dismantle the air arm, Mitchell returned to a hero's welcome. He found an Army preoccupied with demobilization and returning to a peacetime posture. The General Staff was in no mood for the turbulence Mitchell was prepared to put in motion, if necessary,

While serving as Chief of Air Service in 1919, Gen. Charles T. Menoher convened a board to evaluate congressional proposals to create an aeronautical branch in the War Department. The board recommended additional study. *(NASM photo)*

to promote his ideas on an independent air role. En route home, Mitchell visited General Trenchard in London where he observed the prominent role the British high command gave to military aeronautics. As head of the RAF (which was part of the Air Ministry), Trenchard controlled British military aviation, including that of the Royal Navy. A biographer wrote that Mitchell saw "a similar organizational approach [as] the answer to American postwar needs." Military officers and legislators in Washington debated the future role of military aeronautics, and the British example had prompted Indiana Senator Harry S. New to propose a Department of Aeronautics. According to his biographer, Mitchell was ready "to take over the leadership of the work New and others had begun."[69]

Not all Army flyers shared Mitchell's early enthusiasm for the British model. In January 1919, Brig. Gen. Foulois argued that creating a separate and independent air force under the British Air Ministry had failed "the acid test of field service in war." Foulois observed that the "Naval Wing of the British Royal Air Force has practically carried on its operations independent of the Army Wing." Furthermore, Foulois noted that fielding an independent air force under control of the British Air Ministry rather than the Supreme Commander of the Allied Armies, Marshal Foch, was unworkable. He concluded:

> This practical failure of the British Royal Air Force to operate efficiently in active service, as an independent force, directly under the control of a civilian body, is in my opinion a sufficient argument against any such experiment in connection with the creation and establishment of a similar American Air Force.[70]

At the time, Foulois thought a more mature air arm with stronger representation on the General Staff would best serve the future of Army aviation. A board of senior officers convened by General Pershing to record the lessons of World

Roles and Missions

War I heard Foulois' views. Foulois felt most combat units should be assigned to armies, corps, and divisions, with a GHQ reserve independent of these units. The Dickman Board report defined the wartime roles of the Air Service as "observation, distant reconnaissance and bombing, aerial combat, and combat against ground troops." The Board concluded that the Air Service's wartime experience did not offer evidence to support "aerial activity...independently of ground troops, to such an extent as to materially affect the conduct of the war as a whole."[71]

After returning to the United States, Foulois changed his mind and joined other flying officers advocating a separate air arm. This is apparent from Foulois' testimony to a House of Representatives subcommittee investigating military aviation. The subcommittee reported that practically every witness before it—including Mitchell, Kenly, and Foulois—urged the creation of a separate air service to work with the Army, Navy, and appropriate civilian agencies to develop aviation. Senior Army officers looked upon Foulois and Mitchell as "firebrands" for their criticism of the General Staff at these hearings. In its February 1920 report, the subcommittee concluded: "The striking failure of the War Department to rise to the aircraft emergency, either in peace or in war, has made necessary the creation of a separate bureau or department of aeronautics."[72]

Concerned with agitation in the Army air arm, in August 1919 the Secretary of War directed General Menoher to convene a board of officers to report on congressional proposals to create an aeronautical department. The Menoher Board, comprised of nonflying officers, issued its report to Secretary of War Baker in October 1919, proposing that the Army and Navy should "retain as integral and essential elements of their organizations and operating respectively under their complete control all military and naval forces that may be provided by Congress." To be an effective arm of either service, the board reasoned, required an air force to be "an integral part of a command not only during battle but also during the entire period of doctrinal training." The board recommended, however, that the General Staff undertake a more detailed study of the internal Army air organization to give existing air service personnel "an adequate voice in the final determination." "A military air force is an essential combatant branch of the service," the report said, "and should, in so far as may be practicable, be placed on equal footing with the Infantry, Cavalry, and Artillery."[73]

Secretary of War Baker addressed the theoretical role of independent military aviation in his report for fiscal year 1919. While acknowledging that aerial bombardment had "carried the war into the third dimension" and "raised new questions as to the relation of aircraft to the prewar military and naval establishments," he cautioned that aerial bombardment had no appreciable effect on the war and did not justify "reliance upon it to the detriment of the traditional military arms." Aerial bombardment, as yet, was "not an important military effort," Baker said. The infantry remained "the backbone of military effort." Other land, sea, and air components were "mere aids to its advance." While Baker mentioned the attack roles of military planes, he contended that the only indispensable aviation roles in World War I were observation and control of artillery fire.[74]

"It seems quite clear that the time has not come to set up an independent department of the air," Secretary Baker concluded. He left the door open to technology, however, observing that the art of military aviation was "so new and so fascinating" that it was "difficult to reason coldly" concerning its future. Ongoing experimentation already had made the aircraft used in the war "practically obsolete." Baker pointed to successful experiments with radio-controlled "pilotless bombs" as one example of progress in aviation roles that could "necessitate even more radical modification of military practice than those already in use."[75]

Other prominent figures opposing the creation of a separate, autonomous air arm included General Pershing and Assistant Secretary of the Navy Franklin D. Roosevelt. Pershing told Congress he thought it might be wise to consolidate appropriations for aviation to encourage research and development but argued against creating a new combatant force. He supported the Menoher Board's proposal to make the Air Service a separate Army branch similar to the Infantry, Cavalry, and Artillery. Like Pershing, Roosevelt opposed a third organization that would compete with the traditional arms. Roosevelt urged full cooperation and interchange between the Army and Navy air arms, but saw no justification for "unification of the two."[76]

Congress defeated eight separate measures to create an independent air force in the 15 months following the Armistice. Advocacy within the Army was primarily among the flyers, and their cause did not have enough support to win in Congress. The Army Reorganization Act of 1920 became law on June 4, 1920, giving the Air Service statutory recognition as a combatant arm but without changing the Air Service's basic standing with the War Department. The act authorized a chief of the Air Service at the rank of major general, an assistant at the rank of brigadier general and a peacetime force of 1,516 officers and 16,000 enlisted men. It required that 90 percent of Air Service officers qualify as pilots or observers and that all flying units be commanded by flying officers. Many aviators considered the act a setback for Air Service aspirations. As one official historian wrote, "It marked the victory of the old order in military circles over the proponents of a separate air force."[77]

Framing Postwar Roles and Missions

Amid debates over the status of postwar aeronautics, the War and Navy departments resumed deliberations on formalizing the roles and missions of Army, Navy, and Marine Corps aviation and their joint relationships. The absence of Mitchell and other officers who advocated an independent air service from these deliberations was conspicuous. Mitchell's fervent and often exaggerated claims about the efficacy of independent air power tended to alienate senior

Roles and Missions

Navy officers as well as his superiors. The Navy's wartime experience was distinct from the Army's, although both suffered from the lack of men, planes, and equipment. The Navy adopted its own method to correct its mobilization problems by opening the Naval Aircraft Factory at the Philadelphia Navy Yard in August 1917 to construct and repair airplanes and perform experimental work. During the war, Navy pilots flew some bombardment and attack missions but primarily they patrolled the seas. Like the Army, the Navy developed aviation as a supporting arm of the fleet, its primary force. The Navy centralized aviation as a branch in the Office of Director of Naval Aviation under the Chief of Naval Operations in March 1917.[78]

Navy flyers did not join their Army colleagues in crusading for an independent air force. Although Mitchell later claimed that many naval aviators supported his views but feared to speak out because it would jeopardize their careers, his claim was not substantiated.[79] Mitchell had shown he was not above stretching the facts to support his arguments. "If we are allowed to develop essential...means of fighting in the air, we can carry the war to such an extent in the air as to almost make navies useless on the surface of the waters," Mitchell told a Senate subcommittee in April 1919. "The Navy General Board, I might say, agrees with me on that." Closer investigation of Mitchell's proposition reveals that it was based solely on one admiral's agreement that airplanes of the future could make direct attacks on ships.[80]

In dividing responsibilities with his assistant, Menoher tried to distance Mitchell from policy matters. Policy was Menoher's domain, although he was not always successful in keeping Mitchell from interfering. Menoher served on the Joint Board with his Navy counterpart. Neither Mitchell nor any of the officers aligned with his cause served in any capacity with the Board.[81] Joint considerations were politically sensitive during this period. In July 1919, the secretaries of War and Navy broadened the scope of the Board's responsibilities to encompass the full range of policy matters relating to aviation roles and missions. Specifically, the secretaries charged the Board

> with the duties of originating considerations for the advancement of Army and Navy missions and with the responsibility of recommending action in all matters whatsoever which it considers essential to establish efficient cooperation, and the elimination of unnecessary duplication.[82]

In early 1920, the Board published a pamphlet entitled "Joint Army and Navy Actions in Coast Defense," clarifying earlier guidance and reflecting policy that the Board, under its new charter, had developed for operations by the air services of the Army, Navy, and Marine Corps. This policy, as approved by the Secretary of War and the Secretary of the Navy, allotted functions for Army, Navy, and Marine Corps aircraft. Essentially, Army aircraft operated from bases on shore as an arm of the mobile army, while Navy aircraft operated from ships or shore stations as an arm of the fleet. Army aircraft defended shore establishments against enemy air attack; Navy aircraft protected coastal sea lanes by scouting, convoy operations, and attacks on enemy submarines, aircraft, or surface vessels. Navy planes also could attack enemy establishments ashore if related to naval operations. Either service, jointly or alone, could attack enemy vessels engaged in hostile actions against the coast. Marine aircraft performed functions normally assigned to the Army when operations occurred at an advance base where Army forces were not present. When Army and Marine aircraft cooperated on shore, control of their operations was governed by the 120th Article of War.[83]

The new policy "intended to prevent duplication of work without unduly restricting essential freedom of action" of either service. Henceforth, the Joint Board reviewed policy questions concerning the tactical and strategical functions of aircraft and recommended appropriate courses of action to the secretaries of War and Navy. Another board, the Army and Navy Aeronautical Board, was responsible for coordinating the construction of aircraft experimental stations and all operational air stations used by either service. The Aeronautical Board also determined which service would be responsible to develop new types of aircraft, coordinated procurement and purchase of aircraft, and reviewed appropriations estimates for aviation programs before submission to Congress.[84] Appropriations dropped sharply during the return to a peacetime economy. The Army Appropriation Act for 1920 provided $772.3 million for the Army, with only $25 million for the aviation program. Appropriations for the Navy totaled $616 million, with $25 million designated for aviation.[85]

A Turning Point for Roles and Missions

The immediate postwar recognition of military aviation's importance-culminating in the issuance of joint policy and the Army Reorganization Act of 1920-was a turning point in the evolution of air power roles and missions. The policy and the act were disappointments for proponents of a separate air force, who viewed these developments as the handiwork of the General Staff and others who did not comprehend "the full value of military aviation." Recognition of the Air Service as a combatant arm of the Army did not dispel fears that aviation development would remain forever subordinate to the needs of the parent services. The exclusion of experienced Army air officers from policy making left Mitchell and other seasoned airmen with the impression that the War Department did not want their views. The reduction in aviation appropriations and a subsequent realignment of Army aviation which favored observation over offensive capabilities and placed air squadrons under the Army's divisions and corps seemed to confirm these fears.[86]

The Navy Department, on the other hand, viewed the Army separatists as a threat to naval sovereignty. In his annual report for fiscal year 1920, Navy

Roles and Missions

Secretary Josephus Daniels complained about "inaccurate and misleading statements concerning naval aviation" in the *Congressional Record* and the public press. Although the Navy challenged these misstatements, Secretary Daniels feared that the unfavorable effect upon the public and Congress had already been harmful. The Navy protested vigorously to change a clause in a House appropriations bill giving the Army control of all aerial operations from land bases, with the Navy relegated to controlling aerial operations attached to a fleet. The Navy won its protest because the clause was in direct conflict with War and Navy Department policy. Secretary Daniels noted that had the bill passed as written, naval aviation ashore would have come under Army control.[87]

The roles of Army aviation eclipsed those of Navy aviation during World War I because the belligerents fought predominantly a ground war. After the Armistice, however, public awareness and national policy turned to defense of American shores. This raised the importance of the naval air role to the level of the Army's. Perhaps influenced by the Army aviators postwar agitation for autonomy, the Navy Department accelerated its naval aviation development. Secretary Daniels discussed aviation progress at length in his 1920 annual report, saying he was determined to resolve "the difficult problem of molding a new and important branch into an old organization not designed to care for it." He believed that the Navy would be best served by creation of a Bureau of Aeronautics, with money given directly to the Secretary for aviation purposes and handled as a single fund. The Navy established the Bureau of Aeronautics the following year.[88]

Meanwhile, if Mitchell's extensive lobbying did not further the cause of Navy aviation, it undoubtedly raised public awareness about the naval air role. His writings included articles on air power versus sea power, and he proposed developing "airplane carriers to carry bombardment aviation" to replace battle-

Despite the best efforts of Billy Mitchell's to perform a convincing display of strategic airpower bombing capabilities, the USS *Indiana* stubbornly remained afloat in the Chesapeake Bay. *(NASM photo)*.

ships. "When this comes about, the air force will constitute the first line of defense of the country," Mitchell wrote in October 1920. "The Navy may be second, or it may be entirely eliminated."[89]

Mitchell clamored for a bombing test to prove his point. In November, the Navy scheduled a secret test, inviting Mitchell to observe. Navy planes dropped dummy bombs on an old battleship anchored in the Chesapeake Bay, the USS *Indiana*. Bombs laid on and near the ship were exploded. The ship did not sink. The Navy contended that the results demonstrated "the improbability of a modern battleship being either destroyed or completely put out of action by aerial bombs," but Mitchell argued that the test was unrealistic and inconclusive.[90] The War and Navy Departments hoped the bombing test would bring a quiet conclusion to the unwanted roles and missions controversy, but public airing of the test by the news media turned the event into a dramatic transition to the second chapter. As for what lay ahead, a Navy historian noted that the basic roles and missions problem confronting the services was:

> which Service was to be responsible for certain phases of defense and for specific areas of strategic importance as well as the extent to which cooperation between the Services was required in certain areas and the means by which such cooperation could be carried out. It was, in addition, the beginning of a long controversy between the Army and Navy in which protagonists of a separate air force later joined.[91]

Within the span of a decade, the military airplane emerged from the drawing board of a bicycle factory in Dayton, Ohio, to become more than just another promising new weapon in the U.S. arsenal. When the Army Signal Corps accepted its initial Wright Flyer in 1909, only a handful of officers dared speculate on the flying machine's potential lethality in modern war. Tentative acceptance, however, led to development of sturdier machines, to experimentation with new equipment and new roles, and to cautious integration as supporting arms of the Army and the Navy. From 1914 to 1918, Europe became the cradle for three-dimensional warfare, and the European skies, a crucible for exploring the full range of aerial combat roles, including rudimentary tactical and strategical bombardment operations.

The transition from war to peace closed the first chapter of military aviation and opened another. The Mitchell-led crusade for postwar independence stirred the first signs of interservice rivalry over aviation, at a time when the War and Navy Departments recognized the need to formalize roles and missions responsibilities between the two air arms. Since the Army Reorganization Act of 1920 and the joint policy for coastal defense fell far short of their expectations, Mitchell and the separatists prepared for a greater challenge to the status quo as the postwar transition came to an end.

CHAPTER II

TRANSITIONS: EVOLVING INTERWAR ROLES AND MISSIONS

Reflecting on the interwar years, Maj. Gen. Orvil A. Anderson, veteran air planner and founding commandant of the Air War College, wrote in 1956 that military aviation "grew within the confining grounds of a roles and missions garden, effectively fenced in by traditional values, and nurtured from the vantage point of hindsight." According to Anderson, air doctrine was flawed at the start of World War II because inexperience formed "the frame of reference" for training and equipping the air arm between the wars. He explained that because interwar air forces conformed to a prevailing surface strategy, they were organized and equipped for roles and missions to support that strategy. The result, he said, was that the designated roles and missions did not contribute to effective air warfare. The air forces had to improvise to win supremacy of the skies in World War II and then exploit that victory in the full-scale support of surface forces.[1]

Anderson's interpretation of roles and missions development between the wars is consistent with the doctrinal theme running through much of Army aviation history after World War I. That theme was the air arm's enduring quest for autonomy, the cause which Brig. Gen. William Mitchell championed after returning home from France in 1919. Lieutenant General Ira C. Eaker recalled in later years that the quest for autonomy was the heartbeat of the fledgling air arm, and that "Mitchell was our great leader and tutor in this enterprise."[2]

A companion theme was the emerging independent air mission, with roots in the GHQ Air Service Reserve formed during the war to distinguish between air forces assigned to field commanders and those held in reserve for other missions. Commonly identified with strategic bombardment, the independent air mission meant more than that to Mitchell and other proponents of an autonomous air force. Mitchell stated that the principal function of an air force was to win a decision over the hostile air force, thus enabling "airplanes to observe, to drop bombs, or attack troops' uninterrupted." He believed this was essentially an air problem which provided the rationale for a distinct air mission.[3] The definition matured between the wars to mean air missions separate and distinct from missions flown in direct support of surface action. Army airmen visualized that the forces flying independent missions or supporting surface action would be used interchangeably, as required.[4] Mitchell's command of the multinational force at St. Mihiel and in air operations during the Meuse-Argonne offensive validated the concept of flexibly employing military aviation where it was most needed.

Mitchell, Foulois, and other officers put forth compelling arguments to create an autonomous air force. They believed the future of United States military aviation depended on fully developing potential air roles and missions and that a separate air force was the only effective means to institutionalize that development. If the Air Service remained a supporting arm of the Army, they believed that aviation resources would remain parcelled out among field commanders and that the mission to support infantry would take precedence over other roles and missions. In their view, this would harness military aviation to the support of surface action, stunting the air arm's technological and doctrinal growth.[5] General Anderson later explained how this happened to roles and missions between the wars, particularly during the years before the GHQ Air Force was established in 1935.

General Anderson's point of view did not go unopposed. Infantry commanders complained that Army airmen neglected the air-ground role between the wars because of their preference for strategic bombing and other aerial missions. Lessons learned from the Army GHQ maneuvers of 1941 and in reports from the first months of fighting in North Africa during World War II reflected this inattention.[6] Not all airmen agreed that the air arm was neglected because it remained a component of the Army. General Eaker, for one, called this claim a "myth" which had been "considerably overblown." Eaker acknowledged problems with some members of the General Staff, but he had high praise for "a large number of these military seniors" for their treatment of the air arm. "We could not have accomplished the things we did, in selling military aviation and its requirements, had it not been for a considerable group of the best Army officers who helped us instead of opposed our efforts," he said. "If they were approached in the right way, were convinced of your sincerity, and above all, of your facts, they would listen and they would respond."[7] Most, but not all, flying officers of the early 1920s agreed with the advocates of a separate air force. Lieutenant Colonel Oscar Westover, who headed the air arm from 1935 to 1938, accused the separatists of insubordination and supported the War Department's position against autonomy.[8]

In reality, advocates of a separate air force did not have a large following outside their own circle of aviation enthusiasts. The airmen's combat exploits received wide public acclaim, but postwar interest in military aviation waned as the government began dismantling the huge wartime Army, returning the country to normalcy. While the separatists had some support in Congress, the postwar hearings on military aviation and passage of the Army Reorganization Act of 1920 proved that military and political leaders were united against them. A war-weary constituency offered no political encouragement for legislating radical change in the established military order. The effects of demobilization were not long in coming. The Air Service was reduced from 190,000 to 27,000 when the Army discharged over 2.7 million troops in 1919. Army appropriations dropped from a high of $10.2 billion in 1919 to $392.5 million in 1921. Included in these reductions were $952.3 million for Army aviation in 1919 and $33 million in 1921.[9] At the same time, the signing of the Armistice ended the only visible threat to national security that might have justified the costs of building and maintaining a third military arm. With the return to normalcy, the focus of U.S. security turned inward to the defense of America's coasts and interests in outlying possessions.

A variant theme resulting from Mitchell's campaign for an autonomous air force was a lasting suspicion among Navy flyers that Army airmen coveted naval aviation and were scheming to wrest control of it. Little rivalry existed between the two air arms before the postwar debates, but Mitchell's efforts to prove the airplane's supremacy over the battleship changed that. Even more disquieting was Mitchell's claim that all military aviation should be unified into one department of air. Mitchell's testimony before Congress and his published writings left no doubt about his goal. Soon after returning from the war, Mitchell proposed that the Air Service produce airplane carriers for use overseas and argued persuasively that all aviation should be combined under one chief:

> The present system of overlapping and duplication of duties gains nothing in comparison with the singleness of purpose and the unity of action that would ensue from the adoption of a separate air service embracing the Army and Navy Air Services.[10]

The burgeoning roles and missions rivalry between the two air arms centered on their overlapping responsibilities for coastal defense. Before the development of military aviation, the armed forces had drawn clear lines of responsibility for national defense: the Army defended the shores from invasion and fought on land; the Navy patrolled the ocean approaches and defended the seas. The lines were not so clear after the air forces became active in coastal defense, prompting both services to become more territorial in preserving their traditional roles. The Army grew suspicious of naval aviation coming ashore; the Navy was wary of Army flyers encroaching over water. Competition for scarce defense dollars was blamed for intensifying that rivalry, although the two air arms seem to have shared equitably in military spending, at least from 1923 until the creation of the GHQ Air Force in 1935. Budget figures for those years reveal that total defense authorizations averaged just over $900 million annually, including $45 million for aviation.[11]

As for arguments that roles and missions rivalry and duplication impeded the growth of air power between the wars, evidence shows that building competing air forces was not altogether counterproductive. Even those who deplored "the wasteful duplication" conceded some advantages to having two air arms, including the knowledge and benefits each service gained from the tactical and technical advancements of the other. A noteworthy example was the Navy's development of the Norden bombsight, which the GHQ Air Force adapted for use on Army bombers. The bombsight became an indispensable instrument for successful precision bombing operations in World War II. In 1955, Gen. Carl A. Spaatz admitted that "competition for faster, better planes and improved flying techniques between the Army and Navy" between the wars probably was a boon for U.S. air power.[12] Nevertheless, interservice rivalry and duplication were very real concerns as military aviation progressed through the uneven prosperity of the 1920s, the Great Depression, and the road to recovery leading into World War II.

Mitchell, Moffett, and Patrick: The Postwar Denouement

The two most active officers in advancing Army aviation roles and missions during the difficult recovery from demobilization were Generals Patrick and Mitchell. These were men of markedly different temperaments who played contrasting roles in the postwar roles and missions dispute. Foulois' assignment to a four-year tour as air attache in Berlin after the 1919 hearings on aviation kept him out of the fray during these years. Unlike Mitchell and Foulois, Patrick had supported the Army-sponsored legislation to keep the Air Service under its control, having become weary of the feuding when he led the Air Service in France. After the war, Patrick denounced the "self-serving motives" of Mitchell and other officers pursuing a separate service in a communication with General Pershing.[13]

Naval aviation roles and missions during the 1920s were shaped by the policies of Rear Adm. William A. Moffett, who became chief of the Bureau of Aeronautics when it began operating as part of the Navy Department in September 1921.[14] As director of naval aviation since early March, Moffett joined the fight with Mitchell over the bomber versus the battleship. Moffett's unequivocal belief that naval aviation should be developed as an integral part of the fleet pushed him to become an arch rival of Mitchell. The enmity between the two grew so acerbic that Moffett once stated that Mitchell was "of unsound mind and suffering delusions of grandeur."[15] A Moffett admirer wrote that he meant "to build naval aviation without tearing anything down." Moffett later claimed that the Bureau's advancements in aviation were "the result of the experience of naval men, including naval aviators, trained to the habits, requirements and customs of the sea." He believed this contributed to "sound and constructive development" of the naval air arm.[16]

General Patrick became Chief of the Air Service in October 1921 after Menoher asked to be relieved because of his problems with Mitchell. When Mitchell returned in 1919 as Assistant Chief of the Air Service, Menoher put him in charge of flying operations as Chief, Operations and Training Group. Menoher thought this would keep Mitchell out of policy matters and make best use of his flying knowledge. Although Mitchell's operational duties distanced him from decision making, they allowed him and other veteran flying officers (including Thomas DeWitt Milling, Charles deF. Chandler, and William C. Sherman) to dominate tactical thought and experiment with new aviation roles. Staff officers taught tactical doctrine (gleaned from Mitchell's writings on the employment of aviation) at the Field Officers' School which opened at Langley Field, Virginia, in November 1920.[17] The school became the Air Service Tactical School in 1922 and the Air Corps Tactical School in 1926. Mitchell was so headstrong and his views so contrary to Menoher's that constant feuding resulted between the training group and Air Service headquarters. Menoher's assistant executive officer, Lt. Col. Oscar I. Westover, complained about Mitchell's lack of coordination, communications with members of Congress, and disregard for Air Service policy. He went so far as to recommend that Menoher demote Mitchell, remove him from the training group, and post him to the Philippines.[18]

Apparently neither Menoher nor the War Department thought it wise to say or do anything to attract greater attention to their problems with Mitchell. On April 9, 1920, Secretary Baker ordered Army personnel to refrain from public statements which would discredit or reflect upon other departments and warned that individuals would be "strictly accountable" for their public utterances. In a terse note, Menoher told Mitchell to coordinate his official activities with Air Service headquarters and observe Air Service policy.[19]

To Menoher's chagrin, Mitchell's attacks against the Navy and his agitation for autonomy did not end after Congress voted to keep the Air Service as a combatant arm of the Army in mid-1920. From later that year when he published his first book, *Our Air Force*, until his court-martial in the fall of 1925, the defiant Mitchell waged a relentless public campaign for a powerful and separate air force. Mitchell's book, which characterized air power as the sum of the nation's military aviation (land and sea), expounded the familiar theme that victory on land or sea could not be had without command of the skies. Mitchell believed the development of sufficient air forces for that role demanded a separate Department of Air, coequal with the War and Navy Departments. This was necessary, Mitchell said, for the United States to field air forces able to defeat a hostile air invasion. He postulated that the air forces would be the first to engage the enemy in a future war, and that the "whole fate of war" might depend upon "a favorable air decision" at the outset. Mitchell wrote,

> Our doctrine of aviation, therefore, would be to find out where the hostile air force is, to concentrate on that point with our Pursuit, Attack, and Bombardment Aviation, to obtain a decision over the hostile air force, and then to attack the enemy's armies on land or navies on the water, and to obtain a decision over them.[20]

Mitchell further antagonized Navy officials by trying to discredit the role of the battleship in coastal defense. He agitated for a more realistic test of the bomber versus the battleship than the 1920 Navy experiment with the *Indiana*.

Roles and Missions

The Navy was embarrassed by a December article in the *London Illustrated News* with pictures which showed extensive damage to the *Indiana* after it had already released a statement that the experiment demonstrated the battleship's invulnerability. Mitchell was suspected of leaking the story since no reporters witnessed the secret tests, but the charge went unsubstantiated. Nevertheless, the story aided Mitchell's cause, as did subsequent articles in American newspapers which pointed to discrepancies between the Navy claims and photographic evidence. A naval aviator noted the incongruity between Mitchell's highly publicized claims and the fact that nobody proclaimed battleships obsolete after coastal defense batteries at Pensacola, Florida, sank the *Massachusetts* two miles offshore in tests during January 1921.[21]

Mitchell stepped up his criticism of the Navy experiments in early 1921. Testifying before the House Appropriations and Naval Affairs Committees, he suggested that the Navy had rigged the *Indiana* test, urged support for an Air Service bombing test, and repeated his arguments for a separate air arm. Mitchell appealed to the War Department for a battleship and other naval vessels for Air Service testing. The request was referred to the Joint Board for consideration, which recommended on February 28 that the Navy conduct additional tests with Army Air Service participation. Secretaries Baker and Daniels approved the proposal and announced seven tests to be held during June and July 1921. Plans called for aerial bombing and naval gunfire against obsolete U.S. naval vessels and sequestered German warships allocated to the United States under the Treaty of Versailles. The main targets were the light cruiser *Frankfort* and the battleship *Ostfriesland,* which were to be positioned sixty miles off the Virginia coast. The War and Navy Departments ordered a total news blackout on the tests until the results and conclusions had been passed upon by the Joint Board.[22]

Mitchell and the Navy were clearly at cross purposes over test plans and objectives. Mitchell's goal was to attack and sink the test targets, thus proving the airplane's mastery at sea. In contrast, the Navy planned the tests as scientific experiments to gauge the capacity of the ships to withstand attack from naval gunfire and aerial bombardment. According to the Navy's plan, the tests would proceed methodically, allowing construction engineers to examine structural damage at intervals between attacks. To appease Mitchell, the Joint Board promised him an old battleship for separate testing but deferred delivery until after the summer events. The Navy's strict rules for the tests and the delay in turning a battleship over to the Army made Mitchell suspect that his rivals intended to use the air and naval trials against the *Ostfriesland* to validate their findings from the *Indiana* experiment. Mitchell was determined to outmaneuver the Navy by sinking the *Ostfriesland* in a dramatic demonstration of air power's supremacy over the battleship.[23]

After news reports reflecting unfavorably on the Navy appeared in early May, Secretary of War John W. Weeks (who replaced Baker in March) warned Army airmen again not to violate the restrictions on public statements. On May

29, Mitchell caused another uproar when he blamed the crash of an Army plane and the deaths of seven servicemen on the War Department's failure to equip the Air Service adequately. Furious, Menoher called for Mitchell's removal. Weeks, however, downplayed the seriousness of Mitchell's offenses and persuaded Menoher to withdraw his complaint. Mitchell blamed "departmental politics" and the Navy for plotting to have him removed.[24]

Under Mitchell's direction, Army aviators made exhaustive preparations for the upcoming tests during the spring and summer of 1921. Air Service squadrons trained at air stations across the nation. In early May, the hand-picked airmen began arriving at Langley Field to form the 1st Provisional Brigade and to complete final arrangements. Near the end of the month, Mitchell took charge of the Brigade as planes and crews readied for their missions against naval targets. Leaving nothing to chance, Mitchell sought technical advice from experts outside the Air Service, including Alexander deSeversky, a Russian naval aviator in World War I. Army ordnance rushed production of 2,000-pound bombs, which experts claimed were needed to sink a ship of the *Ostfriesland* class.[25] The Washington Naval Gun Factory produced 2,000-pound bombs for naval aviators.[26]

From June 21 through July 18, Army and Navy planes sank three smaller vessels-a surfaced U-boat, a destroyer, and the light cruiser *Frankfort*-before aerial attacks against the dreadnought *Ostfriesland* commenced on July 20. Mitchell declined to participate in an earlier search and attack mission against the *Iowa*, an old battleship converted into a radio-controlled target vessel, because the Army flyers lacked experience and equipment to locate ships on the high seas, and the attack formations were not permitted to carry live ordnance. Mitchell concentrated on the *Ostfriesland* because it would demonstrate the Army's bombing effectiveness against battleships, and it offered the most publicity. Dozens of reporters joined a large group of dignitaries to observe the test as the news blackout was lifted. One newspaper called the bombing of the *Ostfriesland* the most important test ever conducted by any government. Mitchell promised a sensational story.[27]

During the first day-and-a-half, however, Army, Navy, and Marine Corps planes expended a variety of bombs against the *Ostfriesland* without sinking it. Mitchell grew increasingly impatient over delays imposed by the command ship, *Shawmut*, because of high seas and approaching storms. By noon on July 21, the stubborn *Ostfriesland* began to take on water but was still afloat when the *Shawmut* ordered Mitchell to launch his attack with 2,000-pound bombs. Ignoring radio instructions from the *Shawmut* that his planes were to leave Langley with no more than three 2,000-pound bombs, Mitchell ordered a formation of eight Martin bombers and three Handley-Pages into the air. Each was loaded with a 2,000-pound bomb. Within minutes after arriving over the target, the formation completed its mission and headed back to Langley. Six bombs dropped by Mitchell's aircraft (four near misses and two direct hits) rolled the

In 1921, General Billy Mitchell's successful bombing raid on the dreadnought *Ostfriesland* enhanced his reputation in the public eye but further damaged already strained relations with the Navy. *(NASM photo)*

Ostfriesland over and sent it to the ocean bottom. The near misses were intentional because experts told Mitchell bombs exploding next to the ship's hull would do the most damage. In a final salute, the formation dropped a seventh bomb into the water where the dreadnought had anchored.[28]

Sinking the *Ostfriesland* enhanced Mitchell's public standing, but his handling of the affair poisoned already strained relations with his superiors and the Navy Department. Not surprisingly, the conclusions drawn from the bombing tests were as contradictory as the cross-purposes for conducting them. Barely a week after sinking the dreadnought, Mitchell led mock air raids on cities along the Atlantic Coast to demonstrate their vulnerability to hostile air attack and to raise public awareness of the need for a strong national air force. On August 29, he submitted a report on the 1st Provisional Air Brigade's operations to Menoher. He believed the exercises proved that "none of the seacraft would have lasted ten minutes in a serviceable condition" had the brigade been allowed to plan and execute the attacks with that in mind. Moreover, he claimed, the brigade "could have put out of action the entire Atlantic Fleet in a single attack." The advantages were obvious, he said, considering that the total monetary value of the provisional unit's airplanes was no more than a modern destroyer.[29]

Calling the 1st Provisional Brigade "the first real Air Force ever in being in the United States," Mitchell said its performance validated his arguments for revising national defense and establishing a separate, coequal department of aeronautics. Mitchell asserted that the roles and missions in national defense were distributed between the services "in such a way as to make it impossible to function efficiently in an emergency." He recommended redistributing functions to give an independent air force primary responsibility for frontier and coast defense, against seacraft and against aircraft, and for air defense. "A Navy should be organized and equipped to take the offensive on the high seas, and not be employed along and close to the coast," Mitchell said. "Such Air Forces should be assigned to the Navy as can go to sea with it and fight with it on the high seas." He suggested that the Navy's role in coast defense should cease 200 miles from shore and that a Navy driven from the high seas should be protected by an independent air force and the Army. The Army would have complete responsibility for defense of the land and would be so organized.[30]

The Joint Board agreed that the experiments proved the necessity "as a matter of national defense to provide for the maximum development of aviation," but it recommended that aviation be developed under the auspices of the Army and the Navy. The experiments did not diminish the Navy's mission "to control vital lines of transportation upon the sea," beyond the radius of shore-based planes. The Joint Board encouraged the Navy to develop "aircraft carriers of the maximum size and speed...as an effective adjunct of the fleet." Responding to Mitchell's claim that air forces provided "an economical instrument of war leading to the abolition of the battleship," the Board said that aircraft had "but added to the complexity of naval warfare." Asserting that the battleship remained "the bulwark of the Nation's sea defense...so long as safe navigation of the sea...is vital to the success of war," the report concluded:

> The airplane, like the submarine, destroyer, and mine, has added to the dangers to which battleships are exposed, but has not made the battleship obsolete. The battleship still remains the greatest factor of naval strength.[31]

Despite directives that only the official report would be made public, Mitchell's conclusions were leaked to the newspapers soon after Menoher forwarded them to Secretary of War Weeks on August 30. The War Department investigation into the unauthorized disclosure failed to implicate Mitchell or his subordinates, but Menoher believed that Mitchell's relentless agitation had put him in an untenable position. Once more he sought Mitchell's removal, insisting that either he or Mitchell had to go. Mitchell offered to resign, but Secretary Weeks accepted Menoher's resignation instead. Weeks wanted Mitchell to stay, at least until he completed additional bombing tests against the USS *Alabama*, scheduled for late September.

General Patrick succeeded Menoher in October. Mitchell threatened to resign when Patrick refused to let him dictate his own terms, but changed his mind after careful reflection.[32] The *Alabama* bombing tests were anticlimactic and the popular appeal of the tests peaked with the sensational sinking of the *Ostfriesland* in July.[33] One Mitchell scholar noted that "people were interested only so long as they were entertained and even then they exerted little pressure on their representatives in Congress."[34]

The sinking of the battleships neither aroused the outpouring of public support Mitchell sought nor diminished the role of the battleship in the Navy's wartime planning. Although the United States built no new battleships between

Roles and Missions

A Martin bomber lays a smoke screen in preparation for bombing the Naval warship *Alabama* on September 23, 1921. *(NASM photo)*

1922 and 1939, the lapse in ship construction was unrelated to Mitchell's bombing tests or his claim that military aviation had rendered the pride of the fleet obsolete. The construction gap resulted from ceilings set by the Washington Naval Treaty of 1922, limiting the naval armament of its signatories: Great Britain, France, Italy, Japan, and the United States. Imposing a tonnage ratio of 5:5:3 for capital ships of Great Britain, the United States, and Japan respectively, and a lesser figure for France and Italy, the treaty limited the U.S. Navy to fifteen battleships, none of which could be replaced until it was at least twenty years old. To satisfy the limitations of the treaty, the Navy decommissioned thirty battleships and cruisers, and cancelled those under construction with the exception of two cruisers to be converted into aircraft carriers.[35]

Contrary to Mitchell's ambitions for a separate air force, the bombing tests and the Washington Treaty encouraged the Navy to accept the growing importance of aviation to naval warfare and thereby influenced long-range modernization of the Navy air arm between the wars. The Naval Appropriation Bill for 1922, passed in July 1921, authorized construction of the Navy's first aircraft carrier. This bill also centralized naval aviation in a new Bureau of Aeronautics. While blocking modernization of the traditional fleet, the Washington Treaty allowed construction of aircraft carriers. Signatory nations could build two carriers of not greater than 33,000 tons each or convert existing or partially constructed ships, so long as total carrier tonnage did not exceed the ceiling of 135,000 tons. In March 1922 the Navy commissioned its first carrier, the USS *Langley* which was converted from the collier *Jupiter*. In July Congress authorized conversion of the unfinished cruisers *Lexington* and *Saratoga* to aircraft carriers, as permitted by the treaty.[36]

General Patrick was as forceful in developing aviation capabilities within the Army as Moffett was in building the Navy air arm. In later years, General Ira Eaker spoke highly of Patrick's effective leadership during the years of heightened public interest in military aviation, from 1921 to 1927. By the time of Mitchell's court-martial in 1925, Army flyers began to see slow, steady progress in aviation growth and modernization. Patrick was an intelligent, sympathetic leader who understood the needs of the Air Service and knew how to convey them to the Army General Staff. While he did not condone Mitchell's public agitation, he shared his enthusiasm for developing the air arm's roles, missions, and capabilities. Veteran Army aviators respected him. Patrick cemented this rapport in 1923 when at the age of 60 he became the oldest officer to qualify as a pilot. A classmate of General Pershing's, Patrick had access to the highest circles in the War Department. He used this influence to gain recognition for the Air Service and to strengthen relations with the General Staff. Eaker said of Patrick,

> We were able to convince him of some of these new ideas we had in mind and he had the great faculty of being able to talk to the military leaders, the Chief of Staff of the Army, the chiefs of other services, the Secretary of War, the Assistant Secretary of War, and members of Congress. Had it not been for General Patrick and his attitude toward us and toward our ideas, we may very well have failed and we may not have had a suitable beginning for World War II and people may not have had the confidence to give us the funds we required to get ready for the conflict.[37]

For almost two years Patrick defused the roles and missions controversy by keeping Mitchell busy with special assignments at home and abroad. Mitchell's brief attendance at the Washington naval conference as a member of the aviation committee was curtailed in December 1922 when he sailed for France to study aeronautical progress in Europe. Upon returning to the United States, Mitchell was sent on an extensive inspection tour of Air Service operations nationwide. In the summer of 1923, Patrick put Mitchell in charge of bombing tests against two surplus warships, the USS *New Jersey* and the USS *Virginia*. The sinking of these vessels by Martin bombers flying off Cape Hatteras, North Carolina, elicited little reaction. Patrick then sent Mitchell on a six-month study of American defenses in the Pacific.[38] Meanwhile, Patrick took firm command of the Air Service and worked diligently to strengthen the air arm's role in the Army and to clarify its responsibilities for coastal defense.

Some of Mitchell's ideas about aviation roles and missions were apparent in views expressed by Patrick after becoming chief of the Air Service. Army regulations as of November 1921 divided the Air Service into air force and auxiliary units. The principal role of air force units, according to the regulations, was to attack enemy air and ground components and protect friendly air auxiliary units, ground troops, and establishments by destroying enemy aircraft. Air auxiliary units were assigned to aid "directly the strategic and tactical operations of ground troops, by observation, photographic reconnaissance, regulation of artillery fire, and similar activities." While Army regulations appeared to acknowledge the quasi-independent nature of the air force role, it cast the assignment of air force missions generally in relation to ground action.[39] General Patrick, who became an active spokesman for military aviation, mapped a more ambitious course for Air Service roles during his tenure as chief than outlined in Army regulations.

While Patrick did not advocate immediate separation of the air component from the Army, he supported the concept of an independent air role embodied in a GHQ Air Force, which would report directly to the Army General Staff. In his first annual report as chief of the Air Service, Patrick complained that demobilization had reduced offensive aviation in the Army to the minimum of one pursuit group, one attack group, and one bombardment group, creating an imbalance between air force and auxiliary units. Patrick believed that in a properly balanced Air Service, 20 percent of total strength should be comprised of observation units with 80 percent devoted to air force or combat aviation. Instead the postwar Air Service was operating with a 40:60 percent ratio.[40]

The war organization approved in 1920 was "unbalanced and entirely inadequate," Patrick argued, pointing out that the six field-army plan included only one bombardment group of 46 airplanes. To resolve this, Patrick submitted a proposal to provide an adequate air force of pursuit, bombardment, and attack aircraft. The plan called for all air force units to be concentrated in two divisions under GHQ rather than under control of the field army. Subsequently, General Patrick submitted his plan for a revised peacetime establishment representing the minimum aircraft capability he believed necessary to meet the requirements of wartime expansion. While Patrick's plan did not include aviation for coast defense, it postulated that Air Service mobility would permit it to accomplish this mission.[41]

In March 1923, Secretary of War Weeks referred both Air Service plans to a special board headed by Maj. Gen. William Lassiter for review. Upon completing its study, the Lassiter Board agreed with the need to strengthen the Air Service and recommended support for legislation, but it disagreed with Patrick's proposal to centralize combat air forces under the Army General Staff. The Board concluded that observation, attack, and pursuit aviation should remain with the Field Army, with reserves assigned under General Headquarters. To perform the quasi-independent mission, the Board made the following recommendation:

> An air force of bombardment and pursuit aviation and airships should be directly under General Headquarters for assignment to special and strategical missions, the accomplishment of which may be either in connection with the oper-

ation of ground troops or entirely independent of them. This force should be organized into large units, insuring great mobility and independence of action.[42]

After Secretary Weeks approved the Lassiter Board's findings in principle, General Patrick approved a "fundamental conceptions" paper prepared by his staff, which recognized two distinct functions for military aviation. One function included units designed for offensive fighting and operating more or less independently of ground troops. This offensive force would attack and destroy enemy air forces, damage ground components, attack concentration points and lines of communication (LOCs), destroy supplies and munitions, and prevent enemy observation of friendly troops. The other force would serve as an auxiliary to other Army branches.[43] General Patrick noted that "in all cases the missions...were prescribed by the commander of the forces to which these organizations belong."[44] It was clear that Patrick thought the idea of a central air force reporting to the General Staff had War Department approval and was accepted doctrine.

By the end of 1924, however, Patrick was impatient with the War Department's failure to act on the Lassiter Board's recommendations. In December, he submitted strongly worded support of the Lassiter Board's version of an independent strike force to the Adjutant General. In a turnabout from his earlier positions, Patrick said he was now convinced that a unified air service was the solution to the nation's coastal defense problems. He conceded that such a radical reorganization was unacceptable in the immediate future, but he urged that certain preliminary steps be taken, "all with the ultimate end in view."

The crux of the problem, which the Lassiter Board recognized, was that combat air forces were spread thinly through the Army-a self-imposed fragmenting of the force that negated the mobility of the Air Service and the missions it could perform. Reasoning that future emergencies would require the maximum application of strategic missions, Patrick was concerned that war plans contained no provisions for initial operations or for the satisfactory command of air forces. "We should gather our air forces together under one air commander and strike at the strategic points of our enemy-cripple him even before the ground forces can come in contact," he wrote. In conclusion he said, "Air power is coordinate with land and sea power and the air commander should sit in councils on an equal footing with the commanders of the land and sea forces."[45]

The ideas expressed in the letter to the Adjutant General reflected a fundamental change in Patrick's outlook on roles and missions since taking command of the Air Service. In an address sponsored by the Franklin Institute in September 1924, Patrick presented a treatise on "Military Aircraft and Their Use in Warfare" which sounded much like Mitchell. Patrick prescribed missions for Army aircraft against both land and naval objectives. While little use was made of aircraft against hostile shipping during World War I, Patrick pointed to the successful experiments against the *Ostfriesland* and other warships as conclusive evidence that bombers could put naval craft out of action. Those tests confirmed the important role of the Air Service in coastal defense, Patrick said. He envisioned that airplanes scouting as far as 200 miles out to sea could provide timely warning of an approaching enemy fleet, enabling a commander to concentrate opposing air forces. To test this theory, the Air Service moved a bomber group from the Chesapeake Bay to Bangor, Maine, in approximately eight hours, with the group ready to overpower an imaginary enemy within an hour after reaching its destination. The Air Service flew nonstop across the continent in about 26 hours and was completing an around-the-world flight. Patrick proclaimed this flight showed "that no distances or no difficulties" were great enough to make any country immune from air attack.[46]

The Navy, and to a lesser degree the Coast Artillery, resisted overtures for a more prominent Air Service role in coastal defense. Having long shared responsibilities with the Navy, the Army's area of operations traditionally extended seaward to the range of its coastal batteries. Coast Artillery commanders controlled these specialized Army operations and wanted similar control over coastal air defense.[47] This was unacceptable to General Patrick because it ran counter to his plans to centralize offensive aviation to enable it to mobilize its air forces in an emergency. But the War Department's failure to act on the findings of the Lassiter Board, already approved in principle by Secretary Weeks, stymied Patrick's plans.

Some officers on the General Staff opposed the GHQ Air Force concept because financing would come at the expense of other Army requirements and because it implied more autonomy for the Air Service. Nevertheless, Secretary of War Weeks had approved the concept, and the Joint Board had endorsed the long-range aviation programs of both services. The War and Navy Departments reached an impasse, however, when Secretary Weeks proposed a single appropriation for all military aviation and asked the Navy to adjust its program to accommodate early funding of Army aviation requirements. He thought the appropriations "should be considered at the same time by the same Congressional Committee," and Congress should make a suitable division of funds "based on the requirements of each service and their combined needs."[48]

Aided by the debilitating effects of the Washington Naval Treaty and by Mitchell's successful bombing demonstration, Admiral Moffett persuaded his superiors that the Navy needed a more ambitious aviation program to support fleet operations and prevent Army aviation from encroaching on roles and missions that traditionally belonged to the fleet. The Navy saw Weeks' proposal as an Army scheme to undermine Moffett's program and allow Army aviation to usurp the entire coastal air defense role. Secretary of the Navy Edwin Denby responded in February 1924 that he saw no relation between funds appropriated for Army aviation and those appropriated for Navy aviation. Nor did he see any reason for proportioning the monies to the two air arms. "There seems to me to be no more reason for pooling appropriations for Fleet and Shore Aviation than there is for pooling appropriations for battleships and forts," the Navy Secretary wrote.[49] Failing to change Denby's mind, Weeks also tried unsuccessfully to convince the new Secretary of the Navy, Curtis D. Wilbur. Wilbur argued that Week's proposal would require the creation of a separate Congressional air committee or subcommittee. "Such a step would, in my opinion, lead inevitably toward removal of Naval Aviation from control of the Navy Department," Wilbur wrote, adding that this was a "conclusion to which I am unalterably opposed."[50]

Mitchell, who returned from his extended Pacific tour in mid-1924, saw the impasse between the War and Navy Departments as vindication of his arguments for a unified air force. The Assistant Chief used his interlude from Washington to study air power and disseminate his theories within the Air Service. After completing his 1923 European trip, Mitchell distributed an unofficial manual among Army airmen entitled, "Notes on the Multi-Motored Bombardment Group," which defined bombardment aviation as that branch "of the offensive air force of the nation" whose function was "to attack enemy objectives by day and by night, on land or water." The mission of bombardment aviation, according to Mitchell, was to sink or disable all types of seacraft and to attack troop concentration centers and land targets "for destruction, conflagration, evacuation, dispersion, intimidation, and reprisal." Mitchell noted that bombardment aviation also could be used "as a means of transportation and supply."[51]

From observations during his Pacific trip, Mitchell wrote a critical report citing the inadequacy of American defenses and warning of inevitable hostilities between the United States and Japan. Running out of patience with what he considered official indifference to his assessments of the Pacific threat and lingering inaction on the Lassiter Board's findings, Mitchell began to agitate even more vigorously for a strong and independent air force.[52]

Ignoring General Staff directives, Mitchell repeatedly attacked existing aviation policies in the months following his return. By early 1925, he had so alienated top government officials, including President Calvin Coolidge, that the Secretary of War opposed his reappointment as Assistant Chief of the Air Service. Mitchell's indiscriminate and often unsubstantiated statements to the press and members of Congress exasperated Secretary Weeks. Testifying before a House of Representatives Committee chaired by Congressman Julian Lampert, Mitchell accused the Bureau of Aeronautics of muzzling naval aviators and of making misleading statements to the committee. He claimed the War Department neglected Army aviation and failed to act on the findings of the Lassiter Board. These and similar charges outraged his superiors. Not only had Mitchell become an embarrassment to the Secretary of War, his attacks on the integrity of fellow officers exacerbated already strained interservice relations over coastal air defense and appropriations for military aviation.[53]

President Coolidge was fed up with Mitchell's agitation and concurred in Secretary Weeks' decision not to reappoint him as assistant chief. When Mitchell's tour ended in April 1925, he reverted to the permanent grade of colonel and was posted to Fort Sam Houston in San Antonio, Texas. Secretary

Roles and Missions

The crash of the *Shenandoah* near Ava, Ohio, on September 3, 1925, pushed General Mitchell to lodge charges of incompetence and negligence at the military establishment, which, in turn, prompted President Coolidge to charge Mitchell with insubordination. *(NASM photo)*

Weeks appointed Col. James E. Fechet to replace Mitchell and elevated him to the rank of brigadier general. Over the ensuing months, Mitchell published his second book, *Winged Defense*, and sporadically broke his silence to speak out about air power. The administration tolerated these occasional outbursts until Mitchell charged the War and Navy Departments with "incompetency, criminal

General Billy Mitchell's court martial in 1925 was a sensational trial that captured the attention of the nation and served as a trial for the future of military aviation as well as for General Mitchell's military career. *(NASM photo)*

negligence and almost treasonable administration of our national defense" when the Navy dirigible *Shenandoah* crashed in September 1925. President Coolidge ordered Mitchell's court-martial and charged him with willful insubordination. The sensational seven week trial began in Washington, D.C., on October 28, 1925. The court found Mitchell guilty and he tendered his resignation, effective February 1, 1926.[54]

Mitchell's court-martial put the future of military aviation on trial since the proceedings delved into the role of aeronautics in national security. Mitchell's supporters believed he had deliberately provoked the President into preferring charges so the full case for air power could be argued before the American people. Younger Air Service officers, including Henry H. Arnold and Carl A. Spaatz were steadfast in their loyalty to Mitchell, but they also considered the court-martial justified.[55] Admiral Moffett denounced Mitchell as a "military demagogue" who got what he deserved.[56] Speaking as an old rival and colleague, Foulois had "no quarrel with Mitchell's championing the need for air power before the American public," but deplored "his methods and his lack of judgment about what he said."[57] General Patrick could no longer apologize for Mitchell. The charges against the War and Navy Departments were "most intemperate and in many ways unjust," he conceded, and he described the sensational trial to a friend as a "rather messy time."[58]

The irony of the trial for Mitchell was that it did not accomplish what he evidently hoped for. Nothing was said during the proceedings that had not been said before, either in congressional testimony or in published writings, and the trial attracted little public or official response. It resulted in middle-of-the-road statutory resolution of the postwar roles and missions struggle through enactment of the Army Air Corps Act of 1926, legislation fashioned from the findings of the President's Aircraft Board. It fell far short of Mitchell's expectations.

The Morrow Board and The Air Corps Act of 1926

At the request of the War and Navy secretaries, President Coolidge ordered his own investigation into military aviation to coincide with Mitchell's court-martial. On September 12, he appointed a board to be headed by influential banker and lawyer Dwight D. Morrow to study "the best means of developing and applying aircraft in national defense." The board was to report to him by the end of November. During four hectic weeks of public hearings, the President's Aircraft Board (popularly known as the Morrow Board) heard testimony from 99 witnesses-including Patrick, Moffett, Mitchell, the Secretaries of War and Navy, the Secretary of Commerce, the Postmaster General, aircraft industry representatives, and others-and reviewed stacks of testimony from previous hearings. The Morrow Board sent its report to the President on November 30, as Mitchell's trial was under way. Acknowledging the controversial nature of its inquiry and "the great conflict in testimony," the Morrow Board pointed to the "violent wrench of postwar retrenchment" which curtailed opportunities in the Army and the aircraft industry. The Board noted that various causes had been assigned for the controversy:

> the prejudice of the older arms of the service against the new arm, the lack of discipline of the new arm, the fact that the casualties in the new arm are much greater than in any other arm of the service, the sensational character of [the] airman's work even without exaggeration, the readiness with which that work may be exploited by those seeking sensation, the violent propaganda of interested parties.[59]

"It is not unnatural that the controversy which arose between the newer and the older arms...should have raged with some bitterness," the Morrow Board reported, suggesting that such "conflicts of thought" might even be desirable as long as the armed forces retained "that essential discipline without which an army becomes a mob." The board urged patience and "more generous appreciation by each side for the difficulties of the other side." Conceding that aviation created "overlapping of the Army and Navy," the board did not find the duplication unwieldy, but thought that "an element of competition in certain matters has its advantages." Therefore, the board saw no need for a separate department for air or for a Department of National Defense. Saying that "armaments beget armaments," the Board argued that there was no potential threat from air attack which would justify building up disparately large air forces. "The next war may well start in the air," the report concluded, "but in all probability will wind up, as the last war did, in the mud."[60]

The Morrow Board recommended changes in the Army air arm, including a name change to the Air Corps to eliminate confusion between the auxiliary air role and the separate air mission. Another recommendation was to create an additional Assistant Secretary of War to coordinate aviation matters. The board also proposed special representation for aviation on the General Staff and recommended developing a five-year plan to modernize the air arm, in contrast to the ten-year plan endorsed by the Lassiter Board.

The Morrow Board also recommended changes in naval aviation, noting there was "unrest and dissatisfaction among aviation personnel in the Navy". Navy flyers felt their devotion to aviation reduced their chances for promotion and opportunity for high command. They objected to the appointment of non-aviators to command flying men. Among its recommendations, the Board proposed that an additional secretary of the Navy coordinate aviation and that aviators be given stronger representation in the Office of the Chief of Naval Operations and the Bureau of Navigation.[61]

There was a wide divergence of opinion between the Morrow Board report and the findings of the Lampert Committee, which were announced in

December 1925 after eleven months of hearings and less than a month after the Morrow Report appeared. Although the two investigative bodies sifted through much of the same evidence, the Lampert Committee's conclusions were diametrical to those of the Morrow Board. The Lampert Committee endorsed a unified and independent air force, with a department of defense to coordinate the three services. The Morrow Board, however, had more influence because it gave President Coolidge the middle course he was seeking and favored the status quo. The President's endorsement of the Morrow Board report helped blunt Mitchell's allegations and limit the political repercussions of his trial.

Coolidge's influence on the legislative process was apparent when the 69th Congress passed the Air Corps Act of July 2, 1926, bringing only nominal changes. The act renamed the Air Service the Air Corps, created an assistant secretary of war for air matters, increased Air Corps representation on the General Staff, and authorized a five-year expansion program for Army aviation.[62] Concurrently, Congress created an assistant secretary of the Navy to foster naval aeronautics, requiring that command of aircraft carriers, tenders, aviation stations, and tactical flight units be assigned to naval air officers, and establishing a five-year expansion program for naval aviation.[63]

Privately, General Patrick expressed great disappointment in the Morrow Board report and the resultant legislation. "While composed of good men, most of them had preconceived ideas of the proper solution of the matter," Patrick wrote an acquaintance, "and the opposition to what I consider constructive recommendations was too great for those who favored such action to bring about anything really worthwhile."[64] Patrick, who admitted he had changed his position since becoming Chief of the Air Service, believed a department of national defense was the solution to the defense problem. For the time being, Patrick wanted a "semi-autonomous" air organization "somewhat analogous" to the Marine Corps.[65]

Merely changing the name from Air Service to Air Corps was not what he had in mind, but he did tell the House Military Affairs Committee that the five-year development program and other aspects of the Air Corps Act were "a long step in the right direction" which would "very materially increase the efficiency" of the air arm.[66] Under the five-year programs, the Army would be equipped with 1,800 newly designed planes and the Navy with 1,000 new planes.[67]

Neither the Morrow Board nor the Act of 1926 addressed the question of a GHQ air force or an independent air mission. Nor did they broach the problem of overlapping roles and missions between the Army and Navy air arms. Who was responsible for what in defending the nation's coasts remained unresolved. The issue of a single appropriation for military aviation was dead. Passage of the Air Corps Act brought the Mitchell era to a close. Army airmen embarked on an extended journey into what one historian called "a decade of patience and progress."[68]

Roles and Missions

Joint Action of the Army and the Navy

"The defense of the coast itself may rest with the Army Air Service," Admiral Moffett told the Morrow Board in September 1925, "but the offense of the coast should rest with naval aviation." The high-water mark had long been the dividing line between Army and Navy control, he explained, with the Navy responsible for protecting sea lines of communication, including convoy, patrol, and scouting. Moffett accused the Army air arm of wanting "to restrict naval aviation to the high-seas fleet, and to take over convoy, patrol, and scouting, using land planes for these purposes." The Admiral saw no need to change the traditional Navy missions. If an enemy air offensive escaped the fleet at sea and pressed against American shores, he said, then both Army and Navy forces would be called to repel it.[69]

In contrasting testimony, General Patrick said there should be three fundamental phases-the "sea action phase," the "air action phase," and the "land action phase"-to defend an attack on the United States or its territories. He thought primary responsibility for each phase should be fixed on the arm with the dominant role and the actions of other arms would be subordinate to the dominant arm's policies. Theoretically, Patrick envisioned the sea action theater as extending seaward from the effective range of shore-based aircraft, or approximately 200 miles out. The air action had this range as its outer limit, with the inner limit determined by the range of coast artillery. The effective artillery range created the outer boundary of the land action theater, which covered the total land mass. Patrick noted that no important air or land phase would be fought if the high-seas fleet secured a favorable decision over hostile naval forces.[70]

When asked how a foreign power could attack from 200 miles out, in view of existing aviation limitations, Patrick pointed out that the USS *Langley* had launched aircraft from that distance during a recent mock raid against Hawaiian bases.[71] Furthermore, aviation technology was progressing rapidly, with steady improvements in aircraft capabilities. Since the war, Army and Navy aviators experimented with increased speed, altitude, distance, and duration. The Army completed a historic world flight in 1924 while the Navy demonstrated the feasibility of aerial refueling in 1921. Army pilots improved the technique to transfer fuel from one plane to another while airborne in 1922; Major Spaatz tested the use of drop-tanks in 1924. These and other efforts to improve operational capabilities spawned a healthy competitive spirit between the air arms, unlike the often brusque exchanges over roles and missions during the postwar hearings.[72]

From the Navy's vantage point, Army air actions against ships at sea were an encroachment on their mission and they sought to limit the distance that Army planes could operate from shore. The limitation, which Army aviators considered arbitrary and restrictive, became a major point of contention. Army airmen saw an incongruity in joint planning which used carrier aircraft to attack inland targets but restricted land-based planes from offensive action at sea.

Problems with the Navy aside, General Patrick admitted to difficulties convincing his own superiors of the importance of the offensive air role in planning for war. The peacetime mission of the Air Corps, as Patrick summarized it, was to prepare for war by training an adequate nucleus of personnel, developing and maintaining suitable aircraft and equipment, testing and perfecting operational plans, and fostering an adequate aircraft industry. In time of war, he said, the mission was "to further the national war policy by our offensive and defensive action, and by assisting the military forces...in land or sea action." Impugning "the motives of no one," Patrick said he believed the War Department had "done the best it knew how," but had treated the air arm "as a stepchild" because it did not understand its importance. Patrick believed that patience was needed and that the General Staff was "being educated." He pointed to his own experience in gaining acceptance for the ideas that commended an air force rather than merely an auxiliary arm. "The term [air force] is used now by the Army Staff, is used by the schools," Patrick said, "but I had to fight for it for about three years before I could get it adopted and get it realized that there was such a thing."[73]

General Patrick and his successors found it frustrating to get the General Staff to follow its own policies on aviation. The new Army regulation governing the organization and functions of the Air Corps defined a wartime role for GHQ air forces, but the War Department made no provision for an organization to plan, equip, and train for this role in peacetime. The forces assigned to GHQ aviation in wartime executed aerial missions, including operations in defense of coastal frontiers, in furtherance of the strategical and tactical plans of the Commander in Chief. The GHQ air forces also could be employed in support of or in lieu of naval aviation. In the absence of a peacetime GHQ air organization, however, Air Corps units normally were assigned or attached to armies, corps, or divisions and charged with executing aerial missions in support of the Army, corps, or division commanders. The General Staff rebuffed attempts to change the peacetime tables of organization to place attack aviation under one command until General Douglas MacArthur became Army Chief of Staff in November 1930.[74]

Moffett encountered similar misunderstandings about the status of aviation from senior officers in the Navy. Commenting on the Morrow Board report, Adm. S.S. Robison, Commander in Chief, U.S. Fleet, objected to testimony that only naval aviators should command aircraft carriers and that control of aviation personnel be placed under the Bureau of Aeronautics. In a letter to the Secretary of the Navy, Robison denounced the command issue as "tainted by self-interest" and "bred of insubordination...injected by the Mitchell school and by yellow press clamor." Robison praised the accomplishments of the Bureau of Aeronautics, but warned that it was not "their duty to determine the qualifications of commanding officers of ships, nor to spend...their time in attempting to establish and secure exclusive privileges for aviators through class legislation."[75] Moffett later said that Robinson's remarks "explain to me now the attitude of the

Gen. James E. Fechet, between Maj. Gen. Benjamin Foulois and Brig. Gen. Henry C. Pratt, became the new Air Chief at the end of 1927. *(NASM photo)*

high ranking officers towards the Bureau of Aeronautics and myself during the past few years." Moffett claimed he spoke with the Secretary of the Navy, who said that Robison "did not know the situation and was entirely mistaken."[76]

Neither Moffett nor Patrick were dissuaded by opposition to their respective aviation programs. When General Patrick retired in December 1927 and relinquished command to General Fechet, both air arms had embarked on the congressionally approved five-year development programs. Apart from material and operational growth, however, it appeared that the Army Air Corps inherited little else of substance from the "storms of controversy" over postwar roles and missions. Conceptually and doctrinally, Army aviators had convinced the General Staff that aviation could play a valuable offensive role in war as well as in supporting ground forces, but the air arm failed to resolve the question of a GHQ air force, as recommended by the Lassiter Board, or the overlapping responsibilities for coastal defense. Still, in *The United States in the Air* published in 1928, General Patrick expressed "hope and belief" that the day would come when the United States would establish three military branches, "the Army, the Navy, [and] the Air Force," under a single Department of Defense.[77]

Meanwhile, the Navy and Marine Corps air arms were being forged into able fighting forces in their own right. After over two years of testing, the converted carrier *Langley* reported for duty with the fleet in November 1925 and became an integral part of fleet war planning. Pilots aboard the *Langley* developed tactics and techniques to attack hostile naval forces. In October 1926, pilots from VF Squadron 2 simulated dive-bombing attacks against heavy ships of the Pacific Fleet when Curtiss fighters swooped down in almost vertical dives from

12,000 feet, catching the ships by surprise even though they had been fore-warned. In May 1927, the Chief of Naval Operations ordered tests to evaluate dive bombing against moving targets, leading to the adoption of dive-bombing as a standard method of attack. By the end of 1927, the Navy had placed the air-craft carriers USS *Saratoga* and USS *Lexington* in commission, adding muscle to naval aviation's fighting capabilities.[78] Marine Corps aviators showed their fighting skills in support of Marine operations in Nicaragua in 1927 and 1928. A Marine squadron also accompanied the 3d Brigade to China in 1927, flying nearly 4,000 noncombat sorties to support the peacekeeping mission.[79]

Because of their more extensive combat experience in World War I, Army airmen were ahead of their Navy counterparts in roles and missions development when the war ended. Admiral Moffett and the Navy aviators closed this doctri-nal and technological gap as their service-awakened by the *Ostfriesland* affair and the agitation for a unified air force-recognized the potential of carrier avia-tion and aircraft facilities ashore in aiding fleet missions at sea. Passage of the Air Corps Act and equivalent Navy legislation in 1926 pushed the air arms onto parallel development tracks. The formation of joint policy procedures reflected the integration of aviation functions into the larger mosaic of Army and Navy operations.

In April 1927, the service secretaries issued new joint guidance in a land-mark document titled *Joint Action of the Army and Navy*. The new guidance addressed common missions and defined the general functions of the Army, the Navy, and the Marine Corps, with a separate chapter devoted to Army and Navy air components. The intent was to assemble in a single volume all approved joint policies, agreements, and instructions, "with a view to securing effective coordi-nation" between the services. The document provided flexibility to expand or revise guidance, as necessary.[80]

The traditional demarcations between Army and Navy responsibilities, including air operations, remained unchanged. It was axiomatic, however, that the President was empowered "to make exceptions to any general allocation of functions" or that an emergency might require one service to perform the func-tions of another. For instance, the Marine Corps normally operated as an adjunct to the Navy, but it could be called upon to perform "such duties on land as the President may direct," as an adjunct to the Army. This happened when President Wilson ordered Marines to duty with the Army expeditionary forces in World War I.

Another exception concerned overlapping Army and Navy functions in coastal defense and joint overseas operations. Generally, the Joint Board ruled, the principle that guided functional exceptions was that Army operations at sea or Navy operations on land were "proper only when immediately auxiliary to the normal functions." The board ruled that coordination of joint operations would occur under the principle of "paramount interest," favored by the Navy, or the principle of "unity of command," favored by the Army. Under the principle of paramount interest, authority was vested in the commander whose function was of greater importance. Under unity of command, the President appointed either an Army or Navy officer to command forces engaged in joint operations. The method of coordination was to be specified in joint war plans.[81]

The new guidance reaffirmed that the primary function of the Army air component was to operate as an arm of the mobile Army and that of the Navy air component, as an arm of the fleet. The Marine Corps air component was an element of the naval component, employing land-based aircraft to support Marine actions. Each air component had secondary functions and was subject to the policies governing its parent service, including coordination under the principles of paramount interest or unity of command. The joint policy guidance acknowledged the special character of independent operations, but made no reference to an independent air mission. Joint operations were classified as joint overseas movements, landing attacks against shore objectives, attacks against a shore objective by land and sea, coast defense, and special situations in which Army and Navy forces combined to accomplish a task normally assigned to one service.[82]

Starting with the five-year development programs, the Joint Board sought to minimize duplication among air components by jointly considering the procurement of aircraft and aviation appropriations for both services. Disagreement continued over the common use of facilities, the duplication of aircraft operations, and other overlapping functions. In one disagreement, Army airmen challenged the Navy's procurement of torpedo bombers to use from shore bases charging that it duplicated the role of Army bombers in coast defense. After over a year of deliberation, the Joint Board concluded there was no duplication.[83]

Overlapping roles and missions in coastal defense continued to foster interservice disagreements during joint maneuvers. After signatories of the Washington Naval Treaty signed another agreement in London in April 1930, providing for additional reductions of naval armament, Admiral Moffett created a stir by proposing that a large fleet of aircraft carriers was needed to defend the coast from enemy attack. In an article published in the *Los Angeles Examiner* in August of that year, Moffett claimed that Navy carriers had demonstrated they could execute a successful bombing raid against shore objectives without interference from land-based aircraft. Moffett was quoted as saying that the only way to stop such a raid was "to go out and meet the enemy" with airpower at sea. "The airplane cannot fly there and maintain itself," Moffett said, "It must be carried there on ships, on aircraft carriers and other combatant vessels of the Navy."[84]

Major Carl Spaatz, who commanded Air Corps squadrons during Army-Navy maneuvers on the West Coast, disagreed with Moffett. He said that recent joint exercises in the San Francisco area demonstrated conclusively that a small formation of land-based pursuit planes could follow carrier-based planes to their ship and put it out of commission. Furthermore, the carriers were at a disadvantage because they could only launch one plane at a time, while large formations could take off from land-based squadrons. Naval aircraft had to recover and rearm at sea, but land-based planes could recover safely at any field in range.[85]

In his report on the San Francisco maneuvers, Spaatz said his strategy was to ignore air operations by the enemy, relying upon antiaircraft artillery to defend military objectives and initially expend the entire air effort on the theoretical destruction of carriers. By attacking carriers rather than meeting enemy planes, Spaatz claimed that Air Corps squadrons demonstrated:

> that unless the Navy is willing to sacrifice its carrier based air-craft, and carrier, after one mission, it is impossible for them to attack shore defenses even with an overwhelming superiority of airplanes, *providing* the defense is willing to submit to one air attack by the airplanes from each carrier in order to effectively prevent further attacks.[86]

Eighteen months later, in a report on joint maneuvers in Hawaii, Spaatz said that the experience confirmed his earlier conclusion that land-based planes had to be properly dispersed and have proper radio equipment, but they could defeat an attacking enemy force by concentrating on destroying the carriers. Spaatz believed that the strategy of attacking carriers rather than planes should be basic in coastal air defense doctrine.[87]

While the services pondered their operational differences, the simmering controversy over coast defense aviation heated up in Washington after Secretary of War Patrick J. Hurley asked President Herbert Hoover to halt the Navy's plans to procure torpedo bombers and develop air stations. Hurley believed such action would duplicate functions assigned to Army aviation. President Hoover, whose administration was burdened with a severe economic depression, saw an opportunity to cut military spending, but he wanted the services to resolve the issue themselves. Secretary of the Navy Charles Francis Adams maintained that the War Department should abide by the Joint Board decision that the Navy's program was not duplicative of the Army's. After conferring through the spring and summer of 1930, Secretaries Hurley and Adams reached an impasse as both refused to retreat from their positions.[88]

In August 1930, with the dispute unresolved, Admiral Moffett complained to a friend that the Secretary of War (whom he described as a member of the President's "medicine ball cabinet") had "entree to the White House" and acted "in a most unprecedented manner" in trying to make naval aviation "move entirely from the shore and take all our air stations with us." Moffett hoped that Adm. William V. Pratt (Hoover's nominee to be the next Chief of Naval Operations) could influence the President's decision when he came to Washington in September. Secretary Adams told Moffett that "the matter would be settled before Pratt could get here," implying that the President might have already decided in favor of the Army.[89] Adam's prediction proved accurate.

Roles and Missions

On January 9, 1931, the War Department announced that the new Chief of Staff of the Army, Gen. Douglas MacArthur, had reached an agreement with Admiral Pratt "assuring the fleet absolute freedom of action without any responsibility for coast defense." The War Department said that discussions leading to the agreement had "resulted in a clearer evaluation of the fundamental principles involved in the use of the air weapon" and that the agreement left the Army and Navy air forces "free to develop within well defined limits and each with a separate and distinct mission." The agreement was heralded "as the beginning of the closest cooperation that has ever existed between the two great branches of our National Defense."[90]

Against Moffett's wishes, Admiral Pratt had already issued a new policy on naval aviation establishing it as an integral element of the fleet under the direct command of the Commander in Chief, U.S. Fleet. The new policy charged naval aviation with developing the offensive power of the fleet and advanced base forces to protect the United States and its possessions against invasion. Naval aviation's participation in coast defense was relegated to a secondary mission element. Air stations in strategic naval operating areas were assigned to the U.S. Fleet. Only stations necessary for training, test, aircraft repairs, and similar support functions remained under shore command.[91]

Difficulties in locating and sinking an old freighter, the *Mount Shasta*, in August 1931 raised doubts about the Air Corps' ability to perform the coastal air defense role. On August 11, because of inclement weather, a provisional squadron of nine planes failed to locate the *Mount Shasta*, about 55 miles out to sea. Three days later, the squadron found the freighter but was unable to sink it because the planes were armed with 300-pound bombs, known to be ineffective against naval vessels since Mitchell's sinking of the *Ostfriesland* a decade earlier. The squadron's poor showing embarrassed the Air Corps. "The bombing episode on the East Coast has left a very sour taste in our mouths here," Major Spaatz wrote to Colonel Arnold from California on August 31. "Naturally we are called upon to absorb a lot of disparaging remarks delivered by Navy officers and civilians."

The Air Corps had demonstrated its prowess in locating naval vessels on other occasions. Spaatz recalled that only the previous summer "we were able to locate Navy carriers, at will, without much difficulty, even though at times they operated under cover of fog and were well off shore."[92] Nevertheless, the *Mount Shasta* failure convinced the General Staff that the Air Corps needed to be properly equipped and trained to fulfill its expanded coast defense responsibilities. The more expansive aerial role also helped Maj. Gen. Benjamin Foulois win War Department support to develop and procure long-range bombers after he succeeded General Fechet as Air Corps Chief of Staff in December 1931.

While Air Corps officers were pleased with the decision making the Army responsible for the coast defense mission, they were unsuccessful in attempts to formalize arrangements with Navy members in the joint area. The MacArthur-

Pratt agreement was informal, binding only while Admiral Pratt was in office. Both Moffett and Rear Adm. Ernest J. King, who became Chief of the Bureau of Aeronautics following Moffett's death in the crash of the airship USS *Akron* in 1933, fought against giving up aerial coast defense to the Army. When Admiral Pratt retired in June 1933, his successor, Adm. William H. Standley, repudiated the agreement. With President Hoover out of office, the Navy was more comfortable in its relationship with the White House. President Franklin D. Roosevelt had served as Assistant Secretary of the Navy from 1913 to 1920 and had opposed the drive for a unified air force.[93]

Admiral Standley supported Admiral King's contention that only naval aviation could adequately perform the functions of patrolling, scouting, and defending against hostile forces over water. After the MacArthur-Pratt agreement, the Air Corps wanted to extend the range of its coastal defense operations as far as 300 miles out to sea. The Navy vigorously opposed this encroachment, wanting instead to impose even greater limits on Air Corps activities off the coasts. At the same time, General MacArthur unequivocally supported Air Corps plans to expand its unique aerial defense responsibilities, which included developing new airfields, purchasing long-range bombers, and reorganizing its forces for the coastal defense mission. These and related developments came together as a prelude to establishing the long-awaited GHQ Air Force.

Prelude to the GHQ Air Force

Doctrinal underpinnings for Air Corps roles and missions came from a mix of operational experience, command and staff insights, and formal learning at the Air Corps Tactical School. During the various investigations into military aviation in the 1920s, General Patrick and others voiced a need to create a separate college to study air doctrine and provide education about the broad air power contribution to warfare. The Tactical School, which moved from Langley Field, Virginia, to Maxwell Field, Alabama, in 1931, was the sole facility available to fulfill that institutional requirement through the interwar period.

Mitchell's teachings and writings strongly influenced curriculum development at the Tactical School. Brigadier General Laurence Kuter spoke of this influence during an interview in 1942. He recalled that both Maj. Thomas DeWitt Milling (who was sent to Langley in 1921 to start the school) and Maj. William C. Sherman (who wrote the first major text on air tactics in 1921) participated in sinking the *Ostfriesland*, and both had integrated Mitchell's doctrine into the curriculum. Subsequently, at Langley and at Maxwell, the faculty expanded this instruction and separated it "into its several components, including tactics and techniques of attack aviation, tactics and techniques of bombardment aviation, and the employment of air forces." Kuter remembered the school as a center for serious thought and lively debate on air power topics during the 1930s.[94]

Students work in the Map Problem Room of the Air Corps Tactical School at Maxwell Field, Alabama, in the early 1930s. *(NASM photo)*

While the curriculum embraced a variety of aviation roles—attack, pursuit, bombardment, and observation—the faculty and students began to concentrate on the holistic aspects of air power after they settled in at Maxwell. The MacArthur-Pratt agreement, increased emphasis from General MacArthur on war planning and his support for Air Corps' procurement of long-range bombers converged with other developments to nurture the shift of doctrinal priorities from air-ground orientation toward GHQ aviation and a more independent air mission. During this juncture, when other courses began losing ground to bombardment aviation, an internal roles and missions feud erupted between fighter and bomber advocates.

The feuding began with the fighter pilots' belief that the Air Corps' long-range bomber program was being developed at the expense of pursuit aviation. In this charged environment, Capt. Claire Chennault earned his reputation as the champion of pursuit aviation while teaching pursuit tactics at the Tactical School from 1931 to 1936. Speaking and writing prolifically, Chennault authored a classic text that became a bible for fighter tacticians in World War II. His dogged drive for fighter equivalency antagonized Air Corps officers who perceived that a broader view of air force employment was prerequisite to wider understanding and acceptance of the independent air role.[95]

Among the critics of Chennault's parochial approach to aviation was Lt. Kenneth Walker, who believed Army airmen should think "in terms of air force" rather than have narrow functional viewpoints. Walker wrote Major Spaatz in 1934 that he thought the Air Corps "should stop graduating bombers and pursuiters, but graduate all as air force officers." Referring to an article by

Captain Claire Chennault
pushed for recognition of
the tactical fighting capabilities of aircraft, in both
his teachings at the Tactical
School and in his writings.
(NASM photo)

Chennault on pursuit aviation, Walker said, "One big reason why we in the Air Corps can't get together is because of prejudices we have built up in considering ourselves as bombardiers or pursuiters and we quarrel and wrangle amongst ourselves." Walker was confident that Spaatz shared his views:

> I know damned well that you are as confident of your ability to command a bombardment, observation or attack group as well as a pursuit group...You informed me at Dayton last year that you had gained a broad air force point of view primarily because in your command you had to think in terms of air force because you had two types of units therein.[96]

Feuding within the Air Corps made explaining the independent air role to other Army officers more difficult. General Kuter credited the Tactical School with spreading the broader view of air power during the 1930s, saying the school "was the point from which Air Force thought was formulated and disseminated throughout the Air Corps and to some extent throughout the Army." Before World War II, other Army schools began to acknowledge the importance of the Tactical School's instruction as some blocks of instruction were inserted into courses at the General Staff School, the Army War College, and the Industrial College.[97]

No one promoted the total air force concept more actively than General Foulois after he became Chief of Air Corps in 1931. Believing as strongly as his predecessors in service unification and an autonomous air force, Foulois was no more successful than earlier air leaders had been in overcoming entrenched opposition from the War and Navy Departments. As General MacArthur explained, strong air units were essential to Army and Navy combat operations, and the services were not going to support any organizational change they feared would diminish the quality of air support they received. As an interim solution,

Roles and Missions

Foulois argued for the next best thing: activation of a peacetime GHQ Air Force. The General Staff resisted this because they thought it might encourage neglect of the air-ground role.[98]

During General MacArthur's tour as Chief of Staff, however, the General Staff moved progressively, though cautiously, toward an understanding of the advantages of a GHQ aviation organization to prepare and plan for the wartime role. As General Foulois and others before him argued, the GHQ air forces had to be armed and ready to strike at strategic points early in a conflict. General MacArthur's increased emphasis on war planning underscored the inconsistency in preparing air forces to support field armies while leaving them unprepared to perform the more critical GHQ aviation roles at the outset of hostilities.[99]

A top priority during MacArthur's second year as Chief of Staff was to weld Army forces into "an integrated tactical machine", ready to respond instantaneously "to the orders of the President" and to deal with "all emergencies short of a general mobilization." To accomplish this, General MacArthur devised the Four-Army Plan, dividing the United States into four strategic areas with a field army in each area under the Chief of Staff's tactical control. Within each region, the senior corps commander served as the field commander reporting directly to General MacArthur. The War Plans Division comprised MacArthur's GHQ staff. This restructuring of the peacetime Army provided the impetus that the Air Corps needed to justify establishing the peacetime GHQ Air Force.[100]

March Field, California, became an active Air Corps base of operations in 1933 with the formation of the GHQ Air Force. *(NASM photo)*

In keeping with General MacArthur's policies, the Air Corps began to concentrate on war planning and refining the GHQ aviation concept. During two weeks of intensive training in May 1933, the Air Corps formed a GHQ Air Force (Provisional) at March Field, California, and exercised the full range of wartime missions, including attacking airdromes and aircraft carriers. The General Staff showed greater interest in the Air Corps' wartime role after a War Department Board headed by Deputy Chief of Staff Maj. Gen. Hugh A. Drum endorsed the GHQ Air Force concept in August 1933. The next summer, the War Department included the GHQ Air Force as part of its GHQ command post exercise. Meanwhile, problems in early 1934 with carrying the mail prompted serious concerns about the operational capabilities of the Army air arm. After twelve deaths and over sixty crashes in the mail operations, the Air Corps came under critical review by Congress and the War Department.[101]

In the spring of 1934, as the Air Corps' performance in the airmail project worsened, the Secretary of War appointed a board, chaired by former Secretary of War Newton D. Baker, to study the air arm as an agency of national defense. Between April and July, the Baker Board heard testimony from over 100 witnesses and analyzed an extensive body of evidence, including the reports from sixteen previous boards and committees. These historical analyses of Army aviation ranged from the Dickman Board findings of 1919 to the Drum Board report of 1933. The final report that the Baker Board submitted in July 1934, drew the disturbing conclusion that Army combat aviation had fallen below "other leading aviation powers of the world in strength." Naval combat aviation, on the other hand, was numerically and qualitatively superior to that of foreign powers.[102]

Optimistically, the Baker Board concluded that the understanding between the higher command of the Army and the Air Corps was greater than it had ever been. There was hope that this sympathic relationship would "progressively diminish difficulties" which had "heretofore seemed obstinate, if not chronic."

Too many crashes and too many casualties incurred while delivering the U.S. mail brought questions and criticism to the Army airmen.

Roles and Missions

While naval power remained the first line of national defense, the Baker Board emphasized the imperative nature of ground and air roles:

> Since ground forces alone are capable of occupying territory, or, with certainty, preventing occupation of our own territory, the Army with its own air forces remains the ultimate decisive factor in war.[103]

Citing the 1933 War Department study chaired by General Drum, the Baker Board defined the normal mission of the Air Corps as "air operations over the land or the sea, functioning as air units of the Army, in the conduct of land-based operations." Corollary special missions included joint air operations over sea or land with naval air forces against enemy forces, naval vessels, or ground forces. The report repeated the conclusion of the Drum Board and its predecessors that an independent air force was not necessary to defend the United States against air attack. Using the experience of World War I, the report said that while the air arms were powerful components on each side, independent air missions had "little if any effect upon the issue of battles and none upon the outcome of the war."[104]

Suggesting that the Air Corps had "virtually been independent since its inception," the Baker Board did not support more autonomy for the air arm. The board, however, did believe that the combat air forces should be separate and distinct from having to develop, procure, and supply equipment and trained personnel, as was true in other arms and services. The board, therefore, advocated organizing Air Corps units into a GHQ air force without delay. Under this concept, the GHQ Air Force commander would report to the Army Chief of Staff in peacetime and to the Army commander during war, while the Chief of Air Corps would handle development, procurement, and supply functions. This arrangement, the board said, would enable the GHQ Air Force, when adequately equipped and organized, "to carry out all the missions contemplated for a separate or independent air force, cooperate efficiently with the ground forces, and make for greater economy."[105]

In the fall of 1934, as the War Department moved toward implementing the Baker Board's recommendations, General MacArthur published guidance on "doctrines for the employment of the GHQ Air Force," as interpreted by the Joint Board and concurred in by the service secretaries. The Joint Board, of which General MacArthur was a senior member, stipulated that establishing the GHQ Air Force did not contravene existing policies governing Army and Navy functions, as set forth in *Joint Action of the Army and the Navy*. While recognizing that the Army was responsible for the "direct defense of the coast," joint planning emphasized that the fleet, if positioned to defend against enemy forces, had paramount interest in operations at sea. Air forces would join such operations under the temporary command of the naval commander. If naval strategy positioned the fleet elsewhere, Naval forces supplemented by Army Air Corps units would monitor hostile fleet movements. In either situation, the GHQ Air Force would perform reconnaissance.[106]

If hostile naval forces escaped detection or engagement at sea and a major assault upon the coast ensued, joint doctrine called for employment of the GHQ Air Force in three phases. During the first phase, it would conduct reconnaissance over sea approaches and attack enemy elements, when opportunity presented. In the second phase, the GHQ Air Force would support fixed and mobile artillery by conducting observation, reconnaissance, and offensive operations. These operations would last from the time the enemy came within range of ground weapons until he was driven off or the third phase developed. If the enemy persisted, the GHQ Air Force would carry out joint operations on the coastal frontier.[107]

Thus, the Army prepared to organize the GHQ Air Force in early 1935-reaching a new milestone and opening a new chapter in the roles and missions history of the Air Corps. For Army airmen, this momentous act formalized its independent air mission. On the eve of this historic development, however, the Joint Board's guidance enforced strict boundaries on the employment of GHQ Air Force units. Interpretation of these boundaries promised to add lively debate to the interservice roles and missions experience in the months ahead.

General Frank M. Andrews became the first commander of the General
Headquarters (GHQ) Air Force upon its creation in 1935. *(NASM photo)*

CHAPTER III

PATTERNS: WORLD WAR II AND THE DAWN OF GLOBAL AIR POWER

Speaking at the Army War College in 1936, Maj. Gen. Frank M. Andrews explained why the GHQ Air Force had been created and the role it was "destined to play in national defense." He told the audience that to understand the role of the GHQ Air Force, they had to understand air power. This meant accepting the premise that the airplane was not just another weapon but was "an engine of war" which "brought into being a new and entirely different mode of warfare-the application of air power."

"It is another means, operating in another element, for the same basic purpose as the application of military power or sea power-the destruction of the enemy's will to fight," he said. The depiction of air power by General Andrews reflected the doctrine expounded by Mitchell, Patrick, and other airmen since their initiation to aerial combat in World I. The potential of military aviation as a third dimension of war, now organized within the U.S. Army to include the first named air force, was more credible in 1936 than it had been in years past.[1]

As Commander of the GHQ Air Force since its inception in March 1935, General Andrews concentrated more time and resources toward planning, equipping, and training the air forces for the independent air role than previously had been possible. He received more support from the members of the General Staff, who concurred with the recommendations of the Drum Board and Baker Committee to establish the GHQ Air Force as a "highly mobile and powerful striking force" under direct control of the Army Chief of Staff in peace and the Commander in Chief of the field forces during war. General Douglas MacArthur, who led the way to establish the GHQ Air Force, claimed the new organization could perform "every mission that could be carried out" by a separate air force. In granting the air arm this "special consideration," however, he cautioned that "to an increasing extent it should become an integral and vital element of the organization through which teamwork is assured." He believed that air operations, including those beyond the sphere of influence of ground forces, existed to support the land campaign. Opposed to a separate air force, MacArthur declared, "The group of aviators who are to cooperate with land forces, to be truly efficient, must be qualified soldiers, in all that the term implies."[2]

Major General Oscar Westover, who succeeded General Foulois as Chief of Air Corps in 1935, agreed with the Army Chief of Staff about the role of the air forces. Known as a stickler for official military channels since his early days in the Air Service, General Westover supported creating the GHQ Air Force but opposed its separation from the Army.[3] In a paper written before his 1938 death in an air crash, he defended the Army against criticism that it had neglected development of military aviation. He stated unequivocally that "military leaders are fully conscious of what the nation needs for air defense and they are sparing no effort to provide it."[4] Maj. Gen. Henry H. Arnold and Col. Ira Eaker co-authored a book which said, "In the light of succeeding years," the establishment of the GHQ Air Force "proved to have been a wise and prudent step."[5] Air Corps officers generally agreed with this assessment even though most-like Arnold and Eaker-believed an autonomous air force to be the ultimate solution to the nation's air power problems.

General Andrews advocated greater autonomy during his command of the GHQ Air Force and championed development of the long-range bomber. He believed the bomber would be a vital force in future wars. In October 1935, he obtained Gen. Malin Craig's (MacArthur's successor as Chief of Staff) approval of a revised training regulation. The new regulation was bolder than previous Army manuals in its treatment of air power doctrine, defining air power as the capacity of a nation "to conduct air operations; specifically, the power which a nation is capable of exerting by means of its air forces." Although the efficacy of air power had not been fully tested, the regulation predicted "that skillful use of air forces will greatly affect operations in future wars" and stressed economy of force and other principles related to the use of air power. "Whereas it is always unwise to fritter away military forces, it is dangerous in case of air forces," the regulation stated. "Air Forces should accordingly be concentrated against the primary objective, the

Reconnaissance missions remained a critical function of Army aviation. In 1936, an aerial photographer at Maxwell Field, Alabama, prepares a camera for a training mission. *(NASM photo)*

one most advantageous in the situation, and not dispersed or dissipated in minor or secondary operations."[6]

An earlier version of this regulation, published in 1926, framed Army aviation roles and missions within the doctrinal dimensions of World War I. The GHQ Air Force was defined as an air reserve for field armies to assist "directly the ground forces by joining in the ground battle and indirectly by operating against hostile lines of communication." The 1926 regulation implied an understanding of the inherent flexibility of the air weapon in its statement that GHQ Air Force possessed "great freedom of movement, making it possible to rapidly concentrate superior forces at important points when necessary," but it left no doubt that employment of the air reserve was responsive to the needs of the field armies. By comparison, the 1935 version centered on the roles and missions of the new GHQ Air Force.[7]

During his 1936 talk at the War College, General Andrews described the GHQ Air Force as the "medium" for "the application of air power" in the continental United States. He emphasized the role of bombardment aviation as "the principle force employed in independent air operations," but he was careful not to minimize attack, pursuit, or reconnaissance missions, which he knew were more familiar to field Army officers. "They all have their roles, and importance," he said, but he stressed that "the measure of air power of a nation is really that of its bombardment." Pointing out that the bomber forces were "the striking arm-the arm with the punch," Andrews predicted that long-range bombers were "destined to play a large part-and exert a tremendous influence-in any future war between great powers."[8]

General Andrews' views were consistent with emerging strategic air warfare doctrine taught at the Air Corps Tactical School before World War II, doctrine that served as a point of reference for Air Corps training and operations under the new regulation. Decades later, Maj. Gen. Haywood S. Hansell, Jr., recalled the American theory of strategic bombing as it evolved in the 1930s by framing it within three basic precepts: that modern military powers depended upon their industrial capacity to wage war; that sustained precision bombing sorties could cripple or destroy a nation's industrial systems; and that striking forces could penetrate enemy defenses and drop bombs without unacceptable losses. Hansell said that differences of opinion existed among airmen as well as among members of the other arms.[9]

New technology during the 1930s—the introduction of the B–17 Flying Fortress and a program to develop larger airplanes—gave the Army air arm the means to perform the long-range strike mission. The largest plane built for the Army since the Barling Bomber in 1923, the B–17 had a range of 2,480 miles and could carry up to five tons of bombs.[10] Critics of the larger bombers argued that their only purpose was for "aggressive action," but General Andrews called such criticisms "unfortunate and misleading." He explained that operational factors limited the tactical employment of fully loaded B–17s to only 750 miles from their home base. While the B–17 was a formidable addition to the nation's air arsenal, Andrews believed that planes with the range and speed to reinforce Alaska, Hawaii,

The Boeing B-17 Flying Fortress quickly became the primary bombardment aircraft for the Air Corps. *(NASM photo)*

Panama, and the Caribbean had yet to be developed. Forward basing was essential to employ the new bombers.[11]

Like other military arms, limited appropriations constrained the Air Corps' ability to fund costly experimental programs. Emerging from the depression, the nation's economic horizons were still bleak while the military threat-although building in Europe and the Pacific-did not justify maintaining armed forces beyond those required for hemispheric defense and protection of outlying possessions. Between 1933, when the War Department approved the experimental B–17 program, and 1937, when the B–17 became operational, Army aviation appropriations more than doubled, rising from $25.4 million to $59.4 million. Still, the air arm failed to reach modernization levels recommended by the Baker Board. Total Army appropriations showed a lower increase, rising from $289.5 million in 1933 to $383.1 million in 1937. Strapped for funds and unconvinced of the need for long-range bombers, the War Department trimmed the Air Corps' request for B–17s from 65 to 13, barely enough to equip a single squadron.[12]

Comparable Navy statistics showed a rise in total appropriations from $317.5 million in 1933 to $526.3 million in 1937, with the amounts spent on naval aviation rising from $25.2 million to $38.5 million during the same period. More rigidly fixed than the Army's force levels, the Navy's ship-building programs remained linked to international naval treaties amended in London in 1930. Since the 1920s, the Navy had maintained less strength than was allowed by the treaties, but this began to change by the mid-1930s. The Navy had only one vessel designed and built as a carrier, the *Ranger*, and it was not commissioned until 1934. In June 1933, Congress authorized construction of two 19,000-ton carriers, the *Yorktown* and the *Enterprise*, under the National Recovery Act. Shortly after, the Vinson-Trammel Treaty Navy Bill of 1934 authorized construction to bring the Navy up to treaty strength as well as the procurement of naval aircraft. Sizable increases in both Army and Navy strength did not come until after 1938, however, as planners realized that other nations were increasing the strength of their armies and navies "at an accelerating rate."[13]

The rise of bombardment aviation and the strategic air role nourished doctrinal thinking within the Air Corps and pulled it further from its Army roots. Despite these Army developments, naval air doctrine remained closely integrated with fleet doctrine in the 1930s. As Chief of the Bureau of Aeronautics in the post-Moffett era, from 1933 to 1936, Rear Adm. Ernest J. King kept naval aviation on the conservative course of his predecessor. Entering aviation late in his career when he took command of the aircraft tender *Wright* at age 47, King believed naval air elements "must always be integral and primary components of the fleet."[14] King, who was said to have an "almost pathological suspicion of anything in the form of an autonomous air force,"[15] and other senior Navy officers opposed the tack that Air Corps doctrine was taking because they perceived it as a threat to the sovereignty of naval aviation. King said it was futile "to classify air as a separate entity" because it was "impossible to hold a line of battle in the air" and it was "necessary to hold the surface in order to hold the air." "There are two-and only two-surfaces of the earth," King said, "and 'air power' cannot exist if it has no surface to take off from or to alight on whether it be land or water." He believed, therefore, that it was essential to classify aviation in relation to the forces with which it "must operate."[16]

General MacArthur echoed Admiral King's belief in the inherent division of air power during his tour as Army Chief of Staff. While conceding that "unified air power" might be effective "to meet the probable situations of the earlier stages of war," MacArthur thought that air forces would "necessarily be differentiated more and more into the two categories of Army and Navy aviation" as war mounted. He wrote in 1934:

> Air [power] must be based either on the surface of the earth or on the sea, and its offensive targets are found on these surfaces. This basic law clearly differentiates two categories of air force-one based on the fleet, the other based on land. These two types of aviation are differentiated not only by dissimilarities in objectives and equipment, but also by fundamental and unsurmountable differences between the types of forces with which they must cooperate.[17]

Roles and Missions

General MacArthur acknowledged there would "undoubtedly be occasions in war when air operations beyond the immediate theaters of land or sea forces were desirable." The creation of the GHQ Air Force provided for this potential.[18] While MacArthur and other senior Army officers supported the GHQ Air Force during its brief life-span (from 1935 until the creation of the Army Air Forces in June 1941), they opposed the air arm's growing emphasis on long-range bombardment. Ground officers feared that the GHQ Air Force's concentration on planning, equipping, and training for the independent air role fostered neglect of other flying missions (e.g., observation, reconnaissance, and close air support) which they saw as more critical to the land campaign. The airmen's belief in the primacy of the strategic air role prevailed, however, even though the GHQ Air Force's plans and operations were limited to hemispheric defense.

Despite these limitations, in 1944 General Arnold called the GHQ Air Force's activities the blueprints for global air power in World War II. "In the nineteen-thirties when air power was the unseen guest at those grim conferences which marked the Nazi march to power, the Army Air Corps, which preceded the Army Air Forces, had drawn its blueprints for war," Arnold said-tracing those blueprints to the 1935 establishment of the GHQ Air Force. "Our operations were based on the needs and problems of our own hemisphere, with its vast seas, huge land areas, great distances, and varying terrains and climates," Arnold said. "If we could fly here, we could fly everywhere, and such has proved to be the case."[19]

Prelude to Pearl Harbor: Rethinking Roles and Missions

General Andrews said that the GHQ Air Force's centralized control of air combat units (attack, bombardment, pursuit, and reconnaissance) in the continental United States was key to the effective application of air power. Formerly, the tactical control of air combat units was divided among corps area commanders-a fragmentation of forces which General Andrews believed created "insufficient coordination and direction of tactical thought and doctrine" and a lapse in the development of air power capabilities. While the new command arrangements resolved the fragmented control, the GHQ Air Force achieved "the proper amount of decentralization" by organizing three strategically based composite wings-the 1st Wing on the West Coast, the 2d Wing on the East Coast, and the 3d Wing at Barksdale Field, Louisiana. These wings included attack, pursuit, bombardment, and reconnaissance aircraft.[20]

It was months after taking command before General Andrews was satisfied that he had the necessary span of control to field an efficient striking force. The debate over GHQ Air Force's lines of authority accelerated after Andrews reported to the War Department on the test of his organization in 1936. He claimed that the test proved the soundness of organizing Air Corps tactical combat units into one force, under a single commander, but he complained about lack of authority over basing, inadequate allocation of resources, and problems of coordination with Air

Major General Delos C. Emmons became the second commander of the GHQ Air Force in 1939, replacing Gen. Frank M. Andrews. *(NASM photo)*

Corps headquarters. To resolve these issues, the War Department gave Andrews control over permanent peacetime air stations, formerly under the jurisdiction of Corps area commanders, and approved his request to make tactical combat squadrons self-contained. Before implementing this change, General Andrews had to deflect an attempt to return the peacetime GHQ Air Force to Air Corps control.[21]

After reviewing Andrews' report in January 1936, General Westover complained to the Chief of Staff that "the separate growth of the GHQ Air Force" had created a "cleavage" in Army aviation which only a return of the peacetime force to the Air Corps chain of command could eliminate.

Westover did not believe the GHQ Air Force, which represented about 40 percent of the Corps, should be developed at the expense of the rest of the Air Corps, but he was concerned that he could not assure an "efficient and equitable distribution" under existing arrangements. The Air Corps Chief also worried about two authorities advising the War Department on aviation matters, one on the Air Corps and the other on the GHQ Air Force. Westover opposed assigning bases to the GHQ Air Force because he feared this would further undermine Air Corps control. He told General Craig in April that Andrews earlier shared his views about integrating the two commands but that he had changed his mind. Urging that Craig make a "positive decision...to integrate the GHQ Air Force with the Air Corps at some specified date in the future," Westover thought this should heal the "cleavage," which might "never be eliminated if the present set-up is allowed to continue."[22] Westover failed to bring GHQ aviation under Air Corps control, and the dual-command structure remained until Arnold became Chief of the Air Corps in September 1938. When Maj. Gen. Delos C. Emmons replaced Andrews as commander of GHQ Air Force in March 1939, he became directly subordinate to General Arnold.[23]

The initial progress from the service test of the GHQ Air Force soon faltered because of profound differences between the Army airmen and higher command over development and use of the long-range bomber. For the remainder of his four-year tour, General Andrews' persisted in linking GHQ Air Force roles and missions to "an ambitious program of bomber development" which alienated the General Staff. Unlike MacArthur, General Craig was openly hostile to the procurement of long-range bombers and their employment in the strategic air role.[24]

While MacArthur was Chief of Staff, the Army supported the Air Corps program to develop and procure advanced bombers, agreeing that the Drum Board's recommended goal of 2,320 aircraft, including 400 bombers, should be revised by type to obtain as many new heavy bombers as the Air Corps deemed necessary and as many as funds permitted. But after MacArthur's departure, the General Staff persistently opposed the advanced bomber program. Drastically reducing the purchase of B–17s, General Craig deferred Air Corps plans to develop bombers.[25]

A growing emphasis on the independent "air power" concept among Army airmen contributed to strained relations with the General Staff. The substance of the differing views was presented in an analysis of the revised *Joint Action of the Army and Navy* by the Air Corps Board. In the Air Corps report, which was not meant for outside release, the board contended that the joint document contradicted the meaning of air power because it ignored the importance of air forces "as a powerful weapon of national defense." According to the board, the document's broad classification of the air arm of the Army as "an integral part of the land forces" and the air arm of the Navy as "an integral part of the sea forces" failed to recognize the ability of air forces to operate beyond the sphere of surface forces.[26]

In November 1936, General Westover approved a companion study which examined "probable strategical missions and the broader functional responsibilities of the Air Corps." The study, which was an amplification of doctrine expressed in *Joint Action of the Army and Navy*, was framed within the larger context of air power contained in the new training regulation. "Air forces, as distinguished from our ground and sea forces, may constitute a powerful strategic agency of national defense," the authors explained, "and as such, should be charged with the performance of those functions for which they are peculiarly fitted." While acknowledging the basic roles of Army and Navy aviation, the authors placed air forces on equal footing with land and sea forces. They recommended their study be approved and adopted by the War Department as its "Air Corps Policy" for the functioning and employment of the Air Corps. War Department approval, however, was not forthcoming.[27]

Choosing against referring the study to the Joint Board, the War Department became less reluctant to make an issue of the long-range bomber controversy when it reached a critical juncture months later. In 1937, General Andrews proposed that future bombardment units be equipped only with four-engine bombers, but he was rebuffed by higher headquarters. In March 1938, Secretary of War Woodring, whom critics characterized as parsimonious, uninformed about military matters, and indifferent to the war secretary appointment, approved a five-year modernization program stripping the Air Corps of advanced bomber purchases. He replaced them with less costly planes more suitable for supporting ground forces.[28] The

Secretary restricted experimentation and development for 1939 and 1940 "to that class of aviation designed for the close support of ground troops and the protection of that type of aircraft such as medium and light bombers, pursuit or other light aircraft."[29]

The Woodring Program assumed that long-range bombers were not needed to defend the United States and its outlying possessions and that the Air Corps should not be augmented "beyond the state of readiness established for the other combat arms." The Adjutant General told the Air Corps that the War Department wanted it to prepare for the close support mission "to the same extent" as it was preparing for "strategic and more distant missions." The close support mission did not require equipment with the range, speed, and destructive power of modern, heavy bombers. He believed that "the Infantry Division continues to be the basic combat element by which battles are won, the enemy field forces destroyed and captured territory held," and that the Air Corps would have to adjust its program accordingly.[30] GHQ Air Force training and operations continued to center on the B–17s, and General Andrews tried to save the heavy bomber program.

In May 1938, the bomber dispute spilled into the joint arena after General Andrews held special maneuvers off the East Coast to demonstrate the GHQ Air Force's ability to intercept ships before they reached American shores. Not pleased with the results of a joint exercise a few months earlier when his bombers succeeded only after difficulty locating the battleship *Utah* under fog off the California coast, Andrews hoped for a more convincing demonstration of the B–17's capabilities. The highly publicized maneuvers on May 12 drew immediate reaction from the War and Navy Departments. Three B–17s readily intercepted the Italian liner *Rex* some 725 miles out to sea as it steamed toward New York City. General Craig issued a verbal order "limiting all activities of the Army Air Corps to within 100 miles from the shoreline of the United States."[31]

A month later, the War Department referred the issue of advanced bomber development to the Joint Board, a move the General Staff later admitted was a mistake. Predictably, the Joint Board ruled that the Army did not need long-range bombers, recommending instead that it be equipped with medium bombers and aircraft to support ground forces. The General Staff made its position against heavy bombers clear, while the Navy's reaction to the *Rex* affair denied the Air Corps any mission at sea requiring aircraft with a range greater than that of carrier-based planes. In view of the nation's defensive posture and the strategic situation, the Joint Board reinforced the opinions of Secretary Woodring and the War Department that there was no reason to believe the Air Corps would be called upon to perform missions requiring the use of B–17s or larger bombers.[32] Meanwhile, the Naval Expansion Act of May 1938 authorized the Navy to expand its air arm to 3,000 planes.[33]

To make the case for a valid long-range bomber mission, in June 1938, General Westover asked the Air Corps Board to look at the potential roles of military aviation in enforcing the Monroe Doctrine. Completed shortly after Westover's

Roles and Missions

death in September, the report prompted further study by General Arnold's planning staff "of the size, composition, and capabilities of aviation forces" required to enforce national policy. The board concluded that potential existed for the U.S. military to be called upon to quell internal disturbances and restore order throughout the hemisphere, to prevent the invasion of other American countries by hostile powers, or to eject hostile forces from American countries. This possibility placed a premium on long-range bombardment and reconnaissance forces "capable of offensive air action anywhere on the American continent, from Alaska to the Strait of Magellan." In addition to offensive air operations in theaters adjacent to the United States, the report foresaw the potential for multiple theater operations including distant theaters requiring expeditionary movement of forces.[34]

The fate of the long-range bomber took a new turn after President Roosevelt, in consultation with his military chiefs, began planning for national rearmament during the autumn of 1938. Roosevelt believed that the concessions to Hitler at Munich made war inevitable and that the United States could not stay out of it. Alarmed by the strength of the Luftwaffe, he knew that air power would be essential to defeating Nazi aggression. Under pressure from the White House, Congress authorized $300 million for Air Corps expansion in April 1939. Anticipating authorization to buy more than 3,000 new planes, General Arnold wanted to be sure that the Army bought the best aircraft for the mission. In March, Arnold formed a special board to study how to employ air forces in hemispheric defense. After reviewing the completed study in September, Gen. George C. Marshall, the new Army Chief of Staff, described it as the first clear statement of a wartime mission for the Air Corps that he had seen.[35]

General Marshall's approval of the Air Board report marked a change in the War Department's attitude toward the long-range bomber and its wartime mission. As a refinement of the earlier "Monroe Doctrine" study, the report reaffirmed the primacy of the strategic air role and the importance of bombardment aviation in applying air power. Repeating the assumption that air forces, in addition to their basic responsibility to defend the United States and its possessions, might conduct air operations "over land and sea to great distances beyond the operating bases," the report gave de facto recognition to the menacing global strategic situation. Prospects for sending expeditionary forces abroad were greater than in two decades. Even more striking was the need to be able to conduct long-range missions against warring nations. While addressing all mission potentials, including reconnaissance, close air support, and transport, the report stated Air Corps roles and missions to correspond with the advanced capabilities of bombers and the principles of air power doctrine developed at the Air Corps Tactical School and the GHQ Air Force.[36]

Hitler's invasion of Poland in September 1939 and the Luftwaffe's swift destruction of the Polish air force brought a sobering reassessment of Air Corps mission requirements. The United States moved closer to a war footing as the fall of Norway, Holland, Belgium, and France left only the British free to oppose Nazi aggression in western Europe. The rise in military appropriations over the ensuing months, the lifting of restrictions under the neutrality laws, and the enactment of Lend-Lease galvanized the American aircraft industry as it tooled up to fill orders from U.S. and allied air forces. The Battle of Britain erased any remaining doubts about the impact of air power, while Japan's militarism rounded out the global scope of the conflict. The speed, range, and firepower of modern aircraft in a two-ocean war were obvious.

Within the milieu of burgeoning world conflict, General Marshall showed a greater affinity for air power than any former Army chief of staff. One of his first official acts was to return General Andrews to Washington as senior air adviser to the General Staff. Since leaving the GHQ Air Force, Andrews had reverted to the permanent rank of colonel and was posted to San Antonio, an assignment that invited comparison to the War Department's treatment of General Mitchell fourteen years earlier. Marshall, while serving as Malin Craig's deputy, had formed a high regard for Andrews and valued his advice on air matters during the critical prewar military build-up. At the same time, the bond between Marshall and Arnold grew as the war in Europe unfolded, convincing Marshall that the air arm needed more unity and authority. In November 1940, Marshall made Arnold his deputy for air in addition to his duties as Chief of the Air Corps. The following April, Robert A. Lovett became Assistant Secretary of War for Air, a position that had remained vacant since F. Trubee Davison's departure in 1932. Capping these initiatives, Marshall reorganized the air arm, creating the Army Air Forces on June 20, 1941. As chief of the AAF, Arnold retained a dual hat as Marshall's deputy.[37]

Although Arnold wanted full autonomy, he agreed with General Marshall that it was unwise to undertake such a radical change until the nation was past the war emergency. Meanwhile, creating the AAF gave Arnold the authority to plan and develop the air forces to fight a global war. He answered only to Marshall, and was a de facto member of the Joint Chiefs of Staff, placing him on equal footing with the Army and Navy chiefs.

Much of the impetus for Arnold's new authority came from inroads made by the GHQ Air Force, which passed into history when the Air Force Combat Command was created in June. During its brief existence, the GHQ Air Force had changed the way Americans thought about air power and created patterns for air operations to follow in World War II.

Growing rapprochement between U.S. and British military planners added urgency to reordering AAF roles and missions. Beginning in January 1941, secret American-British conversations produced the basic strategy and a combined plan for Allied collaboration in a two-ocean war against the Axis powers. Assuming Germany was the predominant threat, the Allies identified the Atlantic and Europe as the "decisive theater," and agreed to concentrate on defeating Germany before turning their military power against Japan, if the United States entered the war. Guided by this strategic principle, the strategists stressed the need for rapid achievement of superior air strength over the enemy, "particularly in long-range striking forces" to sustain a combined "air offensive against German Military Power, supplemented by air offensives against other regions under enemy control which contribute to that power." While recognizing the need for multiple air roles to support ground and naval operations, the plan emphasized offensive AAF bombardment units operating in collaboration with the RAF, "primarily against Germany Military Power at its source" to prepare for a land offensive against Germany.[38]

By the summer of 1941, AAF planning had matured enough to reliably predict the numbers and types of planes that the United States and its allies would need to engage "simultaneously in war against Germany and Japan." In August, the newly formed Air War Plans Division (AWPD) produced AWPD-1, a remarkably accurate forecast of force strategy and requirements, as part of an overall Army-Navy estimate of arms production "required to defeat potential U.S. enemies." President Roosevelt asked his service secretaries for a confidential estimate of requirements so the administration could finalize its victory programs and galvanize industry for the task ahead. In their report, the services reiterated "that the first major objective of the United States and its Associates ought to be the complete military defeat of Germany" while holding Japan in check. This confirmed the Germany-first policy, agreed upon in early 1941, which prevailed throughout the war.[39] In a sense, AWPD-1 represented a compromise of roles and missions differences and a recognition that reordering priorities was necessary for victory.

Neither the War nor the Navy Department challenged the priority assigned to the production of heavy bombers for the strategic offensive against Germany. Army planners acknowledged "the important influence" of air power, including both air support and strategical missions. "No major military operation in any theater will succeed without air superiority, or at least air superiority disputed," they noted. Navy planners commented on the "increased fighting potential" of naval aviation and called for a strong two-ocean Navy of fast cruisers, destroyers, aircraft carriers, torpedo boats, and submarines. The planners noted that enemy air power had not yet deprived naval vessels of "their vital role on the high seas," but had "greatly accelerated methods and changed the techniques in their employment."[40] Marine air units, meanwhile, had become vital elements in Marine training for amphibious operations in the Pacific, supporting the ground forces who stormed ashore in World War II.

Other priority requirements outlined in AWPD-1 were pursuit, reconnaissance, and transport aircraft. Since 1939, air planners had reconsidered these mission capabilities, especially pursuit aviation, partly because they were engrossed with long-range bomber development but also because they had miscalculated the requirements for fighter aircraft. Fiscal constraints also influenced the neglect of other missions. When he became Air Corps Chief in 1939, General Arnold was concerned that emphasis on bombardment aviation had caused other missions to lag behind. He saw the need for long-range escort fighters, but recognized that other tactical missions also needed attention. Renouncing the doctrine "widely propounded in certain Air Corps circles for many years" that fighters could not "shoot down large bombardment planes in formations," Arnold said that air warfare in Europe proved this assumption false. Noting "the very great role" that pursuit aviation played in air combat and antiaircraft defense, Arnold directed the GHQ Air Force to study the problem and arrive at a program of "new ideas and initiative" in fighter development and employment.[41] Thus, belatedly, the air arm saw the need to rebuild fighter aviation. It was late 1943, however, before the AAF had long-range fighters to escort heavy bombers on deep penetration missions over Germany.[42]

Army field commanders, who did not share General Marshall's views on air power, were more concerned about the air arm's neglect of weapons and tactics to support troops in battle. Serious misunderstandings remained between air and ground commanders even as the Army prepared for war. Between the wars, Army flyers viewed close air support and other missions in the larger context of air power, viewing the various mission elements as integral parts of an overall air campaign. They believed that, ideally, theater air forces should operate as an entity, similar to the GHQ Air Force, under the direction of an air commander who could use them according to sound air principles.

As inculcated in airmen since General Mitchell's 1918 exploits, the key to a successful air campaign was planning. With proper planning, a commander could take advantage of the inherent flexibility of air power to concentrate forces when and where they were most needed, whether in strategic operations, air superiority, interdiction, or support of ground forces, without disruption from enemy air forces. The best way to protect troops and planes from enemy attack was to wage an early, relentless campaign for control of the air. Field commanders also found that the fight for control of the skies required planning and could not be prosecuted in isolation.

As the Luftwaffe illustrated early in World War II, the campaign for air superiority involved more than shooting down enemy planes. During Germany's invasions of Poland and the Low Countries, the Luftwaffe not only destroyed opposing planes in the air and on the ground, but attacked maintenance and production facilities to keep the enemy from regenerating sorties. Unopposed Luftwaffe planes flew interdiction missions to isolate the battlefield while supporting the conquest of enemy ground territory.

During the Battle of Britain, however, the Luftwaffe failed to win control of the air. As a result, the German air arm suffered unacceptable losses to numerically inferior, but tactically superior RAF fighter squadrons. This setback caused the German high command to call off Sea Lion, their planned invasion of England, and gave the British time to regenerate air forces for action in North Africa and against the continent. More successful in the invasion of Russia the following year, the Luftwaffe readily destroyed the Red air force, but left the Soviet warmaking capacity intact. Aided by a severe winter, the Red army staved off the German advance despite the invading army's superior air and mechanized support and rebuilt their shattered air forces.[43]

Roles and Missions

To American airmen, the opening rounds of air warfare by the Luftwaffe bolstered their theory that wars between industrial powers would be decided not by battlefield attrition alone, but by the destruction of a nation's capacity to make war. Colonel Carl Spaatz, in London as an observer during the Battle of Britain, agreed with RAF leaders that the sustained application of air power on a grand scale against the German heartland would be required to win air ascendancy over the Luftwaffe and then to join with other arms in achieving total victory. When he observed Luftwaffe raids on London in the summer of 1940, Spaatz is said to have exclaimed, "Those damned fools will set air power back twenty years."[44]

Spaatz and other airmen believed that the German defeat over England resulted from the failure to gain air superiority against the RAF, the failure to configure bombers with adequate defensive armament and the failure to provide daylight fighter escort. Rather than concentrating their forces against strategic targets, the Germans sent their bombers piecemeal across the channel, attacking in small groups at different times and places. This enabled British airmen to make maximum use of their limited fighter resources by having their Spitfires recover at dispersed bases, refuel, and attack more than one formation of bombers. Although the Luftwaffe massed its formations in a last desperate raid, it suffered unacceptable losses to RAF fighters. Tactics beget counter-tactics, but in the Battle of Britain the Luftwaffe failed to counter the RAF's defenses.[45]

There were opposing views concerning the initial air campaigns of the war. Naval observers in London reported that the Luftwaffe's defeat in the Battle of Britain and unsuccessful RAF night bombing operations conducted prematurely against Germany proved the fallacy of long-range bombardment. Vice Admiral R. L. Ghormley, the ranking Navy observer in London, urged increased production of aircraft for United States and British carriers instead.[46] Ironically, by steeling the British will to fight rather than striking terror into the hearts of the people, the Luftwaffe's relentless bombing of England's cities had the opposite effect of what was intended.

From their analysis of the opening campaigns of World War II, American ground commanders wanted the AAF to procure more planes like the Luftwaffe's Stuka Ju–87 to support the land battle. Although Germany possessed bombers like those flown in the Battle of Britain, the Luftwaffe's experience in the Spanish Civil War led to the development of a more tactically-based air doctrine. German pilots found that the topography and the lack of clear battle lines in Spain, which was not an industrial power, did not afford lucrative bombing targets. Tactical air operations to support ground combat were effective, while high-level bombing without accurate bomb sights against targets of nominal military value was useless. Tactical air forces with the Stuka as a primary weapon system became the mainstay of the Luftwaffe, whose doctrinal manuals emphasized combined military operations with armor and infantry. In Washington, however, General Arnold and his staff resisted pressure from their ground counterparts to procure large numbers of specialized aircraft like the Stuka because of the plane's lack of versatility and its vulnerability to other fighters.[47]

Doctrinal differences continued to hamper effective air-ground teamwork, as revealed during the Army GHQ maneuvers in Louisiana and the Carolinas on the eve of America's entry into World War II. Commanders still wanted dedicated air units for firepower against opposing forces and to provide a protective umbrella over the battlefield. This meant fragmenting the air forces among field commands, which airmen argued would dilute the theater commander's ability to mass forces offensively against lucrative targets across an entire front. Lt. Gen. Lesley J. McNair wanted tactical air forces subordinated to the field commanders. In his view, the principles of flexibility and massing of forces, which were not unique to air force doctrine, did not obviate the need to integrate combined arms at the corps and division levels. Field Manual 1-5, *Employment of Aviation in the Army*, published in 1941, supported McNair's position. The manual addressed the full range of air missions, but assigned aviation units to the commander of field forces, who could assign them to specific corps and divisions.[48]

Inconsistencies between Field Manual 1-5 and air doctrine were not resolved to the AAF's satisfaction until after U.S. forces went into combat. Meanwhile, the Joint Chiefs provided a framework for change by formulating strategy for a three-dimensional war. In a report submitted to the President in September 1941, the Joint Chiefs concluded that because naval and air forces comprised the principal strength of the United States and most of its allies, "a sustained successful land offensive against the center of German power" in the near future was "out of the question." Until the Allies could build up their armies, the prevailing strategy called for peripheral land offensives where the Germans could not exert their full strength, while air and sea offensives were applied against German military, economic, and industrial resources. The Army doubted that this strategy would defeat Germany, convinced that the Allies would have "to come to grips with the German armies on the continent of Europe." For those who thought a strategic air offensive alone could force a surrender, the Army answered:

> Naval and air power may prevent wars from being lost, and by weakening enemy strength may greatly contribute to victory. By themselves, however, naval and air forces seldom, if ever, win important wars. It should be recognized as an almost invariable rule that only land armies can finally win wars.[49]

At the Arcadia conference convened in Washington, D.C. after Pearl Harbor, President Roosevelt and Prime Minister Winston Churchill reaffirmed their commitment to defeat Germany before unleashing full military power against Japan. A massive buildup under the Victory Program was necessary before the Allies would have the strength to mount a strategic offensive against the Axis. Until then, the Allies were confined to a defensive strategy of engaging enemy forces in outlying areas to check their advance and drive them from contested territories. The Arcadia discussions also reaffirmed the combined bomber offensive from the United

Roles and Missions

Kingdom as prerequisite to undertaking large-scale ground operations on the European continent. The bomber offensive depended on mass production from the Victory Program and the buildup of air strength in the United Kingdom.

The sustained bombardment of Japan's vital centers, meanwhile, had to await the capture of island bases closer to the Japanese homeland. While building up bomber forces in England and preparing for the strategic air offensive against Germany, the AAF cooperated with surface forces, demonstrating the flexibility and versatility of American air power. Among the more unique and controversial efforts during this period was the AAF's participation in the antisubmarine campaign.

The AAF Role in the Antisubmarine Campaign

For nearly two years, from before Pearl Harbor and into 1943, the AAF participated in the Allied campaign against Germany's deadly fleet of submarines in the Atlantic and contiguous waters. Thrown into an unfamiliar, ancillary role under the jurisdictions of the U.S. Navy and the RAF Coastal Command, the AAF adapted quickly to the new mission responsibilities and helped defeat the enemy's underwater fleet. From the start, however, the AAF was at doctrinal odds with the Navy in the antisubmarine war, which prompted a continuation of the roles and missions disputes from previous episodes involving the *Ostfriesland*, coastal defense, and the *Rex*. A running dispute with the Navy over the direction and employment of AAF forces exacerbated a reluctance to divert Army bombers for Navy use. As a result, the AAF's participation in the antisubmarine campaign became one of the most contentious interservice issues of World War II.

German U-boat forces commanded by Adm. Karl Doenitz, were a grave concern after Pearl Harbor because sustaining the movement of troops and war materials to the forward areas depended almost totally on shipping. To counter the growing threat in American waters, pilots of the AAF's I Bomber Command began flying regular antisubmarine patrols off the Eastern seaboard in late 1941. Pilots on the West Coast flew some patrol missions, but Japanese submarines never became a serious threat off America's coastlines. After years of resisting the perceived encroachment of Army aviation at sea, the Navy reluctantly asked the AAF to augment its own scant antisubmarine forces until sufficient naval resources became available.[50]

The AAF's antisubmarine operations raised old questions about jurisdiction over Army planes operating offshore. The wording in *Joint Action of the Army and Navy* remained ambiguous. These rules assigned the Navy primary responsibility for offshore patrol and protection of shipping, with the AAF supporting naval forces as required. In the past, Army airmen interpreted this to mean that the Army retained control over its own planes, especially when they operated in lieu of naval forces. Since it had the paramount interest in operations at sea, the Navy maintained that it had unity of command over all forces engaged in the antisubmarine war. Army airmen were apprehensive, however, fearing this could result in Navy control of land-based air forces used to defend the coasts.[51]

General Marshall believed in unity of command, and during the Arcadia talks he persuaded the combined chiefs to adopt the principle of unified land, sea, and air forces in Allied theaters of war. The combined chiefs had earlier promised to honor the national integrity of Allied forces. Applying these principles to joint operations, General Marshall agreed with his Navy counterpart, Adm. Ernest J. King, that unity of command for the antisubmarine campaign rested with the Navy. On March 26, the Joint Chiefs directed that commanders of sea frontiers had unequivocal jurisdiction over "naval forces allocated thereto and all Army air units engaged in operations over the sea for the protection of shipping and against enemy seaborne activities."[52]

Resources permitting, the Navy preferred to carry out operations at sea without being burdened with participation by AAF units. One means to accomplish this was to transfer planes from the Army. In January 1942, the Navy requested an urgent transfer of 200 B–24s to improve Hawaiian area defenses. Fearing follow-on attacks or possibly an invasion, the commander of the Pacific Fleet wanted the bombers to extend the Navy's long-range search and intercept capabilities "out to about 800 miles"[53]-only 75 miles further to sea than the liner *Rex* had been when GHQ Air Force B–17s intercepted it over three years earlier.

After General Arnold expressed an unwillingness to transfer the B–24s because of heavy demands on scarce AAF resources, Admiral King complained to General Marshall. King insisted that the AAF produce and turn over to the Navy enough bombers to defend Hawaii and help secure sea and air routes to the Southwest Pacific.[54] Arnold continued to resist King's demands, arguing that such a diversion of bombers would be "suicidal" to the AAF's expansion under the Victory Program. Serious shortages of heavy bombers was forecast for the first half of 1942, with no prospect to build up any reserve. Moreover, Arnold believed the AAF could provide air support to protect the sea lanes without relinquishing control of the planes.[55]

Admiral King was adamant and increased the Navy's demands for medium and heavy bombers to 400 B–24s and 900 B–25s for service in the Pacific and the North Atlantic in a March 1942 letter to General Arnold. King argued that the last two winters had demonstrated that "naval aviation missions such as convoy escort, observation, scouting, and patrolling over the sea, and the protection of shipping in the coastal zones" could not be accomplished by seaplanes operating from ice-bound bases in the North Atlantic and Pacific area. Moreover, he wrote, the "purely naval operations" of the RAF's Coastal Command proved that multi-engine, land-based planes had "advantages in increased range, ease of maintenance, and facility of operation over seaplanes."[56] Rear Adm. John H. Towers, chief of the Bureau of Aeronautics, suggested that Marine Corps pilots would fly the bombers.[57]

General Arnold still opposed the transfer of planes, saying that he understood the need for "unlimited cooperation in the present crisis," but did not agree that a

The B–24 aircraft, like these awaiting service on the ground during World War II, were in great demand by both the Army and Navy air arms. *(NASM photo)*

large naval bomber inventory was essential to the war effort. He repeated this concern to General Marshall. Arnold feared that King's proposal, if approved, might be the "forerunner of the Navy assuming the Army's primary responsibilities and functions for the operation and control" of a land-based air force.[58] Arnold suggested instead that the best way to support the Navy might be for the AAF to establish an air organization similar to the RAF Coastal Command. This would be an Army command with aircraft under the control of Navy authorities as the situation required, Arnold explained.[59]

Furious, King penned a stiff reply implying that the AAF's lack of cooperation was destructive to the war effort and reflected "the trend toward a separate air force." Disparaging the Royal Navy's experience with the RAF "for the past twenty-five years," King suggested that Arnold accept that "naval personnel are trained and skilled in things that have to do with the sea." As for Arnold's suggestion for larger AAF role in antisubmarine operations, King said he had been told "that air crews of Army planes cooperating with the Navy are not doing the work which you would expect of them."[60] While Arnold admitted that AAF air crews had been inexperienced and ill-equipped at the outset of the antisubmarine campaign, they picked up valuable pointers in tactics, techniques, and equipment from the RAF Coastal Command and learned from their mistakes. Forced to call on the Army for reinforcements, the Navy was equally unprepared. With the vanguard of the fleet challenging Japanese sea power in the Pacific, the Navy did not have enough carriers to join the battle in the Atlantic until March 1943.[61]

In early April, General Marshall agreed to increase heavy bomber forces in Hawaii to two groups, with one attached to the Pacific Fleet. He insisted, however,

Naval aviation played a critical role in World War II. Here, a North American B–25 lifts off the deck of the USS *Hornet* on April 18, 1942.

that bomber units not be turned over to the Navy, but be made available "in accordance with agreements for unity of command or operational control."[62] The Navy continued to demand bombers, however, and had leverage in the fact that the U-boat threat was undiminished and that ample precedent existed for a mutual exchange of equipment and services. The Navy already had provided the AAF with dive bombers for use in the Caribbean, although not in the numbers requested by the AAF. The roles and missions implications of the carrier-supported raid on Tokyo by AAF B–25s (conceived in January and carried out in April 1942), led by Lt. Col. James H. Doolittle, were not lost on either service. The highly publicized raid revealed just how pliant the functional lines between Army and Navy aviation really were.[63]

In June, Secretary of the Navy Frank Knox and Secretary of War Henry L. Stimson, presumably with encouragement from the White House, finally reached an agreement for the Army to allocate bombers to the Navy. The AAF subsequently arranged for a number of B–24s to be delivered over the next two years. Although the Navy received its initial complement of B–24s in August 1942, only 52 bombers were delivered by the end of the year. The delivery of 308 B–24s in 1943 and 600 in 1944 increased the total to 964 planes, giving the Navy a large land-based air force. Admiral King still complained that "many valuable months had been lost."[64]

Meanwhile, doctrinal differences between the AAF and the Navy over the use of air forces in the antisubmarine role convinced General Arnold that he was right in wanting to pattern AAF operations after the RAF Coastal Command. AAF commanders were dissatisfied with a naval policy that required air forces under Navy control to be assigned to and frozen within specified sea frontiers, a practice equating to the Army's division of tactical aviation among field commands. Counter to AAF doctrine, this policy restricted air mobility, tied air forces to zones where enemy vessels might not be operating, and denied commanders the flexibility to shift resources for effective use against U-boats.

Another divergence from AAF doctrine was the Navy's practice of employing bombers defensively and other protective forces to escort merchant convoys through dangerous waters. Accepting the reality that convoys needed to be escorted, Arnold's staff proposed that the full weight of air operations against U-boats be in the form of offensive operations. The AAF proposed to mount an offensive to seek out the U-boats and destroy them in coordination with the RAF Coastal Command. As part of the combined bomber offensive, Allied planes could attack U-boat ports and berthing facilities, eventually crippling Germany's ability to replenish the fleet. To plan and carry out the offensive, Arnold repeated his proposal for an AAF antisubmarine command.[65]

Admiral King rebuked Arnold for promoting an aviation solution to what he considered a naval problem, arguing that protecting the fleet offered the only "promise of success" at this stage of the war. He believed that only the Navy had the experience and knowledge to employ "the potency of sea-air power in fighting submarines."[66] With shipping losses at an appalling rate in the summer of 1942, however, General Marshall sided with Arnold in proposing a more offensive-minded strategy against the submarines. The buildup for the impending Allied invasion of North Africa was not unknown to the German fleet, prompting Admiral Doenitz to change strategy. Having gradually withdrawn his forces from American waters, Doenitz concentrated wolf-pack attacks along convoy routes in the mid-Atlantic gap and against ships in and around the war theater. General Arnold viewed interaction with RAF Coastal Command activities as critical to the success of an antisubmarine offensive.[67]

On October 15, 1942, over Admiral King's objections, the War Department activated the AAF Antisubmarine Command as a "highly mobile striking force" to seek out and destroy enemy submarines "wherever they may be operating." While the Navy retained operational control over AAF antisubmarine forces, the new AAF command could extend the range of its operations and initiate offensive action against the U-boats. The AAF organized hunter-killer groups to seek out and destroy the U-boats, sending two squadrons of radar-equipped B–24s to England to operate with the RAF Coastal Command off the French coast in the Bay of Biscay and in other waters where the German fleet was active. The British supported offensive action against the submarines, and urged a combined offensive to wrest the initiative from the German fleet. Admiral King, however, was unsparing in his criticism of the AAF. Unreceptive to a combined offensive at sea, King insisted that AAF forces concentrate on providing air cover for convoys.[68]

Through the early months of 1943, as German U-boats launched their spring offensive, the War and Navy Departments were locked in debate over strategic policy and the antisubmarine campaign. In April, General Marshall proposed that the Navy agree to an offensive air strategy against the U-boats and establish a joint command to plan and oversee these operations. Marshall wanted an Army air officer in charge of shore-based aircraft in the campaign, subject to the general operational control of the Navy. Fully supporting the proposal, Secretary of War Stimson argued that the Army was in a better position than the Navy to carry out the offensive, which proposed to attack "at strategic places like the Bay of Biscay and the exits from the North Sea, quite independent of the duty of covering convoys." The offensive, Secretary Stimson explained, required the use of land-based planes designed, built, and operated by the Army along with new air tactics familiar to the Army but not the Navy. Above all, he said, a new offensive to deal with the submarines required "the initiative and inventiveness of a young air-minded commander who could carry out his missions without the geographical limitations of the present Navy coastal frontiers." Secretary Stimson argued that "such an offensive during the coming summer and autumn" was essential to clear "the Atlantic Ocean of submarines in advance of the enormous stream of our troops which will be required to cross that Ocean for the 1944 invasion."[69]

Objecting vigorously, Admiral King declared that any arrangement which placed naval aviation under an Army air commander was unacceptable. As an alternative, King advised General Marshall of his intent to establish the Tenth Fleet under his immediate control, to command antisubmarine operations in the Atlantic under his strategic control. The availability of aircraft carriers for convoy escort and the ongoing program to furnish long-range bombers to the Navy raised questions about the need for further participation in the antisubmarine campaign by AAF units. In June, a joint committee including Generals Arnold and Joseph T. McNarney and Rear Adm. John S. McCain drew up an agreement outlining the conditions for AAF withdrawal from antisubmarine operations. The Arnold-McNarney-McCain agreement proposed that the AAF turn its specially equipped B–24s over to the Navy in return for a comparable number of Navy combat B–24s and assurances that Army land-based planes allocated to the Navy would not duplicate AAF roles and missions.

Admiral King agreed with the AAF offer to withdraw from antisubmarine operations, but refused to accept restrictions on using land-based Navy planes to strike "the enemy in other ways, if opportunity and the successful completion of their primary functions permitted." King said such restrictions implied a lack of confidence in the Navy and conflicted with joint agreements that neither service would "restrict in any way the means and weapons used by the other service in carrying out its functions."[70]

The rigidity of Admiral King's position disturbed Secretary of War Stimson, who said it boded "further trouble between the Army and the Navy over these vital problems of jurisdiction." Believing that an aggressive air offensive against the submarines was vital to "the safety of our great Army movement next year," Stimson said that if the matter went to the President, "I shall desire to be heard by him on the subject."[71] General Marshall told Admiral King that he viewed the Arnold-McNarney-McCain agreement as "a practical solution to a vexing problem which has adversely affected the efficiency of our aerial war effort." Marshall denounced the existing joint procedures between Army and Navy aviation saying they were "neither economical nor highly efficient and would inevitably meet with public condemnation were all the facts known."

"I have been hopeful that during the actual war effort we could manage our business in such a manner as to be spared the destructive effects of reorganizational procedures," Marshall said, "But I am becoming more and more convinced that we must put our own house in order, and quickly, in order to justify our obligation to the country."[72]

On July 9, 1943 the War and Navy Departments accepted the Arnold-McNarney-McCain agreement, leading the way for withdrawal of Army air forces from antisubmarine duty as soon the Navy was ready to assume those duties. The primary responsibility of the Army for long-range bombers operating from shore bases was stated clearly. Long-range patrol aircraft allocated to the Navy were assigned to conduct offshore patrol and reconnaissance and protect shipping. Field commanders, Army or Navy, were not restricted, however, from using "all available aircraft as weapons of opportunity or necessity."[73] By mid-November, the last group of AAF B–24s was withdrawn from antisubmarine duty.[74]

North Africa: Transforming the Tactical Air Role

The intensified campaign to take the initiative away from the German U-boats in the summer and fall of 1942 was a critical factor in planning the first major Allied offensive of the war. In July 1942, President Roosevelt and Prime Minister Churchill decided on a major revision in strategy, leading to rewriting AAF doctrine in the contested skies over North Africa.

Confronted with a deteriorating situation on the eastern front and setbacks in the Middle East, the Allied leaders agreed to mount Operation Torch, the invasion of North Africa, before year's end. Neither the combined bomber offensive nor the buildup in the United Kingdom was proceeding as planned, so the cross-channel invasion of Southern France was postponed until 1944. Offering a better chance of success than the cross-channel landings, Torch had the twofold objective of easing pressure on the eastern front while bringing sufficient force against General Erwin Rommel's Afrika Korps to drive the Axis out of North Africa and the Middle East.[75]

Global air mobility was an essential element of Allied strategy. Bases in North Africa and the Middle East were critical to the invasion of Italy and the southern flank, to protect southern supply routes to Russia and the main air ferry route to India, and to the China lifeline. Air ferry routes were a primary means of reinforcing Allied defenses in the Pacific and China-Burma-India (CBI) theaters where the Japanese advanced more rapidly than anticipated in 1942. The strategic advantage in the Mediterranean also favored the Axis. The Germans had engulfed Yugoslavia

Major General Lewis H. Brereton directed the buildup of U.S. air power in the Mediterranean in 1942, in command of what became the Ninth Air Force. *(NASM photo)*

and Greece, forcing a reassessment of Allied air and sea power in the Mediterranean. They had also moved boldly into North Africa and the Middle East. In June, following his spectacular victory at Tobruk, Rommel had the British Eighth Army reeling back to the central coast of Egypt. When Prime Minister Churchill asked for air reinforcements for a counteroffensive, General Arnold ordered Maj. Gen. Lewis H. Brereton to move with all available heavy bombers from New Delhi to Cairo. In July, as the decision to invade North Africa was being made, Churchill sent Field Marshal Bernard Montgomery to Cairo to lead the counteroffensive against Rommel.[76]

Brereton had been General MacArthur's air commander in the Philippines, moving to Australia with him when the islands fell to the Japanese. He later transferred to India to command the newly formed Tenth Air Force. Brereton's move to Cairo was to be temporary, but he stayed on to take charge of the buildup of American air forces in the Mediterranean. Since the Middle East was a theater of British strategic responsibility, Brereton's planes were employed as "homogenous American formations" under British "strategic control," in accordance with rules for combined operations agreed to at the Arcadia conference. In November, Brereton's command was reorganized into the Ninth Air Force, when Gen. Frank Andrews arrived in Cairo as the new Commanding General of Army Forces in the Middle East.[77]

While preparations were underway for the invasion of North Africa, Field Marshal Montgomery gathered his desert forces for the counteroffensive against Rommel. The limited theater air forces, under the command of Air Marshal Sir Arthur Tedder, were pivotal in the fight to choke off Rommel's supplies and stave off his advances in the Middle East. Before the arrival of American reinforcements, Tedder's air forces were outnumbered but not outgunned by the Luftwaffe. As a partner with Royal Army and Navy commanders, Tedder steadfastly withstood pressure from his ground and naval counterparts to spread air resources over widely dispersed areas. By centrally controlling his limited theater air resources, Tedder concentrated them at critical points. RAF forces on Malta gallantly withstood an awesome concentration of Luftwaffe bombardment; RAF bomber groups inflicted heavy losses on enemy shipping in the Mediterranean; and the desert air forces under Air Vice Marshal Sir Arthur Coningham supported the British Eighth Army in halting Rommel's forces along the El Alamein line inside Egypt. At this juncture, the arrival of American bombers and fighters began to even the odds.[78]

While AAF heavy bombers concentrated on strategic targets supporting the Afrika Korps, AAF fighters and medium bombers joined the British desert air forces to support the ground offensive against Rommel and interdict his supplies. This combined air effort was in its infancy when Montgomery arrived in Cairo with orders to drive Rommel out of Egypt, but soon gained air ascendancy under the seasoned direction of Tedder and Coningham.

The mold for cooperation struck by Trenchard and Mitchell more than 20 years earlier shaped the direction of air combat in the desert fighting of late 1942 and early 1943. With his logistic lines over-extended and under pressure from Allied planes, Rommel met quick and decisive defeat in November 1942 in the "great battle of El Alamein." Spearheaded by Coningham's Anglo-American tactical air forces, Montgomery's Eighth Army drove Rommel's Panza divisions from Egypt, pursuing them across Libya toward the Axis stronghold in Tunisia, where they made a final stand on North African soil. To Montgomery's west, Gen. Dwight D. Eisenhower's forces applied additional pressure on the Afrika Korps when they opened the invasion of Northwest Africa on November 8, 1942.[79]

Under Eisenhower's command, the three-pronged invasion forces met token resistance from French defenders and moved quickly against entrenched German and Italian opposition in Tunisia. Land-based air support was negligible during the Allied landings, but became essential in the ensuing ground campaign. Unfortunately, the Luftwaffe had local air superiority and invasion forces were hindered by a lack of central control of air support. While General Doolittle commanded the Twelfth Air Force in support of TORCH, he did not have centralized control over the air campaign. British and American air forces operated independently, mostly in support of their respective national armies. Further complicating matters, the two air forces followed different doctrines and command reins. The RAF was an independent service, while the AAF remained subordinate to the Army field commanders under War Department Field Manual 31-35. Unlike the desert air forces supporting Montgomery, invasion air forces were not permitted to carry out a coordinated campaign for air superiority or to concentrate attacks on pivotal enemy positions and resupply lines. The result was that control of the air went to the Luftwaffe, helping the Afrika Korps stall the Allied advance into Tunisia.[80]

Unlike British command arrangements in the Mediterranean, Eisenhower had no single air commander at his Gibraltar headquarters. General Spaatz, the senior airman and Eisenhower's "most trusted advisor" on air matters, was left behind in England.[81] Before, during, and after the landings in North Africa, Spaatz faced the challenge of educating Eisenhower's staff and field commanders on the employment of air power, and instilling in them the principle of a single commander. Spaatz was squeezed between Gibraltar and Washington, D.C., when orders came from Eisenhower that air resources in the United Kingdom "must be considered in support of Operation TORCH." This brought a heated exchange with Arnold about the diversion of heavy bombers from the air offensive against the Luftwaffe. Arnold objected to Eisenhower's directive that bombing raids on submarine bases in the Bay of Biscay would be the Eighth Air Force's primary objective until TORCH was completed.[82]

Spaatz pleaded for a more concentrated campaign against the Luftwaffe, but failed to pull Eisenhower away from his belief that the main bombing effort should be against submarine nests in the Bay of Biscay. Eisenhower agreed, however, that German air forces "must be constantly pounded, to give our own air forces freedom of action in carrying out our fruitful missions." Eisenhower authorized minor diversions to force a dispersion of German defenses and to take advantage of weather conditions.[83] When Arnold complained about the misuse of heavy bombers, Eisenhower was a "little bit apprehensive" about Washington's interference. From Gibraltar, he sent his "boundless appreciation" to General Spaatz for the "unselfish and enthusiastic support of TORCH." A postscript enjoined Spaatz to "Keep hammering away at the damned submarine!"[84]

Spaatz knew that a senior air officer should be at Gibraltar, but met stiff resistance from Eisenhower's Chief of Staff, Brig. Gen. W. Bedell Smith, who told Spaatz that there was no need for a special theater staff element to advise on the use of air forces. He thought a small air section might be useful but that it should have no part in recommending the objectives to be attacked by the theater air forces. Smith believed that this was the prerogative of the theater staff and that any reasonably intelligent Army officer who had graduated from the Army War College could advise the theater commander on air employment. Spaatz disagreed vehemently, but Smith deferred action. Spaatz considered this a deliberate attempt to "solve the problem by avoiding it."[85]

Once more, Arnold intervened. On November 15, 1942, he wrote Eisenhower that their differences were "all water under the bridge," and suggested that Eisenhower have Spaatz join him at Gibraltar to obtain the best results from the air forces. "If there ever was a time when we should have planned and coordinated aerial operations against Germany for all of our aircraft, that in England as well as that in North Africa," Arnold said, "it is at this moment." The AAF chief believed that the German air arm was on the wane and "only with the greatest effort" could still concentrate forces to secure local superiority in the air. "On the other hand," Arnold warned, "if our airplanes are sprinkled from hell to breakfast in small gobs here, in small gobs there, Germany will be able to secure superiority of the air anywhere she elects."[86] In a letter to Spaatz, Arnold supported "strong centralized control for air in Europe." He cautioned:

> Unless we are careful, we will find our air effort in Europe dispersed the same way we are now dispersed all around the world. We will find as many different bases of operations operating under as many different directives and commanders as there are land commanders. This must be prevented.[87]

A few days later, Eisenhower directed Spaatz to join his headquarters in the dual capacity of air deputy and commander of AAF components in the European theater. After his arrival in December 1942, Spaatz began advising Eisenhower on all air force matters, coordinating strategic air operations with the RAF, and preparing air plans. Spaatz credited General Arnold's personal appeal for swaying Eisenhower, who preferred to postpone altering air arrangements until after Tunisia was taken.[88]

The inadequacy of air support thus far in North Africa may have helped convince Eisenhower that he needed a knowledgeable air commander to plan, coordinate, and direct the air effort. The Army's practice of parcelling out air resources among ground commanders kept them from defeating the Luftwaffe in the early stages of the invasion. The dissipation of AAF sorties over friendly lines left the Luftwaffe free to mass superior air forces where they could stall the Allied advance against Tunisia.

Field Marshal Montgomery and Air Vice Marshal Coningham, meanwhile, drew an indelible pattern for effective air-ground cooperation in the desert fighting

General Carl Spaatz (middle) was Eisenhower's most trusted advisor on air matters and worked assiduously to convince other field commanders of the value of air power. *(NASM photo)*

against Rommel. Upon arriving in Cairo to lead the British Eighth Army, Montgomery collocated his headquarters with Coningham's to accommodate close air-ground coordination in planning and directing the October offensive at El Alamein. Brereton placed a planning cell with Coningham's staff to integrate AAF tactical operations with the RAF desert air forces. These arrangements afforded centralized direction, with decentralized execution, of all available tactical fighters and bombers. The result was a well-orchestrated air-ground offensive enabling Montgomery to seize the initiative from Rommel and exploit his retreat across Libya into Tunisia. At the theater level, Air Marshal Tedder and his staff pressured the Luftwaffe and exploited the enemy's over-extended supply lines. Anglo-American air forces under Coningham pressured Rommel's lines of communication and provided fluid close air support for Montgomery's army in set-piece battle and pursuit across the Libyan coast.[89]

From Tripoli, in January 1943, Montgomery reflected on his victory and on lessons learned from "months of hard fighting." His troops had been thrown into nearly every type of offensive and defensive maneuver— "except withdrawal." He counseled his senior officers that "the stress and strain of high command in the modern battle" demanded a clear understanding that available air power must be centralized under the air commander, and not be dissipated in small packets under "army formation commanders." Montgomery expounded on the theme:

> The greatest asset of air power is its flexibility, and this enables
> it to be switched quickly from one objective to another in the
> theater of operations. So long as this is realized, then the whole
> weight of the available air power can be used in selected areas in
> turn; this concentrated use of the air striking force is a battle
> winning factor of the first importance.[90]

Spaatz's move to Gibraltar gave Eisenhower a single, knowledgeable spokesman for air matters and improved theater air coordination and direction. It did not centralize control over air operations as practiced by the British. Eisenhower had learned from the British experience, however, and incorporated his knowledge in plans for the final campaign in North Africa. The convergence of Montgomery's army with Allied forces in North Africa, the forthcoming invasions of Sicily and Italy, and the importance of Mediterranean bases to the strategic air offensive, demanded greater unified direction over the combined air forces.

In January at Casablanca the combined chiefs agreed that it was time to merge North Africa and the Middle East into a single theater. Eisenhower was given command of the new theater, with British officers appointed to head the combined air, sea, and land components. Tedder became Commander of the new Mediterranean Air Command. Under Tedder, Spaatz commanded the Northwest African Air Forces and RAF officers commanded the Malta and Middle East air forces. This placed the bulk of combat air forces under Spaatz's control, with Doolittle commanding strategic air forces and Coningham commanding tactical air forces. While some senior airmen criticized the division of tactical and strategic air forces, Arnold and Spaatz believed this was essential to free heavy bombers for the strategic air offensive. This pattern took form in the combat theaters of World War II and was followed by AAF leaders in the postwar drive for autonomy.[91]

Educating officers on the field of battle to the value of centralized air support was no simple task. At Telergma, General Spaatz found that British and U.S. ground commanders did not understand the advantages of centrally directed air support as well as their counterparts at higher levels of command. For the coming spring offensive in Tunisia, U.S. Corps Commander Maj. Gen. Lloyd Fredendall and British Army Commander Lt. Gen. K.A.N. Anderson demanded continuous air cover. General Anderson said that this should be the main effort of all air strength and saw no need to bomb enemy airdromes. Fredendall also wanted full air coverage to protect his troops and artillery from enemy dive bomber attacks. He believed that bombs dropped on positions in front of his troops would bolster their morale. Fredendall complained that he lost 300 men to dive bomber attacks. Without full air coverage for the initial 48 hours, Fredendall did not think an Allied offensive was feasible.[92]

Spaatz explained to ground commanders that he had worn out two fighter groups and one light bomber squadron in air-ground support and the rate of replacement would not allow extravagant dissipation of scarce air resources. The General stressed that the air effort would be most effective by hitting the enemy's soft points, such as airdromes, tank parks, truck concentrations, and troop convoys. Maintaining a constant umbrella over a small section of the front with only shallow penetration by bombers and fighters would dissipate available resources without producing any lasting effect. Furthermore, Spaatz believed that the "hard core of any army" should protect itself from dive bomber attacks but that any offensive which required constant air coverage to prevent such attacks was probably made by a force not strong enough to succeed.[93]

Army officers exposed to theater-level plans and operations had a better view of the overall air situation than commanders who focused on the scheme of battle and protecting their troops. General Fredendall's Chief of Staff, Brig. Gen. Ray E. Porter, confided to Spaatz that the ground forces suffered few casualties from dive bomber attacks, with the exception of a daylight attack on a battalion which received high casualties. Porter blamed this incident on the battalion commander. Spaatz remarked that Porter believed that properly dispersed ground troops with sufficient weapons and taught to open fire instead of taking cover in forward positions should be able to take care of themselves.[94]

Formidable resistance from the Luftwaffe over Tunisia made the transition more difficult. Operating over a wider front, Allied air forces were slower to gain control of the air than during Montgomery's rout of Rommel's expedition into Egypt. While still in its infancy, the new air organization was put to a severe test in February when Rommel's army, reinforced and supported by powerful Stuka formations, made a bold thrust into central Tunisia, overran weaker Allied positions, and advanced through the Kasserine Pass toward Algeria. Allied forces regrouped and halted the advance, but not before suffering a crushing defeat at Kasserine. Ground commanders were quick to blame their defeat on a lack of air cover.

After Kasserine, however, the combined air forces conducted a sustained campaign against the Luftwaffe and gained control of the skies over most of Tunisia by the end of March. Air and ground commanders worked together to plan and execute the spring offensive. Spaatz's Northwest African Air Forces, dubbed the "Spaatzwaffe" by admirers, pounded enemy targets on Sicily and Pantelleria and the Tunisian bridgehead to isolate the Afrika Korps. Montgomery's forces drove north from Libya, while armies under Anderson, Fredendall, and Maj. Gen. George S. Patton closed from the west.[95]

As the armies converged in the final offensive, an incident between General Patton and Air Vice Marshall Coningham revealed the emotions behind centralized versus dedicated air support. Rommel's departure on March 9 augured the end for the Afrika Korps, but the besieged defenders were entrenched and fought back desperately. Allied air forces won air superiority, but Luftwaffe remnants prowled the frontlines. On April 1, a flight of bombers attacked positions in the II Corps area killing an aide to General Patton. When Patton complained about the "total lack of air cover", Coningham defended the performance of American air units under his command and impugned Patton's complaint. A slur about the battle worthiness of the II Corps outraged Patton, and he demanded that Coningham apologize to his troops. Eisenhower sent Tedder and Spaatz to meet with Patton and discuss the need to improve air-ground cooperation. He also ordered Coningham to apologize. Although smoothed over, the incident revealed misgivings about air-ground operations at lower echelons.[96]

By the end of April, however, the combined air forces drove the few surviving Luftwaffe planes back to bases in Sicily and Italy, allowing Allied troops to enter Bizerte and Tunis without fear of attack from the air. Within days, the remaining Axis resistance in North Africa crumbled. As decided at Casablanca, Spaatz's Northwest African Air Forces followed through with sustained bombardment of Pantelleria and Sicily, preliminary to Allied landings on these island steppingstones to Italy. Taking Pantelleria without a fight, the Allies established a beachhead on Sicily with little opposition from the Luftwaffe. By mid-summer, the skies over the Mediterranean were under undisputed Allied control.[97]

While the invasion of Sicily was underway, the War Department issued a new doctrinal manual, FM 100-20, *Command and Employment of Air Power*, pronouncing the principles of flexibility and centralized control which had guided air force operations in the Allied defeat of the Afrika Korps. The new manual, pushed through by General Arnold, was the "Magna Carta" of an independent air force, providing a formal statement of the equality of air power and land power. It linked the interdependence of air and land forces, but declared that "neither is the auxiliary of the other." For the first time, the War Department proclaimed that air superiority was prerequisite to successful land operations, and that air power had to be concentrated against the enemy's air forces until that superiority was achieved.[98]

Another prominent feature of FM 100-20 was a provision that theater commanders control air power through the air force commander to exploit "its inherent flexibility and ability to deliver a decisive blow." This provided centralized control over air forces when a theater commander oversaw combined operations. It also implied centralized control of Army, Navy, and Marine Corps air forces when employed jointly in a theater of war, but ran counter to Navy and Marine Corps doctrine and was not followed in the Pacific campaigns.

For the time being, the lessons of World War I for Army airmen were finally accepted as official doctrine by the War Department. This acceptance came as Allied air forces had gained mastery of the skies over the Mediterranean, the combined land forces were taking Sicily, and intensive bombing operations were underway against the Italian peninsula. Benito Mussolini's Fascist government was overthrown; the stage was set for the Allied invasion of Italy; the ring was beginning to close around Nazi Germany. Allied air and land power jointly turned back the Nazi war machine to the barricades of fortress Europe.[99]

Air Power and the Assault on Fortress Europe

When Spaatz joined Eisenhower's North Africa headquarters at the end of December 1942, he left Eighth Air Force and the strategic bombing operations in the hands of Maj. Gen. Ira C. Eaker. Before the Eighth Air Force arrived in the United Kingdom, Eaker set up the U.S. Army Bomber Command to work with Air Marshal Sir Arthur Harris' RAF Bomber Command. Eaker became Spaatz's bomber commander and was the logical choice to command the Eighth in Spaatz's absence. There was talk of shelving Eighth Air Force strategic operations until successful conclusion of the North Africa campaign but Arnold and Spaatz argued for an uninterrupted bombing campaign. Spaatz wrote Arnold from Gibraltar that nothing changed his view that "the one clear way to win this war in the shortest time and with the greatest economy is by the maximum application of the heavy bomber force from the fixed bases in the United Kingdom."[100]

A major consideration was the long-range affect on Germany's ability to wage war, but the bombing also helped staunch the logistic flow to the Afrika Korps and to the Eastern front by keeping Luftwaffe reserves tied up in defense of the homeland. Still, the results of American bombing operations at this time were negligible because so many resources were diverted to North Africa and the remaining bomber force was concentrated against questionable targets.

A lack of long-range escort fighters, inadequate armor, inclement weather, and chronic maintenance problems also hampered operations. American bombers were not sent against Germany proper until January 1943. It was another six months before the Eighth Air Force and the RAF Bomber Command inaugurated the long-awaited combined air offensive against the German heartland.[101] The importance of England-based air power was reflected in the appointment of Lt. Gen. Frank Andrews as commander of all U.S. forces in the European theater in February 1943. General Andrews served in this post until his death in an airplane crash in Iceland that spring.[102] With the air offensive lagging, President Roosevelt demanded to know why the "efficiency and power of the daylight bombing operations" from British bases were not what he had been led to expect. Marshall explained that Army aviation had been "somewhat misused" around the world, a "constant embarrassment" to the AAF. Pressure continued at the highest levels to resolve problems with better results from the combined bomber offensive.[103]

Before leaving England, Spaatz pressed unsuccessfully for the appointment of a unified commander to control AAF and RAF air forces operating against Germany from the United Kingdom. In October 1942, he told Air Vice Marshal John C. Slessor that until a unified commander for the air offensive was named and given a directive stating the means at his disposal, with a time schedule and specific goals, that the "so-called bomber offensive" might never materialize. The opinion of the Air Ministry, Slessor said, was that commitments should be held to a minimum to accommodate the buildup for the bomber offensive and that any offensive against Italy would absorb so much of the war effort that nothing decisive could be launched in the air against Germany. This would permit the Germans to rest, refit, and prepare for the next offensive.[104]

A few days later, Eisenhower told Spaatz to stop pressing for unified command of the air offensive against Germany. Looking at the larger strategic picture, Eisenhower said he anticipated eventual creation of a single air command over all U.S. air units operating against the European Axis powers, allowing the strategic mobility inherent in the flying echelons of the air force. The military advantage of flexible operations taking advantage of weather and strategic opportunity, Eisenhower reasoned, would influence the chiefs of staff in Washington to send forces to a single, unified military theater engaged in destroying Germany and her allies, rather that diverting them to the Pacific.[105]

British and American airmen had ample time to resolve doctrinal differences before undertaking the combined offensive. The best known doctrinal distinction was a British preference for nighttime bombing as opposed to the United States' insistence on precision daylight strikes. Eaker's time as an understudy to Harris' bomber operations did not alter his belief in American bombing doctrine, but provided him an understanding of the British bias. After more than two years of air warfare, the RAF did not have the planes nor the equipment to conduct precision raids deep in enemy territory. Harris was convinced that night bombing was the most economical and efficient means to disrupt German warmaking capabilities. The RAF's experience in flying American B–17s and B–24s did not change his mind. The Allies compromised by inaugurating a coordinated day-night bombing program, with the advantage of keeping around-the-clock pressure on the enemy while permitting the AAF and RAF to specialize in areas where each was best qualified.[106]

Roles and Missions

No appreciable change in command arrangements for Allied air power occurred until after the invasion of Italy in September 1943. Under Tedder's oversight, Spaatz continued to command the bulk of combat air forces in the Sicilian campaign and in the subsequent offensive against Field Marshal Kesselring's entrenched German opposition on the Italian mainland. Coningham's tactical units continued to support Allied ground forces during both amphibious and land operations, while Doolittle's bombers flew continuous strikes against targets ahead of the advancing armies.

The time for a command shake-up was near and the initial successes of the Italian campaign brought the Allies a step closer in their grand strategy to defeat Hitler. Mussolini's overthrow and the government's surrender in the wake of the landings on the mainland forced a major redirection of German military effort. This, coupled with rising pressure on the Soviet front and the combined strategic air offensive in July, enabled the Allies to turn toward more serious preparations for OVERLORD, the amphibious invasion of southern France.[107]

Some believed that strategic air power alone might bring about Germany's collapse, but this postulate was never tested. From their conferences in 1941, Allied leaders planned the air offensive (POINTBLANK) as a prelude to OVERLORD and never wavered in this strategy. The success of OVERLORD hinged on air supremacy, just as it had in TORCH and the invasion of Sicily. Consequently, the first months of the combined air offensive were concentrated against the Luftwaffe-its planes, fuel stores, airfields, facilities, and factories. The Eighth Air Force carried the early brunt of daylight operations, but bombers staging from Mediterranean bases began limited participation in August 1943 with the costly low-level B–24 raid on the Ploesti oil refineries in Rumania. Their participation grew after Italy's surrender and the formation of the Fifteenth Air Force in December 1943 for strategic operations from the Mediterranean area.[108]

At Casablanca the previous January, Roosevelt and Churchill had settled tentatively on a British supreme commander for the cross-channel invasion. It was assumed that OVERLORD would be largely a British undertaking, but by the time of the Quebec conference (QUADRANT) in August it was clear that U.S. invasion forces would constitute the larger national commitment. Churchill agreed that an American general should be in charge.

Roosevelt named Eisenhower Supreme Commander after the Sextant conferences in Cairo. Subsequently, British concurrence in Eisenhower's choice of Tedder as deputy reflected a wider recognition of air power's role in the war and the need for unified direction of the air effort. Other British officers were assigned as air, land, and naval component commanders. This arrangement generally correlated with the theater structure the Allies had set up a year earlier for the Mediterranean, with the two strategic air forces operating independently under the combined chiefs. Agreement was reached for Eisenhower to direct the strategic forces through his deputy, Tedder, but only when they were diverted to the support of OVERLORD. At the Quebec and Cairo conferences, U.S. chiefs argued unsuccessfully for unification of U.S. and British strategic air forces in the European and Mediterranean theaters. British chiefs conceded the right of U.S. leaders to administer their own strategic bombing operations in both theaters as they saw fit.[109]

Before leaving Cairo, American chiefs created the U.S. Strategic Air Forces in Europe to provide integrated command over the Eighth Air Force in England and the new Fifteenth Air Force in Italy. The British retained their existing strategic air organization under "Bomber" Harris. General Arnold returned Spaatz to England to head the new command, gave Doolittle the Eighth Air Force, and moved Eaker to the Mediterranean to replace Tedder as theater air commander. Eaker went reluctantly, for he wanted to finish his work in England. Facing transfer when he finally was getting the forces he needed, including long-range fighters, added to his hurt and disappointment. Although Eaker viewed his transfer as being fired, the reasons for the command shakeup were not that simple.[110]

Arnold clearly wanted Spaatz to have a greater voice in directing the strategic air offensive because results had not been satisfactory, but Eisenhower's concerns as supreme commander for OVERLORD were paramount. Nearly all veteran air and ground commanders were withdrawn from the Mediterranean to begin building the cross-channel invasion, and Eisenhower wanted Spaatz on hand. He insisted that Spaatz be put in charge of U.S. operations and that Doolittle take over Eighth Air Force. Arnold and Spaatz agreed that Eaker was needed in the Mediterranean for a balanced distribution of senior American air rank and experience between the two theaters. Arnold said that the U.S. command of Allied air forces in the Mediterranean demanded a person of Eaker's stature and skills. Eaker had worked well with the RAF in England, as Spaatz had done in the Mediterranean.

Allied cooperation was the key to the success of combined air operations. The more complex the command arrangements, the more vital this cooperation became. Eaker's new responsibilities removed him from direct involvement in the air offensive against Germany, since the Fifteenth was the only air force in the Mediterranean dedicated to strategic bombing and was under Spaatz's control. Spaatz continued to work through Eaker, however, since the Mediterranean commander was responsible for the air forces under his jurisdiction.[111]

Spaatz called the air command structure that evolved for the European theater "a lousy organization" and told Arnold that he believed the best approach was to obtain integrity of air in each theater rather than forming an overall strategic command. He expressed this to Eisenhower and RAF Marshal Sir Charles Portal, the combined chiefs of staff agent for the air offensive and suggested that Tedder be appointed air commander. Spaatz thought he should be placed under Tedder as deputy in charge of all U.S. air forces. The structure was worked out at great strain between the British and American commands and bore as many scars from political compromise as it did from differences in military doctrine, and these prevailed over Spaatz's concerns.[112]

Spaatz's immediate goal was to achieve decisive results from the combined bomber offensive, by targeting facilities (German aircraft factories, oil, etc.,) that would cripple the Luftwaffe and give the Allies command of the air before D-Day. The campaign was plagued by bad weather and radar bombing through cloud cover lacked precision. The RAF's practice of bombing industrial centers at night was of little or no value to the attainment of air superiority over Western Europe.

Another hindrance was the lack of long-range fighter escorts. Early raids against heavily defended targets such as Ploesti, Schweinfurt, and Regensburg, were costly proof of the folly of deep penetration strikes without fighter escort. As an interim solution, the AAF resorted to drop tanks to extend the range of its fighters, until the first P-51 Mustangs arrived to take over escort duties from shorter-range P-38s and P-47s. General Arnold called the arrival of long-range escort fighters "one of the great miracles of the war" and acknowledged that the failure to provide them earlier was the air force's own fault. Although Arnold moved to correct deficiencies in pursuit aviation before the United States entered the war, the delay in developing jettisonable tanks and procuring long-range fighters to protect the bombers indicates how far behind fighter tactics and technology lagged before the war.[113]

In the months preceding OVERLORD, the air offensive from the United Kingdom and the Mediterranean merged as an orchestrated campaign blending mission elements of bombers, fighter escorts, air intelligence, electronic warfare, reconnaissance, and targeting into a powerful striking force. Spaatz and Harris soon found they faced another challenge in meshing the bomber offensive with planning for OVERLORD, complicated by what they perceived as meddling in bomber affairs by Air Chief Marshal Sir Trafford Leigh-Mallory, Eisenhower's air commander for the invasion and a much decorated hero of the Battle of Britain. Leigh-Mallory contended that the bombers would follow the actual landings on the continent and that they would be put to better use in direct support of the invasion. In January 1944, he introduced Professor Solly Zuckerman's transportation plan to concentrate bombing operations against the German railroad system to isolate the battlefield, rather than targeting the Luftwaffe. This infuriated Spaatz and Harris, who saw these interferences as a stratagem to give Leigh-Mallory control of their air forces.[114]

A political struggle ensued, with Eisenhower supporting Leigh-Mallory while trying to accommodate Spaatz and Harris. Eisenhower understandably wanted the maximum air power available to support his invasion forces. He also wanted Leigh-Mallory's fighters free to form a protective umbrella over the beaches at Normandy. Threatening to resign as Supreme Commander, Eisenhower convinced the chiefs to relinquish control of the strategic air forces for the critical phases before, during, and after the invasion between April 14 and September 15. He remained sensitive to the need for control of the air, however, and refused to concentrate solely on the Zuckerman plan at the expense of other target systems. This permitted strategic forces to sustain their attacks deep into Germany, forcing the Luftwaffe's fighters away from the front to defend the homeland. Capped in late February by Big Week, with strikes by the largest force yet assembled by the U.S.

strategic air forces, the combined offensive neutralized German fighter strength and crippled the Luftwaffe's industrial capacity to regenerate its forces.

On June 6, the Allied air umbrella was in place over the beaches at Normandy, but there were no Luftwaffe fighters to challenge them. The Allies' unwillingness to permit air power's greatest asset-its flexibility-to fall victim to the common foes of compromise of air warfare principles and inflexibility of command enabled them to enter the final exploitation phases of the war with victory in the air assured.[115]

Once OVERLORD's invasion forces were established on the continent, the Allies reorganized for the drive across France and Germany. Spaatz argued unsuccessfully to have Tedder's role of air commander without portfolio as Eisenhower's deputy changed to that of component commander of the overall air effort. Spaatz was also unsuccessful in integrating all U.S. air forces under a single commander. Nonetheless, as the senior American air commander he continued to have administrative control over them. The abolishment of Leigh-Mallory's headquarters in October 1944, required assurances to Eisenhower that this was not done to remove the controversial air hero. A semblance of unity in the tactical air forces was retained through an air chief of staff position held by Air Vice Marshal James M. Robb. Tedder was confined to coordinating the direction of the Allied tactical air forces and stating Eisenhower's requirements for strategic air bomber support. Spaatz remained in charge of the U.S. strategic air forces and Lt. Gen. Hoyt Vandenberg as Leigh-Mallory's deputy for the invasion, took charge of U.S. tactical air forces.[116]

Facilitated by the strategic campaign's crippling of the Luftwaffe, air-ground cooperation proved effective where the air advantage rested clearly with the Allies. During the advance across France, the tactical air forces provided a classic blend of interdiction and close air support, uninterrupted only by weather. In contrast to the criticisms that marred the adjustment period in North Africa, ground officers in the European campaign were "uniform in their praise of the close support fighters." One analyst observed that Maj. Gen. Elwood Quesada, Commander of the Ninth Tactical Air Command in support of the First U.S. Army, had a drawing of a column of tanks, hitched together, with the lead tank attached to the wings of a P-47, which was struggling to bring the tank column up to speed. "This is the kind of war they are fighting," he reported, "and do the ground forces love it."[117]

Another enhancement of lessons learned from the North African campaign was the famed air-ground team formed by General Patton and Maj. Gen. Otto Weyland during the Third Army's race across France. As prescribed by FM 100-20, Weyland collocated his Nineteenth Tactical Air Command headquarters with Patton's, and aimed for a close liaison with the ground commander and his staff. At the next echelon, Vandenberg and his staff operated co-equally with the 12th Army Group headquarters of Gen. Omar Bradley. This intimate command relationship assured effective tactical air support for Patton's Third Army, while Weyland retained the flexibility of command that he needed to apply his forces where they could do the most good.[118]

Roles and Missions

While concentrating on destroying the Luftwaffe before OVERLORD, the strategic air forces supported by tactical fighters conducted sustained interdiction campaigns against the transportation systems and logistics flow to the battle fronts. After D-Day, the strategic bombers diverted to tactical support of the ground offensive, but continued pounding industrial centers and interdicting the logistics flow until Germany's collapse in May 1945. On V-E Day, there was no doubt that air power had made a substantial contribution to the victory. The AAF was no longer a tertiary force, but a coequal arm of national military power.[119]

The lasting impression that air power left with Eisenhower was evident in a statement to newly appointed Secretary of Defense James V. Forrestal in late 1947. The Army depended on the necessary air support from "a practically autonomous Air Force" throughout the war, Eisenhower said, and the experience,

> ....proved that control of the air, the prerequisite to the conduct of ground operations in any given area, was gained most economically by the employment of air forces operating under a single command. This assured a maximum of flexibility, providing a command structure under which all forms of available air power could be concentrated on tactical support missions or on strategic missions, as the situation demanded-in other words, it permitted the maximum concentration of combat air power at the decisive point at the decisive time.[120]

Roles and Missions in the War Against Japan

With the possible exception of roles and missions differences in the antisubmarine campaigns, interservice rivalry was more prevalent in the sprawling theaters of the Pacific than in the war against Germany. "The war in Europe was primarily a ground and air war, with naval support, while the war in the Pacific was primarily a naval war with ground and air support," Admiral King later wrote. With no great naval battles to be won in the Atlantic, the Navy's leaders saw the Pacific as their war. While still recovering from heavy losses at Pearl Harbor, they were impatient to regain control of the seas from the Japanese fleet. Thus, Admiral King vigorously opposed giving the European war first claim on air resources, at the expense of early offensive operations in the Pacific.[121] General Douglas MacArthur, the Army's supreme commander in the Pacific, also criticized the Germany-first strategy, blaming the rapid fall of the Philippines and other Allied losses after Pearl Harbor on this policy. MacArthur was eager to retake the initiative from the Japanese.

Allied strategy was to hold as many key positions as possible against Japanese advances and to take the offensive at the earliest opportunity, with the ultimate objective of conducting an all-out offensive against Japan. At the Arcadia conference, the chiefs established a combined theater under British Gen. Sir Archibald

Wavell, which folded soon after unexpected Japanese gains altered the strategic balance in the Pacific, revealing that the Allies had grossly underestimated enemy capabilities. The instructions to Wavell, approved by Roosevelt and Churchill, identified air superiority as the first priority in the Pacific, to be gained at the earliest possible moment through the use of concentrated air power. From the outset, the chiefs hoped to minimize the piecemeal employment of air power against the Japanese.[122] Through the early months of the war in the Pacific the advantage clearly rested with the Japanese air forces.

When grand strategy was mapped out before and after Pearl Harbor, AAF planners viewed the capture of forward bases in the Pacific as a necessary precurser to unleashing an all-out air offensive against Japan. Although AWPD-1 recognized the potential value of B–29s in Europe, the superfortress was never flown against Germany. The timing of B–29 production and their extended range were more suited to delivering the final blows against Japan. The AAF's combat planes flew many different missions in the war against Japan, but Arnold never lost sight of the final objective of a sustained air offensive to bring Japan to its knees without a costly invasion of the home islands.[123]

Improvements in the air posture followed Japanese advances in the Pacific, but the demands of the war against Germany kept reinforcements to a minimum. Along with the division of the Pacific into two contiguous U.S. theaters, with command split between the Army and Navy, this created a competitive environment wherein scarce air resources shifted between theaters with radically different outlooks toward roles and missions. In the spring of 1942, after the dissolution of Wavell's headquarters, Adm. Chester W. Nimitz took command of the U.S. theater in the north, central, and southern areas of the Pacific, while General MacArthur became supreme commander of forces in the southwest. Although MacArthur commanded an Allied theater, his forces were predominately American. The combined chiefs agreed that the Pacific was primarily an American responsibility. President Roosevelt suggested that his joint chiefs establish two theaters to settle the vexing question of Army and Navy interests. The division was geographic rather than functional, however, with both Nimitz and MacArthur commanding air, sea, and land forces in amphibious landings. In both theaters, air forces were a mix of Army, Navy, and Marine elements subordinated to the iron wills of doctrinaire commanders, one Army and one Navy.[124]

Adding to the complexities of command and to the demands on resources were Gen. Joseph W. Stilwell's anomalous China-Burma-India (CBI) theater and Adm. Lord Louis Mountbatten's supreme headquarters overseeing operations in Burma and Malaya. It is to their credit that the combined and joint chiefs and theater commanders, while airing parochial differences, found common ground in the strategic direction of the war.[125]

Within these sprawling theaters, the air war against Japan assumed many faces. In the skies over the rice fields and jungles of the CBI, Gen. Claire Chennault's Flying Tigers gained lasting fame against superior odds. The AAF's

Roles and Missions

C–46s, C–47s, and C–109s made air transport history flying the hump over the Himalayas, while air commando operations and other air support fathered air doctrine for unconventional warfare. In the southwest Pacific, AAF and Marine planes fought for control of the skies and flew air support for amphibious landings and ground battles. They joined carrier-based planes in providing similar support in the island-hopping drive across the Pacific. Across the ocean expanse, AAF units interdicted sea and air lines of communication and supported invasion forces with pre-assault bombardment, air cover, and close air support missions. The AAF's transports and aerial reconnaissance planes ranged the ocean and land areas in support of joint actions.[126]

Successive Japanese victories extended the enemy's outer perimeter to Wake Island in the Central Pacific and to New Guinea, the Bismarck Archipeligo, and to the top of the Solomon Islands in the South. Meanwhile, U.S. naval intelligence gained an advantage by breaking the Japanese code and plotting the enemy's next moves. In June, the U.S. fleet won its first major Pacific victory with a crippling blow against carrier forces converging on Midway. A month earlier, two U.S. carrier task forces aided by AAF planes thwarted a frontal assault against Allied positions on the southern tip of New Guinea in the battle of the Coral Sea. Within striking distance of Australia, the Japanese army pushed further south to strengthen their hold on the Solomons.[127]

By mid-1942, the Japanese had overextended their forces, spreading them thinly along a wide front from India through Malaya, the Netherlands East Indies, New Guinea, and the Solomons, and northward through the Gilbert Islands to the Aleutians. After the victory at Midway, the Joint Chiefs of Staff approved aggressive action against Japan and ordered limited reinforcements to the Pacific. A two-pronged offensive began with General MacArthur heading inland toward northern New Guinea before returning to the Philippines, while the Navy commanded another offensive up the chain of the Solomans. The objective was to invade Japan.[128]

In July, General Arnold sent Maj. Gen. George C. Kenney to Australia to rebuild MacArthur's air force and to prepare for the offensive. Kenney found MacArthur and his staff had closed themselves off from the former air commander, denying him access to his superiors for weeks at a time. MacArthur's Chief of Staff, Maj. Gen. Richard Sutherland, had usurped command of the air forces. Without consulting the air commander, Sutherland routinely issued orders to the air forces well beyond his knowledge and authority. After Kenney received a mission order from Sutherland dictating such details as the designation of units, the numbers and types of aircraft, take-off times, and ordnance loads, he stormed into the Chief of Staff's office demanding that he rescind the order. Kenney made his point by drawing a black dot in the corner of a piece of paper, telling Sutherland that the "blank area represents what I know about air matters, and the dot represents what you know." Thereafter, Kenney said, there was no doubt who was commanding the air force.[129]

In September, Kenney activated the Fifth Air Force to oversee the build-up of air units in the southwestern Pacific and to insure that AAF policies were followed. He donned a second hat in Brisbane as commanding general of the new numbered air force, and selected Brig. Gen. Ennis C. Whitehead, who had a temporary headquarters at Port Moresby, New Guinea, as his deputy. To enhance flexibility, Kenney formed air task forces for specific missions which could be shifted from one area to another as required. The Fifth Air Force remained the primary AAF organization in the southwest Pacific until June 1944, when the Far East Air Forces (FEAF) was activated to handle the rapid growth in air strength. Kenney assumed command of FEAF, while General Whitehead became commander of the Fifth Air Force. The Thirteenth Air Force under Maj. Gen. St. Clair Street was assigned to FEAF, as was the Seventh Air Force-in preparation for the invasion of Japan. Both the Seventh and Thirteenth Air Forces previously fell under Nimitz's theater command. After the Papuan campaign, Kenney's headquarters moved north with MacArthur to Leyte in October 1944 and then to Luzon in April 1945, as hard-won island victories carried the Supreme Commander back to the Philippines.[130]

Kenney worked hard to indoctrinate MacArthur and his staff on air power. He won their respect by employing his forces to provide the most benefit. MacArthur's confidence in Kenney grew, resulting in virtual autonomy in his direction of the air forces. Kenney praised MacArthur's grasp of the proper use of air power, recalling that the theater air, ground, and sea elements functioned as independent organizations. "I had an independent Air Force, Krueger [Gen. Walter] had an independent Army, and Kincaid [Vice Adm. T.C.] an independent Navy," Kenney said. "MacArthur gave the decisions and ordered the coordinated action, and we worked out the details."[131]

Command arrangements for employing AAF planes in the contiguous Navy theater were more complicated. Major General Millard F. Harmon accompanied Kenney to the Pacific, stopping at Noumea, New Caledonia, to take charge of AAF operations under the Navy's jurisdiction. He found his air forces in disarray and authority even weaker. Harmon reported to Arnold that the Navy had relegated him to being little more than "a trainer and a housekeeper" for his combat units. Vice Admiral Robert L. Ghormley, Nimitz's commander for the Solomon's campaign, gave his top airman, Rear Adm. John S. McCain, control over all shore and carrier based aircraft, including AAF units. From his headquarters aboard the U.S.S. *Tangier* at Noumea, Admiral McCain exercised command directly rather than going through Harmon.

Although they were handpicked, experienced airmen, Harmon and his key staff officers had no part in planning or executing combat operations unless specifically invited to participate by Admirals Ghormley or McCain. Harmon opposed these arrangements in principle, but had specific instructions from Arnold that he was to cooperate fully with Navy authorities.[132]

In August, as the forces under Admiral Ghormley opened the Solomons offensive with Marine landings on Guadalcanal, General Harmon reported "no lack of harmony" in his relations with naval authorities. At Noumea, Harmon established daily contact with Ghormley, who provided him with "full and complete information" on plans and operations. "He never comes ashore," Harmon said, "but we go out and board [his ship] practically every day, frequently have lunch, and go over the whole works." Harmon placed two members of his staff on board the *Tangier* with Admiral McCain, who he described as "a knowledgeable, reasonable, and concerned air commander."[133]

As fighting grew more intense, however, Harmon complained that his planes were being misused. In October, he reported to Arnold that more effective results could be secured only by placing AAF aircraft "wholly and completely" under AAF operational control. The AAF commander was better prepared to direct the operations of his own service, Harmon said, and to fit its capabilities into the overall scheme of battle. He believed it was wrong for one commander to control a unit's operations, while another was responsible for "maintenance, protection, state of training, morale, avoidance of combat weariness, airdrome and flight discipline." Harmon claimed that he and his staff had to practice command by "suggestion or recommendation" under the Navy's control, which, in his view, was inherently wrong.[134]

Admiral William E. Halsey relieved Ghormley of command in October 1942, but there was no substantial change in Harmon's role. Halsey subscribed to the April 1943 JCS directive on unity of command wherein command of all forces under the amphibious commander passed to the landing force commander of the service with a preponderance of troops. According to Harmon, Halsey charged him with the responsibility for and complete freedom to conduct operations on only three occasions, "incident to offensives against Guadalcanal, New Georgia and Bougainville."[135]

The gulf between AAF and Navy air doctrine was central to roles and missions problems in joint operations. Naval aviation wanted to protect the fleet, while the AAF wanted to attack strategic targets. General Harmon expressed disappointment over the Navy's refusal to use heavy bombers to strike at distant enemy bases. While B–17s were flying from Espiritu Santo, months elapsed after the capture of Guadalcanal's Henderson Field before it could accommodate enough bombers to sustain major offensive action. Harmon complained that Navy commanders overtasked B–17s for reconnaissance missions, rather than employing them in an offensive role. As the Solomons campaign progressed, General Arnold intervened with Admiral King to obtain fuller Navy use of Catalinas for reconnaissance, so that B–17s could be released for long-range bombing operations.

As roles and missions differences continued, Harmon pressed for establishment of an air echelon in the South Pacific with authority to formulate plans and to carry out missions in accordance with established AAF doctrine and policies. The Thirteenth Air Force was activated in the Solomons in January 1943, but its operations remained under Navy control until assigned to the FEAF under General Kenney over a year later in June 1944.[136]

Meanwhile, General Harmon sought more autonomy for the Thirteenth Air Force and found McCain's replacement, Rear Adm. Aubrey Fitch, more receptive to his ideas. Fitch told Harmon his main concern was to obtain the highest degree of effectiveness from all air forces under his command. He agreed with Harmon that preserving unit integrity, using forces for what they were trained and equipped, and granting them the wisdom of their own service doctrine and techniques was the way to accomplish this. Harmon reported some initial problems with Fitch's staff who misread his position, but this was soon corrected. In planning for a fresh series of campaigns in the spring of 1943, Fitch and Harmon worked out an agreement that gave Army airmen a stronger voice in joint planning and direction of their own forces. For operations in the forward areas of the Solomons, Halsey appointed a subordinate air commander, whose assignment was rotated regularly among the services. Harmon welcomed the changes, but viewed them as a substitute for true unified command.[137]

The divided theater responsibilities in the Pacific were a source of endless concern and controversy. Competition for scarce resources, interdependence of operations, and the shifting boundaries between MacArthur's and Halsey's areas of responsibility detracted from sound planning. Harmon thought that the frequent shifts disrupted the continuity of air operations. Kenney thought the divided arrangement was "silly" and he believed there should have been one supreme commander for the Pacific. Nearly all service leaders agreed on the need for unity of command, but the Joint Chiefs of Staff were unable to resolve the issue because neither the Army nor the Navy would yield. The resultant two-pronged drive by Nimitz and MacArthur created strategic faults, which a stronger enemy might have been able to exploit.[138]

Of the various theaters during World War II, none was more politically charged and less unified than the one under Stilwell. Never popular with Chiang Kai-shek, Stilwell's efforts to build the Chinese Army into an effective fighting force, while coordinating its combat actions with Lord Mountbatten's and commanding a predominantly American air force theater in the CBI, failed to please the Generalissimo. When President Roosevelt recalled Stilwell in October 1944 at Chiang's insistence and abolished the CBI theater, he ended an era in which "over the Hump" airlift missions from India and Chennault's Flying Tigers overcame seemingly impossible odds to fire the imagination of the American public and to help defeat the Japanese. Chennault's special relationship with Chiang and his constant bickering with Stilwell and the Tenth Air Force marred his success. Arnold opposed giving Chennault an independent air force in China, and was quoted by Stilwell as saying during an early 1943 visit to China that he was "Goddamned" if he would take such a request from Chiang to President Roosevelt. But the message reached Roosevelt who approved activating the Fourteenth Air Force under Chennault.[139]

With the increase in air operations in the CBI, the AAF considered the need for an air component commander reporting to Stilwell, but Chiang would not

General Claire L. Chennault's Flying Tigers flew in the China-Burma-India theater, earning him a place of distinction on the homefront, but his inability to get along with fellow commanders hampered his success. *(NASM photo)*

accept a senior airmen over Chennault, and Arnold was opposed to Chennault as commander of theater air forces. While Arnold acknowledged Chennault's tactical genius, he did not consider him knowledgeable in the use of strategic bombers. In July 1943, Arnold sent Maj. Gen. George E. Stratemeyer to the CBI to oversee air operations, but Stratemeyer had only an advisory relationship with Chennault's Fourteenth Air Force. Further complicating intertheater relationships, the combined chiefs established a supreme Southeast Asia command under Lord Mountbatten after the Quadrant conference in Quebec. Stilwell was given a second hat as deputy of the combined command, which strengthened his role in Burma, but eroded his relations with the Generalissimo. When Stilwell left in October 1944, Allied forces had lost ground in China and were stalled in Burma. As the war wound down in Europe and the Allies turned the tide against the Japanese the situation reversed.[140]

The CBI became an essential element of AAF plans to protect the integrity of the bomber offensive against Japan. When the B–29s entered production in the summer of 1943, a protracted interservice controversy over the basing and employment of the Superforts ensued. Since forward Pacific bases remained in enemy hands, MacArthur and Nimitz wanted the B–29s based temporarily in Australia and New Guinea for tactical and anti-shipping operations. Arnold believed this was a misuse of the super bombers and insisted on their interim basing in the CBI to bolster Chinese morale and to strike strategic targets in Japan. Supported by promises Roosevelt made to Chiang at the Cairo and Teheran conferences, Arnold's arguments prevailed. During the winter of 1943 to 1944, an initial force of B–29s

General Curtis E. LeMay led one of the many B–29 offensives against Japan launched from Chinese bases in June 1944. *(NASM photo)*

deployed under project "Matterhorn" to Calcutta, India, with advanced staging bases in the Chengtu area of China. These forces were placed under Stilwell's administrative control until American advances permitted forward basing in the Pacific.[141]

The B–29 offensive against Japan began from Chinese bases in June 1944, and continued with mounting intensity after November when the bombers began flying from the Mariannas in the central Pacific. Led by a series of commanders, including Maj. Gen. Curtis E. LeMay, the B–29s opened with high-level precision bombing missions against military-industrial targets, achieving devastating results with incendiary raids against major Japanese cities. The bombers also conducted aerial

Sustained bombing by scores of B–29s became a hallmark of the air war against Japan in 1945. *(NASM photo)*

mining operations to support the naval blockade of Japan. Allied leaders hoped the strategic air offensive coupled with the blockade might end the war without an invasion of the Japanese homeland.[142]

As Admiral Nimitz took the Gilbert and Marshall Islands and moved westward to capture the Mariannas in the summer of 1944, the combined U.S. air forces grew stronger while Japanese air strength was depleted. The enemy had sacrificed much of its first-line air strength in the losing battles for the Solomon Islands and New Guinea, while its air forces over Burma had lost control of the skies to allied air forces. Land and carrier-based aircraft continued to take a heavy toll in Nimitz's island-hopping drive across the central Pacific and MacArthur's thrust back to the Philippines.

By early 1945, as MacArthur's forces advanced on Luzon and the island fortress of Corregidor and Nimitz's task force invaded Okinawa, U.S. and Allied airpower had neutralized Japanese air strength and won control of the Pacific skies. In a classic misuse of air power, the enemy dissipated his air strength in a series of widely dispersed battles across the Pacific and the CBI. In the final months, the Japanese resorted to Kamikaze tactics as a fatal salute to their demise. Even before the B–29 offensive, Japan's war industry could not match the industrial output of the United States. In naval air strength alone, the U.S. fleet built a formidable force of approximately 50 aircraft carriers, compared to no more than six carriers constructed by the Japanese.[143]

Anticipating the capture of forward bases in striking distance of Japan, in April 1944 the War Department established the Twentieth Air Force to direct B–29 operations. Remembering Admiral King's creation of the Tenth Fleet to control antisubmarine operations, General Arnold convinced the Joint Chiefs to appoint him commander of the Twentieth Air Force to guarantee that B–29s would be employed according to AAF doctrine and primarily for strategic bombing. By September 1942, during a visit to the Pacific Commands, Arnold decided that he should be personally involved in controlling the strategic offensive against Japan. He later wrote that he reached this conclusion reluctantly, but was forced into it by command disunity in the Pacific.

Navy opposition delayed Arnold's appointment as executive agent for the B–29s for months. Even after Arnold obtained White House support, another month passed before Admiral King relented. The unique command arrangement kept the B–29s from being misused and gave Arnold authority to plan and carry out the strategic air campaign against Japan without interference from theater commanders.[144] It also set the precedent for the Strategic Air Command falling under the Joint Chiefs' control when it was established after the war.

As the B–29 offensive gained strength in the spring and summer of 1945, armed forces in the Pacific began organizing for the planned invasion of Japan. While Arnold hoped the invasion would lead to unified command, with all AAF units becoming part of a coequal air component, the force structure in the Pacific remained divided along service lines. Nimitz remained commander of naval forces while MacArthur commanded Army forces, including the theater air forces under Kenney. Arnold continued as the JCS executive agent for the strategic air forces. A new organization, the U.S. Army Strategic Air Forces, was established to carry out Arnold's directives. Fresh from the victory in Europe, General Spaatz went to Guam to take command of this new organization. When he landed on July 29, Spaatz received the order to drop the atomic bombs on Hiroshima and Nagasaki. The Japanese surrendered as he was getting his new command organized.[145]

The Implications for Roles and Missions

To American forces flush with victory at the end of World War II, the full meaning of atomic weapons within the evolution of service roles and missions was uncertain. The secrecy of the Manhattan Project was guarded so zealously that AAF leaders were uninformed about the new technology, beyond delivery of the bomb by its B–29s and the devastating results achieved at Hiroshima and Nagasaki. Nonetheless, General Arnold understood the roles and missions implications of the bomb. Soon after Japan's surrender, Arnold asked General Spaatz to convene a board to study the bomb's impact on the future of the air force. The Spaatz Board concluded that the awesome destructive power of the bomb reaffirmed the strategic air offensive.[146]

Also unclear in the postwar rush toward demobilization was America's new role in world affairs and the intentions of her wartime allies in the Kremlin. More measurable were the wartime achievements of combined arms, and the roles of air, land, and sea power in defeating Germany and bringing Japan to its knees even before the atomic bombs were dropped. While critics remained, air power was now recognized as an essential dimension of modern war. The strategic air forces proved they indeed had an independent mission.[147]

General Arnold wanted to make certain that this wartime momentum was not lost. In the fall of 1944, he and Secretary Lovett formed the U.S. Strategic Bombing Survey to give the American people a full appraisal of air power's contribution to winning the war. The evaluation of the strategic campaigns against Germany and Japan became a source of endless debate, but helped assure that the strategic air role remained at the forefront of air doctrine and technology. Along with a tremendous swell of operational knowledge from the war came marked growth and maturation in other areas such as logistics, intelligence, and research and development. Germany's introduction of rockets and jet fighters late in the war had far-reaching roles and missions implications for air power. To capture these and other advancements, General Arnold set up a scientific advisory group under Dr. Theodore von Kármán in November 1944 to study and define the long-range research and development programs for the Air Force.[148]

Overarching all roles and missions concerns was the promise of an autonomous Air Force. General Arnold was assured of General Marshall's support and began planning for separation and autonomy before the war ended. Arnold believed an autonomous air force would best serve the nation's defense needs, and that a unified structure was the only way to achieve equality with land and naval forces. The variations and difficulties in each theater supported the need for a unified armed forces structure to provide uniformity in organization, doctrine, planning, and training beforehand, rather than improvising during the heat of battle. General Eisenhower favored unification of the armed forces and autonomy for air forces when he became Army Chief of Staff after the war, but wanted assurances that the Army would continue to receive air support. As a rule, however, Army commanders preferred to have organic aviation dedicated to supporting the Infantry. Their opposing views on roles and missions would rise to the fore in later years.[149]

Naval aviation was a vital element of American air power and made a major contribution to defeating air forces and the victory in the Pacific. The Navy's fast carriers were the vanguard of the U.S. fleet during the war, while Marine Corps aircraft proved indispensable to Marine battalions landing and slugging it out with heavily entrenched defenders on Pacific islands. Their doctrine was different from the AAF's, emphasizing specialization as opposed to the versatility of air power. The Navy and Marines developed a solid body of amphibious doctrine stressing integration of air, sea, and assault forces trained and dedicated to the operation at hand. At the heart of AAF operations beat a diversified air doctrine rooted in the principles of centralized control, economy and concentration of force, and flexibility. The two doctrines were set on a collision course for postwar debate and joint application in future wars.

Fearing that an autonomous air force would swallow up naval aviation and threaten the integrity of their service, the Navy's top brass vehemently opposed unification and coequal air power. Most shared Admiral King's view that unified command was ill-advised and unworkable and believed that air power was valuable only in its relation to naval or ground warfare. King never waivered from his belief in the futility of classifying air power as a separate entity because it was dependent on the earth's surfaces for its operations. He maintained that air power, including the atomic bomb, was just another weapon to be integrated into the Army and the Navy.

A large following in and out of the Navy agreed that the experience with strategic air power and in the end, the atomic bomb, did not demonstrate a need for revolutionary change in the way American forces organized for war. This opposition carried into postwar analyses of wartime air operations and intensified with the ensuing struggles over unification, over air force autonomy, and over primacy in atomic warfare.

CHAPTER IV

FOUNDATIONS: FRAMING ROLES AND MISSIONS UNDER UNIFICATION

While the United States adjusted to its new global responsibilities after World War II, England and France sought to reestablish hegemony over their former protectorates. The Soviet Union expanded its sphere of influence wherever the pullback of American forces would permit. From the Kremlin, an expedient wartime ally watched expectantly as the U.S. Government-responding to pressure from a war-weary public-hastened to dismantle the mightiest air, sea, and land forces the world had ever seen.

Only four months after V-J Day, the AAF had shrunk from a wartime peak of over 2,300,000 men to just under 889,000. The number of combat groups was sliced in half, from 218 to 109. By the end of 1946, the AAF had only 341,421 men and 55 groups. Only two groups were combat effective. General Eisenhower told Congress that the armed forces had demobilized too rapidly, blaming this on "the emotional wave to get men out of the Army" that reached "proportions of near-hysteria."[1]

Military planners in the Pentagon worried over the impact of the demobilization program on American security in an uncertain postwar world. The AAF wanted to avoid the crippling effects of too massive a postwar drawdown and to be ready to meet future air power needs. The solution seemed to rest in the awesome power of an atomic arsenal along with the promise of jet engines, rocket propulsion, and other new technology. The unification of the three military arms under a single Department of Defense was also important. Building an atomic stockpile and fleets of jet-powered bombers or guided missiles would take years. Unification had more immediacy for the AAF because it provided the path to an autonomous, coequal air force. While General Arnold refrained from pressing for autonomy until victory was at hand, he laid the foundation before the war ended, including full assurances of support from Generals Marshall and Eisenhower and other senior Army officers. The confidence these men instilled in the air arm was apparent during the postwar drive for unification and autonomy.[2]

While the war forced deferral of the formal quest for an autonomous air arm, planning for this goal remained on the minds of senior airmen. As the war wound down, autonomy became a topic of more frequent discussion. In February 1944, Assistant Secretary for Air Lovett wrote General Spaatz that the Army General Staff supported a single Department of War with three coequal branches. The Navy had "shouted an angry no." Lovett complained, "if past performance is a fair criterion," the question of unification would "be decided by a mixture of vested interests and compromises rather than on a basis of lessons learned and errors corrected." In discussing the issue with General Arnold, the Air Secretary voiced concern

Robert Lovett, Assistant Secretary
of War for Air (third from left),
was a strong advocate of a separate
air arm. *(NASM photo)*

that the adherents of unified air power were not as aggressive and persistent as they
should be. He thought the time had come "to speak out." He felt "a heavy responsibility on the Air Force to have its say regardless of the consequence." Lovett was
combative on the issue, telling Spaatz:

> One of the principle troubles is that under the present setup deci-
> sions of tremendous importance are reached by old time ground
> and naval officers at the highest levels without considering the
> air early enough. Feeling as strongly as I do about the subject I
> expect to be in more or less continuous hot water from now on
> as I am going to battle for a unified Air Force from here on out
> as long as I can get a handful of people to come along with me.[3]

In early 1944, Spaatz was absorbed with winning the air war against Germany
and preparing for the invasion of Japan, but found time to send Lovett his thoughts
on unification. He concluded:

> I am more convinced than ever that the future of the U.S.
> demands that Air be placed at least on a co-equal basis with the
> ground Army and Navy. We may be able to win this war under
> the present type of military organization, but we will not survive
> as a nation through the next war or wars, which will inevitably
> follow, unless our organization is changed.[4]

Opponents believed that unification and a separate air force would be bad for
the armed forces and bad for the nation. The stiffest opposition came from the Navy
which wanted to protect the integrity of its traditional roles and missions. Naval
officers genuinely feared that an autonomous air force might bring an end to integral Marine Corps and Navy aviation and that the Navy might lose control of its

self-sustaining forces. Since the days of Billy Mitchell, Army airmen had suggested that all military aviation, especially land-based elements, be integrated into an independent air force. The Navy feared the potential compromise of traditional Marine Corps roles and missions. After all, it was the Army which carried out the largest amphibious operations of World War II during the Normandy landings, with land-based air forces providing an umbrella for the invasion. Conversely, Navy flag officers believed they had proved the worth of their own three-dimensional operations and that these operations complemented rather than rivaled those of the Army. Navy carrier squadrons were essential to the success of fleet operations in the Pacific and the defeat of the Japanese air forces. In addressing unification, Admiral King took the position that "any step that is not good for the Navy is not good for the nation." He argued that the Army air arm should remain part of the Army and naval aviation with the Navy.[5]

At the highest levels of government, however, unification found favor within President Harry S. Truman's budget-conscious postwar administration. Under study during the last two years of the war, a reorganized national defense establishment offered the promise of economizing the management and operations of the nation's force structure. Reorganization had gained a broad base of political support plus strong endorsement from all armed forces but the Navy. After Truman became president he moved to restructure the "antiquated defense setup" in favor of unity of command. He did not anticipate the deep-seated resistance he encountered from the admirals and their sponsors in Congress. The shooting had barely stopped when the two sides became locked in heated debate over how to organize the nations's postwar defense structure.[6]

The Unification Debates and the National Security Act of 1947

Upon returning to Washington in October 1945, General Spaatz was thrown into the unification debate with the Navy-a divisive struggle rendered more difficult by postwar demobilization and fierce competition for shrinking defense dollars. Of the unfinished business Spaatz inherited as the new Chief of Staff in 1946, none was more pressing than the unification issue. Spaatz told his commanders that agreement on a single department of national defense, with an independent air force on parity with the other services was his highest priority.[7]

Spaatz believed the wartime experience mandated creation of an autonomous air force. The combined arms of land, sea, and air won the war, he said, but air power "was the spark to success in Europe...Japan was reduced by air power, operating from bases captured by the coordination of land, sea and air forces."[8]

Various committees studied the pros and cons of unification through 1945. Most supported some form of unification and a separate air force. A committee headed by Ferdinand Eberstadt, former chairman of the Army and Navy Munitions Board, proposed an independent air force, retaining some aviation in the Army and Navy to perform their respective missions. Neither the Army nor the Navy agreed completely with the Eberstadt Report, commissioned at the request of Secretary of the Navy James V. Forrestal. Assistant Secretary for Air W. Stuart Symington characterized the report as a Navy document while Forrestal denied both the allegation and the report's findings.

Another committee headed by Army Lt. Gen. J. Lawton Collins recommended a single defense establishment with three military departments, including an independent air force with control of all land-based air forces except supporting elements allocated to the Army and the Navy. The Navy dismissed the Army report as a parochial document supporting the AAF's fight for unification.[9]

In December 1945, President Truman asked Congress to unify the armed forces and create a separate air force, but encountered strong opposition from Navy supporters on the Hill. While Assistant Secretary Symington and General Marshall officially disavowed any desire to bring aircraft carriers into an independent air force, naval officers did not believe them. Any unification that might break up the Navy's integrated team of air, sea and land components was anathema to most flag officers. The war in the Pacific had brought aircraft carriers to the fore of fleet operations, and the Navy was not about to relinquish control to another service. The Navy also feared losing dedicated Marine Corps tactical air support, which was indispensable to successful amphibious assaults against the Japanese. Complaints from the Army about the wartime growth of a "little army" within the Navy heated up the controversy.[10]

Navy fear of losing its organic aviation capabilities was not groundless. General Spaatz later said that he wanted all military aviation to be integrated into the independent air force, but realized this was a "rather remote" possibility because of entrenched Navy opposition. "So remote, of course, that it never happened," he said.[11]

Admiral Arthur W. Radford, a seasoned naval aviator and future chairman of the Joint Chiefs of Staff, said General Spaatz sought his support to merge naval aviation into the new Air Force by offering him the second highest post and promising he would succeed Spaatz as chief of the new Air Force. Radford claimed he was flattered by the offer, but refused, believing that the merger would not be in the best interests of national security.[12]

Spaatz admitted that he approached some key Navy airmen to join ranks on the unification issue, explaining that when General Arnold put him "on this work," he contacted senior Navy officers to inquire, "Are you coming with us to have an Air Force, or what are you going to do?" Spaatz said that he was rebuffed by most, but that "one or two of the admirals" agreed with the need for unification and "thought that the proper organization was land, sea, and air." He recalled that about a month before passage of the National Security Act of 1947, a few senior naval officers approached him about joining the new Air Force. "Well, it was too late," Spaatz said. "The agreement had all been made-cleared by the President-and we could do nothing about it. They themselves wrote in the Bill that Naval officers could not transfer to the new Air Force." In the end, Spaatz said, "We have been open and above board and straight forward with the Navy all the way through."[13]

Rebuffed in his overtures for a single integrated air arm, General Spaatz conceded that carrier planes belonged to the Navy. He remained opposed to the Navy retaining land-based planes which duplicated Air Force missions and had strong concerns about patrol bombers which the AAF had reluctantly turned over to the Navy during World War II. The press reported that the Navy proposed to modify its patrol bombers to carry atomic bombs on long-range missions. Symington let Forrestal know that the AAF thought the Navy intended to form its own strategic air forces. He confided his belief that the Navy opposed unification because it feared that strategic air power would monopolize postwar defense budgets to Secretary of War Robert P. Patterson. Any form of unification required the Navy give up independent appropriations, a tradition it had guarded since the Army proposed a single appropriation for military aviation in the early 1920s.[14]

Compromise appeared to be the only way out of the unification maze for either the Army or the Navy. Spaatz encountered growing pressure to remove obstacles from the bargaining table in 1946 and 1947. Concerns that continued interservice bickering might erode executive and congressional support for autonomy joined with signs that the War Department might be wearying of the struggle. In May 1946, Spaatz warned his staff of deteriorating relationships with the War Department, Army ground forces, and Army service forces. He had heard talk among senior Army and Navy officers about the AAF trying to "hog" national defense. While he privately nursed strong feelings of anger and distrust toward the Navy because of its obstructiveness during the unification talks, Spaatz told the Air Staff he wanted the AAF to approach the subject with maturity. Throughout the debates, he cautioned senior AAF officers to conduct themselves properly in relationships with the War Department and other agencies. He urged the AAF to defend its vital interests on an intelligent rather than an emotional basis. "Our point of view should be presented in a logical and dignified manner," he told his staff, "any tendency to become emotional, engage in name-calling, or to become soreheads must be avoided."[15]

During the spring and summer of 1946, President Truman worked to resolve the unification issue. His patience grew thin as stormy congressional hearings failed to produce legislation. The President ordered the armed services to split their differences and agree on a mutually acceptable approach to unification that could win the approval of the Eightieth Congress when it convened the following January. Major General Lauris Norstad, Chief of Plans and Operations on the Air Staff, and Vice Adm. Forrest P. Sherman received the difficult task of threshing out a compromise plan. The result was an autonomous Air Force without control of Navy and Marine Corps aviation. Still harboring faint hope that the Air Force could later make its case to control all air elements, General Spaatz was pragmatic in his support of compromise legislation. In February 1947, he told his staff that he was "squarely behind" the Norstad-Sherman plan and believed it "a most worthwhile contribution to the interests of the Air Force." Not only did the Air Force become "autonomous and gain parity with the land and sea forces," but Spaatz believed that the plan would give the new Secretary of National Defense "authority and power sufficient to eventually resolve the entire matter so that it more nearly meets the ideal."[16]

Throughout unification talks, General Eisenhower stood firmly behind the airmen, declaring that "the Army does not belong in the air-it belongs on the ground." Eisenhower wanted assurances, however, that the Army would have strong tactical air support. Early planning for the postwar organization envisioned a single air force, but Spaatz met Eisenhower's concerns in March 1946 by reorganizing the Air Force into the Strategic Air Command (SAC), Tactical Air Command (TAC), and Air Defense Command (ADC). Spaatz later denied that he yielded to "pressure" from Eisenhower, saying that it was a mutual understanding. "Well, this was the result of the war-we were thinking along the lines of World War II," Spaatz said. "We thought this was the way that it should be organized."[17]

Some senior AAF officers objected to Spaatz's decision to split the Air Force into strategic and tactical forces. At an Air Board meeting in December 1946, General Kenney, the first SAC commander, said, "I think we are cutting ourselves into two camps that are liable to be gobbled up...I don't think that an airplane should be considered as a tactical airplane and a strategic airplane," Kenney argued, "I think it is an airplane."[18] Major General Elwood P. Quesada, the first TAC commander, agreed in principle but thought that without the distinction, the Army might try to demand its own tactical air forces on the same grounds that the Navy had kept its carrier-based forces.

Not all Army officers favored giving up their tactical air support. Even if the concept of a single, operational air force became reality, Quesada feared that the strategic air effort would be frequently diverted to the tactical role because the Air Force would be outvoted in the joint arena. On the other hand, Kenney feared that breaking air power into functional roles heightened the possiblity of misuse. He felt so strongly about this that he ordered SAC forces not to use the word "tactical" when referring to TAC operations, preferring the term "combat air operations." Kenney was equally averse to the word "strategic," but conceded that "it is on the letterhead and I can't help it." He vowed to avoid using either word.[19]

Another outspoken critic of dividing the operational air forces was Maj. Gen. Orvil A. Anderson, an air power thinker and teacher who had participated in World War II planning and on the strategic bombing survey. As commandant of the Air War College, Anderson taught that the World War II experience was more a history of deficiencies in air power theory and application than of perfection in strategy. His articles and lectures sermonized on failures by both sides. He believed enemy bungling contributed as much to the outcome of the war as Allied brilliance. A prime example, according to Anderson, was the Luftwaffe's failure to take advantage of the American lag in long-range fighter technology. Rather than using fighters to stop Allied bombers, Anderson felt the Germans could have exploited Allied weaknesses to win air superiority. Anderson felt both sides had failed to develop sound air strategy, stunted by the overwhelming influence of traditional military thinking.[20]

General Anderson believed that the harmful effects of "packaging air weapons for precommitment to the direct support of surface" forces was a principal lesson of the air war. "If we package our air force weapons to meet the dictates of competing roles and missions," he said, "we detract from air power, lessen the probability of success, and invite both defeat and disaster." He reasoned that modern air wars could not be fought with the patterns of World War II. "Those patterns were poorly designed, but had they been good, they would still be archaic," he said.[21] Anderson concluded it was wrong, therefore, to structure the new Air Force on World War II experiences. He spoke fervently against the functional division of air power, arguing that the "so-called organizational development of the Air Force into strategical air and into tactical air" was illogical and ineffective. He warned that "these two queer distorting shibboleths" would "hang as lodestones around our necks...long beyond our time." "In a bureaucratic form of government such as ours," he said, "having adopted one of these military structures, we wed it, we assign them roles and missions, and nothing short of revolutionary magnitude will get us to divorce our mistake."[22]

Feelings in the AAF ran strong against "only a measure of unification," as some airmen described postwar compromises on restructuring the armed forces, but General Spaatz saw nothing to be gained from being the only service unwilling to make concessions. In 1946, General Norstad and Admiral Sherman worked out a compromise to create unified commands in overseas theaters where American forces remained after the war. While unified command in Europe was a fait accompli, the divided command left from the war against Japan defied easy resolution. After nearly a year of discussions, Norstad and Sherman compromised by retaining dual theater responsibilities in the Far East to satisfy the lingering division of interests between the Army and the Navy. The plan created the Pacific Command under Admiral Nimitz in Hawaii and the Far East Command under General MacArthur in Tokyo. In addition to the European, Pacific, and the Far East Commands, the plan established the Alaskan, Northeast, and Caribbean Commands, and the Pacific Fleet, all under the strategic direction of the Joint Chiefs of Staff. The plan, which President Truman approved in December 1946, also recognized the special status of SAC, which later became a specified command.[23]

The compromises worked out between Norstad and Sherman were rewarded on July 26, 1947, when President Truman signed the National Security Act (Public Law 253), creating the National Military Establishment, including an Office of the Secretary of Defense and three coequal military departments-the Army, the Navy, and the Air Force. The Department of the Air Force and the United States Air Force were established on September 18, 1947, with Stuart Symington appointed the first Secretary of the Air Force. General Spaatz became the first Air Force Chief of Staff. While the long campaign for independence was over, a new battle over roles and missions was just beginning.[24]

Expecting Secretary of War Patterson to head the new Defense Department, the proponents of unification were surprised when President Truman nominated

Roles and Missions

While the debate over roles and missions continued, and agreement seemed imminent, President Truman signed the proclamation designating August 1, 1947, as Air Force Day. *(NASM photo)*

Navy Secretary James Forrestal for the post. Patterson announced his retirement. Air Force leaders had misgivings about Forrestal because he had led the vigorous Navy campaign against unification. They feared his elevation to Secretary of Defense strengthened the Navy's bargaining position on roles and missions and other unification issues.

While Forrestal was credited with "even-handedness" during his tenure as Defense Secretary, from September 1947 to March 1949, critics charged him with favoritism when he brought his former Navy Department team into the new office. Secretary Symington complained that the Secretary of Defense had no one on his top staff who had served in the Air Force. The turn of events that followed Forrestal into the top defense post dimmed General Spaatz's hopes for obtaining "the ideal" unification of land, sea, and air forces.[25]

Executive Order 9877: Impasse Over Roles and Missions

To guard against erosion of naval aviation and Marine Corps functions, the Navy wanted the specific roles and missions of the armed forces written into unification legislation rather than assigned by executive order. Navy and Marine Corps leaders feared that a future President might arbitrarily reduce their services to roles "of military impotence." General Eisenhower, however, thought it unwise to "freeze" detailed statements concerning roles and missions into law. He argued persuasively that assigning roles and missions was a proper prerogative of the Chief Executive in his capacity as Commander in Chief.

The services compromised when Congress added a policy statement to the National Security Act that it intended to provide three military departments to operate and administer the Army, the Navy (including naval aviation and the Marine Corps), and the Air Force. The law's purpose was not to merge the armed forces, but "to provide for their operation under unified control and for their integration into an efficient team of land, naval and air forces."[26]

When President Truman signed the National Security Act in July 1947, he issued Executive Order 9877 prescribing the functions and responsibilities of the armed forces. The executive order charged the Air Force with preparing to carry out prompt and sustained wartime offensive and defensive air operations. This entailed organizing, training, and equipping air forces for operations unilaterally or jointly with other services. The Air Force was responsible for gaining and maintaining general air supremacy and establishing air superiority where and as required. Other responsibilities included strategic strike and reconnaissance; airlift and support for airborne operations; air support to land and naval forces; air transport for armed forces, except for naval operations; and coordination of air defense among all services.

The Navy retained the Marines and the fleet air arm, including land-based naval aviation for naval reconnaissance, antisubmarine warfare, and protection of shipping. The Navy was to coordinate air aspects of these missions with the Air Force, which would assist when it would increase economy and efficiency. The Navy retained authority to develop organic naval air weaponry, giving it wide latitude to expand its capabilities beyond the boundaries set by the executive order.[27]

Intended to eliminate unnecessary duplication among the services and to secure unified military action, the new law and executive order offered hope that the excessive self-interest and intense rivalry of the interwar years had finally been put to rest. That hope, however, did not last beyond the restructuring of the military establishment in 1947. Soviet truculence caused the Truman administration to put brakes on demobilization, but the armed forces were still undermanned and encumbered by austere defense budgets. At the same time, Army, Navy, and Air Force planners were busy sorting out force requirements to support the emerging doctrine of global containment.

The Soviet Union had embarked on an ambitious program to expand Communist influence in Europe and Asia, smothering hopes of lasting peace kindled by the United Nations charter of 1945 and leading to the onset of the Cold War. In May 1947, Congress endorsed the Truman Doctrine when it approved the President's request for aid to Greece and Turkey to combat Communist terrorism. Three months later, George C. Marshall, who became Secretary of State after retiring from the Army, introduced the Marshall Plan to aid European countries recovering from the ravages of World War II. With occupation forces spread thinly overseas and the mighty war machine in mothballs at home, the United States moved cautiously into the Cold War role as leader of the free world.[28]

Three military arms competing for scarce defense funds only intensified service rivalries. While promoting research and development in new technology such as jet powered aircraft, in-flight refueling, and rocket propulsion, the Air Force placed its highest funding priorities on its strategic air mission. It had a critical investment in the giant, propeller-driven B–36, which the AAF had planned in 1941 to fill the anticipated need for an intercontinental bomber. The burgeoning Soviet military threat made production of an intercontinental bomber that could deliver an atomic strike more urgent because of its deterrent value. Since the B–36 was the only such weapon in sight, the Air Force pressed forward with its program to procure the giant bomber, even though it faced criticism both within and outside the Air Force.[29]

Meanwhile, the Air Force relied on SAC's few Silverplate B–29s capable of delivering atomic bombs to enforce the President's policies. Taking into account the Soviet Union's numerically superior conventional forces, planning by the Joint Chiefs called for use of atomic weapons early in a potential East-West conflict. At the time, strategic forces had only one group, the 509th Composite Group, of specially modified B–29s and less than a dozen atomic bombs, but the Air Force was working to increase these capabilities. In 1946, to prepare for a possible European B–29 deployment, General Spaatz arranged with Air Marshal Tedder to prepare five RAF bases for U.S. use in the event of a crisis, including two for atomic operations. At home, the Air Force prepared for aerial refueling operations to extend the range of its strike forces. By mid-1947, SAC began deploying B–29s to Europe and the Pacific on a rotational basis. Although the bombers did not carry nuclear arms, they became a symbol of U.S. determination to counter Communist aggression.[30]

All three services were involved in costly research and development programs with strategic implications in the 1940s, including guided missile programs. Aided by German rocket scientists brought to the United States by Project Paperclip, work on guided missiles progressed steadily after the war, but did not add greatly to the roles and missions rivalry among the services until the next decade.[31]

The Navy's postwar maritime strategy envisioned building a global forward posture around aircraft carriers which could launch atomic strikes against the Soviet Union and other inland targets. Naval modernization priorities, therefore, centered on construction of a 65,000-ton "flush-deck" supercarrier to add a new dimension to the reach and striking power of fleet operations. The supercarrier was essential in Navy plans to share the atomic strike function with the Air Force. The disclosure that naval strategy envisioned using carrier-launched planes to strike vital inland targets outraged Air Force leaders. General Spaatz angrily accused the Navy of intruding upon the Air Force's assigned responsibilities for strategic bombing operations. Admiral Nimitz argued that Navy carriers added range and versatility to the atomic strike mission, unmatched by land-based bombers. The dispute erupted in hearings sponsored by the President's Air Policy Commission in late 1947 and threatened to disrupt the unity of the new defense organization before it became established.[32]

Secretary Forrestal testified before the Commission, chaired by Thomas K. Finletter, in favor of a balanced force structure with budget expenditures divided

Thomas Finletter, who chaired President Truman's Air Policy Commission, inspects a new Air Force fighter. *(NASM photo)*

evenly among the services. He expressed his disappointment with Air Force opposition to Naval maritime strategy and the Commission's findings. Reporting to the President on January 1, 1948, the Commission agreed that the United States needed a new strategic concept looking toward the day other nations would have large numbers of atomic weapons. The Commission bolstered the Air Force position by supporting the concept that such a position "must be based on air power."

While national defense required adequate naval and ground forces, the Commission believed a larger share of the defense budget should be spent to build up the Air Force. It found the Navy air arm "as presently constituted" adequate, but deemed the Air Force inadequate. The Commission recommended increasing from 55 to 70 groups over the next four years to provide the minimum number of aircraft needed for air defense and "only 700 very heavy bombers for the strategic bombing of enemy targets."

The total defense budget for 1948 was $10.1 billion, with $2.9 billion for the Air Force, $4 billion for the Navy, and $3.2 billion for the Army. Of the Navy's share, $1.2 billion was earmarked for aviation. The Commission recommended immediately increasing the Air Force budget to $4.1 billion and upping it to $5.4 billion in 1949. By comparison, the budget for naval aviation increased only by $192 million in 1948 and $310 million in 1949. The Commission also proposed to consolidate the Air Transport Command and the Naval Air Transport Service to provide air transport for all services.[33]

Navy leaders complained that the report of the Finletter Commission mirrored parochial Air Force views, slighting the strategic contributions of naval air power.

Roles and Missions

While General Spaatz ordered Air Force members to refrain from public comment, he shed his own reserve when Admiral Nimitz released a study which advocated the "use of mobile floating air bases off hostile shores to deal shattering blows at an enemy's industrial potential far inland in an event of war." In a January 1948 note to Secretary Symington, Spaatz expressed dismay that Nimitz would ignore agreements prohibiting the Navy from building duplicative air forces. The Navy's study refuted claims that the supercarrier was intended only for sea warfare or the support of fleet operations. "I don't know when we are going to come out with public comment on it," Spaatz said, "but it is not going to be too damn long if they keep up this way."[34]

While emotions simmered over the Finletter recommendations, Congress drew somewhat different conclusions in its own review. In a report issued on March 1, 1948, the Congressional Aviation Policy Board, chaired by Senator Owen Brewster, agreed that the threat to world peace "in the age of the atomic bomb" and other "new and terrible weapons" demanded the maintenance of supreme air power to "discourage aggression" and to "preserve the national security." After reviewing the exhaustive testimony gathered by the Finletter Commission, as well as "additional testimony and voluminous research data," the Aviation Policy Board declined to make recommendations for "the air requirements of the Navy and the Air Force," citing the failure of the Joint Chiefs to fulfill their obligation under the National Security Act to produce a unified plan for the armed forces. The Aviation Policy Board emphasized that its support for supreme air power was "not to be construed as implying any opinion whatsoever concerning the importance or necessity of any other branches of the armed forces."[35]

The Policy Board blamed the lack of "truly coordinate and integrated" strategic planning on the impasse between the Air Force and Navy over interpretation of roles and missions set forth in the National Security Act and Executive Order 9877. The Air Force believed it had been given exclusive responsibility for the strategic air mission while the Navy challenged that the law permitted "it to develop any type of weapon and to base its plans and requirements on the utilization of any weapon." The Navy contended that it was complying with the law and that it was the law and the executive order which were in conflict, rather than the Navy creating the conflict.

The perceived conflict or ambiguity between the law and the executive order prompted the Aviation Policy Board to call for "immediate clarification" either by amending the act, revising the executive order, or both. "The loyalty of each service to its traditions is understandable," the Board said, but warned that "unyielding adherence to service loyalties at the expense of national security is a luxury the Nation can no longer afford."[36]

Clarifying Roles and Missions: The Key West and Newport Conferences

Seeking to reconcile the differences between the Air Force and the Navy, the Secretary of Defense met with the Joint Chiefs at Key West, Florida, from March

11 to 12, 1948, to clarify roles and missions. Afterward, Secretary Forrestal confidently stated that he believed the conference had produced "general accord on practically all matters which were previously unresolved." The conferees drafted a paper entitled, "Functions of the Armed Forces and the Joint Chiefs of Staff," recommending that the President approve it as a replacement for Executive Order 9877. President Truman approved the paper on April 21 and rescinded the executive order.[37]

The conferees at Key West understood that the "Functions" paper was not "an operational or command document," but would serve as guidance for planners. The conferees agreed that during war the roles and missions of the armed forces would not be governed strictly in accordance with their agreement, "but by the means available at the time, and by the urgency of the situation." Nonetheless, they believed that the delineation of functions would be valuable to planners to determine force requirements and prepare budget estimates based on strategic plans.[38]

The "Functions" paper reaffirmed the Army's primary responsibility for land warfare, the Navy's responsibility for operations at sea, and the Air Force's responsibility for war in the air, including strategic air operations and air defense of the United States. Organic Navy and Marine Corps aviation remained assigned as integral elements of fleet operations. The Army retained a few liaison and spotter aircraft, but the Air Force was primarily responsible for providing "close combat and logistical air support to the Army to include airlift, support and resupply of airborne operations, aerial photography, tactical reconnaissance, and interdiction."

The paper assigned each service collateral responsibilities for "maximum assistance" to other services to enhance effectiveness or to help attain military objectives. To illustrate the principle of collateral functions, Secretary Forrestal referenced the overlapping roles between the Air Force and the Navy. Provisions were made for the Air Force to contribute to antisubmarine warfare as a secondary function, while the Navy could participate in the overall air effort as directed by the Joint Chiefs. Although not spelled out in the "Functions" paper, the Key West conferees agreed that the Navy could attack any targets, inland or otherwise, necessary to accomplish its mission. The paper prohibited the Marine Corps from building up a second land army.[39]

Secretary Forrestal admitted that assigning collateral functions left the door open to duplication and disagreement among the services, but he believed problems would be resolved in the joint arena. The services could not develop additional force requirements solely on the basis of collateral functions, but they might be used to justify primary force requirements. Forrestal explained that the Navy's supercarrier would not be constructed solely "on the basis of its contribution to strategic air warfare." If the Navy could not justify the carrier solely on its naval function, he thought that it's combined contributions to naval and strategic warfare might warrant its construction, if the Joint Chiefs of Staff agreed. When differences over force requirements could not be resolved in the joint arena, the Secretary of Defense would make the final decision.[40]

General Hoyt Vandenberg succeeded Gen. Carl Spaatz as the second person to hold the position of Air Force Chief of Staff. *(NASM photo)*

Secretary Forrestal's confidence after the Key West meetings faded quickly. Rather than subsiding, the controversy between the Air Force and the Navy escalated even as President Truman approved the new roles and missions guidance. Under Adm. Louis E. Denfeld, who succeeded Admiral Nimitz as Chief of Naval Operations, the Navy continued to campaign for atomic strike capabilities and a greater strategic air role. The Air Force continued to oppose the inclusion of Navy force requirements in joint strategic planning. General Spaatz, who retired at the end of April and turned the Air Force reins over to Gen. Hoyt S. Vandenberg, told Secretary Forrestal that the Key West talks had failed to answer the prevailing question of "whether there are to be two air forces or one air force."[41] Spaatz wrote General James Doolittle, who had returned to the Shell Oil Company after the war, that the "big battle now" was "a question of one Air Force and Naval aviation." Asserting that all "compromises so far" had favored naval aviation, Spaatz said:

> There will be lots to do over the next year or two to get this question settled properly for the Country. If it is not, I can see ourselves spent into bankruptcy and the end product being two second-rate Air Forces instead of one adequate for the job.[42]

Secretary Forrestal followed the advice of the Finletter Commission by approving consolidation of military air transportation into a single Air Force command, the Military Air Transport Service, effective in June, 1948, but had serious reservations about the Commission's recommendation that the largest share of the defense budget be used to build up the Air Force. Unyielding in advocating a balanced force structure, Forrestal supported Navy plans to construct a supercarrier that could deliver atomic strikes. Secretary Symington, on the other hand, lobbied for a four-year program of 70 groups and argued against building the supercarrier.

In a July 1948 speech, Symington asserted that air power requirements should be put in balance with the power of potential enemies and not with the other services, so angering Forrestal that he considered asking for Symington's resignation. The two officials seemed deadlocked in their opposing positions. Forrestal remained steadfast in his quest for a balanced force structure. Symington continued to campaign for a larger share of the defense budget for the Air Force.[43]

By mid-summer, the two sides appeared more deadlocked over strategic planning differences than before the clarification of functions at Key West. Another impediment to effective planning came with the Navy's block of a proposal for the Air Force to serve as executive agent for the Armed Forces Special Weapons Project (AFSWP), organized in 1947 to coordinate military handling of atomic weapons. Soon after the Key West conference, General Spaatz proposed that the Atomic Energy Commission transfer custodial responsibility for atomic weapons to the AFSWP and that the Joint Chiefs appoint the Air Force as executive agent to control the weapons. The Navy voiced strong objections.

Seeking to resolve the impasse, Forrestal had a cordial, but unfruitful conversation with General Vandenberg at the end of July. Forrestal told Vandenberg he supported the Air Force's "predominance in the field of strategic air warfare," but believed "it was most important" for the Navy to proceed with construction of its supercarrier. Vandenberg responded that the country could not afford to spend billions each year on its armed forces, particularly when large sums were spent on duplicative programs. Vandenberg reassured Forrestal that the Air Force had no objective to gain control of naval aviation, although Forrestal noted that General Spaatz had once confided as much in private conversations. Forrestal told Vandenberg that without an early resolution by the Joint Chiefs, he would make the decision for them.[44]

Forrestal told Vandenberg that he was considering calling on General Spaatz and Adm. John H. Towers, both now retired and in the public sector, to "assist in defining the issues involved in the differences between the Navy and the Air Force on the use of the atomic bomb."[45] On August 9, the Defense Secretary turned to the two veteran airmen for their "singularly competent views" on the strategic warfare controversy. He asked their advice on the Key West recommendations, the role of carrier aviation in strategic operations, the Air Force's dominant interest in atomic weapons, and the employment of atomic weapons by naval aviation. He asked them to address "the issues involved" and "the decisions which should be made on these issues."[46] Forrestal was concerned that the United States might make too great a commitment to a single weapon, noting that the atomic bomb alone would not deter war.[47]

In a joint response on August 18, Spaatz and Towers advised that they believed that the Key West agreement was a satisfactory document. As to the divergent views between the services, the two former leaders attributed the problem to differing interpretations of the agreement rather than fundamental issues. They explained that the differences were not unique to postwar roles and missions, but were "old ones still unresolved," prevalent in both services, rooted "in jealousy and mutual distrust."

Roles and Missions

The gist of the problem was apparent in the polarized views of Spaatz and Towers over such matters as strategic planning, force requirements, defense budgeting, and the control of atomic weapons, as they related to the Key West agreement. The two men were diametrically opposed on the issue of controlling atomic weapons. Spaatz believed that the Air Force was the only service capable of delivering atomic weapons. Therefore, in his view, it should have sole custody. Towers thought the Army and the Navy should have equal access to atomic weapons based on long-range plans and force development.

Spaatz opposed building the supercarrier solely for strategic purposes on the grounds that the Air Force, as the service with primary responsibility for strategic air warfare, was responsible for determining force requirements. Spaatz believed the large carrier was being constructed for strategic bombing. Statements by some naval officers seemed to bear this out. Towers denied this, arguing that the carrier was essential for the Navy to perform its primary responsibilities in support of joint operations, a mission requiring a capability to deliver atomic bombs "considerably behind the immediate land area to be assaulted." He argued that such bombing was "tactical rather that strategic."[48]

Despite their conflicting views, the two men found common ground to seek compromise. They both interpreted the Key West agreement as vesting in each service "exclusive responsibility and commensurate authority" in "the fields of its primary mission," imposing "not only the right but the responsibility" on each service to determine requirements for its primary mission. In this context, Spaatz and Towers concluded that the Navy would be remiss to not develop a capability to deliver atomic bombs if failure to do so would "jeopardize its ability to perform some of its primary missions." At the same time, the agreement mandated that each service use "all available resources" to contribute to "maximum overall effectiveness." By implementing the principle that "exclusive responsibility and authority in a given field" did not "imply preclusive participation," Spaatz and Towers believed that the armed forces could eliminate "the present difficulties and confusion."[49]

Forrestal convened a conference at the Naval War College in Newport, Rhode Island, from August 20 to 22, 1948, to discuss matters of interservice concern with the Joint Chiefs. Afterwards, in a Pentagon briefing, Forrestal told an audience of senior officers that he was convinced that the top military commanders understood the Air Force's exclusive role in strategic air warfare and its responsibility to seek all the help the Navy could provide using air power, strategically or tactically.

General Vandenberg promised to seek contributions from the other services when they would enhance the effectiveness of the overall air campaign. Likewise, the Navy promised to invite help from the Air Force to carry out its primary mission of antisubmarine warfare. The Navy withdrew its objections to the Air Force having "interim" control of the AFSWP, with an understanding this would not preclude use of atomic weapons by the other services. Praising Forrestal's farsightedness, Admiral Denfeld predicted that "when the history of the early days of the present National Military Establishment is written," this conference would mark the turning point for achieving interservice understanding "for perhaps the first time."[50] Near the end of 1948, however, Forrestal admitted that while "great progress" had been made, there remained "great areas in which the view points of the services have not come together." The most divisive issue, he said, was, "What is to be the use, and who is to be the user of air power?"[51]

The Key West and Newport conferences were held in the shadow of heightened European tensions and strengthening of the Truman Doctrine. In February 1948, the Cold War flared dangerously when a Soviet-instigated coup d'etat toppled the neutral government of Czechoslovakia. The United States and its Western European allies filed diplomatic protests, but took no countervailing action. Two months later, however, the United States and Great Britain set on a firmer course of action when the Soviet Union imposed a land blockade of Allied sectors in Berlin. To counter the blockade, the Air Force, in cooperation with the Army, Navy, and Department of Agriculture, began a sustained airlift, dubbed "Operation Vittles," into the besieged sectors of Berlin. The RAF joined in the airlift, which lasted through the summer of 1949.

A technological triumph for air cargo transportation, the Berlin airlift demonstrated the vital role of air transport in both war and peace, and enabled the United States and its allies to withstand Soviet military pressure without armed confrontation. The Kremlin lifted the blockade, but drew the Iron Curtain tighter as the Marshall Plan took root. The allies formed the North Atlantic Treaty Organization (NATO) for collective security and U.S. strategic bombers returned to European bases to form the salient for nuclear deterrence.[52]

The Strategic Bombing Controversy and the "Revolt of the Admirals"

Within weeks of the Newport conference, dissension between the Air Force and the Navy resumed when they were unable to reconcile differences over allocation of funds for the fiscal year 1950 budget. This was to be the first wholly integrated budget proposal under the direction of the Secretary of Defense. By October, relations between the two services appeared more strained than before Forrestal's August intercession. The dispute centered on the $14.4 billion ceiling on Defense spending imposed by President Truman. Estimates for the modernization programs of all three services, including funding Air Force strategic bombers and Navy heavy carriers, were considerably larger than authorized under the Truman ceiling. Estimates were based on a strategic war plan prepared after Key West which contemplated atomic reprisal strikes from RAF bases joined by naval operations to secure the Mediterranean line of communication in the event of hostilities.[53]

Secretary Forrestal recommended that Truman lift the ceiling, since the $14.4 billion estimate provided "the capability only of reprisal against any possible enemy" by land-based air forces, leaving the Mediterranean line of communication unsecured. Not wanting to raise fears that his administration was preparing for war, particularly during his close 1948 reelection bid against Thomas E. Dewey, Truman refused. Instead, he authorized Forrestal to develop costs for force requirements above $14.4 billion, but told him to hold the estimates in reserve as supplemental appropriations only in the event of a national emergency. This meant that proceeding with full funding for Air Force requirements would come at the expense of other priority programs, such as the Navy's heavy carriers, which might have to be deferred as supplemental appropriations.[54]

Forrestal asked the Joint Chiefs of Staff for their "definitive recommendation...as an entity" on dividing the fiscal year 1950 budget, within the Truman ceiling. Failing to arrive at an agreed program, however, the Joint Chiefs "simply transmitted the separate and uncorrelated budget requests of the three services-totalling, of course, very much larger sums-thus dumping the whole problem on Forrestal's desk." The Secretary of Defense privately expressed grave reservations about the reliance on atomic bombs to deter an enemy as well as the ability of the Air Force to deliver a decisive blow. While working with the Joint Chiefs to reconcile the budget submission, Forrestal sought other counsel, including advice from Secretary of State Marshall and the National Security Council, but came away with no concrete answers.[55] In November, the National Security Council provided general policy guidance in NSC 20/4, a draft paper charting Cold War objectives to deal with the Soviet Union. By framing nuclear deterrence as a national strategy, NSC 20/4 substantiated the programmed buildup of strategic bombing capabilities. Taking steps to put atomic muscle into deterrence, the Air Force brought Lt. Gen. Curtis E. LeMay, a seasoned veteran of the strategic air campaign against Germany and Japan, home from Europe to command SAC and to develop it into a formidable nuclear force.[56]

As the budget dispute dragged on, the Navy became more critical of claims that land-based bombers could penetrate enemy territory and drop atomic bombs on vital heartland targets while Air Force opposition to building heavy carriers hardened accordingly. A revival of old concerns that the Air Force intended to absorb naval aviation exacerbated the dispute.

One such forum was a commission created by Congress in 1947 and chaired by former President Herbert C. Hoover to recommend improvements in the administration of the U.S. government. Questions about the cost and duplication of maintaining more than one air force were raised during Hoover Commission hearings examining the organization and administration of the armed forces. The Air Force denied that it had any intention to take over naval aviation, but contradictory statements by retired officers and advocacy groups from both services kept the controversy alive.[57]

During its annual meeting in Washington, D.C., the Air Force Association added to the interservice furor by advocating stronger unification and integration of naval aviation into the Air Force. In the December 1947 issue of *Air Force Magazine*, the Association's President, Gen. James Doolittle, charged the National

Security Act with failing to establish a strong, coordinating head of the Joint Chiefs of Staff or to designate roles and missions unequivocally. Complaining that the National Security Act had created "two self-sufficient, competing air forces, each planning to win the air war in its own way," Doolittle asked why naval aviation could not be integrated into the Air Force as a special branch, as with tactical aviation in the Army. Doolittle pointed out that compromises "intensified rather than reduced the undesirable effects" of interservice rivalry. Quarreling over funding priorities made it obvious that the Key West and Newport conferences had not put roles and missions disunity to rest.[58]

Although his quest for a balanced force structure did little to reduce interservice rivalry, Forrestal stuck to this policy throughout his tour as Secretary of Defense. He steadfastly supported funding and construction of the Navy's supercarrier, *United States*. He did change his views on the efficacy of Air Force strategic bombing, however, after consulting with former Prime Minister Churchill during a trip to Europe at the end of 1948. Upon his return, Forrestal reported to President Truman that "the only balance...against the overwhelming manpower of the Russians, and therefore the chief deterrent to war, is the threat of the immediate retaliation with the atomic bomb." Abandoning earlier doubts about long-range bombing, the Secretary of Defense said that he now believed "the Air Force can get in with enough to deliver a powerful blow at the Russian capacity to make war."

At this juncture, however, the political climate in Washington, D.C. had eroded the Secretary's influence. Since the November elections, Forrestal had steadily lost favor in the Truman administration. In March 1949, mentally distraught, he stepped down from his post as Secretary of Defense. He died soon thereafter, in a tragic fall or leap from the window of his hospital room at Bethesda, Maryland. Having fallen into disfavor partly because of his lackluster support for Truman's reelection, some felt Forrestal had become a victim of the raging roles and missions feud between the Air Force and the Navy. Forrestal saw himself as "a victim of the Washington scene."[59]

Forrestal's departure set the stage for "the angriest interservice fight...since the Billy Mitchell days." On April 23, 1949, just one month after taking office, Defense Secretary Louis A. Johnson cancelled the Navy's $188 million supercarrier. Johnson, acting on the majority opinion of the Joint Chiefs of Staff, convinced Truman to cut the carrier. Both General Vandenberg and Army Chief of Staff Gen. Omar Bradley voted to delete the carrier while Chief of Naval Operations Admiral Louis R. Denfeld dissented. Bradley and Vandenberg argued that the carrier was redundant because it duplicated the role of Air Force strategic bombers.[60]

Navy officials were outraged. Johnson abruptly announced his decision to cut the carrier without notifying or consulting Navy Secretary John L. Sullivan. Bitter over the handling of the matter, Sullivan resigned in protest, prompting the so-called "Revolt of the Admirals". Navy frustrations led to widespread criticism of the Air Force's intercontinental bomber as angry naval officers intensified their criticism of the B–36 after Johnson killed the supercarrier. Earlier, testifying before the Hoover Commission, Adm. Arthur Radford had attacked Air Force procurement of the B–36, claiming the giant bomber was too slow and too vulnerable to enemy defenses. Fueling the controversy, "ugly and disturbing reports of irregularities" in the procurement of the B–36 began to spread through the nation's capital. Of particular concern was an anonymous document implicating Johnson, Symington, and other officials in possible wrongdoing relating to the bomber's procurement. Johnson had served on the board of directors for Consolidated Vultee Aircraft Corporation, manufacturer of the B–36.[61]

On May 25, 1949, the allegations against Johnson and Symington reached Congress when Representative James E. Van Zandt, an ardent Navy supporter, introduced a resolution calling for a special investigatory committee. Because the B–36 affair was viewed as a threat to the national defense, Representative Carl Vinson, Chairman of the House Committee on Armed Services, had investigative authority assigned to his committee. On June 9, the Armed Services Committee agreed to broaden the inquiry to include "investigations into some of the most vital problems of the national defense," including roles and missions, unification, and strategy. The Committee wanted to investigate the truth about the alleged irregularities by the Secretary of Defense and the Secretary of the Air Force. "The airing of these reports, rumors, and innuendoes had already had substantial deleterious effects upon the morale of the services headed by these men at a most crucial time in international affairs," Committee members said, making it imperative that the allegations be investigated so that prompt and just corrective action could be taken, if warranted.[62]

For three weeks in August, the Armed Services Committee held extensive public hearings into the procurement of the B–36. After testimony from an array of witnesses, including officers who had opposed the bomber and those who would have to fly it, the Committee concluded that the B–36 had been selected on its merits, calling it "the best aircraft for the purpose available to the Nation today." The inquiry exonerated Secretary Johnson and Secretary Symington of any wrongdoing in B–36 procurement. The Committee unanimously concluded that there was "not one scintilla of evidence [to] support charges that collusion, fraud, corruption, influence, or favoritism played any part whatsoever in the procurement of the B–36 bomber."

At a dramatic point in the hearings, Cedric R. Worth, formerly a special assistant to the Assistant Secretary for Air and the Under Secretary of Navy, admitted he was behind the anonymous document that led to the investigation. Under oath, Worth "recanted and repudiated" the charges made in the document. The Navy Department suspended Worth and began departmental inquiries into "the matter of participation of officers and employees of the Navy in the preparation of the anonymous document and distorted propaganda" against the Air Force.[63]

On August 10, while the B–36 hearings were underway, the 81st Congress enacted the National Security Act Amendments of 1949, converting the National Military Establishment into the Department of Defense and strengthening the exec-

The controversial B–36 carried over 21,000 gallons of gasoline and 1,200 gallons of oil when fully loaded. *(NASM photo)*

utive powers of the Secretary of Defense. The amendments made the Secretary of Defense the principal adviser to the President on defense matters and the sole Defense representative on the National Policy Council. The amendments established the position of Chairman, Joint Chiefs of Staff, and three military departments (Army, Navy, and Air Force), with civilian secretaries reporting to the Secretary of Defense.

A primary objective of the amendments was to provide organization and lines of authority for effective strategic direction of the armed forces, unified joint action, and integration into an efficient team of land, naval, and air forces. Secretary Forrestal had recommended to President Truman in February 1948 that the National Security Act be amended to "clarify the powers" of his office and to reform the defense organization. The Hoover Commission made similar recommendations. The Navy opposed the amendments, while the Army and the Air Force heartily approved them. Proponents hoped the new structure would help resolve interservice differences before they became full-blown crises such as the controversies over the B–36 and the supercarrier.[64]

The House Armed Services Committee, having dissipated the cloud over the B–36 program, resumed hearings into broader issues. Concerned about the airing of Navy grievances in the press, Chairman Vinson declared at the outset of the second round of hearings that the Committee was "going to the bottom of this unrest and concern in the Navy." The Committee's agenda called for an examination of roles and missions to determine the soundness of the decision to cancel the supercarrier and for a review of procedures in the joint arena as they related to the development of weapon systems. The Committee proposed to address the effectiveness of strategic bombing and its dominant role in nuclear deterrence. Another item concerned accusations from the Navy and Marine Corps that the Air Force was concentrating on strategic bombing to the detriment of air defense and tactical aviation.[65]

Roles and Missions

There were signs that some Army generals had misgivings about relinquishing control of tactical air forces. An article in a major news magazine warned that while Army leaders were not challenging the Air Force publicly, ground-unit commanders and ranking officers in the Army's planning staff worried about the Air Force trend "away from air units that support ground-force operations and toward air units for long-range bombing."[66]

Two events on the eve of the congressional hearings heightened public awareness of the proceedings and their importance to national security. The September surprise of President Truman's announcement that the Soviet Union had detonated an atomic bomb overshadowed the dramatic success of the Berlin airlift. Another grave development was Mao Tse-tung's defeat of Nationalist forces in China and his declaration on October 1 proclaiming the People's Republic. As the congressional hearings got underway, news reports stirred the public's consciousness with their portrayal of Navy witnesses as "rebel admirals" bent on wrecking unification.

The "considerable public comment...generated by the press" moved the Armed Services Committee to announce that it had solicited the "personal viewpoint" of the witnesses and urged that all "testimony be presented without restraint or hesitation." The Committee cautioned against distorting "the presentation of Navy views" revealing "fundamental disagreements" into charges that witnesses had performed in any manner unbecoming their positions in government.[67]

From October 6 to 17, 1949, more than two dozen Navy witnesses appeared before the Committee. For the most part, their presentations consisted of testimony intended to discredit Air Force programs and actions under unification. An exception was the opening statement by Secretary of the Navy Francis P. Matthews, who had pledged "unqualified approval of the policy of unification" when President Truman appointed him to the post in May. Secretary Matthews admitted there was "limited impairment of morale" in the Navy, but denied that morale was "all shot to pieces" as suggested by news leaks. He believed the unrest was confined primarily to naval aviation and called the manifestations of "some dissatisfaction...on the part of naval aviators" no surprise.

The achievements of naval air power in World War II, contrasted with postwar reductions and a diminished Navy role under unification "were felt most keenly by naval aviation, and naval aviators responded quite naturally," Matthews said. The postwar era was one of great flux for the Navy, he said. The United States ended the war with the greatest Navy the world had ever seen, with no foreign navies to challenge the U.S. fleet's command of the seas. Matthews agreed that the Navy needed "effectively equipped naval aviation, including Marine aviation, in adequate strength" to maintain command of the seas. To this end, Secretary Johnson approved the Navy's proposal for two modern aircraft carriers of the *Essex* class, for a total of eight carriers "capable of handling the new and modern planes which [were] just coming into the fleet."[68]

Admiral Radford, now head of the Pacific Fleet and the joint Pacific Command, followed Matthews before the Committee and set the tone for several days of Navy testimony. Radford launched "a direct attack on Air Force concepts of strategy, unification, tactics, and the capabilities of weapons systems, including the B–36."[69] Statements by other Navy witnesses, described by the Committee as "almost the entire high command" supplemented by lower-ranking officers and civilians, followed the same pattern. Admiral Radford and other naval aviators bitterly resented the cancellation of the supercarrier and expressed concern over what they considered overreliance on Air Force strategic bombers.

Admiral Radford derided the Air Force's concept of strategic bombing, which he described as "blitz" atomic warfare. He argued that Air Force strategic bombers alone would not deter war and postulated that they might invite war instead, a horrifying prospect since the Soviet Union was now an atomic power. Radford bluntly claimed that the Air Force could not win a war. He and other Navy leaders declared that a national strategy based on an atomic offensive was morally wrong and inconsistent with national views toward warfare. They charged that the Air Force obsession with strategic bombing caused it to neglect air defense and tactical aviation.[70]

Secretary Symington and General Vandenberg spoke for the Air Force during the October proceedings. Because Generals Spaatz and LeMay and other Air Force witnesses defended Air Force strategic bombing capabilities during the inquiry into the B–36, their supplemental testimony was not needed during the second round of hearings. While not called to testify, General Spaatz's presence was felt at the hearings when Congressman Vinson read an article by the retired Air Force general in a recent issue of *Newsweek* magazine. Spaatz, who had joined the magazine's editorial staff after retiring, wrote in favor of "pushing unification further" by pooling "military air resources" and placing them under a single organization. When questioned about the article, Secretary Symington said it reflected Spaatz's personal views and was not the official Air Force position. Symington denied that the Air Force wanted to control Navy and Marine Corps aviation, stating emphatically, "I know of no officer in the Air Force who agrees with the position that there should be one Air Force for this country."[71]

General Vandenberg repeated Symington's denial when Congressman Vinson asked him about rumors that "the Air Force was trying to gobble up naval aviation and Marine Corps aviation." Stating unequivocally that the Air Force believed "naval aviation has a place with the fleet," Vandenberg assured Vinson, "We are not attempting in any way to organize any type of movement that would get naval aviation into the United States Air Force." Vinson felt that Symington's and Vandenberg's statements had cleared up "beyond a shadow of doubt this question that has been giving the country and the Navy some concern." "If this hearing does not accomplish anything else but clearing that up," Vinson said, "it has at least done that positively and unequivocally." The Chairman went on to say that he believed the hearings would be of great help at home and abroad and "would put the country in a position to intelligently support a national-defense program."[72]

Responding to testimony challenging the soundness of Air Force strategic concepts, General Vandenberg reminded the Committee that the Joint Chiefs of Staff were responsible for strategic planning and had agreed "separately and jointly...that the concept of strategic bombing, and the extent of its employment as now planned, are sound." Moreover, SAC was a specified command whose directives and targets came from the Joint Chiefs as part of national war plans. As for SAC's role in deterring war, Vandenberg cited Winston Churchill's testimonial "that Europe would have been communized and London under bombardment some time ago but for the deterrent of the atomic bomb in the hands of the United States." To witnesses who "recommended that we cancel out this country's capability of conducting a strategic offensive with atomic weapons," Vandenberg said:

> Adoption of this proposal would, in my judgment, destroy the one greatest equalizing factor in the balance of military power between a potential enemy and the western democracies and could only be received with contempt or despair by those who have joined together for common defense.[73]

Vandenberg characterized assertions of an Air Force focus on strategic bombing to the detriment of other missions uninformed. He explained that the Air Force, within existing ceilings, maintained balanced force levels to perform the roles and missions assigned to it. Of 3,246 aircraft in the active inventory, only 942, or 29 percent, were assigned to SAC. Vandenberg ponted out that the SAC forces included 132 tankers, 96 reconnaissance aircraft, 150 fighters, and 24 transports in addition to its bomber force. The remaining 2,304 aircraft were distributed among three other major commands and the Military Air Transport Service for air defense missions in support of all three services. Furthermore, another 2,258 aircraft in the Air National Guard, all tactical and air defense units, were an essential part of the force. "The Strategic Air Command, on the basis of assigned aircraft, represents less than 20 percent, and the B–36 component only 3 percent," Vandenberg said, which hardly could be misconstrued as an imbalance in strategic air power.[74]

Another factor discrediting "assertions of unbalance and overemphasis" of the strategic bombing role was the often misunderstood Air Force doctrine of indivisible air power. The doctrine gave air commanders the flexibility to apply all available air forces wherever needed in a variety of tactical or strategic roles. Recalling the wartime experience in Europe, General Vandenberg said that flexible employment "characterized the role of air to a singular degree throughout the whole European campaign." He cited examples of interoperability between air forces:

> For weeks preceding the Normandy invasion, strategic air teamed with the tactical air forces in isolating the battlefield in every crisis of the ground campaign. The full weight of the strategic air forces was put on the Normandy beaches in support of that amphibious landing. Again at St. Lo its concentrated attack paralyzed the opposing German forces and opened the

gate for our break-through and Gen Patton's exploitation with rapid advance to Paris.

Its full effort, despite foul weather, was focused on the support of ground forces during the critical period of the Ardennes break-through. Concurrently, it conducted a highly successful strategic campaign into the heart of Germany, destroying its oil industry and in conjunction with tactical air effectively immobilized the whole of his transportation system.[75]

Vandenberg claimed he had no illusions about strategic bombing defeating Nazi Germany without a ground invasion, as some air power theorists said. Nor did he believe that a future war could be won solely by strategic air forces. The objective of the strategic bombardment program, as Vandenberg experienced in battle, was to weaken the sustaining sources of enemy forces so they could be defeated in less time at less cost.[76]

Vandenberg's counterpart, Army Gen. J. Lawton Collins, supported his views. Collins' divisions had received close support from Vandenberg's Ninth Air Force when he commanded the VII Corps of the First Army during the Normandy invasion, through the capture of Cherbourg, to the breakout in France and the closing with Russian troops at the Elbe. Collins testified that the greatest lesson of World War II was that no single service could achieve victory and that future wars would be won by a team of Army, Navy, and Air forces working together under unified direction and control.[77]

Senior Army leaders who testified at the Congressional hearings joined the Air force in refuting Navy criticisms. General Bradley, recently confirmed as the first Chairman of the Joint Chiefs of Staff, chided the witnesses for their lack of team effort and their "public revolt" against the Secretary of Defense. Bradley challenged the demand for larger Marine and Naval forces on the basis that the existing threat did not justify expanding amphibious forces. He questioned the Navy's claim to preeminence in amphibious warfare, reminding the Armed Services Committee that neither Navy carriers nor Marines had been present at Normandy, the largest beach assault in history. Bradley and others suggested that questions about military armament should be left to the newly formed nonpartisan weapon systems evaluation group agreed to at Newport.[78]

Defense Secretary Louis Johnson's testimony was more conciliatory, focusing on his responsibilities to reduce expenditures within Congressionally-imposed ceilings. Johnson defended his decision to cancel the supercarrier and to impose budget cuts on all services. Like Bradley, Johnson called for stronger unity in the joint arena, suggesting that judgments about the B–36 and other military armament be left to the nonpartisan weapon systems evaluation group.[79]

The Armed Services Committee issued the report of its investigation into "unification and strategy" in March 1950, just a few months before the outbreak of war in Korea. While generally supporting unification and a stronger Air Force, the report also endorsed strategic pluralism in national defense, criticized the Defense Secretary's handling of the supercarrier cancellation, and urged less rigidity in the joint arena when dealing with sensitive interservice issues. The report emphasized that Air Force, Navy, and Marine Corps aviation were integral elements of the nation's's combined air power and recommended that greater emphasis be placed on joint planning and training to increase military effectiveness and overcome service differences.

The Committee report asserted that each service was responsible for developing its own weapon systems, subject to evaluation by the joint weapons group. Therefore, the report concluded that the Air Force and the evaluation group were in the best position to judge the effectiveness of the B–36. Similarly, the Committee considered the advice of Navy leaders paramount with regard to naval weapons. The Committee withheld action on construction of the supercarrier "because of the pressure of other shipbuilding programs...and the existing budgetary limitations in the Navy Department."[80]

While deploring the manner in which the supercarrier was cancelled, the Committee found the Defense Secretary's decision to withhold funds "to be entirely within the law as passed on August 10, 1949." The Committee expressed deep concern, however, about the infringements of this practice on "the constitutional responsibility of the Congress to provide and maintain a Navy and to raise and support an Army." Urging consultation with Congress before making administrative changes to appropriations, the Committee said it would sponsor legislation to amend the unification act accordingly.[81]

Another matter of "keen disappointment" to the Armed Services Committee was the removal of Admiral Denfeld as Chief of Naval Operations just one week after the hearings adjourned. In an October 27 letter seeking President Truman's approval to transfer Denfeld, Navy Secretary Matthews stated that he had informed the President before the October hearings that he feared the incumbent's "usefulness as Chief of Naval Operations had terminated." Nevertheless, a Committee majority interpreted the firing as reprisal against Denfeld because of his "frank and honest" testimony and viewed the action as a violation of promises made to witnesses. The Committee said that any repetition of this incident would lead it to "ask Congress to exercise its constitutional power of redress."[82] Meanwhile, Adm. Forrest Sherman, who teamed with General Norstad to draft the unification bill and distanced himself from attacks on the B–36, replaced Denfeld as Chief of Naval Operations.

As for the controversy that spawned the public hearings, the Committee doubted there would be "any early meeting of military and naval minds" on strategic bombing. Sharing the Eberstadt Task Force Committee's view that "difficult problems will inevitably continue to exist between the Air Force and the naval air arm," the Committee blamed the "continuing disagreement" less on interservice rivalry than on "a genuine inability for these services to agree, fundamentally and professionally, on the art of warfare." The Committee concluded, "It is a sad fact that neither can be proved right or wrong except through the supreme test of actual war and the nature of the peace that follows."[83] That test would soon come in the form of a limited war, for which the armed forces had neither planned nor prepared.

On the Eve of Limited War: Tactical Air Role Contested

On the eve of hostilities in Korea, criticism of the Air Force commitment to tactical air support was heard more frequently than before the 1949 Congressional hearings. Senior Army commanders had defended the Air Force's record of support to ground forces, but their testimony did not vindicate the Air Force from assertions that it was "giving inadequate attention to air support of ground forces." The Committee concluded only that closer cooperation between Marine Corps aviators, the Army Field Forces, and the Air Force was needed "for the development of sound close air support tactics and techniques."

Testimony by Navy and Marine Corps aviators that Air Force equipment, tactics, and command procedures to support ground forces were inferior had left some doubts in the minds of Committee members and military planners alike. Presenting the Marine Corps position at the hearings, Brig. Gen. Vernon E. Magee testified that "the present high command" of the Air Force emphasized strategic bombing, while tactical air was "a matter of concern to the United States Navy and Marine Corps and to far-sighted officers of the United States Army."[84]

The role of Marine Corps aviation, as stated by General Magee, was to insure command of the air over the combat zone, to isolate hostile forces from resupply or reinforcement, and to attack hostile forces in the battle area. Marine Corps and Navy air elements were complementary, each trained to fly in support of the other. Operating from aircraft carriers or airfields, Marine squadrons flew missions to support amphibious landings or land combat and supplement operations at sea as needed. Marine Corps pilots had "long specialized in the development of techniques for the close support of ground forces," Magee said, since this was their primary mission. After some early deficiencies at Guadalcanal, Magee claimed that the Navy and Marines had developed a workable system of air-ground control that "improved with each campaign until, at Okinawa, we were able to effectively control as many as 20 squadrons in simultaneous close support of a single army corps."

By contrast, Magee conceded that Army Air Forces had compiled an "enviable record" of air support in Europe during the last months of World War II, but only "finally learned to do so, after three years of battling through Sicily, Italy, and France." He charged that the Air Force record before Normandy was "characterized by indifference to the demands of the ground forces, inability to provide effective close support requested, and a certain ineptness in distinguishing friend from foe."[85]

General Magee stated that he believed the Air Force lacked "an effective air-ground control system," contending that the principle of centralized control was a basic defect in the Air Force system, imposing "command by cooperation" on combat units and depriving commanders of control over supporting firepower. This contradicted Marine Corps air doctrine, which taught that "the ground commander on the spot" exercised operational control of supporting air units, just as he controlled his artillery. Magee said "this basic and irreconcilable difference in the concept of command" made joint operations difficult during the war and hampered "postwar efforts to evolve a workable joint Army-Navy-Air Force procedure for the control of supporting aircraft."

Conceding that some Army leaders were satisfied with the Air Force system, Magee said "certain others" were not. He asserted that tactical air forces earmarked for Army support existed "largely on paper," and that Air Force tactical units were not "properly trained for their assigned missions." "Summed up, if war should come tomorrow," Magee stated, "the tactical air squadrons of the Navy and Marine Corps would have to provide the major part of the troop support even as they did in the beginning of the last war."[86]

The Air Force aroused concerns about abandoning the air-ground commitment when funding constraints compelled it to combine air defense and U.S.-based tactical forces under a single Continental Air Command at the end of 1948. Air defense and tactical commands were stripped of their units and reduced to operational and planning headquarters. While the new arrangement provided a closely integrated fighter force for air defense or tactical air missions, it understandably suggested to Army field commanders that their air support needs were being slighted.

General Elwood Quesada, TAC Commander since March 1946, objected strenuously to the change, believing it broke Spaatz's promise to Eisenhower that the Army would always have strong tactical air support. He felt it could push the Army to rebuild its own tactical air force. General Jacob L. Devers and his staff at Army Ground Forces Headquarters also protested the arrangement, complaining that it retarded tactical air support and development. The controversial organization lasted only two years, with TAC and ADC reemerging as full-fledged commands in December 1950, when the armed forces were six months into the Korean conflict.[87]

General Vandenberg said that General Bradley and Army Chief of Staff Gen. J. Lawton Collins had assured him the grievances attributed to General Devers and his staff were "entirely unfounded" and that the Army was "very happy with the situation as it existed." Responding to the attacks on its doctrine and system of air-ground support, Air Force spokesmen said that Marine Corps criticisms were "based on island warfare experience" having "little application to a war of continental, or even intercontinental, proportions." Marine airmen traditionally operated against circumscribed objectives quite unlike the long Army fronts that had characterized the war in Europe. General Collins, testifying before Congress in 1949, reaffirmed the Army's faith in the Air Force system and "the great flexibility of tactical air forces" it afforded. General Eisenhower reiterated his earlier endorsement for the Air Force concept to employ tactical air in World War II:

> Battle experience proved that control of the air, the prerequisite
> to the conduct of ground operations in any given area, was

gained most economically by the employment of air forces operating under a single command. This assured a maximum of flexibility, providing a command structure under which all forms of
available air power could be concentrated on tactical support
missions or on strategic missions, as the situation demanded-in
other words, it permitted the maximum concentration of combat
air power at the decisive point at the decisive time. Throughout
the war, the Army depended on the necessary tactical air support
from a practically autonomous Air Force. This type of close,
accurate, and effective support of the frontline fighting units
provided and proved an essential element in the achievement of
Army objectives.[88]

General Bradley's wartime experience leading the Twelfth Army Group convinced him that the inherent flexibility and economy of force in the Air Force's use
of tactical air power allowed it to meet the requirements of a sustained land campaign. The Twelfth's combat strength reached as many as 30 divisions, supported
by 14 fighter-bomber groups from the Ninth Air Force in its drive across Europe.
This allowed approximately one aircraft group for each Army division, while other
air forces continued to fly interdiction and fighter escort missions. "In my opinion,
this was a very successful sustained operation in the face of a determined enemy,"
General Bradley said. By comparison, based on its wartime experience, the Marine
Corps organized its peacetime aviation with two wings of approximately 21 tactical squadrons-the equivalent of about seven Air Force groups-to support its two
combat divisions. "If this is a fair comparison," General Bradley said, "then Marine
aviation as part of naval aviation seems to be overwhelmingly out of balance." If
the Army applied the Marine air-ground ratio to its vastly larger support requirements, Bradley said the result would be "fantastic" and cost-prohibitive.[89]

Unlike the heavy artillery and armored support available to the Infantry,
Marine combat units were equipped with light artillery and armor and were accus-
tomed to storming ashore under heavy protective fire from naval gun batteries and
organic tactical aviation. Marine tactical fighters were dedicated to supporting
ground troops. Control of their operations passed to the ground force commander
when the troops came ashore. Marine airmen believed their air-ground system provided the most effective tactical support of troops just as strongly as Air Force flyers believed that centralized control of theater air resources under an air commander was the best way to direct air power.

Both systems evolved from the unique make-up, roles and missions, and
warfighting experience of each service. Both were combat-proven. Unable to reconcile these differences before war broke out in Korea, the joint air forces impro-
vised during the early stages of the first armed conflict fought under unification.
Conceptual differences between the air forces erupted into a major roles and missions controversy as the forces began joint operations in the skies over Korea.[90]

Roles and Missions

A warning of doctrinal issues awaiting tactical air forces in Korea appeared in Gen. Mark W. Clark's book, *Calculated Risk*, published just months before the war started. A veteran Army ground commander, Clark praised the "splendid air support of all kinds" his Fifth Army troops had received in North Africa and Italy, but was highly critical of the "command setup" for air employment. General Clark's description of combat aviation as "auxiliary weapons, as is the artillery" that "should come under the direct orders of the ground commander" indicated that misgivings about the Air Force air-ground system might be more widespread among field commanders than previously thought.[91] Clark's words would haunt air-ground relationships in Korea, as the General became Commander of Army field forces in the United States and later Senior Commander in Korea.

Roles and Missions in the Korean Conflict

North Korea's invasion of the south in June 1950 and President Truman's decision to intervene with American forces on behalf of the United Nations brought the first armed confrontation between free world and communist forces. The war became a test for free world solidarity and for the revised U.S. strategy promulgated in the spring of 1950 by National Security Council (NSC) Memorandum 68. Concern over communist advancements convinced Truman to order the development of thermonuclear weapons and undertake a broad reassessment of national strategy. The formulation of NSC 68 also fulfilled a Congressional mandate for "a firm statement of principles" to guide joint planning under unification.

The NSC 68 review of Soviet aims and capabilities called for a state of national readiness to respond to various levels of political and military conflict, preferably within the framework of international treaties and the United Nations. Korean hostilities came weeks after public disclosure of NSC 68 rearmament planning, forcing the United States into a more sober appraisal of its military programs and the President's call for universal military training. While deterrence remained the core of national strategy and the United States continued to build its strategic capabilities, the Korean War diverted attention from nuclear to conventional military operations, with a corresponding change in focus for the roles and missions of the armed forces.[92]

The air war and the overall military situation on the Korean peninsula were unique in the annals of American warfare. It was the first war fought under unification. It was the first time forces were employed under the United Nations flag. American units comprised the largest United Nations contingent, fighting beside men from other non-communist countries on the ground and in the air. Popularly dubbed a "police action" by the news media, it was war without a declaration of war, fought with conventional weapons under the umbrella of nuclear deterrence.

The war evolved into a limited, stand-off military confrontation that deterred broader hostilities while preventing victory in the classic sense. The Army and Marine Corps made amphibious landings on the peninsula to obtain tactical advantage, but the war began as a fluid ground campaign and settled into a stalemate at the 38th Parallel after communist Chinese forces intervened. Marine Corps units found themselves in a non-traditional role of fighting a sustained ground campaign beside the Army and the armies of other United Nations countries.

The Navy performed a variety of combat roles even without fleet engagements. There was a naval blockade of North Korea; Navy troop ships and transports provided a vital lifeline; and the Navy supported both Army and Marine landings. The most celebrated naval role, however, belonged to aircraft carriers operating off the Korean shores. Planes flying from the carriers, which operated free from reprisal because of United Nations air superiority, flew sustained combat missions normally assigned to shore-based air forces.[93]

Fifth Air Force fighters from bases in Japan and Navy and Marine fighters coming off carriers gave the United Nations Command numerically superior airpower, but the employment of joint theater air forces lacked unity and cohesion during the early stages of the war. Although the Joint Chiefs directed that theater commanders establish unified organizations to employ air, sea, and land forces in December 1946, General MacArthur's Far East Command headquarters in Tokyo made little headway towards this goal before hostilities began. American occupation forces remained in a purely defensive posture, and MacArthur's headquarters remained basically unchanged, staffed almost entirely by Army personnel. The only steps taken by MacArthur's headquarters to comply with the unification directives were to form a tri-service planning group and a joint committee of top-ranking Army, Navy, and Air Force officers. The Joint Chiefs' directive that unified commands have staffs representing all service components was all but ignored.[94]

Unfurling the United Nations' banner over the forces fighting in Korea influenced the strategic direction of the war, but had no effect on the command of U.S. forces. When MacArthur established the United Nations Command in July 1950, he laid the foundation to integrate troops from 15 member countries into the fighting. The forces and the command structure for the war remained predominantly American. Wearing a dual hat as the United Nations Forces Commander in Chief, MacArthur ran the war through his Far East theater organization, answering through the Joint Chiefs to the President. He had nominal air and naval components, but elected to retain land component responsibilities for himself, rather than trust them to a subordinate.

Soon after the conflict began, MacArthur established a subordinate headquarters in Korea under Maj. Gen. William F. Dean, but did not give it component status. The air component commander was Lt. Gen. George Stratemeyer, who rose to three-star rank in World War II and replaced Ennis Whitehead as Commander of the Far East Air Force (FEAF) in April 1949. His naval counterpart was Vice Adm. C. Turner Joy, Commander of Naval Forces Far East.[95]

All Air Force resources deployed to the combat theater were placed under General Stratemeyer's control. Drawing upon the AAF's experience in World War II, Stratemeyer formed the FEAF Combat organization along functional lines, with

Roles and Missions

Major General Earle E. Partridge commanded the Fifth Air Force in Korea. *(NASM photo)*

Fifth Air Force providing tactical air support, FEAF Bomber Command performing strategic bombing, and FEAF Combat Cargo Command flying airlift missions. Stratemeyer's Vice Commander, Maj. Gen. Earle E. Partridge, took charge of the Fifth Air Force, moving his headquarters to Korea after MacArthur established the Army headquarters there under General Dean.

Two other seasoned air commanders, Maj. Gen. Emmett O'Donnell, Jr. and Maj. Gen. William H. Tunner, took charge of the bomber and cargo commands. Tunner restructured the airlift organization in 1951, while O'Donnell's bomber command remained relatively unchanged for the duration of the war. O'Donnell and most of his staff were on loan from SAC, which augmented FEAF's single bomber group with three groups of B–29s, all under the theater air commander's direction.[96]

Stratemeyer's centralized control of theater air resources followed the pattern of Allied air forces in North Africa during World War II, allowing the planned use of tactical and strategic aircraft while permitting their diversion to meet any theater emergency. When Partridge moved his headquarters to Korea, he set up a rudimentary tactical air control system alongside Army headquarters and sent tactical air control parties into the field. When available tactical air assets exceeded the ground commander's needs during the early months, centralized control freed them for other missions such as interdiction and armed reconnaissance. Similarly, from his headquarters in Japan, General O'Donnell directed his bombers in a sustained campaign against North Korean industrial and military targets, but diverted his forces to support ground operations when Stratemeyer directed.[97]

According to Air Force doctrine, however, there could be no truly unified air campaign without giving the component commander centralized control over all air forces. Only then could the theater commander be assured of a well-planned and orchestrated air campaign with the flexibility to direct air assets where and when he most needed them. Although the few Allied air units which joined the fighting were integrated under Stratemeyer, no arrangements existed for the theater air commander to control Navy and Marine aircraft.

When Stratemeyer tried to gain control over Navy planes operating over Korea, he met resistance from Admiral Joy and Maj. Gen. Edward M. Almond, General MacArthur's Chief of Staff. Stratemeyer wrote in his diary that Almond, who criticized the Air Force system of centralized control, tried to dictate air operations in Korea. Stratemeyer took his problem to MacArthur, who assured him that he had full responsibility to command theater air operations. This was difficult to implement, however, because an absence of joint contingency planning in the Far East Command precluded working out the many details necessary to establish unified theater air command.[98]

Stratemeyer complained to MacArthur in early July about FEAF and Seventh Fleet aircraft operating independently against the same target areas, without adequate joint planning and coordination. Insufficient notice of naval air strikes against Pyongyang on July 3, forced FEAF to abort sorties planned for the area. Admiral Joy proposed that an area in North Korea be preserved for the exclusive use of carrier forces, but Stratemeyer argued that the limited land mass prohibited such an arrangement and that it would deny the air commander the flexibility to concentrate air resources where they could do the most good. Stratemeyer wanted operational control over the Navy's planes when they were used for other than purely naval tasks. When Admiral Joy objected, MacArthur instructed Stratemeyer to work things out with Joy and Almond.[99]

Stratemeyer and Joy reached a compromise which gave Stratemeyer "coordination control" of Navy aircraft operating in Korea, but failed to provide a clear definition of "coordination control," leaving Stratemeyer without authority. Resolution of coordination problems rested partly in developing procedures to target air missions. General Almond set up a targeting group in MacArthur's headquarters, comprised mostly of Army officers without experience in air operations. Major General Otto Weyland, on special assignment to FEAF, convinced MacArthur that a more experienced group was needed for a successful sustained interdiction campaign. Joint mission planning and targeting continued through the end of the war, with FEAF gradually assuming responsibility to direct these activities from the joint operations center. The Navy participated in center operations, but the question of the theater air commander's authority over Navy aircraft remained unsettled to the satisfaction of the Air Force.[100]

Early attainment of air superiority in Korea allowed Bomber Command's B–29s to carry out unescorted strike missions, unopposed in the air. Before United Nations forces drove the North Korean Army back across the 38th Parallel and pushed toward the Yalu, the B–29s carried out bombing missions against North Korean industrial and transportation centers. By October, when United Nations forces crossed the 38th Parallel, the B–29s had depleted worthwhile strategic targets, except for those protected by the rules of engagement.

There was never a true strategic campaign in Korea because self-imposed constraints to keep the war from widening prohibited long-range bombers from striking the industrial source of the enemy's warmaking capability, centered in the

Roles and Missions

A formation of B-29 Superfortresses of the Far East Air Forces (FEAF)
Bomber Command flies over Korea in December 1950. *(NASM photo)*

Soviet Union. There was no grand air strategy similar to World War II. It was a tactical, not a strategic war. Even after the entry of Chinese troops, targets in China and Russia remained off limits, which affected air interdiction efforts. Targets of opportunity prevailed over systematic destruction, making interdiction operations more random than methodical. The enemy learned to evade air strikes by moving at night and resorting to unorthodox supply methods. There was some success in stemming the flow of enemy supplies, but isolation of the battlefield was impossible.[101]

The same constraints barred United Nations air forces from conducting a classic campaign for air superiority, although the more powerful American air forces enabled United Nations ground units to operate free of pressure from enemy warplanes. The North Korean Air Force was destroyed in the first days of the conflict, but the air order of battle changed drastically with the Chinese entry. Enemy aircraft factories were free from destruction and enemy airfields in Manchuria became sanctuaries. Without an exploitation phase in the air war, American fighters faced deadly encounters that were unpredictable and disruptive.[102]

Before Chinese MIGs rose to challenge air superiority over the north near the end of 1950, the absence of enemy aircraft allowed Fifth Air Force to concentrate on supporting ground forces. Without adequate field artillery fire, United Nations forces relied on air support to stave off defeat and establish the Pusan perimeter. Tactical air support became critical when the Seventh Infantry Division and the First Marine Division landed at Inchon in mid-September, joining the Eighth Army in driving the North Korean invaders back across the 38th Parallel. By the end of October, tactical air forces were supporting two victorious armies, the Eighth Army to the west, commanded by General Walton Walker, and the Tenth Corps, commanded by MacArthur's former Chief of Staff, General Almond. The Tenth was composed of the Seventh and Third Divisions, the First Marine Division, two Republic of Korea divisions, and a commando group of British Royal Marines. By October 19, United Nations forces took Pyongyang, the North Korean capital, and were poised to destroy the North Korean Army. When the full force of four Chinese Communist armies was thrown against them in November, it changed the course of the war.[103]

As United Nations forces fell back, friendly air forces carried out relentless interdiction and concentrated close support operations to prevent envelopment by the enemy. After a brief stand along the 38th Parallel in mid-December, United Nations forces withdrew further south, giving up the capital city of Seoul. They established a main line of resistance along the Pyongtaek-Wonju line. With air power pounding the overextended supply lines of the Chinese army, the enemy offensive stalled, allowing United Nations forces to mount a counteroffensive which brought them back to a line along the 38th Parallel by April. While communist forces made a stand, they failed to drive further southward during a spring offensive. The first year of the Korean War was over. Over the next two years, the war bogged down into static warfare along the 38th Parallel.[104]

In the first year, Air Force, Navy, and Marine airmen fought a sustained air campaign giving the ground commanders a deadly edge over a numerically superior enemy. Despite the success of the air campaign, the bickering between commanders over how to provide tactical air support and criticism of the Air Force by some Army ground commanders seemed to receive more attention at home. Air-ground disputes in Korea led to Congressional hearings on tactical aviation in August 1950 and the Air Staff renewed efforts to increase air-ground effectiveness.[105]

Before the First Marine Division came ashore at Inchon in September, Marine and Navy airmen operated under the Fifth Air Force's tactical air control system when supporting Army troops. At first the airmen had difficulty scheduling sorties and adapting tactics and techniques to Air Force control methods, but these were eventually resolved. The Marines were doctrinally opposed to operating within the Air Force system and insisted on compatible tactics, techniques, and equipment for their system once operational in Korea. General Partridge welcomed the additional tactical air squadrons, but opposed allowing the Marines to operate independently because it created a gap in the application of tactical air power across the battlefront.[106]

Introducing a Marine division with organic tactical air support into Korea to take over a segment of the front alongside Army and allied units, presented a unique challenge for the United Nations Command. Under Air Force doctrine, the theater commander's air power was not fragmented by limited air resources tied to supporting a single organization. When the enemy attacked, concentration of all available air power was critical. The Air Force system provided flexibility to divert air forces from one area to another to assist troops in trouble. Air Force officials pointed out that although the Marine airmen were tied by their training and weapons to tactical support missions, they benefitted from Air Force and Navy superiority, interdiction, and strategic campaigns. They also benefitted from the diversion of other services' air resources when crises developed. All of this depended upon the flexibility of air allocation that only a single manager for air could provide.[107]

General Stratemeyer learned of Marine intentions to operate their air resources independently when belatedly shown plans for amphibious landings at Inchon. Stratemeyer was infuriated at being left out of the planning. Although Admiral Joy was in charge of the amphibious assault, it was not conducted in isolation, and Stratemeyer's command of the air campaign in Korea made him responsible for air tasks that bore upon the invasion's success or failure. Stratemeyer blamed the oversight on General Almond, who was in charge of joint Army and Marine landing forces. After landing at Inchon, Almond continued to use the 1st Marine Air Wing to support Army and Marine ground forces, relying exclusively on Marine air to support his assault. He refused to place Marine planes in the centralized pool under Partridge's control, violating all joint agreements on unified theater operations, including an earlier directive from MacArthur's headquarters. After United Nations forces moved across the 38th Parallel and Almond's forces made another amphibious landing at Wonson, General MacArthur finally placed all Marine air units under the Fifth Air Force commander's control in October.[108]

Partridge and Stratemeyer believed Almond was deliberately trying to parcel out air power in Korea, to compare his dedicated Marine air support to the Fifth Air Force's centralized system supporting General Walker's larger Eighth Army. Almond said he did not believe in the Air Force method of "support by cooperation," and thought the Marine doctrine of placing aviation under the ground commander was more effective. Without MacArthur's intervention, Almond might have protracted the rivalry and intensified the interservice controversy. The American press wrote about the burgeoning feud between the two services, reporting that the Army was now siding with the Marines. While Army field commanders might have preferred to have dedicated air support directly under their control, there was not enough available air power to satisfy all requirements. The Air Force doctrine of centralized control provided the best assurance that everyone received their fair share and would have sufficient resources in an emergency.[109]

The flexible employment of air power, including the use of B–29s for carpet bombing to support troops in contact with enemy forces, became far more critical after Chinese troops joined the war. The Marine breakout during the Chosin Reservoir Campaign is an example of an emergency ground situation which required support from all available air resources. Transports from FEAF's Combat Cargo Command worked tirelessly to air-drop supplies and evacuate Marine casualties.

Still, centralized control was not resolved to everyone's satisfaction. Marines remained unhappy operating under the Air Force system. A growing number of influential Army generals believed ground commanders should have organic tactical aviation and shared Almond's views. Among them were Gen. Matthew Ridgway, who replaced MacArthur when President Truman relieved him in April 1951, and Gen. Mark W. Clark, who succeeded Ridgway in 1952. Marines remained critical of the air control arrangements in Korea, and the issue remained controversial inside the Pentagon.[110]

Despite their conviction that the Army should have its own tactical aviation, Ridgway and Clark believed in unity of command, reflected in their direction of United Nations forces. General Clark organized the United Nations Command and Far East Command staffs into a unified headquarters and ordered the belated activation of an Army headquarters on a coequal level with Air Force and Navy components. Clark rejected an Eighth Army proposal, similar to Almond's, to experiment by assigning Marine squadrons directly under corps commanders. Not only did Clark wish to avoid the uproar such a test would cause, but he respected the counsel of his theater air commander, Gen. Otto Weyland, who returned to Tokyo to command the FEAF when General Stratemeyer suffered a heart attack in May 1951. General Clark relied on Weyland to make the air-ground team effort work and to maintain pressure on the enemy behind the lines. Weyland blamed most interservice problems in Korea on MacArthur's failure to establish a unified headquarters, observing that the deficiency was corrected by General Clark's reorganization late in the war.[111]

General Vandenberg was concerned that publicity about the tactical air controversy and the political constraints on air power had misinformed the American people about the Air Force's role in Korea. To combat any misperceptions, Vandenberg wrote an article for the February 1951 issue of the *Saturday Evening Post* in which he tried to explain the advantages of flexible application of air power. Vandenberg felt he did not need to apologize for the Air Force's performance in the war, but felt it necessary to challenge misperceptions about the Air Force role and the limits on air power. He admitted that the Air Force was not blameless for misunderstandings about its doctrine of flexible and indivisible air power. As General Anderson and others had cautioned in 1946, the organizational development of the Air Force into strategic and tactical air contributed to the problem. "We don't speak of a 'strategic' or 'tactical' Army or Navy," Vandenberg explained, "yet those terms are constantly applied to the Air Force."[112]

General Vandenberg reiterated that winning the air battle, "on which final victory on land or sea is predicated", and interdicting the enemy's lines of communication required a concentrated effort of theater air forces, but that neither was performed at the expense of providing close air support to ground forces. The Air Force system permitted it to carry out these activities simultaneously, when necessary, and to divert bombers and fighters from other missions to support troops. The flexible application of air resources where most needed served the principle of economy of force by assuring that air resources were not tied down to missions or areas where they were not always in use.[113]

Air Force F–86 Sabrejets such as these flown by twin pilots John and James Kumpf, provided powerful air support in the skies over Korea.

The United Nation's ability to operate in Korea free from the threat of air intervention was a tribute to attainment of local air superiority, made possible by the superior global posture of the Air Force. This posture provided flexibility to cope with other contingencies and helped deter a widening of the Korean conflict. By increasing the range and speed of air weapons, modern technology enhanced their flexibility. The Air Force developed its weapon systems to meet global requirements, giving it the capability to operate in limited war or to meet threatened aggression by selective positioning of counter force. The Air Force did not agree that tailoring its forces should be reordered for limited tasks in limited battle areas like Korea.[114]

Events leading to General MacArthur's recall from the Far East focused public attention on the political limitations of the Korean War. After General Stratemeyer was denied use of his fighters to pursue hostile aircraft across the Manchurian border, MacArthur confided his concern that the politicians were going to dissipate America's superior air and naval power by limiting the conflict to a land war. In contrast to the unconditional use of air power in World War II, air forces in Korea were constrained by the political restrictions of limited war.

General Vandenberg and other service chiefs, following President Truman's orders, resisted pressure from MacArthur for more aggressive air power, including a bombing offensive against mainland China. Air Force strategic planners had targeted mainland China for nuclear strikes, but there was little possibility of launching such strikes unless the Communists widened the war. On the other side, the rules of engagement prohibited pilots flying out of China from attacking United Nations ground forces or striking targets in South Korea. Chinese leaders feared this might lead to lifting the moratorium against air strikes in Manchuria and mainland China.[115]

Granting sanctuaries to the enemy and denying United Nations forces the strategic advantage of a sustained bombing campaign against the enemy's warmaking capability evened the odds in the air over North Korea and blunted the effectiveness of Fifth Air Force and Navy air operations forward of the battle lines. An effective interdiction campaign was made doubly difficult, if not impossible, because the industrially backward Chinese and North Korean forces relied on the Soviet Union to support an endless flow of men and supplies. With constraints on air power dulling the superior technological advantage of United Nations forces, time and attrition in the static, defensive war at the 38th Parallel became negotiating pawns for the other side. President Eisenhower's threat of atomic resolution did little more than bring an uneasy truce which would outlast the leaders who negotiated it.[116]

Another legacy of the war left lasting implications on the roles and missions issue. Judging from the Korean experience, the prepositioning of Army, Navy, Air Force, and Marine combat elements in forward areas and planning for their joint use required participation of all military arms, whether needed or not, when hostilities arose. Joint use of forces within the geographically confined field of battle in Korea placed Navy and Marine forces in nontraditional roles and increased the exposure of all services to interservice rivalries. From the Air Force perspective, the political constraints on air power in limited warfare, the adverse effects of interservice rivalry, and the need for a joint air doctrine were the principal lessons gleaned from the war. More than a decade of joint planning and another Asian war would pass before these lessons were learned with much conviction.

The Pace-Finletter Agreement: Rebirth of Army Aviation

In November 1950, Gen. James Doolittle recalled that General Eisenhower had been pleased when the Air Force achieved autonomy, but had warned General Spaatz, "Always lean over backward to give the Army what it needs in the way of air support or you will be in trouble." Judging from heated controversy over tactical air support in Korea, Doolittle said it was obvious the Air Force had been "remiss in not contenting the Army." He wrote General Partridge that General Vandenberg had tried to rectify the situation by bringing Lt. Gen. John K. Cannon home from Europe to "head up a revitalized Tactical Air Command," but was fighting hard to keep the Air Force from being dismembered. While Doolittle understood that insufficient funds to support the total Air Force commitment demanded compromise, he said he told Vandenberg that the Air Force "wasn't 'leaning over backward' far enough" on the tactical air support issue.[117]

By 1950, General Doolittle said, it seemed that the Army and Navy were "ganging up on the Air Force" to give the Army "control of the equipping, training and operation of Tactical Air."[118] A common criticism of Air Force tactical support in 1950 was the slowness in responding to ground commander's requests. Almond and other commanders in Korea wanted planes based closer to the front, readily available and responsive to their needs. They wanted to direct air attacks to support their troops, rather than having to ask for them. Almond argued that the Army should have control of all air units providing reconnaissance and fire support to its ground forces down to the corps level. Almond's criticisms and lack of cooperation with Air Force commanders in Korea prompted concern that the Army intended to develop its own organic aircraft for tactical support.[119]

Similar criticism was heard from General Clark and other Army commanders in the United States. General Clark complained about the limited range and loiter time of jet fighters, and wanted the Air Force to develop specialized aircraft for close air support. The Army also wanted improved aircraft for tactical airlift support and a larger voice in the design of specialized aircraft. In November 1950, General Collins supported this position in a paper presented to General Vandenberg. Shortly after, an Army spokesman in the Pentagon implied that the Army might be "forced" into the "close support business" unless the Air Force changed its thinking.[120]

Heightening Air Force concerns, the Army began to build a larger force of light planes and helicopters. When the Air Force became independent in 1947, the Army had retained a small number of light aircraft for artillery and liaison. Rotary-wing technology was adapted to perform various ground support missions and by 1949, a small fleet of helicopters had entered the Army inventory. In May 1949, the Army and Air Force issued a joint regulation permitting development of organic aircraft, but imposing weight ceilings to restrict Army aviation from duplicating Air Force missions. For the Army, its fixed-wing aircraft could not exceed 2,500 pounds, while its rotary-wing aircraft could not exceed 4,000 pounds. The regulation recognized the Army's limited needs for organic aircraft in forward areas of the battlefield, but forbade their use to attack enemy forces. When hostilities began in Korea, the Army had 700 aircraft, including 57 utility helicopters.[121]

In September 1950, General Collins asked General Vandenberg to lift these weight restrictions so the Army could purchase larger helicopters for combat cargo operations in Korea. Collins assured Vandenberg that the Army had no intention of duplicating Air Force roles and missions, but Vandenberg was wary of criticisms coming out of Korea and reports that the Army wanted to control tactical operations. Vandenberg turned down the Army's request. The matter was referred to the Secretariat for resolution.[122]

The clamor over tactical air support subsided after Army air-ground experts visited Korea in the spring of 1951 and found Fifth Air Force pilots doing a "splendid job" of supporting the Eighth Army. Their investigation concluded that Eighth Army commanders generally were pleased with the air support they received, and that "virtually all of the personal adverse remarks on air support could be attributed to a lack of information, or even misinformation about the subject." Efforts to judge between Marine Corps and Air Force air support operations were considered meaningless because "the two systems and the means at their disposal were so disparate as to preclude a basis of comparison."[123]

Air Force and Army commanders made good progress in remedying problems in air-ground support. While both recognized there was more to be done, the Air Force believed any air-ground improvements had to come within the framework of Air Force doctrine. Ground commanders determined the requirements for air support while Air Force commanders were capable of managing and providing the support. More effective training for air and ground personnel would improve the situation, but Army leaders believed that more than training was needed. While heading the Far East Command in 1952, Gen. Mark Clark agreed that the Air Force was doing an excellent job, but felt that tactical air support was "wide open for improvement."[124]

Ignoring Army demands for specialized support aircraft, Air Force research and development programs were geared to provide a full range of tactical air capabilities in a single aircraft. Years would pass before the Air Force relented to Army demands for aircraft designed specifically for the close air support mission. Meanwhile, the Army continued to build its own organic air capabilities.[125]

In October 1951, Air Force Secretary Thomas K. Finletter and Army Secretary Frank M. Pace signed a memorandum of understanding to eliminate the weight restrictions on Army aircraft. Defining Army aviation in terms of functions to be performed within a 50-mile radius of the combat zone, the Pace-Finletter agreement stipulated there would be no duplication of the roles and missions assigned to the Air Force at Key West.

This understanding was shortlived and differences between the services persisted. Under pressure from Secretary of Defense Robert A. Lovett, Secretaries Pace and Finletter signed another memorandum of understanding in November 1952 reinstating the weight restrictions at even higher levels of 5,000 pounds and redefining the combat zone to "50 to 100 miles in depth." These changes allowed the Army to proceed with plans to activate helicopter transport battalions and provide additional transport helicopters in Korea.[126]

The Army interpreted the 1952 memorandum as giving it free rein "to develop fully the potential of light aviation within its combat units." When fighting in Korea ceased in July 1953, the Army's aviation inventory had quadrupled to more than 3,000 aircraft. Helicopters accounted for one-third of this expansion. The use of helicopters in the combat zone laid the foundation for regenerating Army aviation. Before the war, the Air Force and the Navy showed greater interest in the fledgling helicopter industry, but the Army's rotary-wing force showed dramatic growth as the war progressed, taking steps to form 12 helicopter battalions in August 1952.

Some senior officers, like Maj. Gen. James M. Gavin, began describing helicopters as the Army's cavalry of the future.[127] The vision of a highly mobile air cavalry ultimately emerged as a controversial roles and missions issue for the next decade, having evolved almost unnoticed through a decade dominated by the nuclear arms race and rivalry surrounding funding and developing strategic weapons.

President Eisenhower inspects a security police honor guard as part of his duties as Commander in Chief during the emerging Cold War years. *(NASM photo)*

CHAPTER V

NEW DIMENSIONS: THE AIR FORCE
AND MASSIVE RETALIATION

President Dwight Eisenhower's years in the White House brought new dimensions to Air Force roles and missions. The Administration's "New Look" at military strategy preserved the Cold War objectives of the Truman Doctrine, but revised fiscal and force priorities, investing in a buildup of nuclear strength to deter Soviet aggression and adventurism. The ensuing nuclear arms race had a profound effect on doctrinal thinking, force planning, research and development, budget allocations, and roles and missions trends. To carry out the revised national strategy, dubbed "massive retaliation," the Air Force experienced unprecedented growth. Within the Air Force, the growth of SAC was most prominent.

While on the campaign trail, Eisenhower invariably pointed to the relationship between fiscal solvency and military strength when discussing Cold War objectives. He wrote to financier and political advisor Bernard Baruch saying that he thought war with the Soviet Union possible, but doubted "the Soviets would in their own best interests, deliberately provoke war." Disagreeing with staff planners who identified any particular year as "our point of gravest danger," as NSC-68 had done, Eisenhower believed "the continuance of various kinds of satellite conflicts" was more plausible. "Consequently, I feel that we should figure out our strength objectives, and push toward them steadily," he wrote, "always having in mind that we must retain a strong and solvent economy."[1] After his inauguration in January 1953, the soldier-statesman worked to build "security and solvency" as twin pillars of America's "Arsenal of Democracy", a policy with far-reaching implications for armed forces roles and missions.

During the campaign, Eisenhower warned against draining America's military and economic strength through small, peripheral wars. He promised to seek an honorable way out of the "Soviet mouse trap" in Korea. The costs of financing the Korean War, NATO, and other global defense requirements had quadrupled military appropriations, which rose from $14.2 billion in 1949 to $59.1 billion by fiscal year 1952. By sending diplomatic signals that he was prepared to widen the war and use nuclear weapons, Eisenhower hastened the armistice.

The Korean experience as well as other trouble spots convinced the new President that the United States should follow a policy of arming and preparing "South Koreans and other non-Communist nations to defend their own front lines and thus minimize, if not eliminate, the drain on Western manpower." Before the election Eisenhower told Richard Nixon, his running mate, that providing "most of the weapons and ninety percent of the manpower" was not his understanding of "a fair distribution of collective security."[2]

Roles and Missions

Eisenhower presumed that other Free World nations shared the "give us the guns and spare your sons" spirit he found during a post-election visit to Korea, and would fight to preserve their freedom if armed, trained, and aligned with their non-Communist neighbors for collective security. Different circumstances existed in places like Indochina, where the Vietminh's armed resistance against French reoccupation after World War II seemed less reprehensible than naked aggression in Korea. The protracted Indochina bloodshed was an economic and political burden to France. The United Nations provided grudging support as many members viewed the struggle more as a return to French colonial rule than a legitimate fight against insurgents.[3]

By the time a ceasefire was reached in Korea, France had depleted its NATO support in Indochina to sustain the war against the Vietminh. Red China, now free of its commitment in Korea, increased support for the Vietminh. The siege of the French stronghold at Dien Bien Phu in the spring of 1954 brought the war to a close. The United States helped finance French military operations in Indochina, and provided airlift and logistics support, but President Eisenhower refused to authorize air strikes to support Dien Bien Phu or to intervene militarily. The French defeat led to the partitioning of Vietnam, with the United States providing economic and military aid through its Military Assistance Program to the Republic of Vietnam and other signatories to the Southeast Asia Collective Defense Treaty of September 1954.[4]

Building collective security through regional and bilateral treaties, bolstering alliances with military and economic assistance, and shielding them with the U.S. nuclear umbrella were the cornerstones of Eisenhower's Cold War foreign policy. While concentrating on Cold War security measures, the administration actively sought rapprochement with the Soviet Union in pursuit of world peace and arms control. The United Nations General Assembly created a disarmament commission in 1953, but remained deadlocked over verification and enforcement. The U.S. government viewed Premier Josef Stalin's death as an opportunity to achieve better superpower relations, but the post-Stalinist regime headed by Georgi Malenkov rejected such overtures. The West decided this meant that the Communist bloc did not want to ease international tensions.

In August, a thermonuclear explosion by the Soviet Union caught Western intelligence by surprise and served as a warning that the arms race was tighter than previously thought. While Eisenhower did not abandon his goal of improved relations with Soviet leaders, these events convinced him that his view of the Cold War as a war of endurance was correct. The ultimate outcome would depend on economic staying power in addition to ideological remission or superior military strength.[5]

For the government to meet its superpower commitments and preserve the staying power of the economy, Eisenhower believed he needed "to overhaul the entire creaking federal establishment."[6] He pursued immediate reform in the Pentagon, simplifying the chain of command, strengthening the authority of the

The Korean experience convinced
Secretary of Defense Robert A.
Lovett that whoever occupied this
position needed greater authority.
(NASM photo)

Secretary of Defense, and facilitating a smooth transition into the strategy of massive retaliation. He planned an early review of military progress under unification. Realizing that the forthcoming military and economic changes could strain interservice relationships, the President wanted to avoid repeating the divisive roles and missions controversy that sparked the admirals' revolt in 1949.

Reorganization Plan No. 6: Tightening Unification's Reins

During his first month in office, Secretary of Defense Wilson set up a committee to study the defense structure, focusing on the authority and procedures of his office and interdepartmental relationships in the Pentagon. Chaired by Nelson A. Rockefeller, the committee began its work in February 1953. Over the next few weeks, witnesses testified and the committee reviewed documents, including an assessment of weaknesses in the Defense Department structure and suggestions for improvement from outgoing Defense Secretary Robert Lovett. His thoughts on reorganizing the Defense Department corresponded with Eisenhower's views, and were reflected in the Rockefeller Committee's final report of April 11.[7]

The Korean War convinced Lovett that the secretary of defense needed greater authority, contending that the secretary should serve as "the deputy to the commander in chief," with full direction over the Joint Chiefs, military departments, and unified commands. Advocating a stronger role for the JCS chairman in the planning and deliberating process, Lovett maintained that the military chiefs should serve "as the principle military advisers" to the Secretary of Defense and the President and be removed from day-to-day command of their services. He believed these changes would give the secretary of defense the necessary "authority and flexibility" to manage the Defense Department and resolve "service conflicts over such problems as budget, manpower, procurement, and logistics."[8]

Eisenhower incorporated the Rockefeller Committee's recommendations into Reorganization Plan No. 6, which he transmitted to Congress at the end of April

Roles and Missions

1953. The President said his objectives mirrored those of Congress when it enacted the National Security Act of 1947 and the amendments of 1949, including strengthening civilian control, establishing clear lines of accountability, implementing economies, and improving the machinery for strategic planning. Reorganization Plan No. 6 took effect on June 30, 1953.[9]

Eisenhower's instructions accompanying the reorganization plan defined the secretary's role as the "principal assistant" to the President in all Defense related matters, and affirmed his "full direction, authority, and control" over the Department and all component agencies. Reorganization Plan No. 6 abolished the Munitions Board and other "unwieldy" boards, vesting their functions in new assistant secretary positions. These new positions were to provide "executive" expertise to oversee and economize defense programs supporting the military arms. The reorganization strengthened the advisory role of the JCS Chairman and streamlined the joint staff for more effective strategic planning. In separate actions, the President broadened the policymaking role of the National Security Council (NSC), adding the treasury secretary and the budget director to the Council. He established the NSC Planning Board and the Operations and Coordinating Board later in the year.[10]

Writing in *Newsweek* in early May, General Spaatz (who served as an adviser to the Rockefeller Committee) described the President's plan as an initial step towards "adequate provisions for the security of the United States without spending so much on the defense establishment that the financial burden wrecks the national economy." This challenge remained "whatever the Soviet peace offensive amounts to," Spaatz asserted, referring to post-Stalinist hopes for rapprochement between the two superpowers. The retired Air Force leader maintained that the National Security Act of 1947 had "federated rather than unified the services" and that the 1949 amendments fell "far short of unification." Spaatz believed that increasing the powers of the secretary would correct many weaknesses in unification and that removing the military chiefs from "the difficult position of serving two masters" would serve "national defense needs and not...service interests."[11]

Eisenhower later wrote that this 1953 reorganization was intended to eliminate "waste and duplication in the armed forces." He said his administration was prepared to do whatever was necessary to defend America, but the nation "could not afford to waste money in any area, including the military, for anything that it did *not* need."

"I knew from personal experience," he recalled, "that there was much duplication among the three services in research and development, in procurement, and even in roles and missions-these last always at least partly self-assigned."[12]

The New Military Team and the "New Look" at National Defense

In view of Eisenhower's commitment to unification and emphasis on strategic air power, supporters and critics alike were surprised by the President's nomination of Adm. Arthur Radford to replace General Bradley as Chairman of the Joint Chiefs on May 11, 1953. Radford's recent experience as unified commander of the Pacific area had not allayed concerns about his reputation as a partisan architect of postwar Navy opposition to unification and as a "hard-hitting leader" of the 1949 admirals' revolt. Reporters lampooned the nomination, portraying Radford as "a man of controversy" about "whom there [was] usually an argument," implying that his nomination "caused tremors" in the Air Force and the Army. One newsman claimed "Men of the Air Force worried...lest the new Chairman of the JCS might attempt to whittle down their functions and forces."[13]

Many, including Radford himself, doubted that the Senate would confirm his nomination. One reporter explained that the Admiral's confirmation was in jeopardy because "some of the Senate's strongest air-power advocates" sat on the Armed Services Committee, "among them Democrat Stuart Symington of Missouri, a Radford foe since his days as Truman's Secretary of the Air Force." Observers questioned how a man who had opposed the B–36 as "a billion-dollar blunder" and who called the Air Force concept of strategic bombing "nonsensical" could serve effectively at the helm of the Administration's "New Look" military posture, which promised to be long on atomic air power and short on conventional arms. Radford had reversed his position on unification issues since 1949, but agreed that his "chances were slim" of becoming the next JCS Chairman.[14]

Eisenhower saw the situation differently. He realized that much had transpired since the 1949 admirals' revolt to temper Naval views on unification and wanted Radford to head the "New Look" military team. It was during his post-election trip to Korea that Eisenhower gleaned that Radford had changed his views on unification and the importance of strategic air power. He believed the Admiral would make a superb Chairman and had no qualms about his ability to win confirmation.[15]

Availability of funds after the start of the Korean War had allowed the Navy to pursue its force modernization objectives. It reinstated its supercarrier program after Louis Johnson resigned as Secretary of Defense in September 1950. Carl Vinson, Chairman of the House Armed Services Committee, supported the Navy, overriding Air Force objections to fund the supercarrier. Vinson said the carrier "would...serve as a highly mobile atomic base supplementing land-based Air Force planes," the role naval planners envisioned for the supercarrier. Christened the USS *Forrestal*, the ship was scheduled for commissioning by the mid-1950s.[16]

Moreover, Naval air support of sustained land combat in Korea proved that its carriers could complement Air Force land-based planes in the overall air campaign. The introduction of tactical nuclear weapons, deployed overseas as early as mid-1952, further assured the Navy of at least a collateral role in atomic strike operations. The Navy looked forward to launching its prototype nuclear submarine, the *Nautilus*, in early 1954, and began experimenting with launching intermediate range ballistic missiles from the new class of underwater vessel.

The Navy had reestablished itself as a full partner in unification by the 1953 Radford confirmation hearings and stood on the threshold of a new era when its

The Boeing XB–52 rises from the ground on its initial test flight on October 2, 1952, from Boeing Field near Seattle, Washington. *(NASM photo)*

nuclear submarines would join the strategic triad along with ground-based ballistic missiles and long-range bombers. Under General LeMay, SAC was on its way to creating a formidable nuclear strike force to provide the muscle in Eisenhower's nuclear deterrence policy.[17]

While fighting the air war in Korea, the Air Force stretched its budget dollars to meet other commitments, to modernize its nuclear strike capabilities, and to build a permanent air defense system at home. Development and production of the next-generation strategic bomber, the jet-powered B–52 Stratofortress, was assigned "the greatest importance" by Secretary Symington in 1948. When President Eisenhower took office, SAC anticipated replacing B–36s with B–52s beginning in 1955. They expected to receive the first KC–135 jet tanker in 1957. Some medium and light jet bombers and F–86s were configured for tactical nuclear operations and tactical air forces planned the transition into the nuclear-capable Century-series jet fighters when they came off the production line. The F–100 Super Sabre entered the inventory in 1954, followed by the F–105 Thunderchief four years later.[18]

The May confirmation hearings on Admiral Radford's nomination also included those of the new military chiefs, Gen. Matthew Ridgway, Army; Gen. Nathan F. Twining, Air Force; and Adm. Robert Carney, Navy. Air Force supporters on the Hill were concerned that the recent defense cuts proposed by Secretary Wilson would delay the buildup to 143 wings. While Wilson assured the Senate Armed Services Committee that the cuts would not jeopardize SAC's mission, they were

A North American YF–100 taxis to a parking ramp after a parachute drag landing. *(NASM photo)*

still on members' minds during the hearings. Senator Symington and others expressed concern that Wilson's plans to slash defense spending were made without consulting General Vandenberg or his successor, General Twining and they sought assurances from the nominees that they would "speak up" if defense cuts endangered national security.[19]

Responding to questions from Senator Styles Bridges, Radford testified that he now viewed SAC as "a primary safeguard to the United States," and that he supported the decision to "go forward with the B–52 bomber." This left only one question for Senator Symington to ask his former adversary-would the Admiral work as hard for the Army and Air Force as for the Navy as Chairman? Radford responded, "I will work primarily for the United States and I will do my best not to favor any particular service." On June 2, the Senate unanimously approved Radford's nomination and those of the military chiefs.[20]

Radford told the Senate that "developments, improvements in material, and other changes" over the past four years prompted him to modify his views. He claimed that he had not opposed unification, per se, but rather, he objected to what he believed was exclusion of the Navy as a full partner. Symington later recalled that Radford kept his promise of impartiality as Chairman, "bending over backwards to be fair to the Air Force." He said that no one could have been "more able" or "more objective" in the Chairman's role than Radford.[21]

After the confirmation hearings, Eisenhower ordered his new military team to Washington, D.C. "to make a completely new, fresh survey of our military capa-

Roles and Missions

General Nathan F. Twining became Air Force Chief of Staff during the Eisenhower administration. *(NASM photo)*

bilities, in the light of our global commitments." At a White House meeting in mid-July, the President told Radford and the military chiefs that he did not expect "a long exhaustive staff study," but wanted to tap their "great collective experience" and to elicit their "individual views, honestly and forthrightly stated."[22]

Eisenhower asked his incoming chiefs to review the recently framed national security policy in NSC 153/1 and the need for austerity in military preparation and operations. Approved by the President in June, NSC 153/1 identified "two principal threats to the survival and fundamental values and institutions of the United States," including "the formidable power and aggressive policy of the communist world led by the USSR," and the potential for "serious weakening of the economy of the United States...from the cost of opposing the Soviet threat over a sustained period."

Seeking a balance, the national security objectives of NSC 153/1 reinforced the President's link between fiscally responsible military programs and credible nuclear deterrence. The paper noted the urgency to develop and maintain "an offensive capability...to inflict massive damage on Soviet Warmaking capacity, at a level that the Soviets must regard as an unacceptable risk in war." In dealing with wars of lesser magnitude, NSC 153/1 identified strengthening other forces to counter local aggression as paramount, but stated that the United States would remain ready to take action, if necessary.[23]

Admiral Radford said Eisenhower's instructions made it clear that military readiness under the New Look "would have to be heavy in air power," and that the Army, Navy, and Marines "would have to adjust to organizations that would be fleshed out in case of emergency." The high cost of strengthening strategic and air defense forces also meant that the Air Force had to settle for less than "it felt it needed" in tactical and logistical capabilities. "In short," Radford said, "after the deterrent forces were decided upon, almost every other activity had to give to a certain extent."[24]

Radford admitted to promoting consensus on the President's tasking by secluding the military chiefs on the Secretary of the Navy's official yacht, *Sequoia*, "provisioned for an indefinite stay in the lower Potomac," until they completed a response. The Chairman said he was surprised that the group reached a unanimous agreement after only three days at sea, in view of General Ridgway's and Admiral Carney's heated opposition during the "long and difficult sessions" of the first two days. General Ridgway's subsequent public contradictions of the agreement disturbed Radford and convinced him that he was mistaken in "trying to achieve agreement on controversial matters brought before the JCS." Thereafter, the Chairman "tried to develop real differences" in the joint arena when he thought they existed.[25]

Conforming to the President's guidance, the JCS paper charted a redirection of national military strategy from "peripheral military commitments" to protection of the continental United States and "the capability for delivering swift and powerful retaliatory blows." After several revisions, the paper provided a strategic framework for national security guidance contained in NSC 162/2 and was approved by the President in late October. The revised guidance called for "a strong military posture, with emphasis on the capability of inflicting massive retaliatory damage by offensive striking power," which Eisenhower interpreted, as a concession to Admiral Carney, to "include all offensive forces, including aircraft carriers."

In January, Secretary of State John Foster Dulles introduced the phrase "massive retaliation" to describe the new military strategy during a speech in New York City. Massive retaliation encompassed the nation's atomic striking power, including the Navy's large carriers and ballistic missiles, under development. The phrase became synonymous with the atomic strike capabilities of SAC in the years ahead, with roles and missions ramifications for all branches of the armed forces.[26]

When sharing General Twining's views on NSC 162/2 with Air Force commanders, Lt. Gen. Earl Partridge, Deputy Chief of Staff for Operations, pointed out that "the basic philosophy running through this paper has long been advocated by the Air Force." The roles and missions controversy from early Air Force arguments to recognize nuclear weapons "as the new and dominant factor" in military planning had precipitated the 1949 admirals' revolt followed by stormy congressional hearings. Now, NSC 162/2 acknowledged that the Soviet Union's "ever-increasing capability...to launch a nuclear attack against the United States, coupled with its efforts to undermine U.S. influence world-wide, by subversion or force," demanded that the West pursue a more aggressive policy. Developing and maintaining a superior nuclear force "to strike an immediate decisive blow at the sources of an aggressor's strength" constituted "the most effective deterrent to war and [the] best assurance of victory should war eventuate" and, therefore, became a national mandate. In the event of commitment of U.S. forces to a limited war, the Air Force interpreted NSC 162/2 as placing no restrictions "on the use of available weapons needed to terminate the action expeditiously and successfully." Nor would limited engagements be allowed to critically compromise the "capability to achieve victory in a general war."[27]

In the spring of 1953, the Air Force published its first manual on basic doctrine, Air Force Manual (AFM) 1-2. A handbook of guiding principles, AFM 1-2 was oriented toward nuclear deterrence and general war, and suited to the strategy of massive retaliation. It was general enough, however, for the Air Force to adapt its roles and missions to any level of conflict. Acknowledging that modern war required "all three of the nation's military forces," the manual asserted that air power was "most likely to be the dominant force in war." The global nature of modern war and the lethality of modern weapons, the manual said, demanded the presence of a strong deterrent force-in-being. If deterrence failed, air forces had to be prepared for use against the "entire spectrum of a nation's strength." Air forces targeted against the enemy's heartland would destroy "the vital elements of a nation's war sustaining resources, including the enemy's long range air force." Simultaneously, air forces would engage in peripheral actions, "not necessarily limited to specific geographic areas," to reduce "the enemy's air and surface efforts" and enforce command of the air. In the foreword to AFM 1-2, General Vandenberg pointed out that Air Force doctrine needed "periodic substantive review" to comply with "the dynamic and constant changes in new weapons."[28]

In his 1954 State of the Union message, President Eisenhower asserted that the great advantage of the policy set forth in NSC 162/2 was that it gave the United States the strategic initiative to control the projection of its military and economic strength, rather than being "limited to mere reaction against crises provoked by others." Eisenhower's objective was "to hold this new initiative and use it" to build the nation's military and economic power "for our own defense and to deter aggression." We shall not be aggressors," he promised, "but we and our allies have and will maintain a massive capability to strike back."[29]

Credible deterrence hinged on the belief that the West would respond with nuclear weapons if attacked, so the incoming Joint Chiefs recommended that the administration form "a clear, positive policy" for their use. The guidelines in NSC 162/2 provided that the United States would "consider nuclear weapons to be as available for use as other munitions." The administration sought the "understanding and approval of this policy" by its allies and began building up nuclear capabilities in strategic forward areas.[30] Beginning in 1948, SAC rotated its long-range bombers to Europe and the Pacific. The services began to deploy tactical air and surface nuclear weapons to forward bases by mid-1952.[31] President Eisenhower said he took "into full account our great and growing number of nuclear weapons and the most effective means of using them against an aggressor if they are needed to preserve our freedom."[32] He later wrote that his "intention was firm to launch the Strategic Air Command immediately upon trustworthy evidence of a general attack against the West."[33]

A vital factor in Air Force nuclear planning which exacerbated roles and missions differences, was the development and availability of guided missiles. The Army Air Forces had primary responsibility for missile research during and immediately after World War II, but passage of the National Security Act of 1947 brought competition in the guided missile field. Despite attempts to gain exclusive claim to missiles by designating them "pilotless aircraft," the Air Force failed in this goal.

Secretary Louis Johnson ordered a review of the guided missile effort when he took over in March 1949, to eliminate "undesirable duplication in research and development." One result of this review was a JCS consensus paper, approved by Johnson in March 1950, assigning guided missile responsibilities on the basis of primary roles and missions. The Air Force became exclusively responsible to develop and employ long-range strategic missiles, while the Army and Navy retained interest in short-range missiles. All services developed and employed guided missiles in shared mission areas.[34]

By 1953, despite progress in technology, funding problems caused missile production to lag. Soon after becoming Chief of Staff, General Twining reemphasized the role of guided missiles and enjoined the Air Staff to "redouble...efforts toward providing at the earliest date the weapon systems to fulfill Air Force mission commitments." While the Air Force responsibility for intercontinental missiles was clear, Twining complained that the role of missiles in air defense and support of Army forces remained unresolved.[35] Competition between the Air Force and the Army intensified as the services realigned force priorities to support "New Look" and massive retaliation.

Continental air defense was another shared mission area with high priority under "New Look". Despite nuclear deterrence, military planners reasoned that the Soviet Union, "through miscalculation, or even desperation,...might still launch a surprise air attack against the United States." Consequently, strong continental air defenses were "a complementary deterrent to aggression" to protect the United States "against the shock effects of a surprise air attack."[36]

Although the Key West agreement gave the Air Force the primary role of air defense, the other services had collateral responsibilities. The Army retained its antiaircraft artillery mission, while the Navy provided sea-based air defense to protect the coastlines. Before the 1949 Soviet atomic test, the services neglected both primary and collateral air defense responsibilities because of funding constraints. Moreover, the Army and the Navy were reluctant to place air defense resources under Air Force control during the unsettled roles and missions era before the Korean War.[37]

Following the Soviet atomic test, Congress appropriated funds to build a modern air defense system to replace the "temporary lash-up" the Air Force had put together after 1947. By 1953, the Air Defense Command, reestablished in January 1951, had approximately 50 interceptor squadrons equipped with jet fighters, but many approached obsolescence. In 1949, the Air Force outlined its requirement for advanced interceptors, resulting in development of the F–102 Delta Dagger and the F–106 Delta Dart, scheduled for operation after the mid-1950s.[38]

In 1950, the Chief of Naval Operations directed fleet commanders to cooperate in air defense during emergencies, but did not agree to place Navy forces under Air Force control. The Army went a step further when its Chief of Staff, General Collins, signed an agreement with General Vandenberg to alleviate conflicts in the air defense mission. The agreement authorized an antiaircraft artillery component

Roles and Missions

An F–102 fighter takes off on a mission. *(NASM photo)*

at each echelon of the air defense system, gave air defense commanders control of antiaircraft artillery in their sectors, and formalized rules of engagement. The two services collocated their air defense headquarters in Colorado Springs, Colorado.[39]

Concerned about the Soviet nuclear threat, in early 1954 Admiral Radford obtained Eisenhower's approval to create a unified air defense command. The Air Force, perhaps fearful of losing its preeminence, had opposed earlier attempts to create a unified command, but reversed its position after Secretary Wilson and Admiral Radford assured General Twining that the organization would strengthen the Air Force air defense role. In July, the Secretary of Defense approved establishment of the Continental Air Defense Command (CONAD), to be headed by an Air Force general. The Air Force became Executive Agent for CONAD, located in Colorado Springs, with Army and Navy forces serving as joint command components. Three years later, after integration of Canadian and U.S. air defenses, the two governments established the North American Air Defense Command (NORAD), headed by an Air Force general and a Royal Canadian Air Force deputy.[40]

In forming the new commands, the Joint Chiefs overruled Army protests against what it saw as an Air Force attempt "to consolidate absolute control over the air defense mission." The Army believed its air defense contributions of antiaircraft artillery and surface-to-air missiles would be subordinated to Air Force requirements. The Army objected to plans to merge the headquarters of the Air Defense Command and CONAD, convincing the Joint Chiefs to provide adequate representation from all of the services in the new headquarters.[41]

While the Army continued to cooperate with other services, emphasis on strategic air power and air defense while scaling down air support for the Army strained relations with the Air Force. The ensuing rivalry exceeded that of previous years.

President Eisenhower announced in his 1955 State of the Union address that future budget messages would reflect the administration's "heavy emphasis" on air power.[42] The budget for the next fiscal year totaled $29.1 billion, based on a projected three-year military program. The Joint Chiefs agreed to reduce total military strength from 3.5 million at the end of the Korean War to 2.8 million by 1957. While all services would be cut, the Army faced the most drastic reductions, a drawdown of more than 500,000 troops, to a strength of only one million within three years. The Air Force dropped to 910,000 from a wartime peak of 977,500, while the Navy reduced from 795,000 to 650,000. The Marine Corps scaled back from 249,000 to 190,000.

These force levels reduced the Army from 20 divisions and the Navy from 1,130 to 1,000 active ships. The Marine Corps retained three divisions and three air wings, while the Air Force expanded from 106 to 137 wings. The National Security Council adopted the reduction program and force levels adhered to these projections through the remainder of Eisenhower's first term.[43]

Air Force expenditures from fiscal years 1955 through 1957 totaled $51.5 billion, almost double Army and Navy expenditures of $26.7 billion and $29.8 billion, respectively. Through the Korean War, Air Force annual expenditures were in balance with the Navy's, but substantially lower than the Army's. Postwar defense budgets averaged about $35 billion each fiscal year through 1957, were smaller than the wartime appropriations of $47.3, $59.9, and $48.4 billion for fiscal years 1951, 1952, and 1953, but more than twice as large as during the lean years before the Korean War. Admiral Radford noted that this was the first time the defense program accounted for more than half of the national budget. The larger share of the budget directed towards the Air Force remained a contentious issue through Eisenhower's White House years.[44]

General Ridgway and the Crack in "New Look" Solidarity

In their "New Look" report hammered out aboard the *Sequoia* in July, the incoming Joint Chiefs agreed that "the existing directive" on roles and missions was "clear" and that it provided "reasonable, workable guidance for service programs."[45] A month later, when Secretary Wilson asked the Chiefs to review a revision to the Key West agreement it became evident that they were not in full concurrence.

When submitting his reorganization plan in April, the President told Congress that he intended to revise the Key West agreement to give the Secretary of Defense authority to appoint military departments as executive agents for unified commands. Former Secretary of Defense Lovett complained that authorizing the Joint Chiefs to appoint one of their members as executive agent would skew unified command arrangements away from the Secretary's direct authority. The President wanted the chain of command drawn "unmistakably" from the White House to the Secretary of Defense to the military departments to the unified commands, correcting the "considerable confusion and misunderstanding" of the past. Eisenhower said it was imperative that the Defense Secretary authorize military chiefs to communicate and act in executive agent capacity for "the strategic direction and operational control of forces and for the conduct of combat operations" in emergency or wartime situations.[46]

Secretary Wilson incorporated the President's guidance into a revision of the Key West agreement, which was coordinated with the new JCS members in August. After obtaining JCS concurrence, Wilson issued Department of Defense

Roles and Missions

Directive 5100.1, affirming the co-equal status of the Commandant of the Marine Corps with JCS members on matters concerning the Marines.[47]

Although the Joint Chiefs concurred with the revisions, General Ridgway recommended giving the Army more authority over supporting arms. The Army Chief of Staff wanted authority "to establish requirements for aircraft and amphibious vessels" supporting ground combat, "to exercise operational control over tactical air power supporting ground troops," and "to acquire and operate such aircraft as were essential to land operations." Ridgway claimed the existing agreement "was ambiguous and inconsistent and that it failed to integrate the Services into a balanced military team." Although his proposal died,[48] Ridgway's dissent revealed an early crack in solidarity toward the emerging strategy of massive retaliation. Before the year was over, Ridgway showed open signs of breaking with "New Look" policy, with its emphasis on atomic air power and the reduction of the standing Army.

General Ridgway began complaining publicly about the President's military policies and what he perceived as a weakening of U.S. ground forces as early as October. In his initial public remarks, Ridgway charged that "New Look" would substitute "new and untried weapons for its foot soldiers." Ridgway was described as a "thoroughly unhappy man" as his tour unfolded and Radford called Ridgway's criticisms disturbing.[49]

General Ridgway claimed he was aware of trends in the Pentagon which "would work long-range injury to the Army and the nation, the full effects of which would not become manifest until too late to correct them" when he returned to Washington, D.C. to take the top Army post. He also knew that the Chief's job was "an extremely difficult one," and that much time would be spent on "the unhappy task of defending the United States Army from actions by my superiors which, to my mind, would weaken it physically and spiritually."[50]

Opposing massive cuts in Army strength, Ridgway argued passionately for larger, streamlined ground forces with greater organic air support capabilities. He envisioned "a totally different Army than any we have known to date-an Army trained, equipped and organized to fight and win in an atomic war." Losing the argument and having to place Army forces in strategic reserve at home, Ridgway said his greatest tasks included deploying the "waning strength in such a way that ground combat units would be as effective as possible in the event of war," while laying the foundation for the new Army on the atomic battleground.

The Army Chief claimed to have "no quarrel whatsoever" with the administration's "concept of a hard-hitting highly mobile force, based in the United States, and ready to put out big fires as well as little ones wherever the Communists might set them," but believed the Army was best equipped service to carry out that mission, but it was being emasculated.[51] Some senior airmen, including Gen. Otto P. Weyland, argued that massive retaliation increased the possibility of small wars with tactical air forces as unprepared as the Army to fight them. Such views were in the minority.[52]

Following General Ridgway's lead, the Army felt wronged by what it saw as an Air Force failure to meet the needs of ground soldiers. The Army Chief said he did not oppose the administration's "emphasis on the air arm," but resented what he "sincerely believed to be an *over*emphasis on one form of air power, the long-range bomber." He charged that the Air Force showed little interest in developing the "low and slow" combat platforms needed by the Army and he felt the Army would have to fill this void on its own to survive on the modern battlefield. Under Ridgway's direction, the Army developed a long-range aviation plan to explore development of fixed-wing aircraft and helicopters, including gunship platforms, to meet Army requirements.[53]

Troubled by the Army's estrangement, President Eisenhower did not reappoint General Ridgway when his two-year term expired. Admiral Radford said he felt the President "had no other choice" and that "General Ridgway himself preferred to retire."[54] General Ridgway claimed the decision to step down was his own, a decision he had made before accepting the post as Army Chief of Staff, allowing that his resignation "may have been accepted by my superiors with a sense of relief."[55] General Maxwell Taylor, no less opposed to massive retaliation than his predecessor, became the new Army Chief in June 1955.

General Taylor recalled being greeted to his new job with a friendly warning from Admiral Carney-"You're one of the good new Chiefs now but you'll be surprised how quickly you will become one of the bad old Chiefs." Like Ridgway, Carney was not reappointed when his two years were up because of friction with Navy Secretary Charles S. Thomas. Admiral Arleigh Burke replaced Carney, serving an unprecedented three terms as Chief of Naval Operations."[56]

As a postscript to his falling-out with the Eisenhower administration, General Ridgway became even more vocal in retirement. In late 1955, in the first of a series of articles in the *Saturday Evening Post*, Ridgway accused Eisenhower of misleading the American people by claiming unanimous agreement on military policy from the Joint Chiefs. Ridgway charged that the "New Look" was politically rather than militarily motivated and that the President "had sacrificed the national defense in the interest of balancing the budget." He suggested a revolt of the generals similar to that of the admirals a decade earlier might be in order.[57]

Writing in *Newsweek* in early 1956, General Spaatz countered General Ridgway's criticisms, arguing that Eisenhower's military policy was the surest way to build "national defense without national bankruptcy" in the atomic age. "Even if we were willing to spend the United States into bankruptcy to maintain a vast standing army in Europe-and elsewhere," Spaatz wrote, it was impossible for the United States to match the Communists man for man around the globe. Spaatz reasoned that "the free world must rely primarily on its economic staying power, shielded by superior air power," rather than on massive ground troops. As more than half of the federal budget was directed towards defense, Spaatz thought it imperative for the government to "get the maximum value in military power for the defense dollars appropriated."[58]

Roles and Missions

Like Eisenhower, Spaatz viewed the Army's dispute as another roles and missions polemic arising from the lack of true unification of the armed forces. He argued that service rivalries and "the partial and halfhearted unification we now have" made it impossible to obtain real economy. In explaining why the present system prevented prudent spending of the $35 billion defense budget, Spaatz wrote:

> Four services-the Army, the Navy, the Marine Corps, and the Air Force-will compete for the $35 billion with overlapping and redundant services. Each, for example, will build its own air force and three of the services will carry on experiments in rocket development. The Navy, competing with the Air Force for strategic striking power, will build its sixth supercostly supercarrier and the atomic plant for a seventh, even though the utility of the first is still in question.[59]

Spaatz's defense of national security policy did not assuage Army grievances left unsettled with Ridgway's departure. More reserved about airing his differences with the administration, General Taylor planted the seeds for a new strategy of flexible response during his four years as Army Chief of Staff and nourished Ridgway's programs and objectives for stronger Army aviation. One principle Taylor prescribed for the Army was to be a loyal member of the defense team, "quick to defend its own legitimate interests but scrupulous in not trespassing on those of the other services."[60] Recalling Admiral Carney's friendly warning, Taylor claimed that by the end of 1955 he was "a bad chief" and remained one until his retirement.[61]

The Symington Subcommittee: Resurveying the Dimensions

When he became Army Chief of Staff, General Taylor was encouraged by recognition of the threat of limited war in NSC memorandumn 5501, issued in January 1955. Relying on "nuclear-air retaliatory power" and continental defense, NSC 5501 acknowledged that the Soviet Union might increase local aggression without fear of retaliation from the United States. While not abandoning programs to "build and strengthen" defensive forces, the Eisenhower administration conceded that some contingencies might require ready, mobile forces to protect vital interests abroad. With each service tasked to prepare mobile strike forces within their force ceilings, the Air Force developed a composite air strike force concept. In July, the Air Force established the 19th Air Force to coordinate field training with Army forces and to serve as a mobile task force headquarters. Plans called for trained forces from TAC units to deploy to trouble spots around the globe under control of the 19th Air Force. The administration still "contemplated reductions in the overall size of the armed forces," and specified that mobile forces be equipped with atomic capability "to perform both contingency tasking and to assist in discharging initial tasks in the event of general war."[62]

Admiral Radford wondered whether nuclear arms were so integrated into military planning that distinct lines of use no longer existed. NSC 5501 did little to clarify the distinctions, but it did address the conditional use of nuclear weapons in limited war situations, taking note of military and political pressures which might influence their use. When revised security guidance in the form of NCS 5602/1 appeared in early 1956, the President and some Cabinet members began to question whether the United States could plan to use nuclear weapons in limited hostilities without forfeiting allied support. Other nations shrank from the prospect of a nuclear war fought on their soil. Still, the administration concluded that the United States could not afford to maintain "different kinds of forces for different kinds of wars" if it hoped to stay in the nuclear arms race with the Soviet Union. The administration's intention to use nuclear arms in both general war and lesser hostilities remained in the final version of NSC 5602/1, with a protocol to consult allied forces before proceeding with the use of nuclear weapons, time and circumstances permitting.[63]

Driven by budgetary constraints as much as by threat assessments, national security policy and JCS planning focused on nuclear options through President Eisenhower's fourth year in office. To the President's consternation, interservice rivalry continued unabated, while the buying power of the defense dollar declined under the burden of rising inflation. Air Force appropriations, totalling $25.7 billion for fiscal years 1955 and 1956, were larger than the Army's $14.9 billion and the Navy's $18.8 billion, but Air Force leaders were apprehensive about the pace of force modernization when measured against the Soviet Union.

Although the Air Force's share of the President's fiscal year 1957 budget request rose to $15.7 billion, General Twining and some Congressmen complained that funding for strategic capabilities was inadequate. The Army budget request was $7.3 billion, with $9.1 billion requested for the Navy. The President asked for an additional $547.1 million, including $248.5 million to speed production of B–52 bombers. At the same time, Air Force supporters pursued a probe into how U.S. air power measured against the Soviet nuclear threat.[64]

In early 1956, while the House of Representatives debated the President's budget request, the Senate Armed Services Committee formed a special subcommittee under Senator Stuart Symington to investigate the "present and planned strength of the United States Air Force." Symington had been a persistent critic of Eisenhower's cost-cutting measures affecting guided missiles and air power. Congressional Democrats aligned with Symington in an otherwise ho-hum election year. The President, expected to announce his intention to run again soon, remained popular despite attacks on his foreign and domestic programs. But Secretary of Defense Wilson was not so popular and his office became an easy target for administration critics. Democrats on Symington's air power subcommittee suggested that the President's supplemental budget request "was a strategic move

W. Stuart Symington served as Chairman of the powerful Senate Armed Services Committee during a critical period of Air Force development. *(NASM photo)*

to counter the Symington subcommittee's investigation" and to "keep the administration in the lead on defense." Senator Leverett Saltonstall, ranking Republican on the subcommittee, defended the administration, while Senator Henry Jackson, second ranking Democrat, said the supplemental request amounted to "confessing that they're wrong."[65]

Beginning on April 16 and continuing into the hot summer months, the Symington subcommittee held hearings on air power. Hoping to shield the proceedings from charges of political partisanship, Symington sought to mute public criticism during the investigation. In his opening statement, the Chairman said the subcommittee would examine various Air Force programs, but would focus primarily on the adequacy of "present and planned strengths...to preserve the peace through the deterrence of aggression." While comparison to the 1949 B–36 hearings was inevitable, news reports in April of another "Battle of the Potomac shaping up" proved hasty and premature. Symington's pledge to conduct the investigation "objectively and impartially" was successful and the lengthy hearings proceeded without rancor or recrimination.[66]

Despite their muted tone, the Senate hearings exposed divergent views, adding occasional spice to the morning news. General Curtis LeMay made headlines when he testified that without "increased and vigorous attention" to reversing current trends, strategic air superiority would shift to the Soviet Union within four years. Lemay advocated accelerated B–52 bomber and KC–135 tanker production to assure the United States of superior strategic forces into the 1960s.

During the hearings and after a visit to a Soviet air show, General Twining corroborated LeMay's claim that the Red Air Force was closing the gap in atomic strike capabilities.[67] Other Air Force generals and Trevor Gardner, former Assistant Secretary of the Air Force, testified that the United States also lagged in research and development. Gardner, who had resigned because of differences with the administration, cited inadequate funding and interservice rivalry as reasons for the lag in ballistic missile technology.[68]

The Eisenhower Administration's response, described by the media as "an apparently carefully-coordinated attack" against critics of its air power program, caused a brief roles and missions stir when the President and the Defense Secretary identified Navy carriers as a vital part of the nation's strategic air strength. They claimed that General LeMay and other critics failed to consider SAC's B–47 medium bombers, missiles, and other forces, including Navy carriers. Lashing out at "fear-mongers" who warned that the Soviet Union was "overtaking U.S. leadership in technology and strategic bombing capability," Secretary Wilson asserted that Navy carriers complemented SAC's bomber forces, serving as "mobile bases for immediate retaliation against enemy attack." Furthermore, Eisenhower and Wilson declared they had no intention of leading the nation into "an all-out armaments race with the USSR," or "trying to match Russian strength in long-range bombers."[69]

When queried by reporters, Air Force spokesmen denied that Navy carriers were a factor in planning for retaliatory strikes because "the fleet would be engaged entirely in its own defense against Russian air and undersea raiders during the initial stages" of general war.[70] Testifying before the Symington subcommittee, General Twining said carrier forces had an important job, but their contribution to strategic striking power was "small." If carriers were employed against Soviet strategic targets, the Air Force Chief believed they should be under Air Force control. Twining did not believe aircraft carriers could survive in forward waters in the initial stages of a Soviet air attack. Secretary of the Navy Charles S. Thomas assured the subcommittee that the 6th and 7th Fleets, deployed in strategic areas, were "strong deterrents in cold war," but were "not trying to preempt the Air Force's mission." Vice Admiral Thomas S. Combs, Deputy Chief of Naval Operations (Air), agreed that the fleet was concerned "with targets of naval interest," but could strike strategic targets on a "very much smaller scale" than could SAC if instructed to do so by the Joint Chiefs of Staff.[71]

During three days of relentless questioning, Secretary Wilson traded barbs with Senate Democrats without satisfying their doubts about the nation's air strength. The Defense Secretary's running commentary on the hearings and his own sometimes hostile testimony antagonized majority members of the subcommittee. Earlier, when a reporter wrote that Wilson had labelled Congressional efforts to increase Air Force appropriations as "phony", a heated debate broke out on the Senate floor with some Senators calling for the Secretary's resignation.

Wilson's charge that the Senate debate was politically motivated brought a heated exchange with Democratic Senator Henry Jackson. During the exchange, Wilson told a story about a "mama whale" saying to her calf that "it is only when you are blowing that you are liable to be harpooned." Senator Jackson retorted, "Mr. Secretary, I think the public knows who has been doing a lot of blowing." In a lighter moment, Senator Jackson admitted there was a propensity in Washington, D.C. to make statements that should be forgotten. "Apparently I am not properly housebroken down here," Wilson conceded, amid laughter.[72]

Roles and Missions

Senator Symington was not amused. He challenged the Defense Secretary's testimony and scolded him for selectively citing General Twining when it suited his purpose, while disavowing him when he did not support his arguments. Symington complained that Wilson's testimony was inconsistent with other leading military witnesses and that he failed to respond to "the expressed intent of the Congress" to modernize the nation's strategic air strength more rapidly.[73]

The subcommittee completed its inquiry during the summer, but postponed its final report until after the election because Symington did not want the subcommittee's deliberations to become embroiled in partisan politics. When the report came out in February 1957, however, it split on purely partisan lines. An editorial described the report as painting "a thoroughly bleak picture" of the Air Force by the Democratic majority while the Republican minority "voiced undiluted optimism on the same subject."[74]

The report dismissed the administration's claim that the Air Force's declining "strategic striking power" could be overcome by using offensive naval aviation. The report charged that the administration had ignored or underestimated "Soviet military progress," and placed financial considerations "ahead of defense requirements to the serious damage of our airpower strength relative to that of Russia, and hence to our national security." It concluded that the United States was increasingly vulnerable because of the lack of an adequate warning system and that "the direction of planning of naval strength" left vital targets vulnerable to submarine missile strikes.[75]

Democratic subcommittee members accused civilian Defense leaders of permitting "duplication, even triplication, among the three services in the development and production of missiles," charging them with intensifying interservice rivalry and giving the Soviet Union a technological edge. While such conclusions dealt primarily with strategic capabilities, the majority members also blamed the administration's "vacillating policies" on limited and unlimited war for "confusion and therefore inefficiency in defense planning." "It is essential that we be prepared for both," they said. In this regard, the subcommittee reported that the Air Force's airlift capacity was insufficient "to maintain the mobility of the Army and enable it to meet overseas commitments." In summary, the report claimed that Defense officials had failed to use the full capacity of the United States to obtain military supremacy over the Soviet Union, which they believed was possible "without jeopardizing a sound economy and without imposing additional tax burdens."[76]

In a minority rebuttal, Senator Saltonstall argued that such an "unduly pessimistic" view of the defense posture ignored testimony that the combined might of U.S. air, naval, and ground forces was superior to Soviet power. Further, he charged that the report failed to consider the total air strength of the Free World, which was greater than that of the combined Communist bloc. Saying that the United States did not want to "engage in a numbers race with Russia," Saltenstall stated, "What we do want are balanced land, sea and air forces which give a visible deterrent and such power to retaliate quickly and devastatingly that no enemy dare attack."[77]

Critics attacked the report for its lack of objectivity and failure to recommend a specific course of action to resolve the nation's air power problems. The report recommended "that the deficiencies in military strength as pointed out in the conclusions be corrected as promptly as possible." An informed observer described the report as "an anti-climax to the 1,863 page record" of published testimony accompanying it. Air Force Secretary Donald R. Quarles said the published testimony was "probably the most comprehensive compilation of expert opinion on U.S. airpower that has ever been assembled for distribution to the American public."[78]

Perhaps the Senate inquiry's greatest service was that it sharpened the focus on strategic air power at a critical point in Cold War history, as the nuclear arms balance threatened to shift in favor of the Soviet Union. At the same time, however, the hearings amplified divergent views within the Department of Defense about SAC's dominant role in national security and its large share of defense appropriations. Congressional lobbying to increase appropriations to speed production of B–52 bombers and strategic missiles added to the frustrations of defense leaders who sought a balanced force posture. In this regard, the air power hearings underscored the prediction that strategic weapons would monopolize defense spending through the next decade. Any remaining doubts that the "New Look" for defense would last at least four more years disappeared with Eisenhower's landslide victory in November.

The New "New Look": Declaring War on Interservice Rivalry

The endless roles and missions controversy was a disappointment to Eisenhower. He had been a champion for unification after World War II and as Commander in Chief hoped that closer cooperation among the services would become a hallmark of his administration. The intense rivalry over missiles and tactical aviation during his first term was particularly annoying. By his second Presidential campaign, Eisenhower's patience was thin from the public airing of divergent views over development and operation of short-range missiles. The President insisted that Secretary Wilson end the dissent among the services, and began his second term with the admonition that the country wanted interservice rivalry to stop.[79]

One of many issues in the smoldering missile controversy was determining what the future Army role would be in atomic warfare. From the Army's perspective, restricting development and use of land-based missiles to the traditional battlefield meant yielding control of new generations of nuclear weapons to the Air Force and the Navy. Engaged in missile research and development since the end of World War II, the Army maintained that it shared roles and missions responsibilities for antiaircraft missiles and intermediate range ballistic missiles. It viewed these as extensions of organic anti-aircraft artillery and tactical guided missiles. The Air Force, on the other hand, contended that land-based intermediate range ballistic missiles and antiaircraft missiles were integral elements of its primary air power and defense functions.

Roles and Missions

The controversy erupted into a bitter interservice row during the congressional hearings of 1956 on the fiscal year 1957 budget fueled by the Air Force's intention to develop an advanced land-based version of the Navy's Talos missile to defend SAC bases. The Army felt that the Air Force did not need its own air defense missile since the Army's advanced Nike was comparable to the Talos and would be adequate to defend SAC strike forces. The public rehashing of the missile arguments during the Symington subcommittee hearing may have induced the leak of partisan Army and Air Force staff studies to the press in May. Allegedly planted by two disgruntled Army colonels, the studies assailed Army neglect in defense planning, devalued the role of aircraft carriers in modern warfare, and called the Nike missile a multi-billion dollar boondoggle.[80]

Puzzled by public release of the indictment of the Nike, Air Force supporters assumed that the Army wanted "to show just how far the inter-service fight had gone." Publication of the leaked documents angered Secretary Wilson, prompting him to call a press conference to "discount the extent of inter-service rivalry" implied by press accounts. Secretary Wilson pointed out that "successful development of a new missile by a specific service [would] not necessarily insure that the particular service [would] operate it in the field." He said a service's mission, the availability of basing, and logistics capacity would be determining factors. Wilson's relations with Congress soured further when he refused to honor Senate demands for tests of the Talos and Nike programs. Wilson said that he "did not see how such tests would serve any useful purpose."[81]

Newsmen covering the Pentagon squabble predicted that the Talos-Nike controversy would pale "in bitterness and significance" to upcoming interservice disputes over jurisdictional responsibilities for intermediate range ballistic missiles. The Secretary of Defense assigned first priority to the Air Force Thor program, but authorized a joint Army-Navy group to develop the Jupiter missile as a back-up. The Army's Redstone Arsenal had primary responsibility for the Jupiter. Wilson had not decided which service should operate intermediate range ballistic missiles in the field when he called his press conference.[82]

Buoyed by the Symington hearings and confident in their dominant role as a deterrent to war, Air Force leaders refrained from public recriminations against the other services. General Twining advised commanders that his pubic relations policy was "to help build confidence not merely in the Air Force but in the entire national security program." Urging commanders to evince pride in the achievements of the Air Force, Twining cautioned, "Negative material will only bring negative results."[83]

General Thomas D. White, Air Force Vice Chief of Staff, told a civilian audience the country needed "more complete unification" and a military structure "that will help us all to be free of conflicting service loyalties and confusing influences." He warned, "with the passing of time, the roles and missions of all the services seem to overlap more and more," and explained that the services needed to support "any actions which will reduce the chances for wasteful duplication and controversy." Otherwise, White reasoned, a day might come "when, for all practical purposes, all three services would have the same weapons, the same capabilities and limitations, and all attempting to do the same job." White made a veiled reference to the missile controversy when he mentioned Daedalus-the mythical inventor who "murdered his nephew," named Talos.[84]

Agitation over the missile controversy overshadowed Army dissatisfaction with air support for ground forces. Divergent views over tactical air support doctrine and weaponry reemerged as a divisive roles and missions issue during the congressional hearings and debates on the fiscal year 1957 budget. Army leaders charged that equipping, training, and deploying tactical fighters for atomic war caused TAC to ignore its responsibility to support ground forces. General Weyland and other generals agreed with the Army complaints, but were overruled by the mobility requirements of deterrence. During a June 1956 briefing, Gen. E. J. Timberlake, Commander of the Ninth Air Force, focused on the overseas build-up of atomic-capable theater air forces. Timberlake said these highly mobile strike elements made deterrent forces readily available to the allies, providing decisive strike capabilities to control the air and support surface forces. He explained:

> The TAC role stresses the utilization of atomic weapons, modern equipment and limited numbers of highly skilled American technicians to help defend our allies overseas, rather than depending upon American infantry manpower.[85]

As the Air Force equipped for atomic operations, the Army expanded its conventional air capabilities. After becoming Army Chief of Staff in 1955, General Taylor reorganized Army aviation and appointed Maj. Gen. Hamilton H. Howze as the first director of Army aviation. As Senate air power hearings began, the Army was granted authority to train fixed-wing and helicopter pilots independent of the Air Force. Army leaders submitted a five-year plan to develop aviation to the Joint Chiefs. In early 1957, General Taylor approved the Army plan, which called for an expansion from 3,516 to 8,486 Army aircraft by 1959.[86]

Meanwhile, the Army sought "unconditional command" of its organic aircraft in combat and lobbied to remove the weight and range limitations imposed in 1952. General Howze argued that the Army needed short takeoff observation planes and larger fixed-wing transports to increase mobility in rear areas and the combat zone. The Army did not see these requirements as encroaching on Air Force responsibilities, because the Air Force had no plans to develop and operate such planes. Therefore, Howze saw Air Force objections to Army expansion of organic aviation as "a misunderstanding" of the ground forces' combat environment.[87]

General Twining opposed the Army's aviation plan because he believed it would breed duplication and waste. He also opposed lifting the weight restriction because he feared this might encourage the Army to build up its tactical air forces. Taylor and Howze presented sound arguments for larger Army reconnaissance and transport planes, but Twining pointed out that planes like the T–37 jet reconnaissance aircraft could be reconfigured for weapons delivery. There was wide speculation that the Army intended to develop its own tactical air capabilities, infringing on roles and missions assigned to the Air Force.[88]

With the White House pressuring to end interservice rivalry, Secretary Wilson and Admiral Radford sought to reconcile opposing views. On Radford's recommendation, Secretary Wilson issued guidance on Army aviation and missile responsibilities in November 1956. In a memorandum to the Armed Forces Council, Wilson stated that the basic roles and missions agreed to in 1948 remained valid, but "the development of new weapons and of new strategic concepts, together with the nine years of operating experience" revealed a need for clearer delineation of responsibilities. Wilson repeated his earlier position that simply because one service developed a weapon did not guarantee that they would operate that weapon. Similarly, peacetime guidance on roles and missions did not predetermine which weapons and forces a field commander could use in war. Such decisions, Wilson said, would be made by the Secretary of Defense in consultation with the Joint Chiefs.[89]

Wilson's memorandum reaffirmed the functions of Army aviation as defined in the Pace-Finletter agreement and established the forward boundary of the Army's combat zone to 100 miles beyond the front line for air operations. The Secretary of Defense decided against modifying the 5,000-pound weight restriction on Army fixed-wing aircraft, but agreed to consider exemptions. Approvals for Army observation aircraft and transports which exceeded the weight limit came almost immediately. Wilson established a 20,000-pound weight limit for Army helicopters, twice Admiral Radford's recommendation, and adopted the Chairman's recommendation that the Army not maintain a separate research and development facility.[90]

In assigning missile responsibilities, Secretary Wilson ruled against the Army on the intermediate range ballistic missile issue. His November memorandum gave the Air Force responsibility for land-based intermediate range missiles, while the Navy retained custody of sea-based missiles. The memorandum confined Army use of surface-to-surface missiles to the 100-mile range limit imposed forward of the front lines. This placed a maximum range of approximately 200 miles on Army missile batteries since they normally fired from a 100-mile radius behind friendly lines. Army planners believed that the 200-mile limit was far too restrictive, contending that battle zones in future wars would "be several hundred to a 1,000 miles deep." Wilson's memorandum allowed the Army to continue limited feasibility studies on intermediate range ballistic missiles, but insisted that the missiles be turned over to the Air Force. Jupitor and Thor missiles were assigned to SAC when they became operational in 1958.[91]

In distinguishing Army and Air Force responsibilities for surface-to-air missiles, Wilson's memorandum assigned point defense to the Army. This meant that the Air Force lost its bid to use the land-based version of the Talos missile. Wilson made the Air Force responsible for area air defense, "a job that would be carried out primarily by its long-range interceptor missile, the Bomarc." The Secretary's guidance on roles and missions mandated that the services develop "balanced and interrelated" forces, rather than pursuing "completely independent" programs.[92]

Despite Army complaints about the adequacy of Air Force support for airlift of ground units and supplies, Wilson concluded that the Air Force provided "adequate airborne airlift in the light of currently approved strategic concepts." The Defense Secretary was concerned about "the proliferation of special-purpose airlift." In an effort to increase "economy and efficiency", he issued a new directive on December 6, designating the Secretary of the Air Force as the single manager of Defense Department airlift. Although the Air Force and Navy transferred some special-purpose transports to the Military Air Transport Service, the directive was never fully implemented. More than 900 transports from both services remained outside Military Air Transport Service control.[93]

The Army position on Wilson's clarification of roles and missions was to "try to live with the new rules." Privately, however, General Taylor and his staff were frustrated by the Secretary's pronouncements, concerned that the Army was now isolated from the decisionmaking process, fearing that the Army had been drawn "into a costly and losing competition with the Air Force" in the ballistic missile field. He claimed that the same "misguided response" had caused him "to conjure up the Madison Avenue adjective, 'pentomic,' to describe the new Army division...with atomic-capable weapons in its standard equipment." The Army believed that gaining part of the nuclear retaliatory role was essential to its survival. "While it was true that at the time the Army had only the cumbersome Honest John rocket and the heavy eight-inch howitzer capable of firing nuclear munitions," Taylor wrote, "nuclear weapons were the going thing and, by including some in the division armament, the Army staked out its claim to a share in the nuclear arsenal."[94]

The transition into Eisenhower's second term was rife with rumors that Wilson was "on his way out as Secretary of Defense," raising hopes that a successor might take "a new look" at the Wilson memorandum. Wilson had served an unrivaled four-year tour as Defense chief and Eisenhower was unhappy with his failure to halt the ongoing strife in the Pentagon. While many thought change at the top was imminent, Wilson surprised his critics by staying on for several months. He was finally replaced by Neil H. McElroy in October 1957.

The change in leadership had little effect on Army roles and missions and General Taylor found he was in "well-nigh continuous conflict" with the new Secretary of Defense. Taylor described his years as Army Chief of Staff as "wearing times," recalling that he had not "particularly minded the conflicts" with his "Pentagon peers," but keenly regretted the "increasing coolness" of his relations with the President.[95]

Before leaving office, Secretary Wilson toughened his stand on the division of aviation responsibilities between the Air Force and the Army. On March 18, 1957, he rescinded the 1952 Pace-Finletter Agreement, issuing new definitions for the scope of the Army aviation program and Air Force responsibilities to support the Army. The Wilson directive confirmed the principles embodied in his earlier memorandum, applying the same weight limitations for Army aircraft and fixing the same boundaries for their range of operations. Wilson stressed that he wanted to insure that the Army could employ aircraft for its combat operations without duplicating Air Force functions. At the same time, ground commanders expected the Air Force to "devote an appreciable portion of its resources" to close combat and logistical support for the Army.[96]

The Wilson directive listed the specific functions that Army aviation was authorized to perform as well as Air Force functions the Army was not to duplicate. The Army could employ aircraft for command, liaison, and communications; aerial observation, reconnaissance, fire adjustment, topographical survey; airlift of troops and material within the Army combat zone; and aeromedical evacuation within the combat zone. Army aviation could not perform strategic and tactical airlift outside the combat zone; tactical reconnaissance; battlefield interdiction; and close combat air support, all of which were functions assigned to the Air Force. The Air Force was not to increase or decrease its forces based on the limited organic aviation available to the Army.[97]

The stipulation in Wilson's directive for no unnecessary duplication or overlapping roles and missions was a sine qua non, but Army planners did not appear bound by it and Force officials were ambivalent about its enforcement. Within the Army, research and development in tactical air surveillance and transportation continued unabated through the 1950s. The Air Force, meanwhile, appeared willing for the Army to assume greater combat air support capabilities while SAC and TAC concentrated on upgrading atomic capabilities. General LeMay proposed merging Air Force strategic and tactical forces into a single offensive force, leaving support of the battlefield to the Army. This proposal died after encountering strong resistance from TAC's General Weyland.[98]

Army interest in developing tactical nuclear missiles clouded perceptions of what was wanted from the Air Force in supporting ground combat. General Taylor implied in statements to Congress that Army-controlled tactical missiles might make Air Force close air support and interdiction unnecessary. General LeMay interpreted this to mean that the Army no longer wanted firepower support from tactical air forces and would provide its own support with short range weaponry. Other signs that the Army intended to dispense with Air Force close support included an incident reported by Brig. Gen. Henry Viccellio, Ninth Air Force Commander. Viccellio complained after a joint exercise that ground commanders had not called for close air support, an indication that they would rely on their own weapons in real combat. Viccellio encouraged ground commanders to exercise close support procedures to insure the art did not become lost.[99]

General Weyland doubted that the Army really intended to supplant the tactical air forces. Other Air Force generals, however, were concerned that the Army wanted to take back the tactical air forces it had released in 1947. When the Army tested divisional combat reconnaissance companies equipped with armed helicopters in 1958, the Air Force interpreted this as the first step towards Army assumption of battlefield interdiction and close air support. The Army had experimented with armed helicopters since the end of the Korean conflict and sanctioned aerial combat reconnaissance units in March 1958.[100]

The Army's Chief of Research and Development, Lt. Gen. James M. Gavin retired in 1958 because he opposed Eisenhower's defense policies. Before his retirement, Gavin had complained that Wilson's directive closed the door to exploring the vast area between the Army's light air vehicles and larger Air Force vehicles. A later Army study, however, documented a different trend:

> Despite the limitations imposed by the Department of Defense, the Army intended to take full advantage of the air for travel, observation, and communication to ensure the success of the land battle. The Army asked private industry for assistance in developing some major technological improvements in aircraft design to tailor aircraft to the jobs they must perform instead of tailoring battle missions to the capabilities of the existing aircraft.[101]

The Reorganization of 1958: "A Pentagon for the Missile Age"

Earlier attempts to reorganize the Defense Department had failed to resolve interservice rivalry and disunity problems. By the start of his second term, President Eisenhower believed that only a more extensive shakeup could attack the root causes of service parochialism and provide a framework for a unified force structure. Various study groups, including the Symington subcommittee, identified unbridled competition and duplication as major obstacles. Still, recommendations to reorganize the Pentagon came from all sides. General Twining became Chairman of the Joint Chiefs in August 1957. He joined with General White, his successor as Air Force Chief of Staff, to promote the concept of a single service as the solution to the unification dilemma. Both generals realized that the concept was too radical for the times so instead, they endorsed the earlier proposal for a single chief of staff, supported by a multiservice general staff. The Army traditionally favored stronger unification, but cooled toward revisions that might diminish its role in national defense. The Navy remained opposed to the single chief of staff concept.[102]

Disclosures of rapid advancements in Soviet space and missile programs in 1957 added urgency to the President's plans to streamline Pentagon bureaucracy. In August, the Soviet nuclear threat became more ominous when the Kremlin announced that Russian scientists had successfully flight-tested an intercontinental ballistic missile. More alarming news came in the fall with the Soviet launch of Sputniks I and II, the world's first artificial satellites.

Roles and Missions

General Thomas D. White, Air Force Vice Chief of Staff, urged stronger definition of the unique roles and missions of each military service. *(NASM photo)*

Congressional committees blamed rampant interservice rivalry. The Symington air power report blasted Defense Department research and development activities for their competitiveness, which promoted waste and retarded modernization. Air Force leaders past and present argued to reorganize the Defense Department to strengthen unification of the military services. Days before the Soviet announcement of its missile capability, General Spaatz wrote in *Newsweek* that the country needed "a Pentagon for the Missile Age" to overcome the Soviet lead.[103]

Spaatz believed that the "new Pentagon" should be organized "not only for economy" but "to facilitate the introduction of new weapons and the discard of old ones." He noted the importance of air power to the modern fighting force, and the harmful competition that modern weapons engendered. Spaatz wrote:

> Today the Air Force gets about 60 percent of the defense dollar. In addition, the Navy and Marine Corps spend about half of their appropriations on their own air arms and the Army devotes 15 to 20 percent of its share to the same purpose. And all three military departments are constantly getting deeper and deeper into the business of missile research, development, and production.[104]

Spaatz backed the official Air Force position on reorganization, although he wanted the defense structure to evolve into a single service. He proposed the "complete integration of the services," but later modified his ideas.

General Eaker also thought that "all three services may one day be in the same uniform with one promotion list."[105] While the President never seriously entertained the idea of merging the armed forces because he knew it was politically infeasible, he believed strongly in unification and suggested that the armed forces send prospective officers to a single academy. A fellow officer quoted Eisenhower as saying that nothing contributed so much to service parochialism as the rivalry engendered in cadets at the military academies.[106]

Accepting that the country was not ready for full merging of the services, at the end of 1957 Spaatz suggested that Congress consider a new reorganization act providing a single military chief of staff to advise the Secretary of Defense. Calling "the middle way the wise way," Spaatz modified his position the following April, conforming to President Eisenhower's more moderate reorganization plan. After the President called for revamping defense in his State of the Union message on January 9, Secretary of Defense McElroy appointed a group to draft legislation. General Twining was alone in calling for the replacement of the existing Joint Chiefs organization with a single military chief and general staff.

The group completed its work quickly, allowing the President to submit a plan to reorganize the Defense Department to Congress on April 3. The President asked Congress to organize "deployed troops into truly unified commands" and do away with "separate ground, sea, and air warfare...forever." While the President's proposal did not provide for a single chief—a man on horseback—Spaatz felt the plan might give the Secretary of Defense enough authority "to weld the individual services into a force sufficiently unified to prepare for a modern war emergency without impoverishing the nation in the process."[107]

As enacted on August 8, the Defense Reorganization Act of 1958 gave the Secretary of Defense greater "direction, authority, and control" over the Defense Department and the military services. By giving the Secretary of Defense more authority for research and development and creating an oversight directorate, the new law institutionalized the power and the structure in the Defense Department to "coordinate weapons planning and development" and to "minimize service rivalries and duplication of effort and expenditure." It gave the Secretary more responsibility to formulate strategy with the aid of the Joint Chiefs.

Removing service secretaries from the chain of command provided a more direct channel from the President through the Secretary of Defense to the Joint Chiefs to the unified and specified commands. While giving more statutory power than granted in the National Security Act of 1947, the new law did not allow the merging of military departments or services, changing statutory functions without congressional review, or establishing a single chief of staff and general staff.[108]

The 1958 law provided the unified and specified commands control over combatant forces, while responsibility for preparing, providing, and supporting forces remained with the military departments. These and other key provisions were codified in a new directive issued by Secretary McElroy on December 31. The new directive lumped the statutory powers of the Defense Secretary into a general statement, giving him "direction, authority, and control" over "all functions in the Department of Defense and its component agencies." It defined the chains of command and addressed the responsibilities of the services, which remained essentially unchanged from previous directives. The primary functions of the military departments included organizing, training, and equipping Army, Navy, Air Force,

Roles and Missions

and Marine Corps forces, along with doctrines and procedures for combat operations. Each service retained collateral functions to support the other services.[109]

The 1958 legislation had little impact on roles and missions issues in the remaining two years of Eisenhower's Presidency, primarily because abbreviated tours did not allow McElroy, or his successor, Thomas S. Gates, Jr., to take advantage of their new statutory powers. Gates was a lame duck, serving from late 1959 until President John F. Kennedy's swearing-in on January 20, 1961.

From the Air Force's perspective, the new law did not achieve the desired unification and control of combat forces sought by President Eisenhower. "The top military body [was] still shot through with interservice rivalry," according to General White. Noting there was "no more agreement in the JCS" than before the reorganization, White observed that legislation alone would not resolve interservice rivalry, duplication, or waste. Nevertheless, he believed the law "was a pretty good step" in the right direction, one that might lead to full unification.[110] Meanwhile, military and political crises in the years before Kennedy's inauguration put national defense and military strategy on a roller coaster creating roles and missions upheaval in the Pentagon and rampant interservice rivalry.

Turning Points: From Massive Retaliation to Flexible Response

When Congress passed the Defense Reorganization Act in 1958, simultaneous crises in Asia and the Middle East put contingency planning in the Eisenhower Administration to its severest test. In the volatile Middle East, Lebanese President Camille Chamoun requested American intervention following a mid-July coup d'etat that toppled the pro-Western regime in neighboring Iraq. President Eisenhower agreed to send troops. Within 24 hours, the Sixth Fleet landed a battalion of Marines near Beirut. By the end of July, the American commitment included an impressive force of Army and Marine combat units supported by an Air Force element deployed to forward bases in Europe and Navy tactical fighters flying from carriers offshore.

At the peak of the Lebanon buildup, the mobility of combat units in the Pacific Command was tested when Communist China provoked a confrontation over the islands of Quemoy and Matsu in the Taiwan Straits. The only shots exchanged were between Communist and Nationalist Chinese forces, but American military elements deployed to Taiwan in a show of force to bolster Nationalist morale and send a signal of American willingness to defend Taiwan against Communist aggression.[111]

The American experience from the two crises, oceans apart, became a turning point in the transition from reliance on weapons of mass destruction to developing flexible capabilities to respond to all levels of military conflict. The transition from massive retaliation to flexible response augured one of the greatest challenges for service roles and missions since President Truman's embrace of nuclear deterrence and the National Security Act of 1947.

After retiring in July 1959, General Maxwell Taylor called for a "complete reappraisal" of national security strategy in his book, *The Uncertain Trumpet*. Taylor's book argued for a ground-oriented strategy of flexible response, emphasizing developing conventional forces and weapons to deal with limited wars while maintinaing a strong strategic umbrella.

The Army's experience during the Lebanon and Taiwan crises provided evidence for Taylor's claim that Eisenhower's "New Look" failed to prepare the armed forces for the kind of war they most likely would be called on to fight. During the 1958 landing in Lebanon, Army combat units were armed with Honest John rockets, but were not allowed to take them ashore. To Taylor and other Army generals, this illustrated the fallacy of depending on low yield tactical nuclear forces in peripheral or small war situations. Critics of the Eisenhower Doctrine pointed to the Taiwan crisis as additional evidence that the administration's policy on the use of nuclear weapons was ambiguous and that non-nuclear readiness of U.S. air and surface units was deficient.[112]

After-action reports on Air Force operations during the Lebanon and Taiwan deployments also backed up General Taylor's charge that American combat forces were ill-prepared for limited war. While the Air Force was ready to deploy to trouble spots anywhere in the world, they were unprepared for conventional operations when they arrived in the forward staging areas in Lebanon and Taiwan. The 1958 emergencies convinced many military leaders that dual forces were needed in forward areas, yet this issue remained unresolved into the 1960s, well after the United States committed to the protracted use of conventional arms in Southeast Asia.[113]

Air Force leaders also saw a greater need for conventional readiness, but interpreted the Lebanon and Taiwan crises differently than General Taylor. While the Lebanon operations revealed training deficiencies in conventional arms delivery by American pilots, the superior flying and shooting of Nationalist Chinese airmen during the Taiwan Straits encounter seemed to bear out Eisenhower's policy to arm and train small friendly nations to counter local aggression. Both crises reinforced the principle "that general war capability inhibits limited war or cold war adventuring." Air Force Maj. Gen. Glen W. Martin explained:

> ...The deployment and increased readiness of U.S. military force having both general war and limited war capabilities prevented both these crises from expanding beyond the cold war operations in so far as the U.S. was concerned since U.S. military forces were not required to do any shooting-nuclear or non-nuclear, but they were ready and the enemy knew it.[114]

Nevertheless, the lessons learned from the two crises supported General Taylor's thesis. Americans began to heed the call of his *Uncertain Trumpet* as the 1950s drew to a close. While Soviet Premier Nikita Khrushchev's "wars of national liberation" speech came days before President Kennedy's inauguration, U.S. policymakers were already heeding General Taylor's warning that low intensity conflicts were unavoidable.

Developments such as Fidel Castro's Cuban revolution, anti-American violence in Latin America, civil war in Laos, and anarchy in the Congo eroded public confidence in massive retaliation before the end of Eisenhower's Presidency. The Army moved toward a more flexible strategy, having developed both ground and air support forces for limited war during Taylor's four years as Chief of Staff. By the end of Taylor's tour, having obtained waivers to procure OV–1 Mohawk reconnaissance planes and CV–2 Caribou transports, the Army had started rebuilding combat air capabilities. Although Air Force tactical air commanders opposed Army purchases of Mohawk and Caribou aircraft, some SAC generals appeared willing to let organic Army tactical air power flourish.

Given the roles and missions implications, the Navy and Marines readily adapted to the limited war trend. The Air Force did so belatedly and somewhat reluctantly. The Army moved quickly to procure more than 5,000 aircraft and developed an air mobility concept founded on organic air capabilities, including armed helicopters for close support.[115]

Adding to the perception that the Air Force did not take its roles and missions responsibilities in support of the Army seriously enough, the 1958 crises strained strategic and tactical airlift capabilities. The problem repeated during airlift support for United Nations movements in the Congo in 1960. In January, the House of Representatives created a subcommittee to investigate airlift forces, including complaints of inadequate support from the Army. Headed by Mendel Rivers, the committee urged that airlift forces be modernized and that the Air Force and the Army coordinate more closely in airlift matters. The Air Force made TAC the single point of contact for joint airlift operations and TAC officers worked more closely with their Army counterparts to resolve airlift issues as the Eisenhower era drew to a close.[116]

General Taylor's book castigated Air Force support for the Army. Describing the Navy as a "satisfied service" that "successfully fought for the concept of balanced, self-contained naval forces," Taylor complained that the Air Force failure to discharge its responsibilities left the Army a "dissatisfied customer." Taylor believed the Army needed its own tactical air support and airlift forces, rather than remaining tied to the vagaries of the existing unhappy arrangement. He proposed not to "take over the obsolescent weapons and equipment" used by the Air Force in these functions, but thought the Army should develop its own resources over a period of time.[117] Steadily gaining a larger audience and representing views shared by most Army generals, Taylor's book threatened to impact Army-Air Force roles and missions in coming years.

The Army's new Chief of Staff, General Lyman L. Lemnitzer, embraced Taylor's vision. Lemnitzer established a general officer review board under Lt. Gen. Gordon B. Rogers to study Army aviation requirements for the coming decade and to develop a coherent aviation policy. Taylor wanted roles and missions rewritten to define the Army responsibilities for land combat "as including the land itself and the contiguous layers of air and sea necessary for use in ground operations." He wrote that each service had "the right" to develop "all the weapons and equipment" that were "habitually necessary for combat in its particular medium," recognizing that "more than one service might properly possess the same weapons." The Rogers Board recommended developing and testing "air cavalry" units for combat, attesting to widespread institutional interest in and support for General Taylor's views.[118]

Lemnitzer made it clear that the Army did not want to usurp Air Force roles and missions. When a House Committee suggested merging the Air Force with the Army, Lemnitzer objected strenuously:

> ...I think the division among the services is a perfectly natural one-one service to fight on land, the Army; one service to fight on the surface of the sea, over it and underneath it, the Navy; and one in the air, the Air Force.[119]

As a concluding note on Army-Air Force relations under the Eisenhower Administration, the isolation that Army leaders felt in the joint arena began to fade in the twilight of massive retaliation. General Taylor complained that he and the Army staff chafed under the impression that the Secretary of Defense and the Chairman of the Joint Chiefs paid little attention to their objections or recommendations. Taylor struggled to reverse this trend as Army Chief of Staff to no avail. The reversal began in 1960 when President Eisenhower nominated General Lemnitzer to succeed Twining as chairman, but a full turnaround would not come until after President Kennedy's inauguration and the onset of flexible response.[120]

Meanwhile, interservice relations between the Air Force and the Navy, once stormy and strained to the breaking point, began to mature. By the end of the decade, joint air and naval power was a reality. The Navy developed the Polaris missile for its nuclear-powered submarines and the George Washington became the first Polaris-equipped submarine.

The Air Force successfully fired its new Atlas medium range ballistic missiles in early 1960 and prepared to introduce longer range Titan and Minuteman missiles into the strategic inventory. These new weapons could reach targets in the Soviet Union from the United States. Attaining the strategic triad of manned bombers, land-based missiles, and submarine-launched missiles effectively closed the research and development gap implied by the Soviet's intercontinental ballistic missile test and the Sputnik launches of 1957.[121] It also meant that the Air Force and the Navy had reached a new plateau in the evolution of strategic roles and missions.

Activating the nuclear triad demanded cohesion in joint planning, as war planning was a polemical issue in the joint arena since the end of World War II. While some joint planning existed for nuclear strikes before and during the Korean War, SAC maintained an almost exclusive role in this area until other forces began to

An Atlas intercontinental ballistic missile at the Air Force Missile Test Center at Cape Canaveral, Florida, in November 1959. *(National Archives photo)*

field nuclear arms in the 1950s. Even then, procedural changes did little more than encourage interservice coordination on targeting matters. Problems with duplicative strategic planning prompted Eisenhower to give the Joint Chiefs and the Secretary of Defense greater direction and authority by enacting the new defense reorganization law in 1958.[122]

Stronger unified direction over nuclear planning was a high priority when Secretary of Defense Gates took office in 1959. Secretary Gates approved a new

Joint Strategic Target Planning Staff (JSTPS) under the Joint Chiefs in August 1960. Composed of Army, Navy, Marine Corps, and Air Force planners, the JSTPS was collocated with SAC headquarters and charged with producing the joint strategic war plan, the Single Integrated Operational Plan (SIOP), and the National Strategic Target List (NSTL). The SAC commander directed strategic target planning, while a Navy admiral served as vice director, providing day-to-day administration of the staff. The JSTPS assigned integrated planning for nuclear strike forces, including submarine-launched ballistic missiles, land-based strategic bombers, and intercontinental ballistic missiles. No sooner had it incorporated the "massive destruction" strategy of the Eisenhower era into its planning process, the JSTPS transitioned into the "assured destruction" philosophy of the Kennedy era.[123]

As service roles and missions evolved, milestones such as the strategic triad suggested that modern arms might dislodge doctrinal boundaries between land, sea, and air warfare-even though the services were more divided than ever before on some issues. This might help explain why the Air Force and the Navy were more accommodating than in years past. Although the Air Force received the largest share of defense appropriations, the arms race with the Soviet Union produced ample budgets for funding both services' programs. The Air Force remained wary of the Navy's ambitious supercarrier program, which boasted four *Forrestal*-class carriers and three under construction by the end of the 1950s. One of these carriers was the nuclear-powered *Enterprise*, the prototype for seven more ships.[124]

The Atlantic and Pacific fleets argued that their carrier forces and the Marines were best prepared to deal with emergencies such as Lebanon and Taiwan Straits, yet the Navy was no better prepared to fight small wars at the start of the 1960s than the Air Force. Both services modernized their forces for nuclear conflict, but were slow to follow the Army's lead in reorienting doctrine, weapons systems, and training to respond to lower conflict levels. The Air Force rewrote its basic doctrine to conform to national strategy, only to find it unsuitable for the limited war joint forces would have to fight.

Air Force mobile tactical air forces and their fighter posture overseas were geared for nuclear strike operations. Counter to traditional doctrine, the Air Force had not developed a versatile air superiority fighter and would have to rely on the F–4 Phantom, introduced by the Navy as an interceptor in 1958, as its mainstay in the Vietnam era. Air Force tactical air forces centered their 1950s research and development on the F–100 Super Sabre and the F–105 Thunderchief, designed to deliver nuclear bombs. Both aircraft had to be reconfigured for conventional operations.[125]

Headway by the Air Force and Navy in strategic arms teamwork under massive retaliation was not lost in converting to flexible response. By substantially widening the window of armed commitment, the revised national strategy prompted larger defense budgets and a panoply of conventional weapons. One unintentional result was the rise of intensified roles and missions rivalry among the services as they competed for defense dollars and force levels to wage either nuclear

Roles and Missions

or conventional warfare. Through the transition to flexible response, the Air Force bore the brunt of mounting criticism that massive retaliation had emphasized the buildup of nuclear power at the expense of forces needed to confront non-nuclear aggression. Answering these critics, Secretary of the Air Force Dudley C. Sharp said that he believed history would that show massive retaliation was "the wisest way to keep peace." General White said simply, "The payoff has come in the cold clear fact that this nation has been militarily safe throughout some of the most critical years in history."[126]

Nevertheless, the mood of the nation was changing and General Taylor's views on military strategy were more in tune with the public. Alarming developments such as Sputnik, Khrushchev's missile rattling boasts, and the Soviet downing of an American U–2 spy plane in May 1960 shook the public's faith. The Soviet nuclear buildup created a superpower stalemate, making the prospect of nuclear war even more abhorrent, especially to allies who feared their homelands might become battlegrounds. Fidel Castro's takeover in Cuba and the threat from a Communist toehold on America's doorstep, also increased the likelihood of non-nuclear military initiatives closer to home.

During the 1960 presidential campaign, John F. Kennedy used Taylor's criticism and reports of an alleged "missile gap" between the Soviet Union and the United States to punctuate attacks on Eisenhower's military policies. Days before Kennedy's inauguration, a bellicose Khrushchev declared Soviet support for "wars of national liberation", convincing the President-elect that small wars were inevitable. His blueprint of a "New Frontier" strategy was the right direction, Kennedy believed. The nation was moving closer to sub rosa military involvement in Southeast Asia, and into a new chapter on roles, missions, and interservice relations.

CHAPTER VI

NEW DIRECTIONS: THE VIETNAM WAR AND FLEXIBLE RESPONSE

The redirection of national defense policy under President John F. Kennedy turned the nuclear "overkill" era around, altering the course of air power history. While serving in the Senate, Kennedy's thoughts on military strategy had been influenced by General Taylor's book, *The Uncertain Trumpet*, and other proponents of a more flexible military posture. During the 1960 Presidential campaign, the Democratic hopeful adopted the strategy of flexible response as his own. After his inauguration, Kennedy committed to a defense policy to maintain strong forces ready to respond to a full range of military contingencies, from low-intensity conflict to thermonuclear war. For the Air Force, whose strategic bombers and missiles dominated the 1950s, this redirection meant a turnabout in doctrinal thinking, defense budgeting, force planning, and interactions within the joint arena.[1]

In his State of the Union message on January 30, 1961, Kennedy presented his blueprint for the "new frontier", calling for a reappraisal of defense strategy. In addition to defending against all levels of aggression, Kennedy pledged to seek alternatives to the arms race by starting arms reduction talks with the Soviet Union. He believed that by maintaining strength and the will to counter the Soviet threat, the United States could use conventional readiness as a complement to strategic deterrence and arms control initiatives to avoid nuclear holocaust. Kennedy's new frontier offered a fresh approach to government service, including the Peace Corps and a reinvigorated space program. While his ideas made no quick or radical changes to existing roles and missions directives, the Kennedy doctrine portended adjustments ahead during the transition from massive retaliation to flexible response.[2]

Reappraisal and Redirection: Flexible Response Takes Root

The Air Force began to experience the effects of shifting roles and missions priorities early in the new administration. Kennedy ordered Secretary of Defense Robert S. McNamara to reappraise national defense and the Soviet military threat and directed interim actions to increase military airlift and accelerate missile programs and Polaris submarine production. The President told McNamara that he expected "cost-conscious and efficient" management of the Pentagon, but wanted to build a superior force structure unhindered by arbitrary budget ceilings. By early 1961, it was clear that the cost of strengthening the conventional force posture would take its toll in other areas, including reducing or killing some cherished Air Force programs.[3]

In the White House Rose Garden, Secretary of the Air Force Eugene Zuckert swears in Gen. Curtis E. LeMay as Air Force Chief of Staff as President Kennedy and Vice President Johnson look on. *(National Archives photo)*

When he succeeded General White as Air Force Chief of Staff in July 1961, Gen. Curtis LeMay found himself in a desperate fight to save manned bombers. Speculation that strategic missiles made manned bombers obsolete was heard even before the new frontier was announced. In April, after the Administration completed its review of military programs, President Kennedy cancelled the Air Force B–70 Valkrie advanced bomber program, under development since 1954, and cut another wing of B–52s from the defense budget. Naval strategic programs were also cut back as Kennedy cancelled a nuclear-powered aircraft carrier.[4]

General Taylor's growing influence on Kennedy's military policies did not bode well for the strategic-minded Air Force. The management style of Secretary McNamara, whose decisions were influenced more by systems analysis than by sound military advice, also concerned the Air Force. Both men contributed to the strategic vision and force posture gravitating toward American military intervention in Vietnam.[5]

Seasoned early by the Bay of Pigs debacle in Cuba, President Kennedy returned General Taylor to active duty as his special military representative in July 1961. Taylor brought an orientation which continued to deflate the hyper-nuclear doctrine of the past decade. Taylor's 15 months as White House military adviser, including a fact-finding mission to Saigon, coincided with budding counterinsurgency operations in that region. At the direction of the President, the

Secretary of Defense Robert S. McNamara approached management of the Defense Department from an analytical business perspective, evoking concern among many career officers. *(National Archives photo)*

services began to develop counterinsurgency capabilities. By the fall of 1961, the Air Force introduced a counterinsurgency detachment known as Farm Gate into Vietnam. This detachment joined special forces from other services to train South Vietnamese to fight the Viet Cong. Although General Taylor has traditionally been identified with the decision to send U.S. special forces to Vietnam, he gave President Kennedy full credit for the counterinsurgency role. Taylor later recalled that when Kennedy first inquired about counterinsurgency, "he had to beat me over the head before I understood what he was talking about."[6]

General Taylor served in his special advisory capacity until October 1961, when Kennedy appointed him as Chairman of the Joint Chiefs. For an officer to come out of retirement to assume the top military post was unprecedented, but the youthful President believed these were uncommon times demanding vision and bold, imaginative action from government. Serving as Chairman allowed Taylor to exert greater influence over planning the force posture and shaping military policy. Dispensing with the NSC papers Eisenhower had used to guide policy, President Kennedy relied on a tightly knit group of national security advisers.[7]

The President and his advisers used many of Taylor's ideas to shape a new strategy of "graduated deterrence." Designed to respond to a complete spectrum of military force, graduated deterrence became best known for its application to the Cuban missile crisis and the subsequent buildup in general purpose and counterinsurgency warfare abilities. Its greatest impact was felt in conventional force planning, modernization, and readiness. The effect on Army programs, including organic aviation, was electric. When General Taylor became Chairman, General LeMay was the odd man out and Air Force strategic programs suffered the consequences.[8]

Taylor claimed to have mixed feelings about returning to the Pentagon "Bear Pit" where the "orthodoxy" of flexible response under Kennedy had been "heresy" when he served as Eisenhower's Army Chief of Staff. The new Chairman was also concerned about "allegations which floated about

Roles and Missions

Washington" that McNamara's "Whiz Kids had taken over much of the advisory role of the Joint Chiefs of Staff." Taylor said, however, that McNamara seemed "genuinely pleased" with his appointment, and assured him that the statutory obligation of the Joint Chiefs "to serve as the principle military adviser to him, the National Security Council, and the President" would be honored. Taylor expressed "high regard" for McNamara, describing him "as a man of decision who tackled fearlessly the tough problems of defense."[9]

Air Force leaders saw McNamara in a different light. General White thought it ironic that the Air Force, the only service to back greater centralized authority for the Defense Secretary during Eisenhower's 1958 reorganization, now suffered the most under McNamara's tighter control. White decried McNamara's "hardhitting" style of centralized authority and propensity for disregarding advice from top military leaders.[10]

Secretary of the Air Force Eugene M. Zuckert complained about McNamara's high-handed treatment of service secretaries and military chiefs. "So overpowering was McNamara and his centralized system," one historian wrote, "that Zuckert seriously considered resigning." Instead, he decided to "help the Air Force adapt to McNamara and cope with the fact that it was no longer the dominant service that it had been in the 1950s."[11]

General White believed the Air Force was right to place "major emphasis on strategic forces and atomic weapons" and that it had done "exactly what it was supposed to do under the then current national policy." The Air Force had evolved from "a purely flying force" into "an organization of vast technological complexity," and had "turned a corner" that would change its character even more. He reminisced:

> I remember well telling the Air Staff on many occasions that the build-up in strategic missiles such as the Atlas, Titan, and Minuteman was not good for the traditional Air Force but it was vital for the nation. The Air Force did not default this mission, though it began a radical change in its character.[12]

The Kennedy Administration did not abandon strategic nuclear forces, but changed the immediacy of its military requirements to a buildup of conventional capabilities, with a greater range of options and flexibility in force planning. Air Force planners rediscovered the special air warfare doctrine fashioned in jungle fighting of World War II. An air commando unit activated at Hurlburt Field in April 1961 was a throwback to such doctrine used against the Japanese in Burma. With the build-up of conventional forces in Europe and the deployment of the Farm Gate detachment to Bien Hoa Air Base in South Vietnam, a buzz about counterinsurgency warfare began to be heard above debates over nuclear roles and missions. In discussing accommodation to these changes, General White drew the lines together for the old and the new Air Force:

...for many years it was perhaps a fact that what was good for the Air Force was good for the nation. But that was the infant Air Force struggling for true recognition of air power.

Today aerospace power has proved itself, and it is clear that what is good for the nation is good for the Air Force. The President, the Secretary of Defense, and the Congress determine what is good for the nation. The country and the Air Force stand to profit from the sound attitude which prevails in Air Force recognition of its new role.[13]

At the other end of the spectrum, the new Air Force had to prepare for a role in space warfare. In March 1961, without consulting the Joint Chiefs, Secretary McNamara issued Directive 5160.32 assigning control of military space development to the Air Force. The Army and Navy objected, fearing their capabilities might be neglected. Both services contended that space was "an environment, not a function, and that all the services should be permitted to use space in pursuing their missions on or near the earth."

Secretary McNamara reassured the Army and Navy that their space requirements would not be slighted while General White promised that the Air Force would "bend over backward to meet the requirements of the Army and Navy." During House hearings on the space program, Republican Congressman James Fulton commented that the Air Force might be trying to "find a place" for itself, since manned aircraft might one day be obsolete. Lieutenant General Arthur G. Trudeau, director of Army research and development reportedly replied, "That's why we must be bighearted and accept the directive. We would hate to have them known as the silent silo sitters of the seventies."[14]

While taking the lead in military space development, neither White nor LeMay was unyielding in opposing the build-up of limited war forces. Their concern was that the build-up came at the expense of general war capabilities. When President Kennedy cancelled the B–70 Valkrie after approving more Polaris missiles, White warned that the Air Force would be crippled without an advanced manned bomber. It was not simply a matter of de-emphasizing strategic air forces, he argued, but a question of the strategic mix. "If the overall U.S. general war capacity can be maintained by use of the Polaris and aircraft carriers," he said, "then it would be all right to use funds from SAC for limited war forces." White believed there were ways to fund the limited war build-up without sacrificing effectiveness.[15]

Reversals in strategic air force modernization created consternation in the Chief's office, but airmen outside SAC welcomed the changes. In TAC, the lone proponents of flexible response in the 1950s, airmen felt stifled by the overpowering influence of strategic air forces and they were relieved that the yoke of general war budgeting was lifted from the rest of the Air Force. Although discouraged by the setbacks, General White was proud of the maturity shown by the Air

Roles and Missions

President Kennedy raised concerns throughout Air Force leadership when he cancelled the B–70 program. Here, a prototype XB–70 is open for inspection at North American Aviation. *(National Archives photo)*

Force by not engaging in public recriminations "despite pressure from within and without." He recalled that "reverses of no greater consequence have resulted in an admirals' or generals' revolt with an inspired press joining the fray," in the past.[16]

Roles and missions differences were plentiful as flexible response took root and the armed forces moved to implement McNamara's policies. Some of his decisions, such as those governing development of aircraft for counterinsurgency warfare, encouraged competition and duplication in developing weapon systems. Others, like his guidance on advanced systems like the F–111 sought commonality in development and use but showed a lack of understanding of individual requirements.

While the F–111 was in the conceptual stage, McNamara pushed for tri-service development, believing the multi-purpose aircraft could fulfill all fighter roles, even close air support. While protests from all services convinced the Defense Secretary that close air support was not a suitable role for the F–111, he refused to budge from development of a common airframe to meet requirements of both the Air Force and Navy. As a result, the F–111 satisfied neither service and the Navy refused to purchase the aircraft.[17]

Revival of rivalries with the Navy in the early 1960s was not as embittering for the Air Force as the continuing roles and missions struggle with the Army over tactical aviation. The doctrinal turnabout giving tactical aviation prominence in conventional and counterinsurgency roles when President Kennedy's military policies took root was traumatic for the nuclear-oriented Air Force posture. Strengthening Air Force tactical air capabilities became more urgent after the administration began to build-up conventional forces in response to the Berlin crisis, assessed smoldering aggression in Southeast Asia, and weighed the lessons of the Cuban missile crisis. Fueling the burgeoning rivalry between the Army and the Air Force, Secretary McNamara directed the Army to develop organic air support capabilities to compete with tactical air forces.[18]

McNamara, Taylor, and the Howze Board: Army Aviation Takes Off

During the few months he served as Air Force Chief of Staff in the Kennedy Administration, General White felt threatened by increased support for organic Army aviation and attempted to mend relations between the services. Seeking an alliance against threatened cuts in tactical squadrons, White offered to let the Army select aircraft to equip and train tactical squadrons to support its ground forces. White's offer was a concession to the long-standing Air Force policy of developing and employing multipurpose aircraft rather than aircraft designed for specialized missions.

Army Chief of Staff Gen. George H. Decker rejected the offer, claiming the Army's primary concern was not aircraft selection but the lack of a system of control to give ground commanders responsive tactical air support.[19] To the Air Force, Decker's rejection meant that the Army still wanted to take dedicated squadrons from centralized Air Force control, putting them under ground commanders. Although no formal revision of the Key West provisions made the Air Force less responsible to support the Army, concern persisted in the Air Force that the Army intended to build its own tactical air support capabilities.

Secretary McNamara's policy decisions seemed to disregard the Key West agreement. From the Air Force's perspective, McNamara appeared to encourage roles and missions duplication by giving the Army virtual free rein to develop air mobility capabilities for the build-up in Europe and the budding counterinsurgency in Southeast Asia. In a memorandum that mirrored General Taylor's influence, if not his actual words, McNamara directed the Army to develop and test its long-range air mobility requirements for land warfare immediately. He urged a bold "new look" at Army aviation programs without regard for "traditional viewpoints and past policies, and free from veto or dilution by conservative staff review." McNamara asked Gen. Hamilton Howze to chair a board for this tasking.[20]

Joint review of the Howze Board report in 1962 caused a stir in the Pentagon. The report proposed to modernize ground forces with new aviation and airmobile units, including air assault divisions and urged maximum use of armed helicopters, fixed-wing aircraft, and organic air transport. The expanded combat role for helicopters and light planes, considered "sitting ducks" in a hostile environment by the Air Force, raised questions about what the Army really wanted from Air Force tactical air forces.[21]

Roles and Missions

Vice Commander of TAC, Lt. Gen. Gabriel P. Disosway, chaired a board which helped clarify roles and missions issues in the early 1960s. *(National Archives photo)*

Many tactical air commanders wondered how General White's successor would react to this new round of Army initiatives because of his reputation for single-mindedness in building the world's most powerful strategic air forces. While General LeMay opposed the initiatives he realized that the Air Force had to compromise. Although the Air Force expanded tactical aviation and airlift to accommodate ground requirements, it did not give the Army everything it wanted. LeMay believed it was essential for the Air Force to continue providing support because it could do the job better and at less cost than the Army. Cautioning the Air Staff to keep the matter within military channels, LeMay formed a board under TAC Vice Commmander, Lt. Gen. Gabriel P. Disosway, to prepare an Air Force response to the Howze Board report. He negotiated with General Decker and his successor, Gen. Earle G. Wheeler, to keep Army-Air Force disagreements from becoming a public spectacle.[22]

The Disosway Board clarified the Air Force position on issues which divided the services. Of concern was whether armed helicopters and light planes could survive to deliver fire support in a hostile environment. Demands for a permissive operating environment and greater aerial firepower required more, not less, of Air Force tactical fighters. Air Force arguments did not dissuade McNamara, who authorized the Army to test and evaluate the British V/STOL prototype fighter, the P-1127, for close air support in 1962. The Army also developed in-house aviation engineering and procurement capabilities duplicating those in the Air Force and the Navy. The Air Staff protested:

> ...in our view, which we are certain Secretary McNamara will share, it is both undesirable and unnecessary for the United States to spawn and support an increasing number of modern air forces with all the implications of steadily increasing complexity and cost.[23]

McNamara did not agree. He told the Army in April that it should turn to aviation to improve its tactical mobility. He thought aviation offered "the opportunity to acquire quantum increases in mobility, provided technology, doctrine, and organization are fully exploited."

Rebuffed by the Defense Secretary, General LeMay encountered similar resistance when he met with General Wheeler to suggest that the best air-ground team at the lowest cost could be achieved if the Air Force performed all of the air tasks. Throughout LeMay's tour as Chief of Staff, from 1961 to 1965, the Army warded off persistent Air Force efforts to take over all aerial vehicles. LeMay believed the Air Force should operate "everything that flies, down to the last puddle jumper," but found no support from the Secretary of Defense or the joint arena. Ironically, Air Force development of counterinsurgency capabilities brought Congressional protests that it might be encroaching on Army responsibilities.[24]

Meanwhile, McNamara's office facilitated two landmark decisions pushing towards development of joint plans, procedures, and operational doctrine. These included activation of the Strike Command in September 1961 and establishment of close air support boards in April 1963. The impartiality of Strike Command was soon found wanting after McNamara ordered joint tests of Air Force and Army air mobility concepts. After the Army tested its capabilities in the fall of 1964, it refused to participate in Strike Command's joint evaluation the next January. Strike Command Commander Gen. Paul J. Adams explained that the Army viewed air mobility as a unilateral rather than a joint concern. Yet General Adams assured the Air Force that the Army wanted full support from the Air Force during joint operations.[25]

The Army clung to the special status of its air mobility and assault forces in the 1960s. Because these were dedicated forces not to be placed under the control of an air support component commander, speculation grew about Army intentions to develop a capability to provide its own air support, despite reassurances that ground commanders depended on the Air Force for tactical air support. The Army's emerging concept of air-land warfare visualized units fighting on a battlefield much like a checkerboard, without fixed battle lines or clearly defined forward and rear areas, but with rapidly changing tactical situations. Under this concept, the Army proposed to concentrate highly mobile forces to take an objective, dispersing them before they became a target for the enemy. Immediate reaction was key to the success of such operations. The Army maintained that air units deployed from fixed bases could not survive or respond effectively.[26]

Conceived for nuclear or general purpose wars, the Army's mobility concept appeared uniquely suited for low intensity efforts such as Vietnam. Air mobility was promising in an environment where the Viet Cong owned much of the countryside and controlled most surface lines of communication. Some Army strategists felt air mobility offered the only advantage to wrest the initiative from insurgent forces. Thus, with McNamara's encouragement, the Army used its expanding advisory role in South Vietnam to test the air mobility concept in actual combat. The other services did the same for their unproven low-intensity warfare capabilities.

McNamara's policy of having each service develop whatever unique capabilities it needed turned the jungles of Southeast Asia into a deadly laboratory for military doctrine and arms development, lasting through escalation of the conflict in 1965.[27]

Roles and Missions in Southeast Asia: The Advisory Years

When the Air Force's Farm Gate detachment deployed to Vietnam in 1961, it operated in a hotbed of interservice rivalry, where services were sorting out counterinsurgency roles and missions, and testing concepts and techniques on the battlefield. This rivalry extended through America's protracted military involvement in Southeast Asia, exacerbated by the uneven progress of the war, lack of a coherent strategy, and unorthodox command arrangements and rules of engagement.[28] From the introduction of special forces in 1961 through 1973, American combat units operated in a highly competitive roles and missions environment outside the unified chain of command established by the 1958 Defense Reorganization Act.

The theater structure for U.S. forces in the Pacific and Far East changed between the end of the Korean War and the beginning of American combat in Southeast Asia. Just before the 1958 defense reorganization, the Eisenhower Administration dissolved the Far East Command and made the Pacific Command the single unified authority over the Pacific, including Japan, Korea, and Southeast Asia. The Navy became executive agent for the sprawling new theater, with an admiral as its supreme commander. The Pacific Command headquarters at Camp Smith, Hawaii, included a joint staff of senior officers, with component Army, Navy, and Air Force command headquarters at nearby installations. When the Pacific Air Forces at Hickam AFB absorbed the Far East Air Forces, all Air Force tactical forces in that area were consolidated under a single commander. Still, this did not unify the direction of theater-wide air power.

True unified command, according to Air Force doctrine, included land, sea, and air components, with all theater air assets under the air component commander. This was not the case in the Pacific Command. Commanders of the Pacific Air Forces and the Pacific Fleet had to cooperate on air tasks. The latter was responsible for developing indigenous air forces in Southeast Asia. General Emmett O'Donnell attempted to get the Pacific Air Forces more involved in preparing indigenous forces after he became commander in 1959, but made few inroads before the Kennedy Administration moved toward greater military commitment in Vietnam and Laos.[29]

Besides giving America her most controversial war, the Southeast Asia conflict left military scholars pondering one of history's most fragmented chapters on air warfare strategy and direction. The fragmentation was born of the sub rosa entry of U.S. military forces in the region, compounded by protraction of the war and the ambivalent policies of three successive Washington administrations.

Forward strides in planning and preparing for unified theater warfare had little influence on introduction of combat units into Vietnam or their use in battle. American units first entered under the guise of advising country forces and to test counterinsurgency doctrine and techniques. The fact that counterinsurgency operations sprang from a ground strategy was evident in the top-heavy Army command structure, in which Brig. Gen. Rollen H. Anthis operated as the first Air Force commander in the war zone.[30]

Anthis headed the Air Force element of the Military Assistance Command, Vietnam (MACV), established in February 1962 as a subordinate theater command. In its initial configuration, MACV was layered on top of the existing advisory group, which was already dabbling in counterinsurgency activities. It was not a truly joint headquarters, with little conformity in component service lines.

The Joint Chiefs conceived the Saigon headquarters as a joint structure, but it was dominated by Army officers, just like the advisory group and the Vietnamese high command. The first MACV Commander, Gen. Paul D. Harkins, reported through the Navy theater Commander in Chief in Hawaii to the Joint Chiefs. This arrangement brought tighter controls from Washington and relegated Adm. Harry D. Felt and component commanders to little more than senior consultants on service operations. Felt opted to keep peripheral naval involvement in Southeast Asia under his Navy component rather than under Harkins, while the Army component in Hawaii was divorced completely from Harkins' reporting chain. This gave Harkins control over all Air Force operations in Vietnam, with direct command of Army forces because there was no Army component commander in the Saigon headquarters.[31]

Anthis reported for duty in Saigon as the only recognizable component commander under Harkins. He remained responsible through his own service channels, the Thirteenth Air Force in the Philippines, to Admiral Felt's theater air component headquarters, the Pacific Air Forces in Hawaii. Since Vietnam was a proving ground for special air warfare equipment and techniques, Anthis was placed in the unenviable position of serving under his competitor. This position was even more awkward because of Air Force reluctance to fit its budget to a tenuous military role. The Army spent liberally to pursue roles and missions which the Air Force undertook with mothballed aircraft from World War II.[32]

In 1961, the Army began deploying a variety of planes and helicopters to Vietnam. By the end of 1964, this force included more than 400 aircraft, including armed Huey helicopters, OV-1 Mohawk surveillance aircraft, and CV-2 Caribou transports. The Air Force protested Army procurement of the Mohawk and Caribou because these fixed-wing airplanes were exceptions to agreements between the services. The Mohawk was particularly controversial because it

Roles and Missions

The expansion of American involvement in Vietnam in the mid-1960s led to many scenes such as this in which a C–123 lands on a small airstrip at Dau Tieng, aided by a mobile air traffic team.

could be used as an attack or electronic surveillance platform in addition to its primary role of visual reconnaissance.[33]

In early 1962, after deploying its first special air warfare unit to Vietnam, the Air Force introduced a rudimentary tactical air control system, with a joint operations center in Saigon staffed by Americans and Vietnamese. Air Force expectations to centralize control of air operations under Anthis were dashed when the Army set up its own system with an aviation headquarters for each Army senior advisor in the four corps tactical zones. The Air Force also organized its system to conform to operations in the four corps areas, with central control from Saigon.

The Army's overpowering influence extended to Anthis' advisory role and the direction of Vietnamese Air Force operations. An early lesson of the war was that American advisors imposed tactics, techniques, and doctrine, including roles and missions biases, on country forces they were training. When Anthis left Saigon at the end of 1963, he spoke favorably of relations with Harkins, but urged strengthening the Air Force component role, to correct the imbalance of Harkin's headquarters and to assure the integrity of Vietnamese Air Force training and operations. Anthis criticized Pentagon policy which encouraged rivalry

198

General William W. Momyer, commander of the Seventh Air Force in Vietnam, feared that fragmentation of command hindered the ability of American forces to conduct the war. *(National Archives photo)*

in an active combat theater, costly in lives and resources and interfering with war objectives.[34]

Anthis' departure came during political transition at home and at a turning point for American intervention in Vietnam. President Kennedy's assassination coincided with the deterioration of the political and military situation in South Vietnam. American troops assumed a larger, more active role in the fighting, prompting concerns about the war and its management at home. There were no clearly defined objectives for American involvement. The policy of self-sufficient forces was not working in Vietnam even in these early years. Ten years later, as the United States sought to extract its forces, it was still not working. The Air Force sought a stronger voice in air matters, but McNamara controlled the size and composition of the Saigon headquarters. He viewed the war as an investment in advisory and counterinsurgency capabilities.[35]

In January 1964, the Air Force sent Maj. Gen. Joseph H. Moore to replace Anthis, partly because of Moore's friendship with Harkins' new deputy, Lt. Gen. William C. Westmoreland. Harkins stayed in command until June, but Westmoreland was slated to take over MACV, with orders from the Joint Chiefs to settle the disagreement over air doctrine and turn the war around. In retrospect, this was the period most favorable to define a workable strategy for American intervention and for organizing forces in the war zone. General William W. Momyer, who took command of the Seventh Air Force in July 1966, believed the failure to establish a unified theater command for Southeast Asia was one of the greatest mistakes of the war. The period between the summers of 1964 and 1966 was the crossroads for making that decision.[36]

When Lyndon B. Johnson took office after Kennedy's assassination, he retained key members of Kennedy's cabinet, including Defense Secretary McNamara and Secretary of State Dean Rusk as well as many of the slain president's military policies. Seeking an early resolution to the Southeast Asia predicament, President Johnson appointed General Taylor ambassador to Saigon

Roles and Missions

in July 1964. Taylor's assessment, with that of others, convinced Johnson that a larger commitment of military force was necessary. It could be argued that Johnson's subsequent escalation of the American commitment strayed from Kennedy's policy, but this is a moot point as the two presidents shared the same circle of close advisors and the situation in Vietnam changed markedly after Kennedy's death.[37] It was perhaps inevitable that regular forces would take control of the war the longer the fighting lasted. The build-up of American forces and the start of the air war against North Vietnam in 1965 changed the character of the war.

While fighting throughout Southeast Asia retained some elements of counterinsurgency warfare, the air war against the North was altogether conventional, as were the bulk of combat operations after 1965. After a series of unproductive air strikes against the North, the Air Force found itself tied in a doctrinal knot of its own making with the start of the on-and-off Rolling Thunder campaign against the North. Post-Korean nuclear thinking was evident in the decision to undertake this campaign of graduated response against North Vietnam, placing the Air Force in the untenable position of conducting conventional strike operations with a nuclear-oriented doctrine and aircraft designed for tactical nuclear operations against targets with little or no strategic value. Graduated response was logical for some nuclear crisis situations but proved unworkable against North Vietnam. Political constraints on U.S. military power and the tenacity of an enemy secure that the highest level of response would never come had grave consequences for American air power and the outcome of the war.[38]

There were more contrasts than parallels between the air war in Southeast Asia and the Korean experience. Conducted under the Southeast Asia Treaty Organization umbrella, the war's objectives were more blurred than those in Korea. Three successive presidents and national security advisers ran the war from Washington, D.C., without developing a sound strategy to bring it to an acceptable conclusion. So-called theater arrangements to prosecute the air war combined with geographic divisions in command responsibilities to provide a patchwork affair that worsened as the war wore on.

Politically divided into the in-country war in South Vietnam, with no clear battle lines, and the out-country war in North Vietnam, Laos, and eventually Cambodia, the maps of the two wars subdivided into a mosaic of battle zones and operational areas. Fragmented application of air power in both the in-country and out-country wars made it seem that roles and missions lessons from Korea were never learned.[39]

Commanding the Air War: A Roles and Missions Throwback

When General Momyer left Saigon in mid-1968, after two years as Seventh Air Force Commander, he reported that the use of air power in Southeast Asia was more fragmented than during the Korean War. The massive buildup in air power after the Gulf of Tonkin incident included a vast array of Air Force warplanes based in South Vietnam and Thailand, a mix of Army helicopters and fixed-wing planes, a Marine air wing in the northernmost province, and Navy fighters flying from offshore carriers.

By the end of 1966, the Air Force had 1,249 aircraft in the war zone. The air order of battle included both modern and vintage warplanes, supported by an assortment of transports, tankers, and other aircraft. Conventionally armed B–52s from bases in Guam and southern Thailand complemented this force. The maze of command and control arrangements for employing this panoply of Air Force, Army, Navy, and Marine air forces, provoked Momyer's parting complaint about air power fragmentation and was a throwback to the diffusive air command relationships of the war against Japan in World War II.[40]

The heart of the air control problem in Southeast Asia was hidden in anomalous command layers and political constraints that evolved with escalation of the conflict. In South Vietnam, the designation of MACV as a subordinate unified theater command, for example, was a misnomer. Neither General Westmoreland's authority nor that of his successor, Gen. Creighton W. Abrams, extended beyond the borders of South Vietnam, except for MACV's designated responsibilities for interdiction of an area (Tally Ho) just north of the DMZ and a contiguous pocket (Tiger Hound) in the panhandle of Laos in part of the Steel Tiger sector through which the Ho Chi Minh Trail wound from North Vietnam to the South. Westmoreland and Abrams delegated their interdiction responsibilities to Momyer and successive Seventh Air Force commanders, in their dual role as the MACV deputy for air operations.[41]

Momyer found that the air deputy's control of interdiction was better defined and more integrated than in the four corps areas of South Vietnam. In South Vietnam, the Seventh Air Force controlled only Air Force operations, although the improved tactical air control system was tailored to satisfy recommendations from the Army's close air support board. The services failed to settle old differences such as who should have operational control over close air support resources, how much and what type of supporting firepower was needed, and whether aircraft should be designed and employed exclusively for close air support. They did agree on improving the responsiveness to air requests from the Army and incorporated these into the tactical air control system beginning in 1965.[42]

Once operational in Vietnam, Seventh Air Force controlled Air Force tactical forces through the tactical air control center at Tan Son Nut Air Base, near MACV headquarters on the outskirts of Saigon. To facilitate responsiveness to Army requests, subordinate air support centers were established in each tactical zone, with tactical air control parties operating with Army units down to battalion level. The joint staff at the tactical air control center used daily requirements from ground commanders to allocate resources for preplanned and immediate support missions, while air control parties obtained diversions when additional support was needed.[43]

A C–123 aerial spray aircraft is readied for a Ranch Hand mission in January 1969. *(National Archives photo)*

The Army relied on its own system to control air operations in Vietnam after the force buildup. Organic aviation became the mainspring of Army combat operations after Secretary McNamara approved the air cavalry concept and use of armed helicopters as standard equipment in June 1965. The Army deployed its 1st Air Cavalry Division to Vietnam that August and air assault operations became a regular feature of Vietnam ground offensives.

The Army operated its organic aviation units independent of Air Force activities for the duration of the war. McNamara's decision took an ironic twist when Air Force plans to deploy helicopters for rescue work and tactical airlift brought a polite protest from Deputy Secretary of Defense Cyrus Vance that the Air Force should be careful not to encroach on new Army roles and missions obligations.[44]

In Saigon, Momyer and his successors had no recourse but to follow MACV's rules for control of Army air resources. Not only was MACV in charge of combat operations in South Vietnam, but Air Force Chief of Staff Gen. John P. McConnell instructed his field commanders to stay out of roles and missions quarrels and devote their attention to combat operations. He promised to deal with interservice issues at the Washington level.[45]

A more vexing problem, from Momyer's point of view, concerned MACV's reluctance to integrate the Marine air wing into support of the total ground battle in South Vietnam. Joint air lessons from the Korean war were forgotten as the Marines landed with dedicated tactical air units in South Vietnam in 1965. The Marines settled in South Vietnam's northernmost provinces in I Corps, where the

Rows of F–104s such as this scene at Udorn, Thailand, were only a small part of American airpower used in Vietnam.

III Marine Amphibious Force became the sector's senior headquarters under MACV. For two years, the Marines retained control of organic air units while fighting their own small war against the Viet Cong and North Vietnamese regulars in I Corps. Army forces in I Corps received the bulk of their tactical air support from Seventh Air Force, whose tactical units also supported Army troops in the other corps areas.[46]

Prior to the siege at Khe Sanh and the Tet Offensive of early 1968, Momyer encountered a stone wall at MACV when he proposed that Marine air units be brought under his control. Westmoreland was reluctant to force the issue because he believed that Army forces had sufficient tactical air support from Seventh Air Force and Army gunships. Momyer's argument that Marine proprietary air control diminished flexibility and the ability to concentrate air power where it was most needed failed to persuade Westmoreland that a change was necessary. The Marines retained control of their assets and argued that they should also control air strikes in the lower part of North Vietnam because this represented the forward edge of the battle area.[47]

Divided arrangements to control other air operations weakened the case to place Marine air operations under MACV centralized control. The Navy retained control of its aerial missions except when flying close air support. The B–52 bombers and KC–135 tankers were controlled from Thailand and other Pacific Command bases. While Navy carrier squadrons flew most missions outside MACV's area of responsibility, nearly all Army missions to support ground battles and B–52 strike sorties were flown against targets in Laos and South Vietnam. This remained unchanged until air resources were unleashed against North Vietnam during Linebacker II in 1972.

Air Force tankers were an integral element of Seventh Air Force strike forces flying out of Thailand, but only coordinated their schedules with the tactical units they refueled. Similarly, B–52 Arc Light strikes were coordinated through an office in MACV headquarters. A complicated but effective system was established to divert B–52s to support emergency battlefield situations. The Seventh Air Force, however, had no authority to plan, target, or schedule B–52 operations. Lack of unified direction over Air Force forces in Southeast Asia, unlike Korea where General Vandenberg placed all Air Force aircraft under Fifth Air Force control, prompted General Momyer to complain that "the first step in getting the forces properly organized was for the Air Force to get its own organization straightened out."[48]

Momyer's complaints did not stop SAC, the Army, or the Navy from operating independent air forces. He did convince Westmoreland that it was essential to give MACV's air deputy control of Marine tactical fighters when the decision was made to defend Khe Sanh in early 1968. The enemy's siege of the Marine stronghold at Khe Sanh, in the northwest corner of I Corps, and simultaneous assaults during the Tet offensive, placed inordinate demands on air power flexibility. Seventh Air Force was called on to support Army troops in the southern, central, and northern provinces, and provided the bulk of air support for Marines at Khe Sanh. The inherent flexibility of the Seventh Air Force to respond to in-country emergencies, while flying to interdict enemy reinforcements, convinced Westmoreland that having Marine air units dedicated solely to support other Marines was a luxury he could no longer afford.[49]

The decision to defend the besieged Marine outpost at Khe Sanh was symbolic of the ground war's dependence on air power. Since the enemy owned the countryside, tactical airlift often provided the only secure lines of communication for friendly forces in Vietnam. Fire support from the air often meant the difference between surviving an enemy assault or being overrun. General Momyer recalled, "If Khe Sanh was to be held, it would be held by air power or not at all because there was no means of providing supplies, munitions and heavy fire support except by air power."

President Johnson demanded assurance that the outpost would not fall and General Westmoreland held General Momyer responsible for the air effort in its defense. With air resources stretched by the Tet Offensive, Momyer knew that he needed all available air resources to provide sustained air support of Khe Sanh. The Marine air wing could not support the Marines at Khe Sanh independently, nor could it support Army reinforcements in the northern corps area. Momyer had sought centralized control over tactical air resources since his arrival in Vietnam and now General Westmoreland agreed.[50] Momyer still did not have control over SAC B–52s, which provided overwhelming firepower in Khe Sanh's defense.

During the massive defense of Khe Sanh, restrictions on the use of Thailand-based forces were temporarily lifted. Although the restrictions had been imposed by the Thai government, Momyer viewed them as contrived arrangements to keep Air Force forces in Thailand from coming under MACV control. He believed that the Navy's persistence in controlling naval air power under the Pacific Command had convinced the Air Force to keep its Thailand-based forces under control of the Pacific air component commander. Unlike Marine air units in Vietnam, the rules governing employment of Thailand-based Air Force units were reimposed after the Khe Sanh emergency ended.[51]

Khe Sanh was saved by one of the greatest concentrations of air power in military history, while the air forces kept constant pressure on reinforcements coming from the north, turning back the enemy's widely dispersed Tet initiatives against major urban centers. While Tet was a major defeat for the North Vietnamese, it created an image at home in the United States that American fire-power had to destroy South Vietnam's cities to save them, turning it into a pro-paganda victory for the enemy and escalating opposition at home against further military intervention. From the Air Force's perspective, Tet provided an out-standing demonstration of its single manager system and the flexible application of air power.[52]

While Marine air remained under centralized control of the MACV air component commander through the war, their service never fully subscribed to the single manager arrangement. Nor were the Joint Chiefs ever in full agreement on the issue. Momyer felt that "the problem with the Marines should never have been allowed to develop." They were engaged in a land campaign under direction of a field army commander, which made the Air Force air component commander the legitimate central authority for air operations. Momyer also noted that the Marines seemed willing to turn their fighters over to his control when they were diverted to interdiction missions in Laos or North Vietnam. There was a reluctance to employ Marines in the interdiction role because their tactics, training, and ordnance were tailored to close air support for Marine ground forces.[53]

Momyer believed the services had to agree to centralize air operations under the air component commander before the next war. In Korea and Vietnam, the failure to resolve this in peacetime brought an unhealthy airing of service differences in the press and congressional hearings as the war was being fought. More importantly, lack of agreement diminished the flexibility of air power by freezing air assets in a particular war zone when they might have been more useful else-where. Ideally, resolution of these issues should occur before the heat of battle.[54]

Arrangements to fight the out-country wars were even more fragmented. There were two distinctly different air wars fought in Laos, with the U.S. ambassador running one with mixed Air Force, Laotion, and CIA-contracted planes in the north, while the Seventh Air Force conducted interdiction operations in the panhandle. Most Air Force strike aircraft operating over Laos and North Vietnam belonged to the Thirteenth Air Force in the Philippines and were based in Thailand, with their operations controlled by Seventh Air Force. A special head-quarters was set up at Udorn, Thailand, to manage this unwieldy arrangement, with a task force at Nakhon Phanom to coordinate activities in the panhandle and another in Vietnam to oversee the interdiction campaign above the DMZ. Operations in Laos required close coordination with those in North Vietnam, with diversion from one area to the other often required. The merging of battles near the borders also involved limited use of air resources in South Vietnam.[55]

The American ambassador's unique air war in northern Laos, with the assistance of Air Force officers in Vientiane, consisted of overt and covert air operations to support government forces in the northern area. In addition to providing preplanned sorties, the Seventh Air Force and Navy task force commanders diverted aircraft to support Laotian government and paramilitary forces. Thus, distinctly separate air wars evolved in the skies over South Vietnam, North Vietnam, Laos, and Cambodia, all bound to a common enemy but divided among U.S. command authorities.[56]

The desultory Rolling Thunder campaign against North Vietnam steeled the enemy's will to fight and was as compartmentalized as the rest of the war. Air operations against the North were not unified under the theater air component, the Commander in Chief, Pacific Air Forces, whose authority was limited to Air Force operations through Seventh Air Force. The Seventh Fleet's Task Force 77 in the Gulf of Tonkin coordinated with Seventh Air Force through a committee arrangement, carrying out independent Navy air strikes. The fleet succeeded in isolating naval air operations under a senior flag officer serving as theater commander in the air war against North Vietnam.[57]

In December 1965, Adm. Ulysses S. Grant Sharp, who replaced Admiral Felt as Commander of the Pacific Command in July, approved a plan to divide North Vietnam into sectors known as route packages, with Air Force pilots flying strike missions in all but one sector, reserved for Navy jets operating from carriers in the Tonkin Gulf. Although Navy planes could be diverted to other areas as needed, they were scheduled primarily against coastal targets in Route Package 6. The Air Force concentrated its forces against longer-range inland targets.

This compartmentalization added a competitive edge to the joint effort, further weakening air operations already divided by piecemeal direction from Washington, D.C. While command headquarters and its Navy and Air Force components participated in planning for air strikes, they often functioned merely as conduits through which targets and rules of engagement funneled from the President and his national security advisers to Seventh Air Force in Saigon and Seventh Fleet in the Tonkin Gulf.[58]

The breach of air doctrine on unity of command left its greatest imprint in the hotly contested skies over North Vietnam. The skies over South Vietnam and parts of Laos, while hostile, were available for all aircraft because of uncontested air superiority. The piecemeal pattern of the air war over the North allowed the enemy to build a formidable air defense system. The rules of engagement were more stringent than in the air war against North Korea and frequent bombing halts ordered by President Johnson allowed enemy defenses time to regroup. Protraction of the conflict meant that air forces on both sides had to adjust to changing tactics. The arbitrary division of operating areas worked to the enemy's advantage since it alerted him to ingress and egress routes, allowing him to adapt his defenses accordingly. Thus, American airmen were robbed of the vital element of surprise in a war where the enemy already enjoyed the initiative.[59]

Divided responsibilities and the policy of graduated response deprived the air component commander discretion to plan and execute a fully integrated campaign against North Vietnam. Senior military leaders joined in opposition to the vacillation and political constraints imposed on air operations, even though they did not agree on overall command and control issues. Admiral Sharp was outspoken in his belief that proper use of airpower against the North might have ended the war as early as 1967. Yet, neither Sharp nor his successors were willing to unify the campaign if it meant yielding control of naval air power to the Air Force component commander.[60]

The arbitrary compartmentalization of the air campaign was born of the technicality resulting in a naval officer commanding the theater with authority for the air campaign against the North. It could be argued that the commander should have delegated responsibility to the air component commander, an Air Force officer. The delineation of service roles and missions in President Truman's executive order and agreements at Key West and Newport 20 years earlier clearly gave the Air Force responsibility for air superiority and interdiction in support of the land battle.

Naval aviation was to support the naval campaign, including attainment of air superiority at sea. Both services were to support the other, and lines of responsibility were clearly drawn. There was no naval campaign in Southeast Asia. It was a land war, supported by the air campaign against the North and interdiction of communication lines. Therefore, it was consistent with law and the principle of unity of command for the air component commander to have full responsiblity to plan and execute the air campaign.[61]

In the policy of graduated response, the end clearly did not justify the means. In December 1972, when President Nixon ordered the first B–52 strikes against Hanoi and Haiphong as part of Linebacker II, he hoped to force the North Vietnamese back to the negotiating table and gain release of American prisoners of war. Nearly eight years had passed since American airmen first flew north with Flaming Dart reprisal strikes and the Rolling Thunder campaign. When U.S. involvement ended in 1973, six generals had followed Momyer in commanding Air Force operations. One was relieved for authorizing air strikes in a prohibited zone, symbolizing the frustrations of an air campaign so restricted that it was doctrinally bizarre. Political restrictions invited the protraction of the air war, which should have been predictable from the outset. Unfortunately, the voice of experience was not the word of authority in Vietnam.[62]

Final responsibility for the piecemeal application of air power in Southeast Asia must rest with the political leaders who placed limits on U.S. intervention. Nonetheless, parochial service interests also contributed to the uneven growth and direction of the war. It may be difficult to reconcile the armed forces' recognition of the need for a unified theater command in Southeast Asia with the failure to agree on this basic issue or the inability to communicate this to higher authorities. Laws enacted under Truman and Eisenhower put the pieces in place to solve the puzzle of unity in theater warfare, but there was no cohesive attempt by the Pentagon to fit the pieces together.

While the armed forces might be stuck with the legacy of political constraints, it remained within their ability, by commitment and by law, to work out the details of unity of command and to fulfill history's promise that separate service warfare was in the past. Until this was done, the nation's wounds from Vietnam may have cut deeper than abandoning an unpopular war by striking at the heart of military procedures to organize and prepare for war. Until this was settled, the quest for unified air power would remain a dream.[63]

Roles and Missions Notes From a Forsaken War

For the informed airman, air power roles and missions lessons from the Vietnam conflict were learned in the skies of wars past. The overall air pattern was different in Vietnam, developing like a patchwork quilt as Washington reacted to enemy initiatives. The air war see-sawed as fighting escalated from an advisory role to covert air commando to a complex proving ground for tactics, techniques, and weapon systems.

Aged fighters and bombers returned from the graveyard, retrofitted with electronic weapons and other high-tech wizardry, to be tested in battle. A variety of hybrid gunships entered the fray. Retrofitted C–123 Ranch Hand transports sprayed the jungles with Agent Orange to kill vegetation and reveal enemy movements. Century-series fighters designed for tactical nuclear use were reconfigured for non-nuclear combat. Airmen weaned from conventional tactics in the 1950s relearned old lessons, putting guns back on their fighters. Giant B–52 bombers carpet-bombed enemy concentrations.

Limited tactical and technological gains, however, were small consolation for the grief caused by political constraints, a fact of modern war. In battle after battle, American air weapons helped defeat an outgunned but resourceful enemy, yet could not decide the final outcome.

Short of destroying warmaking centers or invading the North, unacceptable political options, the air campaign against North Vietnam offered the only hope to wrest the initiative from the enemy. The campaign was reactionary, with policymakers failing to exploit the dominant air power advantage of the United

States until it was too late. Lessons from past air wars were lost on those who defined the graduated campaign as an instrument "to destroy the North Vietnamese will to make war." Only later was the objective revised to include destruction of the enemy's capacity to make war. The Rolling Thunder campaign degenerated into a protracted, desultory application of air power, punctuated by false starts and stops. Little wonder that in 1967 American airmen in Southeast Asia thrilled to hear of the Israeli Air Force's decisive use of air power in their six-day war.[64]

Restrictive rules of engagement, random targeting, and politically inspired standdowns gave the enemy time to harden his defenses and regenerate military pressure against the South. Reminiscent of the Battle of Britain, Rolling Thunder air strikes-although performed with greater precision than ever before-hardened the enemy's resistance. Lacking systematic strategic targeting, armed reconnaissance against military targets of opportunity took precedence, with difficult to measure results, prompting accusations of a "sortie race" between Air Force and Navy airmen.[65]

Friendly air and ground operations in South Vietnam and Laos and Navy carriers in the Tonkin Gulf were free from the threat of enemy air action, but the protracted air war over the North was a battle for air superiority. Flying restricted profiles over an enemy land mass of 61,000 square miles, American pilots were denied the element of surprise and often found the tactical advantage rested with the North Vietnamese. Given the time and wherewithal to build elaborate surface-to-air missile and MIG fighter defenses around key target areas, North Vietnamese air forces proved a worthy foe. Tactical ruses such as the simulation of F–105 flight profiles by F–4s in Operation Bolo were no replacement for a well orchestrated campaign to win and maintain air superiority.[66]

In their concern to protect American lives, commanders seemed to confuse the principle of mass with the massive use of firepower in Vietnam. More bomb tonnage was expended in a few weeks in 1968 at Khe Sanh, defending an outpost of questionable strategic value, than was dropped on Japan in World War II. Commanders followed the principle of mass to send strike forces, escorted by air-to-air cover and missile suppression, against heavily defended targets, including the 1972 Linebacker raids when B–52s massed against the North. General Westmoreland and other commanders praised the use of the nation's foremost strategic weapon to deliver massive fire support but invited criticism that the Air Force destroyed more jungle foliage than legitimate targets.[67]

The air war, right or wrong, came to be seen as a wanton abuse of American military might against a smaller nation. What began as a stand against communist aggression foundered on a sea of political and military excess. One can only speculate how the war might have progressed if fighting had remained at the counterinsurgency level. Would a classic air campaign against the North, planned and executed according to proven air power principles, have made a difference? After all, U.S. leaders had the warmaking capacity of Moscow and

Peking to worry about. Destruction of North Vietnam's forces might have prompted the enemy to move into Chinese sanctuary.

A classic bombing campaign at the outset might have helped interdiction halt the flow of reinforcements and isolate the battlefield, rather than reducing it to impeding the flow and making it costly for the enemy. Whether more aggressive action would have convinced the North Vietnamese to accede to an early political solution is another question.

The lesson appears to be that air power, while still the most flexible military force available to policymakers, must not be employed in isolation. Without an invasion of North Vietnam, it is doubtful that the United States could have entered an exploitation phase of the war. In the final analysis, however, the nation's air leaders are the authority on air power and they must advise without axe to grind and without equivocation.[68]

Given the redundancy of air power in Southeast Asia after 1965, it is surprising that interservice rivalry was not more rampant. Other than jurisdictional problems of command and control, Air Force, Navy, and Marine airmen generally put aside doctrinal differences and worked together to plan, schedule, and fly combat missions. Interaction with Army aviation was more complex since the Air Force had a statutory obligation to provide the Army with air support. General McConnell made clear that roles and missions issues with the Army were to be worked out in Washington. Air Force commanders in Vietnam resigned themselves to the fact that armed helicopters were an integral element of Army combat forces.

In 1966, the Army and Air Force chiefs of staff agreed to give the Army an exclusive claim to the helicopters it needed for intra-theater movement, fire support, and resupply. In return, the Army transferred its CV–2 and CV–7 transports to the Air Force and agreed to relinquish claims on future fixed-wing aircraft for tactical airlift. The Air Force reassured the Army that it would limit its use of helicopters to integral missions such as air rescue and administrative support and agreed not to expand their use to fire or logistics support for the ground battle. The two services agreed to jointly develop an Air Force tactical support aircraft acceptable to the Army. The Air Force developed and procured the A–10 Thunderbolt, which entered the inventory in 1976 as the first jet attack plane designed exclusively for close air support.[69]

The 1966 agreement did not satisfy all Army and Air Force officers. In 1970, Seventh Air Force Commander Gen. George Brown said that he thought the agreement should be "torn up and abrogated." Although it presumably "got the heavy, fixed wing aircraft out of the Army," Brown noted that some still remained in the Army's inventory. More importantly, the agreement allowed the Army to develop attack helicopters-an experiment that many airmen frowned upon as an inferior and duplicative form of tactical aviation. At the time of the agreement, the Army planned to equip its units with AH–10 Cobra attack helicopters for the gunship role. Among its many uses, the Cobra protected maneuver units and suppressed enemy fire in Vietnam. Army plans to develop and procure the AH–56 Cheyenne composite aircraft to attack tanks and fortified ground targets was a greater concern to the Air Force, leading General McConnell to agree to a specialized Air Force close air support aircraft, the A–10.[70]

Some Army commanders viewed Air Force development of the Thunderbolt as a threat to its plans to procure the Cheyenne and provide air support in the immediate battle area. General Westmoreland, who became Army Chief of Staff after leaving Vietnam in 1968, opposed A–10 development, claiming that the Army did not need a specialized Air Force close air support aircraft. He and Gen. John D. Ryan, who replaced McConnell as Chief of Staff of the Air Force, exchanged memoranda in 1970 which reversed the arguments used before the Vietnam War. In a statement that could have been lifted from Air Force tactical manuals, General Westmoreland extolled the multi-mission capabilities of Air Force weapons systems and placed close air support lower on the priority list.[71]

This odd reversal demonstrated the complexities of the joint issue, as well as the extremes both services were willing to go to protect their special interests. It added to the perception that the services were less than forthright in confronting this sensitive problem. Long before the American withdrawal from Vietnam, the Army came to view the attack helicopter as indispensable, a vital extension of their organic firepower. There still was no clear demarcation between Army and Air Force aviation responsibilities. The Army coined the term "direct aerial fire support" to distinguish its gunship operations from Air Force close air support and for the time being, wanted the benefits of both.[72]

Escalation of the war increased Army dependence on firepower provided by the Air Force's system of centralized control and decentralized execution, even though Army gunships continued to operate independently. Senior Army commanders criticized the Air Force system before the force buildup, but those who later served in Vietnam praised the single manager concept for providing flexible air support in a shifting combat environment. There were the inevitable complaints about response times and ordnance loads, but ground forces were never without the air power edge when engaging the enemy. The lack of clear battle lines made short rounds more prevalent in the earlier part of the war, but these misfortunes were the exception, not the rule. General Westmoreland recognized the need to integrate tactical air operations when he placed Marine air units under General Momyer's centralized direction during the siege at Khe Sanh. Although Momyer and his successors were never given command of B–52's, SAC commanders developed procedures to integrate their strike operations with tactical units and make them more responsive to the ground situation.[73]

"The centralized control of the application of air power is an important feature and a critical one for efficient use of air power," General Abrams said during his tour as MACV commander. "The air is really a powerful weapon," he said, "but to use this power effectively, you need both integrated all-source intelligence and an integrated all-resource reaction." Abrams explained that integration of the total air effort was essential, with interdiction and close air support to obtain the best results. Comparing the Air Force system to a "faucet of tremendous firepower," Abrams described his use of air power as MACV commander:

> Fortunately, we've had centralized management of the air effort and this has been important to me personally. While air is powerful, it is also flexible. From this level, air power can be moved with ease. For example, our arena includes Barrell Roll [northern Laos], Steel Tiger [Laotian panhandle], and South Vietnam. Where the enemy puts the heat on, whether it is the Plain of Jars [Laos] or Duc Lap [South Vietnam], it is only a matter of hours until tremendous shifts of power can be made. We realize it's not all that effortless on the part of the Air Force. You have to arrange for tankers and that sort of thing, but the whole system is geared to do precisely that, with no long warning to the enemy. It's done right away.[74]

In a war abandoned by the United States, particularly one in which secondary explosions were as common as body counts in reporting the results of air strikes, the views of Vietnam ground commanders are perhaps as good as any to judge air support. Vietnam, after all, was essentially a ground war. The advantage in firepower and flexibility provided by air power was unfortunately not decisive in the war's outcome. Before drawing conclusions about what Army commanders wanted from the Air Force, one should ponder what one architect of U.S. involvement in the war said on this subject. In contrast to Westmoreland's and Abram's views, Gen. Maxwell Taylor thought it was a mixed blessing:

> ...I would say certainly the net effect has been good from the military point of view, and I think from the political point of view inside of Vietnam, but another thing, like artillery support, of course, it could be ruinous to the infantry. Too good artillery and too good air support can ruin the infantry, because they sit down and wait for it. They get in their foxholes, and call for air support. And we have taught that habit to the Vietnamese.[75]

A New Spirit of Unity in the Post-Vietnam Era

When James R. Schlesinger became Secretary of Defense in the summer of 1973, one of his stated priorities was "to achieve a greater degree of force interdependence" without intruding upon "the delicate area of roles and missions."[76] Faced with soaring costs of military programs, Schlesinger said the nation could

As the new Secretary of Defense in 1973, James R. Schlesinger had his work cut out for him, facing soaring budgets for military programs and continuing debate over roles and missions. *(National Archives photo)*

not afford "each of the services to build into itself capabilities that will permit it to be independent of the other services."

As armed forces regrouped after Vietnam, the Defense Secretary wanted them "to look at the larger view," and "to think in terms of a common national defense rather than in terms of their separate interests." He hoped to draw them closer to "get the beneficial effects of interservice competition while avoiding the nefarious effects of interservice rivalry."[77] Thus, leaving the Vietnam era to history, the defense establishment entered a period in which greater unity proposed to mend the roles and missions fences of wars past. For the Air Force, this was a stark contrast to the unsettling opening of the decade which led into Vietnam.

As the war wound down, the armed forces reoriented doctrine and planning to the NATO and European theaters. The Air Force retained a forward nuclear deterrent posture in Europe, but escalation in Vietnam had forestalled plans to strengthen Air Force conventional forces in NATO. In 1966, the Air Force began to withdraw some fighter squadrons from Europe to meet air power requirements in Vietnam. To compensate, the Air Force earmarked some U.S.-based squadrons for deployment to European bases in an emergency. The forward basing situation worsened in 1967 when Charles de Gaulle denounced United States intervention in Southeast Asia, divorced France from the NATO Alliance, and demanded withdrawal of American forces from French bases. The United States sought to reassure Europeans that America would honor its NATO commitment by deploying dual-based forces to and from Europe. There was growing concern in Washington about the diminishing availability of overseas basing.[78]

On the eve of America's withdrawal from Vietnam, the Air Force resumed building conventional capabilities in Europe, strengthening NATO's force posture, and increasing the survivability of forward bases and aircraft. Air Force commanders in Europe focused on improving NATO interoperability, hoping to avoid recreating the fragmented command and control situation that persisted through the war in Vietnam. They worked with the Army to develop joint air and land doctrine for NATO operating areas. Despite the focus on the threat to NATO countries, crises such as the 1973 Arab-Israeli war and the 1979 upheaval in Iran directed U.S. attention to NATO's southern flank and the bottled-up Mediterranean. There, Navy carriers and other warships fulfilled their NATO commitments and protected U.S. interests in the Middle East and Africa.[79]

In the background, strategic arms limitation talks between the United States and the Soviet Union continued at an uneven pace. Struggling with runaway inflation at home, President Richard M. Nixon sought to ease international tensions and slow the arms race by improving relations with the Soviet Union through detente and opening the door to rapprochement with Communist China. Not surprisingly, the core of the Nixon Doctrine resembled Eisenhower's policies of a decade earlier. After his inauguration in 1969, Nixon told Congress that the United States would honor its security treaties and provide a shield against regional or global aggression, but individually threatened nations would be expected to defend themselves. The central focus remained on NATO interests. In May 1972, the United States and Soviet governments signed an interim SALT I treaty, but the Soviets continued to modernize their force capabilities. The Warsaw Pact posed a formidable nuclear and conventional threat to world peace through the 1970s, particularly to the NATO Alliance.[80]

The changing strategic environment challenged the quest for greater unity. NATO's shrinking base structure rekindled the debate between the Air Force and the Navy over which service should take the lead in projecting U.S. military power abroad. When French President de Gaulle ordered American forces off French soil in 1967, Adm. Thomas H. Moorer, Chief of Naval Operations, campaigned for a stronger naval presence in foreign waters to offset the "shrinkage of overseas bases available to U.S. forces" and counter the growing Soviet threat. Moorer was concerned about increased Soviet activity in the Mediterranean and argued that problems of overflying friendly or neutral countries to reach military targets made sea power a more reliable and politically acceptable instrument of national policy.[81]

Years earlier, while planning the buildup in Southeast Asia, the Navy had argued for the deployment of more aircraft carriers instead of building air bases in the war zone. This particular roles and missions issue encompassed a full range of issues, including airlift and close air support for ground forces, interdiction, and strike operations against the enemy. Beyond the operational advantage of land basing were the less tangible political and psychological benefits derived from permanent bases. The Johnson Administration decided to build permanent bases in South Vietnam and Thailand as a signal of commitment that could not be duplicated by aircraft carriers.[82] No one knew in these early years that the Vietnam base complex would one day become a painful reminder of U.S. abandonment.

Proposals to expand the role of sea power transcended fiscal self-interests. The Vietnam War and flexible response produced larger and more evenly distributed defense budgets than in previous years. Appropriations during the peak buildup years gave the Air Force a slightly higher budget than the Army or the Navy, but the margin was smaller than the lopsided defense budgets of the 1950s. The Air Force share of appropriations for fiscal years 1967 and 1968 was approximately $24 billion, compared to about $23 billion for the Army and $20.5 billion for the Navy. At the beginning of the 1960s, the Air Force received $19 billion during fiscal year 1960, compared to $9.3 billion for the Army and $11.6 billion for the Navy.[83]

The quest for a larger global Navy presence and counter-arguments from the Air Force lay in the realm of high policy and strategy, which was where such issues were decided. For now, the global threat required the sustained presence of land, sea, and air power on a scale sufficient to protect America's national interests.

During the early 1970s, however, U.S. policymakers returned to political goals that would not require a massive commitment of American military force. Through the 1960s an Army general headed the Joint Chiefs, mirroring the prominance of the ground war in Vietnam. President Nixon took office committed to gradual withdrawal of U.S. troops. He appointed Admiral Moorer as Chairman of the Joint Chiefs in 1970 and he served until mid-1974. Moorer was followed by two Air Force generals, George S. Brown and David C. Jones, whose terms spanned the next twelve years. During their combined terms, serving three Presidents—Gerald Ford, Jimmy Carter, and Ronald Reagan—there appeared to be greater emphasis on unity among the military services.

The Air Force suffered its share of budget defeats during the post-Vietnam era, including President Carter's 1977 decision to cancel the B–1 advanced strategic bomber. General David Jones, then serving as Air Force Chief of Staff, recalled that the Air Staff had put together "the finest argument possible" in support of the B–1, but Carter had announced his opposition to the bomber during his 1976 campaign. Jones said that he believed it was appropriate "to continue advocating the B–1 and giving our views" in congressional testimony, but after the President announced his decision, he did not allow Air Force members to lobby Congress to overturn it.

"This country is built on compromises and consensus," Jones said. "It is up to the military to make its case, and then salute smartly once that case is made." The exception, according to Jones, would only be if there was "something illegal, immoral, unethical" or if the services were prohibited from presenting their case. An "attempt to muzzle you before the Congress" would be an ethical issue, according to Jones.[84]

Asked if he considered resigning over the B–1 decision, Jones said that the idea had never crossed his mind because "it would have been totally inappropriate." Jones recalled a previous incident in which an admiral had threatened to resign if Congress did not agree to an additional carrier task force he had personally championed. The carriers were cut, but the admiral did not resign. Eventually, the carriers were reinstated. After Ronald Reagan was elected President, the Air Force got its B–1. Jones said he considered the Vietnam War to be the only event he experienced during his military service that might have warranted a protest resignation. If a military leader had resigned, Jones believed it would probably have been for the wrong reasons, such as the political constraints and tight controls placed on prosecution of the war. He concluded:

> The more fundamental reason is how in the world did we get ourselves involved in a land war in Southeast Asia where we tried to fight the war rather than let the Vietnamese fight the war and we support them. To have avoided Vietnam in retrospect was so important that anything that could have helped avoid Vietnam was almost worth doing.[85]

Before becoming Air Force Chief of Staff in 1974, General Jones had served as Commander in Chief of the United States Air Forces in Europe, where he spearheaded efforts to build greater unity into NATO air forces. As Chief of Staff, he sought cohesion between the Air Force and other services. As JCS Chairman after 1978, Jones built on his tradition of championing unity and jointness among the armed forces.

In 1975, Jones negotiated an agreement recognizing increased Air Force collateral responsibilities in naval warfare. Since World War II, the Air Force had supported various maritime operations, such as aerial surveillance during the Cuban missile crisis, but the support was sporadic and of short duration. In the early 1970s, however, two successive Chiefs of Naval Operations, Adm. Elmo Zumwalt and Adm. J.L. Holloway, welcomed Air Force assistance in meeting the Soviet maritime threat. With Secretary of Defense James Schlesinger's support, General Jones and Admiral Holloway formalized arrangements for the Air Force to participate in maritime operations.[86]

After this agreement, the Air Force increased joint training with the Navy, using B–52s for aerial surveillance and mine laying. It increased the capabilities of the B–52 to include an offensive naval warfare role. Although Schlesinger approved arming B–52s for sea interdiction, progress in working out the agreement with the Navy was slow. Jones recalled:

> At first the Navy didn't want any part of it…We finally decided to go ahead…[but] had to promise that… we would not claim that we could have sunk the U.S. Navy on every sea surveillance mission, or that we would not use sea surveillance as a force structure builder. On the other hand, the Navy would not claim they easily shot down every B–52 that came within 500 miles.[87]

General Jones carried out his initiatives to upgrade and unify the conventional NATO air posture in the shadow of Soviet control over employment of Warsaw Pact air forces, especially in the vital central European region. NATO flanks presented special problems for unity of command, with American forces in the southern area adding to the complications. It was difficult to rationalize the need for unity with U.S. carriers operating independently in the Mediterranean or when U.S. Marines resisted placing their air forces under centralized NATO direction. Never satisfied with the control arrangements imposed by General Westmoreland in Vietnam, the Marines continued to challenge joint planning which gave the Air Force control of their aircraft. Still organized and equipped primarily for amphibious operations, the Marines remained ready to fight, but wanted to be employed as integrated air-ground teams.

The rigidity of this position brought the Marine Corps and the Navy into dispute with the Air Force and the Army, impairing JCS efforts to develop contingency plans for the Rapid Deployment Joint Task Force formed in 1980 to deal with military threats outside NATO and Korea. Thus, there remained serious doubts about Allied unity as long as U.S. armed forces could not work out their own problems with unity of command.[88]

The Marine Corps position on command and control in joint force situations was that Marine air power was "subject to the joint force commander's direction as to the application of that air power...wherever it is most needed," but not under the control of the air component commander. The Marine Corps Deputy Chief of Staff for Air, Maj. Gen. H.S. Hill, reiterated this position before a Senate subcommittee investigating close air support in 1971, contradicting General Momyer's interpretation of his responsibilities as Air Deputy for Marine air resources during and after the 1968 defense of Khe Sanh. The Marines interpreted the command arrangements in Vietnam as placing "the assignment of priorities" for Marine air power directly "underneath the joint force commander General Westmoreland, and later, General Abrams," not the MACV Air Deputy.

"The Marines retained sorties necessary to support [Marine Corps] peculiar operations," Hill said, while the MACV Commander allocated "the other remaining sorties" through the Tactical Air Support Element in Saigon. According to Hill, Momyer's responsibilities entailed coordinating "the fragging of these aircraft with the 1st Marine Air Wing." Hill's argument ignored Momyer's responsibility to the MACV commander for allocation and application of tactical air power.[89] Such differing interpretations remained unresolved well into the 1970s.

The 1971 Senate hearings dealt with "the thorny issue of roles and missions," in the context of close air support. At this point, the use of the Army's advanced helicopter, the Cheyenne, as a close air support platform provoked opposition from some congressmen who felt the helicopter duplicated the Air Force's proposed close air support aircraft, the A–10. Although the Air Force withdrew its objections to Army development of helicopter gunships in the 1966

Roles and Missions

McConnell-Johnson agreement, Senator William Proxmire and a small group of colleagues renewed the challenge.

Concerned with the soaring costs of new weapons, Proxmire's group recommended terminating the Cheyenne and designating the A–10 "as the primary system for the future support of Army ground troops in Europe." This group of politicians believed that the Air Force should retain "the primary close support mission" if it demonstrated "it will give the Army adequate and continued support." They also recommended that the Defense Department "clarify the responsibilities of the Navy and the Marines, respectively, in providing close air support for Marine Corps infantry operations."[90]

Army witnesses testified that the Cheyenne performed a different role than Air Force tactical aircraft, although both provided battlefield support. When someone suggested that the Army be given primary responsibility for providing close air support for its own troops, the Army Assistant Chief of Staff for Force Development, Lt. Gen. Robert R. Williams, strongly disagreed. "They are two different missions," he explained, pointing out that Army gunships provided mobility and firepower which could not be duplicated by fixed wing aircraft.

Air Force tactical fighters, on the other hand, provided essential firepower support to ground troops and were "an integral part of the whole combat air mission," to include "air superiority, tactical reconnaissance, and interdiction." Furthermore, tactical air force missions were "closely related to the more strategic mission, escorting of the bombers." Williams explained that tactical aircraft and missions were interchangeable and that assigning the close air support mission to the Army "would be quite troublesome" in the total air battle, "particularly in the form of where does close air support end and where does interdiction start."[91]

Marine Corps witnesses defended the need for close air support from both Navy and Marine tactical air forces with similar arguments. Marine airmen flew close support for Marines on the ground, while the Navy was responsible for the full range of aerial missions. Testimony by Marine witnesses seemed to support the Army argument that its helicopter gunships were not categorized as close air support aircraft. The Marines had used Cobra gunships in Vietnam for "close-in fire suppression support for troops and cargo carrying helicopters," but General Hill told Congress that the Marines did not consider armed helicopters as "close air support aircraft within the same context as fixed-wing jet aircraft."[92]

While witnesses made convincing arguments that the Army's employment of armed helicopters did not duplicate the Air Force's A–10, the old question of competition among the services to develop aircraft to support surface operations would rise again as costs soared higher and budgets grew thinner. For the time, each service made a good case for their roles and weapons. It was generally agreed that the Air Force should retain responsibility for close air support to the Army.

Overall, the 1971 hearings strengthened the existing assignment of roles and missions. Admiral Moorer saw no reason to tamper with this issue, saying that in more than four years of attending meetings of the Joint Chiefs, he had not seen an agenda to address revision of roles and missions. Deputy Secretary of Defense David Packard said, "We look to the Chiefs as our advisors in these matters." For now matters stood.[93]

Having resolved their basic differences during the Vietnam War, the Air Force and the Army reached a new plateau of cooperation even though there remained contentious issues to be settled before the services would agree on air-ground roles and missions for the future. The Air Staff appeared to accept armed helicopters as an integral part of Army firepower, but doubts persisted about these weapons. The Army believed that their helicopters gave ground forces in Vietnam an edge in maneuverability against an enemy who retained the advantage of sanctuary, initiative, movement, and surprise. From the Air Force perspective, Army plans to extend the helicopter's use into more sophisticated air and ground environments was another matter.[94]

The Air Staff cautioned against taking lessons from Vietnam out of context. Lack of enemy air capability outside North Vietnam had given the Army a permissive air environment for its helicopters and the Air Force "some extra freedom" in employment of its tankers and other vulnerable planes. While Seventh Air Force Commander General Brown acknowledged the "good job" the helicopters were doing, he doubted they could survive without absolute air supremacy.[95]

The measurement of helicopter attrition rates in Vietnam was at times as controversial as "body counts." The Army admitted high helicopter loss rates in areas of intense enemy air defense fire, but allegedly concealed some combat losses through a reporting system that listed only aircraft that were totally destroyed. The Army also found that it needed "the equivalent of several major airfield complexes" to operate its air mobility units in Vietnam. The question of base survivability, used by the Army to argue against Air Force tactical capabilities in the early 1960s, now reflected upon itself, but this did not hinder Army helicopter research and development. During the war, the Army's inventory grew to 12,000 aircraft, mostly helicopters, and the Army modified its doctrine to emphasize use of the attack helicopter and developed the Cheyenne for more intense combat conditions.[96]

Among the most useful lessons from Vietnam was the melding of Air Force and Army air support capabilities. Despite their differences, the two services developed and implemented effective joint doctrine. General McConnell and Army Gen. Harold K. Johnson established joint coordinating teams under project New Focus in August 1965. Progress was evident in 1973 testimony before the House Armed Services Committee when Army leaders defended both services' capabilities in the close air support role. General Abrams, now Army Chief of Staff, told Congress that there was "nothing in the world" like the Air Force's centralized system of air support, and it could not be replaced by helicopters.[97]

Responding to suggestions from a House Committee member that development of the advanced helicopter might be a subterfuge to replace tactical aviation, Secretary of the Army Robert F. Froehlke countered that the Air Force had a definite role in close air support. At the same time, Froehlke believed that the Army needed its own air support capabilities. There was room and need for both, according to Froehlke. "I think that a helicopter and fixed wing is as good a line as you can draw," he said. "I think it is a sensible arrangement whereby we say the organic Army unit will be helicopter, the Air Force will have fixed wing."[98]

In 1971 Senate hearings on close air support General Momyer's voice stood apart in challenging Army development of the Cobra and the Cheyenne. Momyer had served as TAC Commander since returning from Vietnam, and steadfastly opposed the Army advanced helicopter program. He believed that Army helicopter gunships flew close air support, duplicating the Air Force's assigned mission. He warned that the Cheyenne, like the Cobra, was "just an interim step."

"An army aviator is no different than any other aviator," Momyer said, "He is going to want to go faster; he is going to want to go farther and he is going to want to carry more bomb load." Momyer criticized the 1966 McConnell-Johnson agreement and saw no need to change the assignment of roles and missions as agreed at Key West in 1948. Drawing the relationship between new weapon systems and assignment of roles and missions, Momyer said:

> I don't think we ought to let hardware determine the roles and missions. I think hardware is a manifestation of the roles and missions and every organization or endeavor has got to have a clear objective; and I think that the roles and missions states the objective and then the hardware is developed to the objective and not vice versa; and the development of the helicopter, it seems to me, is no different in terms of the performance of close air support than any other type of aircraft. The fact that it takes off vertically is only a means to get into the air so that it can deliver the firepower.[99]

General Momyer explained that the roles and missions problem did not lie in the various acts and agreements between the services since World War II, which "properly elaborated on the intent of the congressional acts," but that it came from not following these directives. Momyer pointed to the "four air forces performing tactical air operations, one each in the Air Force, Army, Navy, and Marines," and contended that the nation could not afford "such needless duplication," even though it came from "honest differences of opinion between professional military men and their desire for organic firepower in their own aviation." This seemed evident in the fact that the Senate was "trying to decide between three weapons systems, each from a different service, all competing for the same mission, close air support." Momyer concluded that close air support was:

> A mission, in my judgment, properly assigned to the Air Force by the intent of the National Security Act of 1947 and subse-

quent DOD directives. So we are really deciding which service is going to be given equipment to perform the Air Force mission.[100]

Senator Symington agreed with General Momyer, saying that it was "clear as light" that an effort was underway "to usurp the assigned mission of ground support the Air Force was given in the Key West agreement." As the first Secretary of the Air Force, Symington said he had learned long ago "the conviction that air power is indivisible," and that "if we follow every engineering theorist and every planebuilder, we are going to end up not only bankrupt, but we will jeopardize the mission." He predicted that the Senate hearings would result in a decision to "keep everybody happy." "We cannot decide which of these three airplanes we want most, so let's build them all," he said.[101] Senator Symington was correct as the consensus went against his belief that close air support was a roles and missions issue.

General Brown's appointment as Air Force Chief of Staff in August 1973 brought together a veteran air-ground team from the Vietnam War. Brown and General Abrams ordered a continuing dialogue on areas of mutual interest in the Pentagon and between the Air Force and the Army. They hoped to improve cooperation and resolve issues where divergent views persisted. Their goal was "to reduce unnecessary overlap and duplication of effort...and to seek more effective and efficient methods for designing, developing, procuring, and employing combat and combat-related systems."[102]

This dialogue continued after Gen. David C. Jones became Air Force Chief of Staff in 1974. While building conventional NATO force capabilities, Jones planned for the Air Force's A–10 close air support aircraft and the Army's Cheyenne attack helicopters to be deployed to Europe when they became available. Jones and Army Chief of Staff Gen. Frederick C. Weyand asserted that these new weapon systems were not duplicative in a joint statement released in April 1976. General Jones acknowledged that the Air Force did not believe that Army attack helicopters duplicated Air Force close air support because of their "limited range, speed and firepower." Together, the two systems offered "a complementary capability in terms of a wider spectrum of fire support, enhanced responsiveness, flexibility and capability."

The two chiefs agreed that attack helicopters were integral to Army ground maneuver units and would be employed with or behind forces on the forward edge of the battle area. They would provide escort and suppressive fire to counter enemy armor. It was understood that Air Force close air support resources were essential to fully exploit the capabilities of tactical air power.[103]

Meanwhile, the Army began to reorient its doctrine to accommodate the advanced technology of its attack helicopter forces. This reorientation owed more to lessons from the brief 1973 Arab-Israeli war than from Vietnam and corresponded with a renewed emphasis on the conventional land battle in Europe.

Roles and Missions

The Mideast experience convinced Army leaders they needed to revise their doctrine to reflect technological changes brought to the field of combat.

General William E. DuPuy led this doctrinal revision as Commander of the Army's Training and Doctrine Command. His guidance resulted in publication of Army Field Manual 100-5 in July 1976. The Manual envisioned a rapidly shifting combat environment where victory would demand swift concentration of combined arms, principally air mobile anti-armor weapons, attack helicopters, and close air support aircraft.[104]

While doubts remained about helicopter survivability in a high-threat environment, the Air Force agreed that the new Army manual provided a good doctrinal foundation within the firepower mix available for battlefield support in Europe. Senior American ground commanders in Europe, however, soon found the new doctrine too defensive. Their experience convinced them that a more offensively minded air-land battle doctrine, integrating Army helicopters into the total air engagement was necessary.

They had learned during NATO war games that Army commanders had to extend their attacks beyond the forward edge of the battle "into the zone of the enemy's second echelon forces" to halt a Warsaw Pact advance. Ground commanders coined a new phrase-"battlefield air interdiction," to distinguish between the air operations area and deep interdiction zones that were the responsibility of the air component commander. In 1978, NATO air forces in the central region revised their operational doctrine accordingly.[105]

At home, the Army hastened to rewrite its operational doctrine to capture the NATO experience and expand the air-land battle concept worldwide. DuPuy's successor oversaw these efforts under the direction of the new Army Chief of Staff, Gen. Edward C. Meyer. Reflecting the joint spirit, the Army kept the Air Force informed of its progress on the new manual, allowing both TAC and the Air Staff to comment on the revised version before its publication in 1982.

Concerns remained, however, before the air-land battle concept could be defined as joint doctrine. Treating close-in interdiction as part of the total battlefield dynamics obscured the lines between corps and air component control and was a potentially disruptive problem which required close monitoring at the theater level. Questions of resource apportionment and allocation also required theater-level coordination between corps and air component commanders. The new doctrine added complications to joint air-ground cooperation, but the Air Force and the Army appeared dedicated to making the air-land battle concept work.[106]

While the end of the Vietnam War brought greater unity to roles and missions progression, the rise of military space technology opened a new frontier of interservice competition. In the aftermath of Sputnik, Presidents Eisenhower and Kennedy had accelerated U.S. space efforts, taking steps to avoid another arms race with the Soviet Union. In 1957, Eisenhower sponsored a United

Nations resolution and treaty prohibiting member nations from placing offensive weapons in space. In 1958, he formed the National Aeronautics and Space Administration (NASA) to oversee the national space program. Kennedy challenged NASA to create a dynamic program leading to a lunar landing by the end of the decade.

In the Pentagon, Secretary McNamara set new space policy for the armed forces-limiting development of defensive systems to those which held "a distinct promise of enhancing military power and effectiveness", and requiring them "to mesh with NASA's program in all vital areas." McNamara hoped to control the cost of military space systems as well as avoid rivalry and duplication.[107]

In March 1961, McNamara issued Department of Defense Directive 5100.32 designating the Air Force as the central point of contact for military space development programs and projects, but reaffirming that other services retained vital interests in space technology, principally through the use of satellites "for strategic intelligence, surveillance, communications, navigation, western, and other similar activities." One exception to Air Force space responsibilities was the Navy's Transit family of navigational satellites which became operational in 1964.[108] Officially, the Air Force's strategic concern in space "was to deny hostile use...to other nations by maintaining certain defensive systems and by using space for surveillance." Tactically, the Air Force deployed "communications satellites and other vehicles...in support of terrestrial operations."[109]

Competing priorities such as the Vietnam War and NASA's Apollo program stifled progress in military space programs through the 1960s and the Air Force lost two costly projects. In 1963, McNamara terminated the Air Force's Dyna-Soar experimental space glider program, yet approved an Air Force effort to develop a manned orbital laboratory. As the 1960s drew to a close, a new Secretary of Defense, Melvin R. Laird, cancelled the orbital laboratory citing funding limitations.[110]

In September 1970, a new directive replaced the 1961 space directive. Issued by Deputy Defense Secretary David Packard, the revised directive did not change "existing assignment of responsibilities for on-going space systems," but required that future "development and acquisition of space systems" follow the same "functional responsibilities within OSD and the Military Departments for acquiring major weapon systems." Packard reaffirmed the Director of Defense Research and Engineering as "focal point for space technology and space systems" to "monitor all space activity to minimize system technical risk and cost, to prevent unwarranted duplication, and to assure that a space program assigned to one department meets the needs of other departments."

The Air Force was assigned "responsibility for development, production and deployment of space systems for warning and surveillance of enemy nuclear delivery capabilities and all launch vehicles, including launch and orbital support operations."[111] The Air Force became the Defense Department Executive Agent for the space transportation system under development by NASA.[112]

A trail of doctrinal revisions over two decades led to the formal declaration of the Air Force mission in space in 1979. Twenty years earlier, the Air Force had replaced the phrase "air power" with "aerospace power," to capture the extension of Air Force operations into space. Until 1979, the Air Force treated space as a medium rather than a mission, defining aerospace "as the region above the earth's surface, composed of both atmosphere and space," providing "a unique medium for military space operations."[113]

The first formal treatment of space as an Air Force mission appeared in an updated version of Air Force Manual 1-1, *Functions and Basic Doctrine of the United States Air Force*, published in February 1979, which listed "space operations" as one of nine basic operational missions. The Air Force mission in space was "to conduct three types of space operations: space support; force enhancement; and space defense." The Manual stated that space systems multiplied the effectiveness of surface, sea, and aerospace force, performing global surveillance, serving as penetration aids, enhancing global communications and worldwide command and control, serving as positioning and navigational aids, and producing detailed, timely meteorological information.[114]

Thus, as the 1970s ended, the Air Force had responsibility for "development and deployment of space systems" and had defined its space mission. There still was no formal statement of space roles and missions in other joint directives.[115] Not unlike the early years of military aviation, the Air Force had primary responsibility for space, while each service retained a vital interest in systems related to their assigned roles and missions in space.

To summarize, the center of gravity for the 1970s was a lodestar of unity rising from the turbulent 1960s, a roles and missions sequel to the Vietnam War. While the war divided the nation, it brought the armed forces closer. Opening in a vortex of interservice rivalry, the war evolved as a costly, painful, unwanted offspring of the transition from massive retaliation to the strategy of flexible response. The new strategy emerged as a centrifugal force of competing roles, missions, weapons systems, and force objectives. As U.S. forces withdrew from Vietnam, the rivalry subsided, allowing the maturation process to begin. While minor differences remained, the armed forces demonstrated a greater propensity to pull together than at any time since enactment of the National Security Act of 1947.

While increased consensus on roles and missions eased the burden of joint concerns awaiting future airmen, enough unreconciled issues remained to ensure a suspenseful future. Open to contention was the position that Army helicopter firepower did not constitute close air support. That issue remained potentially divisive because it permitted independent Army air operations to go uncontested, while Air Force doctrine required that Navy and Marine Corps tactical air forces be subject to centralized control during joint operations. At the same time, all services wondered how far the Air Force would allow the Army to expand its airland battle concept.

Increasing interest in space systems honed the competitive edge in the roles and missions medium, while a consensus was building for legislation to streamline command lines and strengthen the role of the JCS chairman. In addressing these and other issues, closer cooperation among the services was the key if flexible response was to mature as a viable military strategy.

CHAPTER VII

CHANGE AND CONSEQUENCE: THE MATURING OF ROLES AND MISSIONS

Before the guns fell silent, the American failure in Vietnam conditioned U.S. forces for years of change and consequence ahead. Admitting that "we made an awful lot of mistakes" in the war, Gen. David Jones recalled that realization "came home" to him when he returned to Saigon in early 1975 to find a "smell of defeat in the air." President Gerald Ford had diverted the Air Force Chief of Staff from a Pacific trip to Saigon to assure the demoralized government of Nguyen Van Thieu of unwavering support, a promise the Ford administration was unable to keep.

General Jones said that this visit along with the fall of Saigon four months later convinced him that American forces had failed to build "confidence into the Vietnamese forces." At the same time, U.S. forces had spent "an awful lot of money on Vietnam that drained us in lots of areas-the Army more than others."

"Post-Vietnam was a traumatic period where it was clear that a lot of things had to change," Jones said. "It was a time of some real fundamental looking at where we were going and to try and rebuild confidence in ourselves, in the country, and in the military."[1]

General Jones played a central role in reversing the erosion of confidence spawned by the Vietnam experience. He believed that rebuilding confidence required the armed forces to stop arguing among themselves and to meld their combined resources into an efficient engine of war. Problems he experienced as Commander in Chief of the United States Air Forces in Europe from 1971 to 1974 made Jones determined to remove obstacles to cohesive air warfighting. Mindful of the "five separate air wars" fought in Vietnam, Jones integrated allied tactical air power in NATO's central region during his tour in Europe. On NATO's southern flank, however, an attempt to bring Navy and Marine forces under allied command and control encountered difficulties not unlike those which had fragmented air operations in Vietnam. Jones' quest for greater interoperability and more cohesive joint warfighting extended through his years as Air Force Chief of Staff from 1974 to 1978 and as Chairman of the Joint Chiefs of Staff until 1982.[2]

The matter of "jointness" took on added weight after the Vietnam War. Extension of the flexible response strategy into the forward areas to counter "the modernization, expansion, and forward deployment" of Soviet forces made joint doctrine and interoperability more compelling than in the fog of Vietnam jungle combat. Even more critical was the "relentless and aggressive strategic buildup by the Soviet Union" believed to have altered the balance of power in favor of the Kremlin.

Roles and Missions

By 1981, the Reagan Administration reported "an unabating diminution of the capability of United States strategic forces relative to like Soviet forces." While U.S. forces had been "living off the weapons and technology lead...carefully developed in the 1950s and early 1960s," the Administration said, "the Soviets [had] never reversed, slowed, or even perturbed their robust strategic development and deployment programs in spite of detente, ongoing arms control negotiations, or the self-imposed restraints in our own strategic programs."[3]

Adding to East-West tensions, the 1979 Soviet invasion of Afghanistan unmasked Kremlin aggression at a crucial point in U.S. relations with the oil rich Persian Gulf states and the volatile Middle East. While not a direct threat to regional interests, the invasion damaged U.S. policy and prestige in a pivotal, unstable area of the world.

The United States suffered a major strategic setback in the region when Islamic fundamentalists toppled Reza Shah Pahlavi's pro-Western government in Iran. In his 1980 State of the Union message, President Jimmy Carter had warned against "any outside force" attempting "to gain control of the Persian Gulf region." He stated that any such attempt would be "regarded as an assault on the vital interests of the United States" and would be "repelled by use of any means necessary, including military force."

The aggression against neighboring Afghanistan, already in the Soviet camp, was a different matter. The Carter Administration followed by the Reagan Administration, settled on a strategy to arm and equip Afghan guerillas to resist the Red Army.[4] No one knew that a protracted war in Afghanistan would eventually burden the Soviet Union with its own "crisis of confidence," not unlike the American experience in Vietnam.

The Iranian crisis, prompting suppression of Western influence and seizure of the American embassy in Tehran, escalated when Iraqi forces invaded western Iran in September 1980. While both the U.S. and Soviet governments tacitly supported Iraq, neither country supported an all-out victory by either side. After the Shah's ouster in 1979, deployment of two carrier battle groups into the Indian Ocean created a more visible American military presence in the Gulf region. At MacDill AFB, Florida, the newly formed Rapid Deployment Joint Task Force (RDJTF) rushed into action. An abortive mission to rescue American hostages in Iran, however, added to post-Vietnam perceptions that the armed forces were "inept" at carrying out even small joint operations. While naval deployments and the failed rescue mission opened a new era in the projection of U.S. military power into the troubled Gulf region, the perceived "ineptness" of military capabilities carried over into the first term of the Reagan Administration.[5]

"The perception of our inability to respond adequately and promptly has served to encourage Soviet and Soviet-inspired exploitation of areas of instability," Secretary of Defense Caspar W. Weinberger stated in early 1981. Testifying before the Senate Armed Services Committee, Weinberger said there was "clear evidence of aggressive Soviet activity around the globe." The United States and its allies faced "a spectrum of threats-from covert aggression, terrorism, and subversion to overt intimidation to use of brute force."

At the lower end of the spectrum, Third World violence was a leading export of rogue states across the Middle East and surrounding areas. The "massive arms build-up" by the Soviet Union was a more pressing concern. Weinberger warned that the Soviets were dangerously close to achieving "clear military superiority" and could be expected "to exploit that military capability even more fully than they are now doing."[6]

Weinberger later said that the early Reagan defense program had "but one overriding priority: to rebuild American military strength as rapidly as possible." A near-term effort to modernize and achieve "counter-balancing strength" was part of a long-term strategy "to invest in those new forces required to bring us safely into the next century and beyond." Weinberger said that coupling reinvigorated armed strength "with such a clear determination to resist aggression that we discourage challenges" was a central thread in Reagan's defense strategy. Negotiations for strategic arms reductions from a position of strength provided a complementary thread. Acknowledging that rethinking strategic concepts would take time, Weinberger's declaration promised that the armed forces would no longer be haunted by the ghosts of Vietnam:

> ...once a decision to employ some degree of force has been made and the purpose clarified, our government must have the clear mandate to carry out, and continue to carry out, that decision until the purpose has been achieved.[7]

With a strong NATO-Europe bearing its share of the collective security burden and "the rearming of America" underway at home, the Reagan defense strategy brought unexpected consequences for the Soviet Union. By the mid-1980s, a failing Soviet economy showed the strains of the arms race. By the end of Reagan's second term, economic decline, ethnic unrest, and a new Kremlin policy of openness contributed to the collapse of the Soviet empire, bringing an end to the Cold War.

Without fanfare, the global threat receded to the shadows of regional tyranny and international terrorism, but U.S. armed forces were prepared for the new threat and adept at wielding military power against any level of aggression. The Air Force experience in using joint air power against Iraqi aggression during the 1991 Persian Gulf War attested to the wisdom of technological growth in the 1980s and the maturing of roles and missions.

New Initiatives in Jointness and Interoperability

The Reagan Administration's blueprint for "rearming America" mandated "heavy defense spending" through the 1980s and beyond. The staggering cost of

Roles and Missions

maintaining conventional readiness on a global level and funding the strategic weapons needed to overtake the Soviet lead encountered increasing congressional resistance as the decade wore on. Nevertheless, landslide elections in 1980 and 1984 along with success in communicating the extent of the Soviet threat enabled Reagan's programs to withstand partisan opposition. At the start of President Reagan's second term in 1985, Secretary Weinberger still voiced concern about the Soviet's "increased numbers of supersonic bombers and increasingly accurate nuclear ballistic missiles launched from hardened silos or from mobile launchers." Weinberger warned that the Soviet Union had, through "strategic force deployments and exercises, given clear indications it believes that, under certain circumstances, nuclear wars may be fought and won."[8]

Reflecting both inflation and resurgent growth in military strength, defense budgets in the 1980s eclipsed Vietnam-era outlays. The Reagan Administration's proposal to bring the strategic Triad into balance against the Soviet nuclear threat was reflected in larger appropriations for the Air Force and Navy than for the Army. Budget authorizations for fiscal year 1983, for example, totaled about $74 billion for the Air Force, $81.9 billion for the Navy, and $57.5 billion for the Army. Over the next six years, the Army's share of the budget averaged $74 billion, while the Air Force and Navy averages rose to $93.2 billion and $94.3 billion respectively.[9] Ample defense budgets funded an array of new weapon systems which increased the reach and readiness of air power and alleviated the interservice rivalry and air weaponry debates of past years.

The transition to flexible response guided the development of modern tactical fighters. In addition to the A–10 to meet the Army's close-air-support requirements, the Air Force acquired the F–15 Eagle and the F–16 Fighting Falcon as its primary tactical fighter aircraft. Designed as an air superiority fighter, the F–15 could be used in a variety of tactical roles. The F–16, a compact, versatile aircraft, was an advanced lightweight fighter. Some Air Force tactical units still flew F–111s, introduced in the late 1960s and combat-tested in Vietnam. These aircraft deployed to Europe in the early 1970s.

Increased appropriations permitted the Air Force to explore technological breakthroughs to give its tactical forces a decisive combat edge before the end of the decade. In Panama and Iraq, force enhancements including new F–117 stealth fighters proved the value of state-of-the-art lethality and survivability and air power's readiness for the roles and missions challenges of the next generation.[10]

To strengthen strategic deterrence, President Reagan revived the B–1 advanced bomber and approved acquisition of the B–2 stealth bomber. Programs brought forward from the 1970s included the E–3 airborne warning and control system, the KC–10A extended aerial refueler, and the air-launched cruise missile. The Air Force still flew B–52 bombers, some of them older than the pilots who flew them.

Secretary Weinberger considered the President's antimissile Strategic Defense Initiative (SDI) to be "this administration's boldest departure from the past." Costly deterrent programs like SDI and the MX missile contributed to dismantling of nuclear arsenals and to the end of the Cold War, but support for these expensive programs wavered as the Soviet nuclear threat diminished.[11]

Because strong naval forces remained essential to the projection of military power in the post-Vietnam era, the Reagan defense program called for the Navy's "expansion to 600 ships." Nuclear-armed Trident submarines were part of this expansion and helped to counterbalance Soviet gains in underwater nuclear strike capabilities. The Soviets anchored their forward strategy to a menacing submarine fleet, which reportedly outnumbered the Navy's by three to one in the mid-1980s.

As the superpowers negotiated to reduce or eliminate land-based missiles, Defense Department statistics revealed that the balance of U.S. long-range striking power was "shifting almost unnoticed from land to sea." This shift, which raised the Navy's strategic nuclear warheads to nearly half that carried by land-based missiles or bombers, "had taken place as eight Trident submarines...joined the fleet, each with 24 missiles with 8 warheads."[12] By the end of the 1980s, the nation's strategic forces included 584 fleet ballistic launchers on Poseidon and Trident submarines, 1,000 ICBMs, 154 B–52s, and 90 B–1 Bombers.[13]

American naval capabilities clearly prevailed over those of the Soviet Union in carrier aviation. While U.S. maritime strategy emphasized development of larger and faster aircraft carriers, the Soviet navy did not put aircraft at sea until 1967, when it deployed "the 17,000-ton aircraft-carrying cruiser or helicopter carrier *Moskva*, joined by a sister ship the following year." In 1974, the Soviet navy commissioned the 37,000-ton *Kiev*, the first of four second generation heavier aircraft-carrying cruisers equipped with vertical take-off and landing aircraft. Economic and political upheaval jeopardized a 1980s Soviet program to build its first large-deck carrier, the 64,000-ton Admiral *Kuznetsov*, and two additional ships.[14]

Meanwhile, U.S. Navy carrier forces continued their prominent role in projecting military power and protecting vital interests overseas. By President Reagan's second term, the Navy boasted that aircraft carriers were the "big Stick" against "terrorism and global tensions" during an "era of violent peace." Flexible use of sea power to deal with minor crises in regions like the Mediterranean and the Persian Gulf was deemed expedient because carriers could land Marines and launch air strikes without having to obtain host-country approval or overflight rights. The tragic loss of Marines in the terrorist bombing of a military barracks in Lebanon in 1983 warned of the perils of basing token forces for protracted periods in hostile land.[15]

That Air Force F–111s based in the United Kingdom were part of the joint strike force employed against Libya was nearly lost in the attention focused on the Sixth Fleet afterward. The Navy declared the Libyan raid was "more than just a victory over Muammer Gaddafi." Admiral William J. Crowe, Chairman of the Joint Chiefs, and other naval officers viewed the raid as vindication against critics who charged that the United States was financing history's "most expensive

General Charles A. Gabriel worked to develop stronger cooperation between the Air Force and the other services during his tenure as Air Force Chief of Staff in the early 1980s. *(National Archives photo)*

naval museum" after the Battle of the Falklands. If British losses to Exocet missiles in the Falkland Islands campaign made aircraft carriers obsolete, the admirals pondered why Gaddafi "dared not send his 535-plane air force aloft to challenge the Sixth Fleet." The media reported that the *Carl Vinson*, the newest and most powerful aircraft carrier, was "a symbol of the Reagan Administration's new globalism, in which the 19th century notion of gunboat diplomacy has been transformed into one of aircraft carrier diplomacy."[16]

From the Air Force perspective, the carefully orchestrated air raid against Libya exemplified advancements made in joint operations with the Navy. Another milestone came in 1982 when Air Force Chief of Staff, Gen. Charles A. Gabriel, and Chief of Naval Operations, Adm. James D. Watkins, signed a comprehensive agreement to formalize joint maritime operations involving Air Force aircraft employed in an offensive maritime role. "We will be putting more emphasis on such collateral roles as sea-land protection, aerial maneuvering, and ship attack," Gen. Gabriel said, noting that the Falklands demonstrated the contribution that land-based airpower could make to ocean warfare. Although Congress killed plans to arm B–52s for anti-ship operations, Navy Secretary John F. Lehman and Congress backed the agreement.[17]

The push to formalize Air Force and Navy cooperation came from Secretary of Defense Weinberger who believed "the Soviet threat [had] become too large for either service to handle by itself." Weinberger felt it was essential for the Navy to take advantage of Air Force capabilities in ocean warfare, and that the Air Force needed to rely on Navy aircraft and cruise missiles to assist in striking inland tactical targets.

In 1982, Weinberger urged the services "to work more earnestly at melding their systems, doctrine, and weapons" to get "their combat effectiveness and efficiency up," and "their costs down." On another occasion, the Defense Secretary stated that no service would ever "go to war by itself." "Military objectives can be achieved only by joint planning and operations that integrate all combat arms," he said.[18] In 1984, the Air Force included expanded maritime roles in its doctrine.[19]

General Gabriel and his Army counterpart, Gen. John A. Wickham, Jr., were intent to make further improvements in jointness and interoperability. During the spring of 1981, Air Force and Army staffs adopted a NATO tactical doctrine relating to offensive air support. Among other changes, the new doctrine distinguished between battlefield air interdiction against an immediate threat of advancing second-echelon enemy forces and traditional interdiction operations to interrupt lines of communication and the arteries of resupply and reinforcement. Ground commanders requested missions designated as battlefield air interdiction but the air component commander allocated such missions under centralized control.[20]

The 1981 agreement clarified the air component commander's role in allocating and apportioning air missions. While the unified commander was responsible for theater-wide application of air power, the air component commander made recommendations for apportioning the air effort consistent with the Air Force doctrine of centralized control and decentralized execution. Another initiative that same year clarified the authority of the air component commander to suppress enemy air defenses beyond the limits of Army responsibility for observed ground fire.[21]

After revising Field Manual 100-5 to embody air-land battle doctrine in 1982, the Army announced a reorganization of its organic aviation, including 8,100 rotary-wing and 500 fixed-wing aircraft, consistent with the new doctrine. The Army explained that the doctrine broadened Army aviation's role as a combat maneuver element and mandated "single manager responsibility for aviation matters." In April 1983, Secretary of the Army John O. Marsh, Jr. approved a separate aviation branch and announced plans to centralize the "proponency, or responsibility, for aviation matters" at Fort Rucker, Alabama. In 1984, Maj. Gen. Bobby J. Maddox, Commander of the new Aviation Center, described Army aviation as "landpower's third dimension," claiming that Army aviation was now "a full-fledged member of the combined arms team."[22]

On May 22, 1984, Generals Gabriel and Wickham signed a landmark agreement on 31 joint initiatives the Army and Air Force had identified as essential to development and "fielding of the most affordable and effective air-land combat forces." The initiatives addressed a variety of joint concerns, including theater air interdiction, battlefield air interdiction, manned tactical reconnaissance systems, intratheater airlift, air base ground defense, point air defense, surface-to-air missiles, and rear area close air support. The agreement evolved from two years of working on budgets "to ensure coordination and reduce overlap in the acquisition and development of systems." Hailed as a "revolutionary approach" to force cooperation, the agreement formalized the "participation of each service in the other's budget process" and committed them to a "long-term, dynamic process" to exchange, review, and update initiatives.[23]

Roles and Missions

Although critics complained that the initiatives ignored the root problem of functional duplication, Air Force acquiescence to the Army's air-land battle doctrine settled this issue, at least temporarily. The initiatives led to an agreement on manned aircraft two years later, replacing the 1966 McConnell-Johnson agreement, reaffirming the dominant role of the Air Force in providing close air support to the Army, and leaving rotary-wing development to the ground forces. The Air Force continued to operate a small force of about 100 helicopters for such specialized missions as search and rescue. General Gabriel wanted to develop a similar agreement with the Navy and the Marine Corps,[24] but burgeoning military competition in space and the Goldwater-Nichols reform of 1986 overtook this effort.

Roles, Missions, and the Unified Space Command

As the armed services reconciled their old rivalries in the post-Vietnam era, competition escalated in the military application of space technology. Cold War adversaries relied increasingly on space satellites to gather intelligence so that by the late 1980s, the military use of space included an array of communication systems, surveillance, and navigation. Space-based systems were a vital element of national security, opening "a new medium of warfare", over-arching the mediums of land, sea, and air. Anti-satellite and other space weapons systems were being developed in the 1960s, and the Reagan Administration's support of the anti-missile SDI program brought the advent of weapons in space a step closer.[25]

From the earliest days of U.S. space exploration, the Defense Department worked on research and development programs to adapt new technology to military operations. Not unlike the birth of military aviation, each service pursued technological breakthroughs in space to support their unique mission and each "envisioned its own independent role in space." While Eisenhower was the strongest proponent of military unity, his administration killed a 1959 Navy proposal to create a unified space command. Defense officials saw "little need for joint control over operational space systems that did not exist." Secretary of Defense McNamara issued Directive Number 5160.32, giving the Air Force primary responsiblity for space systems development, but interservice rivalry continued and accelerated after Secretary of Defense Laird opened up space systems development to the other services in 1970.[26]

In November 1984, the Pentagon announced President Reagan's approval of a unified command to manage space operations. A full quarter of a century after the Navy first proposed to centralize control of military space activities, the President made his decision as NASA prepared to launch its initial secret shuttle mission into space.[27]

Established on September 23, 1985, the United States Space Command centralized "operational responsibilities" formerly shared between the Air Force and the Navy.[28] With "over half of everything" sent into space having "military application,"[29] Pentagon officials felt they could no longer tolerate fragmented control of military space operations. They studied "the idea of a joint command for years, but reportedly were confronted with intransigence on the part of the two services to any merger."[30]

Only in the 1980s did the services begin to attach "the same operational emphasis" to space as they did to other missions. Galvanized by "increasing military dependence on space systems, new Soviet threats and far-reaching changes associated with space shuttle operations," the Air Force had activated its own Space Command in September 1982. Controversial even in the Air Force, the new command was expected to merge "into a unified command involving all the branches of the military with the Navy a leading partner."[31]

A year later, the Navy formed the Naval Space Command, with the understanding that it was also a prelude to a unified command structure. Viewing "space operations as an extension of the sea-an important role in keeping open lines of communication in space and protecting its assets," Navy hierarchy expressed concern that "ocean surveillance activities would get short shrift in a unified command" since the Air Force did not "strongly support its own space command."[32] Following activation of the unified space command, the Army moved to reestablish "its high level of space involvement," and three years later activated its own space command "to serve as the third major command component to the unified command."[33]

The mission of the unified Space Command was to support other unified and specified commands and "to enhance the use of space systems for all the armed forces." An Air Force general officer headed the new Command, with an admiral as deputy.[34] Widely reported as a "shift toward dominance by the Pentagon" in space programs,[35] the Space Command's birth was seen as a "shift toward non-nuclear defensive systems-many based in space-to serve as a defensive umbrella or shield" over the United States and its allies.[36] It was also a manifestation of the maturing military roles in space and their increased value to the combat effectiveness of land, sea, and air forces.

Goldwater-Nichols: Strengthening the Joint Structure

Before retiring in mid-1982, General Jones took an unprecedented step by criticizing the joint military structure before the House Armed Services Committee. The General testified that the joint system needed reform to strengthen both the JCS Chairman's role as well as the commanders in chief of the combatant commands. Jones felt that the only change of consequence since Eisenhower's reorganization was the granting of full member status to the Marine Corps commandant in 1978.

A lingering dispute under Jones' tenure was the Marines' unbending resistance to integrate their air support under Air Force control in joint operations. Concerned about the services' failure to resolve their differences, Jones believed that an overhaul of the joint structure was long overdue and would exorcise the ghosts of Vietnam and the botched rescue mission in Iran.[37]

In his proposal, General Jones did not advocate creating "an all-powerful Chairman", but believed it was essential to develop "a joint staff and a joint system that [were] not beholden to the services." He believed the reorganization should promote jointness, dispose of parochial service influences, and build greater cohesion into joint warfighting.[38] He argued that "we need to spend more time on our warfighting capabilities and less on intramural squabbles for resources."[39]

The Jones argument came as criticism of "the useless nature of compromised military advice, logrolling that takes the place of serious budget decisions, and service parochialism undercutting the authority of unified commanders" intensified.[40] Defense officials were well served by advice from individual members of the Joint Chiefs, but found corporate decisions less reliable. Air Force Chief of Staff General Lew Allen described such joint decisions as "mush."[41]

General Edward Meyer, whose tour as Army Chief of Staff was drawing to a close, shared Jones' concerns and urged sweeping reform. Arguing that "major surgery" might be needed, General Meyer recommended replacing the Joint Chiefs with an independent military advisory council with members divested of all service responsibilities. Prompted by the Jones and Meyer proposals, the House Armed Services Committee opened hearings on reorganization of the Joint Chiefs in 1982. A bill addressing some concerns passed in the House, but died in the Senate at the end of the 97th Congress opposed by Secretary of Defense Weinberger as well as past and present Navy leaders. Former Chairman Adm. Thomas Moorer argued that periodic calls to reorganize the Joint Chiefs "makes about as much sense as reorganizing Congress or the Supreme Court to stop disagreements."[42] Even the new Joint Chiefs rejected most reforms suggested by Jones and Meyer. General Jones' successor, former Army Chief of Staff General Vessey, told the House Armed Services Committee in 1983 that Joint Chiefs members agreed that his office should be part of the formal chain of command, but did not believe that he should be the principal military advisor because it would stifle the flow of advice from service chiefs.[43] Opposition to "major surgery" on the joint structure persisted through Reagan's first term, followed by a turnabout after the President's reelection in 1984.

President Reagan allowed Secretary Weinberger to make decisions on Pentagon reform, and the Secretary's resistance to radical change withstood mounting pressure from Congress. In addition to the proposals of Generals Jones and Meyer, congressional reformers heard recommendations from former defense officials and "various independent reports...nearly unanimous in calling for strengthening [the] JCS."[44]

Secretary Weinberger made modest structural reforms, including strengthening the involvement of service secretaries and commanders in chief of the unified and specified commands in deliberations of the Defense Resources Board.

He consulted with the Joint Chiefs and professed to "rely on the Joint Chiefs of Staff for military advice on a range of issues that I believe transcends those with which their predecessors have normally dealt." Such issues, Weinberger said, included "weapon system programs and the relative priorities among competing claims for our scarce resources."[45]

A pivotal influence in the wake of Reagan's reelection was a study conducted under the auspices of the Georgetown University Center for Strategic and International Studies which called "for a sweeping restructuring of the American military operation." Conducted by a distinguished panel of former defense officials, members of Congress, and academics, the Georgetown study was released in January 1985 and found the military structure "stagnated" and "paralyzed" by interservice rivalries, a condition pinpointed as "the underlying cause of bloated budgets, poor combat readiness, and a lack of coordination in operations."

Congressional participants included Democratic Representative Les Aspin of Wisconsin, the new Chairman of the House Armed Services Committee; Senator Sam Nunn of Georgia, ranking Democrat on the Senate Armed Services Committee; and Republican Senator William S. Cohen of Maine, Chairman of the subcommittee to oversee naval forces. Senator Barry Goldwater, Chairman of the Senate Armed Services Committee, was receptive to proposals for a major defense shakeup to make the Chairman of the Joint Chiefs the principal military adviser to the Secretary of Defense and the President and to give combatant commanders "more authority to override quarreling among the services and to influence the military budget."[46]

Consistent with their opposition to reorganizing the JCS, Navy leaders argued against the Georgetown reforms as Secretary of the Navy Lehman claimed they "would centralize too much power in Washington and diminish civilian control." The "man on horseback" argument had plagued attempts to strengthen the Chairman since the National Security Act of 1947.

The reorganization study created a dilemma for Secretary Weinberger, who just two weeks before its release told an interviewer he would not support major changes in the Joint Chiefs.[47] The release of the study, however, marked a turning point which led to a change in the Defense Secretary's views before the year ended.

The Senate Armed Services Committee issued another pivotal study on defense reorganization in October 1985, recommending changes to "the structure of America's military leadership" which were even more radical than the Georgetown report. The Senate study echoed Meyer's plan to replace the Joint Chiefs with a military advisory council, recommended strengthening the Office of the Secretary of Defense, and sought more power for unified commanders. The study found the position of Secretary of Defense weaker "today than when it was created by President Truman in 1947." It cited problems of coordination among the armed forces and questioned a predisposition to include all services in combat operations whether or not they were needed. The report suggested that the Navy and Marines could have operated alone in missions such as the 1983 invasion of Grenada.[48]

The Senate report met resistance from the Navy and its supporters in Congress. Admiral Moorer called it "the worst report I have ever read since I have been involved in Washington activities." Moorer reminded proponents of reform to remember that "the services are not organizations-they are institutions."[49] Virginia Senator John W. Warner, a former Secretary of the Navy, called the report a prescription for "open heart surgery" on a military system that had "given us 40 years of peace in Europe." Proponents of reform, with Senator Goldwater and Representative Bill Nichols leading the charge, saw this as a chance to achieve "the first comprehensive changes to how the military operates" since the Defense reorganization of 1958.[50]

A month after public release of the Senate report, the House of Representatives approved a bill to reorganize the Joint Chiefs along the lines drawn by General Jones and the Georgetown study group. Confronted with a lopsided defeat of 383-27 in the House and the probability of a more radical version by the Senate, Secretary of Defense Weinberger abruptly announced that the Administration had changed its stance on reform. In early December, he informed ranking members of the Senate Armed Services Committee that while he remained opposed to legislation abolishing the Joint Chiefs, the Administration was now amenable to moderate improvements, including measures to strengthen the Chairman's authority. Conceding that the Joint Chiefs "should be truly joint in composition and motivation," Weinberger said reforms "should avoid parochialism, but should fully consider competing service interests." Senator Goldwater welcomed Weinberger's change of heart, calling the Secretary's letter the start of a "comprehensive dialogue" toward enactment of meaningful legislation.[51]

President Reagan's endorsement of a report by his Blue Ribbon Commission on Defense Management sought to "preempt a growing congressional clamor for reform of the Pentagon." Chaired by former Deputy Secretary of Defense David Packard, the Commission proposed strengthening the authority of the Chairman and theater commanders to "overcome the interservice rivalry that has impeded military planning by the Joint Chiefs and execution by commanders in the field." The Packard Commission proposed creating an Under Secretary of Defense "to oversee the purchase of new weapons systems for all service branches", charging that "all too many of our weapons cost too much, take too long to develop and by the time they are fielded, incorporate obsolete technology."[52]

Different versions of reform legislation arrived on the floors of Congress. In May 1986, a bill to replace the Joint Chiefs with a senior body of advisers received unanimous approval in the Senate, with a vote of 95-0. In August, the House voted 406 to 4 to approve a defense authorization bill with a military reform amendment less extreme than the Senate version. A compromise resulted in the Goldwater-Nichols Reorganization Act of 1986, which was signed by President Reagan on October 1. Senator Nunn, a leading architect of the compromise, announced that Congress had finally given the nation a joint military structure reflecting the vision of unification Eisenhower had evoked when he signed the Defense Reorganization Act of 1958.[53]

The final wording of the Goldwater-Nichols legislation did not compromise the nearly universal mandate to strengthen the Chairman and combatant commanders. It designated the Chairman as the principal military adviser to the President and the Secretary of Defense, but failed to end the controversial practice of dual-hatting service chiefs as members of the Joint Chiefs or allowing them to express dissenting views to the Secretary of Defense.

The Chairman became responsible for overall strategic and logistical planning, for assessing budget requests and making budget recommendations to the Secretary of Defense, and for overseeing joint staff activities. For continuity, the law created a four-star Vice Chairman, to be filled from a different service than the Chairman. Both the Chairman and vice-Chairman could serve three two year terms, in contrast to the previous two term limit. Service chiefs served four-year terms.[54]

The commitment to improve the operational effectiveness of joint military forces was the most important promise of Goldwater-Nichols. Toward this end, the law clarified the chain of command and strengthened the authority of combatant commanders. The Joint Chiefs and service chiefs remained outside the chain of command, which ran from the President to the Secretary of Defense to combatant commanders. Senator Nunn explained that Goldwater-Nichols confirmed the responsibility of the four services to train, equip, and organize military forces, while "the operational command of those forces was clearly reserved to the war-fighting commanders."[55] The law mandated that the Chairman perform periodic reviews of the unified and specified commands and submit an indepth report on the roles and missions of the armed forces every three years.[56]

Other provisions of Goldwater-Nichols sought to improve the quality of joint or multiservice staffs by broadening personnel policies and providing career incentives for officers in joint duty assignments. Among the incentives provided by Goldwater-Nichols, the law mandated that joint duty officers be promoted consistent with their contemporaries and that officers not be promoted to brigadier general or rear admiral without serving in a joint assignment.[57] These provisions were aimed at countering ingrained assumptions that joint duty assignments woud not enhance an officer's career, leading to avoidance of these assignments by the most qualified officers.

Air Force Gen. Robert T. Herres, the first officer to occupy the new position of Vice Chairman of the Joint Chiefs, described "the essence of the intent" of Goldwater-Nichols was to "be less talk of so-called roles and missions of the services and more meaningful, aggressive action to support the combat commanders." Herres felt that the framers of the legislation believed that "service inter-

Roles and Missions

ests" had been "served at the expense of joint responsibilities." They also perceived,

> ...that the Department of Defense was emphasizing functions rather than missions; the resources managers were believed to hold too much influence at the expense of the warfighters, and the acquisition process was producing equipment with insufficient thought to effective joint integration and interoperability."[58]

Senator Nunn pointed out that Presidents Truman and Eisenhower had advocated strikingly similar reforms in 1947 and 1958, but Congress blocked any action. "It is an interesting paradox but a tribute to our system of government," Nunn said, "that Goldwater-Nichols reform finally came about on the initiative of Congress over the objections of many in the executive branch."[59]

During his tenure, General Herres reserved judgment on the Goldwater-Nichols reforms saying it was too early to gauge the results. Herres did feel that charges that the Joint Chiefs were "bound up in purely parochial interests and incapable of providing sound military advice," were overblown. Nevertheless, there were, in his mind, "enough kernels of truth in them" to bring evolutionary change.[60]

Requiem for the Cold War: Roles and Missions Ramifications

Implementation of the Reorganization Act of 1986 intersected with yet another roles and missions crossroads. On the world stage, the strategic threat and balance of power shifted from a superpower stalemate to a denouement in the four-decade-old Cold War. Beset by serious economic and political troubles, exacerbated by the Kremlin's escalation of the arms race and futile intervention in Afghanistan, the Soviet empire was in turmoil when a new leader came to power in the mid-1980s. Mikhail Gorbachev's domestic reforms, expressed by the terms perestroika (reconstruction) and glasnost (openness), his democratization of the U.S.S.R., and his renewed detente with the United States, led inexorably to the end of the Cold War in 1989 and the collapse of the Soviet empire soon after. These astonishing events brought a far-ranging reassessment of U.S. national security interests around the globe, of post-Cold War force composition and requirements, and of roles and missions alignments among the armed services.

The effect of post-Cold War strategy on roles and missions remained uncertain at the end of the 1980s. The military worked toward full implementation of the 1986 reorganization act, but a report on roles and missions, as mandated, by outbound Chairman Crowe rekindled the debate. The Crowe report concluded that the "roles" of the armed forces as crafted in law were fundamentally sound, but assignment of "functions" should be changed "to achieve a greater degree of effectiveness and enhance the capabilities of the combatant commanders to carry out their missions." Crowe recommended that:

> The functions of the Armed Forces contained in DOD Directive 5100.1 should be revised and updated to more clearly reflect current US military strategy, our efforts to harness technology, and our responses to new threats to the national security.[61]

Although Admiral Crowe consulted each service chief about the report, he did not seek a consensus. One of the most contested issues was the recommendation to assign primary responsibility for space functions to the Air Force. Crowe anchored this proposal to the growing importance of the space mission, reasoning that nations no longer would be fully able to control their own destinies without significant space capabilities. He wrote:

> From a strictly military perspective, the use of space is now necessary, even mandatory, for the success of global military operations. And because of the capabilities of our most powerful potential adversary, space is now a contested medium, exactly like those of air, sea, and land. Our objective for space must mirror that which we have long held for the sea-to ensure free access to space for all nations in time of peace, but to be able to deny access to space for our enemies in time of war.[62]

While Crowe insisted that the Army and Navy retain responsibility for space functions involving land and maritime operations, critics feared that his proposal would consolidate all space authority in the Air Force, leading to replacement of the Space Command with a specified commander under the Air Force.[63] General Colin Powell, who followed Crowe as Chairman, considered the dissenting views, but reported to Secretary of Defense Richard Cheney that he believed the space proposal made "effective but also efficient use of our military forces."[64]

The Joint Chiefs split over a recommendation to add language to defense policy to reflect that all four services performed close air support, acknowledging a long-standing Navy and Marine Corps position not shared by other services. In a dissenting view, Gen. Larry Welch and Gen. Carl Vuono, the Air Force and Army Chiefs of Staff, opposed this recommendation. The Army believed that the Air Force responsibility for close air support for ground forces was as valid in the 1990s as it was when President Truman signed the National Security Act of 1947. Both Chiefs felt that Crowe's contention that the Army performed close air support was doctrinally incorrect because they regarded Army helicopters as integral elements of a ground commander's combat power. Only fixed-wing Air Force assets could provide the flexibility needed to cover an entire theater, they said.[65]

General Powell considered the close air support issue the most controversial question of the roles and mission debate. Agreeing with Generals Welch and Vuono, Powell saw no reason to alter the close air support function. Powell argued that even though any service could provide close air support "as a matter of theology," this did not mean that each service "must have close air support assigned to it as a primary function to be performed." The Army and the Air Force had made progress in resolving the issue in recent years, Powell noted, and felt that Crowe's proposal would "sow considerable confusion."[66]

While differing with his predecessor on the close air support issue, General Powell praised "the meaningful perspective" contained in Crowe's report. "The report should be viewed as the first iteration in a process that will remove 'Roles and Functions of the Armed Forces' from the status of icon," Powell wrote, "and will place it in a context as a working document of the Department of Defense." Powell reiterated that the purpose of Crowe's report was "to provide forces to the combatant commanders which are capable jointly of performing all the missions assigned to them."[67]

The periodic roles and missions reviews mandated by the Goldwater-Nichols bill were to provide a compass to deal with issues such as duplication among the armed services and the demands on this guidance increased as the United States scaled down its military in the post-Cold War era. The Crowe report confined its comments to redundancies in the intelligence and special operations fields and strategic nuclear capabilities. The Admiral recommended investigating new opportunities to reduce "duplication of effort among DOD intelligence activities" and the duplicative functions "necessary to maintain U.S. special operations capabilities." He acknowledged redundancy within "the strategic triad of land, sea and air-deliverable nuclear weapons," but did not feel it was excessive, defending the triad as a "force multiplier" which gave the United States a strategic edge and "a greater range of capability against a given threat."[68]

Close air support persisted as the most contentious issue facing the services and budget-minded members of Congress remained unconvinced that separate arms were necessary. Duplicative tactical air capabilities became a prime target for cost reductions in the post-Cold War environment. Nonetheless, the roles and missions debate was temporarily laid aside when Saddam Hussein invaded Kuwait in August 1990 and threatened oil-rich neighbors in the Persian Gulf. The impact of Goldwater-Nichols and other initiatives to strengthen joint military action was that combatant commands were better prepared to respond to aggression.[69]

The measure of the success of the Goldwater-Nichols act would come on the battlefield. Except for limited use of military force to bring Manuel Noriega to justice in Panama, the first test of the new law on combat operations came when President George Bush deployed U.S. forces to the Persian Gulf to drive the Iraqi army out of Kuwait.[70] Although the success of the Panama operation pleased the Bush Administration, the joint assault against Noriega's military defenses encountered such inept resistance that it could not be considered a real test for joint operations.

The provisions of the Goldwater-Nichols Act made the Central Command more responsive as a unified command. Headquartered at MacDill AFB, Florida, the Command replaced the Rapid Deployment Joint Task Force in January 1983. With no forces assigned in peacetime, the Command relied on designated components to provide combat forces during wartime. Senator Nunn believed that the most significant reform of Goldwater-Nichols for the Gulf War was "the strengthening of the command and personnel authority" of the Commander in Chief, Central Command, and other field commanders. General Norman Schwarzkopf, who commanded Central Command during the Gulf War, "clearly had the authority necessary to carry out his demanding responsibilities." In contrast to Vietnam-era commanders, Schwarzkopf had unity of command in the Gulf War, and "the chain of command above...worked in the clear, direct manner prescribed by the Goldwater-Nichols Act."[71]

The new Transportation Command, headquartered at Scott AFB, Illinois, performed the massive movement of personnel, equipment, and supplies to the Persian Gulf. Acting on a recommendation of the Packard Commission in 1987, President Reagan had directed that air, sea, and land transportation be integrated into a unified command. The Transportation Command, headed by the dual-hatted commander of the Military Airlift Command, became operational in October 1988. The Goldwater-Nichols Act also influenced Reagan's decision to create the new command, which Senator Nunn claimed improved the movement of joint forces in the Gulf War.[72]

Despite its success, some remained concerned that Goldwater-Nichols would create a new careerism in which officers did "not compete for joint duty assignments," but took them "because they are required to by law," but most senior officers believed that the new career incentives attracted better officers to compete for joint assignments. General Colin Powell credited Goldwater-Nichols "with making the Joint Staff one of the best staffs in the world." A Marine Corps general agreed, noting that his service "used to send officers who were retiring to work on the Joint Staff," but now sent "our sharpest folks and so do the other services."[73] General Ronald R. Fogleman, who became Air Force Chief of Staff in 1994, credited Goldwater-Nichols with changing the American way of war, claiming that the Air Force was committed "to put our very best people" on joint staffs and in unified commands.[74]

The Persian Gulf crisis came too soon after the end of the Cold War and diminished Soviet threat to have any material effect on U.S. strategic planning or budgeting. The defense budget reached an all-time high when President Bush ordered the buildup of American military forces in the Persian Gulf in response to Iraqi aggression against Kuwait. Rising from $239.5 billion in 1985 to $283.8 billion in 1988 under the Reagan Administration, the defense budget continued to climb after the election of George Bush, reaching $293 billion by 1990.

The Air Force share dropped from $94.7 billion in 1989 to $92.9 billion in 1990, while the Navy allocation rose from $97.7 to $99.9 billion. The Army budget remained at $78 billion. While Saudi Arabia and other coalition partners bore much of the financial burden of the Gulf War, the incremental costs of the war kept the Bush Administration from cutting defense spending until submission of the fiscal year 1992 budget.[75]

The rising costs of force modernization added to the fiscal burden of national defense. Holding the edge in state-of-the-art technology was considered fundamental to Cold War survival and strategy. Technological advances such as stealth aircraft and laser-guided weaponry sharpened the teeth of American air power and gave the nation an advantage in air superiority over its adversaries. Having been developed and produced in secrecy in the late 1970s, the Air Force unveiled its first-generation stealth fighter, the F–117, in 1988. The deadly radar-evading fighters flew their first missions in December 1989 and became combat-ready with the buildup of air power in the Persian Gulf the following August.

Air Force plans called for B–2 stealth bombers, a $70 billion program, to become operational in the early 1990s. Navy development of stealth aircraft, the A–12, followed in the wake of the Air Force programs. With all four services competing to modernize their air capabilities, the multibillion dollar stealth and other advanced aircraft programs became prime targets for budget cutters, but the onset of the Gulf War deferred these and other cost savings.[76]

Moving into an era dubbed by President Bush as a "New World Order" brought the armed forces to a new crossroads in the evolution of roles and missions. Change was in the air, but much depended on the post-Cold War threat and whether the shifting balance of power would lead to a less dangerous or more perilous world. That Soviet nuclear warheads were no longer targeted against the United States did not remove the peril of nuclear proliferation in rogue nations. In 1988, U.S. and NATO leaders reaffirmed their commitment to flexible response, requiring a readiness to respond to all levels of armed conflict.[77] Potential trouble spots, including former Soviet bloc countries, abounded around the globe, requiring readiness to intervene.

The U.S. military also remained active in lesser roles such as counter-narcotics. State-sponsored terrorism continued to be an international menace and humanitarian operations responded to a need that would not go away. The scope of post-Cold War roles and missions became clear in the afterglow of air power successes in the Persian Gulf.

Unified Air Power in the Gulf War

When he became Secretary of Defense in the spring of 1989, Richard Cheney upheld a pledge by his predecessors to not commit American forces to battle without clear-cut objectives and a political resolve to see them through. In a restatement of the Bush Administration's evolving post-Cold War strategy, Cheney said that the United States "must be ready to show moral and political leadership; to reassure others of our commitment to protect our interests; and, if necessary, to respond to threats resolutely with forces for deterrence or defense."[78] This pledge, along with the fabric of unity spun from the Goldwater-Nichols Act, prepared the way for integrated and effective air power in the Gulf War.

Since the overthrow of the Shah of Iran by Muslim extremists in 1979, the Persian Gulf region had rivaled the Middle East in violence and volatility. The fall of the Shah's pro-Western government altered the balance of power, destabilized the region, and threatened the security of U.S. regional interests. During a decade of instability, punctuated by eight years of Iranian-Iraqi hostilities and sporadic attacks against shipping in the Persian Gulf, U.S. efforts to protect its strategic interests and keep the war from spilling into friendly Gulf states centered on the Navy's forward maritime strategy and its "forward deployed and rapidly responsive naval forces." Air Force forward-based planes were active in the area and the Central Command was ready to deploy up to its full complement of land, sea, and air forces.[79]

The first full-scale deployment of Central Command forces came in response to the Iraqi invasion of Kuwait on August 2, 1990. Over the next five months, the Bush Administration worked with the United Nations to impose sanctions against Iraq, putting together a powerful coalition and building up forces in Saudi Arabia and neighboring states. President Bush issued an ultimatum to Saddam Hussein to withdraw his forces by January 15. On August 8, the President succinctly presented U.S. objectives: to secure the complete and unconditional withdrawal of Iraqi forces from Kuwait; to assure the security and stability of the Gulf Region; and to protect American lives.[80]

While the linkage Senator Nunn drew between Goldwater-Nichols and victory in the Gulf War had merit, the five-month hiatus from August to January formed an important nexus to the decisive use of air power against Iraq. The protracted build-up gave Iraqi forces time to dig in and tighten their grip on Kuwait, but also enabled the coalition to mass superior air, sea, and land power. Five months gave the Central Command a wide margin to prepare an air campaign to destroy Iraqi warmaking infrastructure and isolate the battlefield.[81]

Central command warplanning heretofore confined air resources to tactical roles supporting surface operations. Options for employing Air Force tactical units focused on Army air-land battle doctrine while options to use strategic air power were not considered because of low threat levels in the Central Command area. Iraqi aggression against Kuwait, however, convinced General Schwarzkopf that he must prepare to deal Saddam a punishing blow from the air if the Iraqi dictator widened hostilities or defied the ultimatum. When the crisis broke, Schwarzkopf sent his top airman, Lt. Gen. Charles A. Horner, to Riyadh, Saudi Arabia, to coordinate the initial force beddown with the Saudis.[82]

Air Force planners were already at work on a strategic campaign for possible use in the Gulf War. They completed an initial plan and briefed General Schwarzkopf on August 10, envisioning a sudden massive strategic air campaign to destroy Iraq's command and control centers and warmaking infrastructure. The plan emphasized the use of precision guided weapons to assure destruction of military targets and to "minimize civilian casualties and collateral damage" and General Schwarzkopf approved it on the spot.

The concept was then presented to General Horner and integrated into the planning process in Riyadh. The strategic air campaign became the first phase of Central Command's Desert Storm offensive war plan. Other phases maintained air superiority over Kuwait, prepared the battlefield, and executed the ground offensive to eject Iraqis from Kuwait. General Powell asked that the strategic air compaign concept be expanded into a joint plan and include a maximum air effort to destroy Saddam's elite Republican Guard and formidable armored capabilities. Secretary of Defense Cheney and President Bush gave Powell and Schwarzkopf approval to proceed with preparations for the strategic air campaign if Saddam's forces remained in Kuwait past the deadline.[83]

Decisions about the use of force against Iraq were not constrained by the fear of superpower confrontation that had blunted the edges of air power in Korea and Vietnam. The end of the Cold War narrowed the political concerns about widening the war, while the Goldwater-Nichols act created a less parochial doctrinal climate, more conducive to planning and executing a decisive air campaign against Iraqi military power. By giving the Joint Chiefs more authority and assuring that unified commanders had full authority over their forces, Goldwater-Nichols strengthened the decisionmaking process.[84]

For reasons of diplomacy, the Central Command agreed to a dual command arrangement in the Gulf War with a Saudi general serving as theater and joint forces commander and General Schwarzkopf commanding all U.S. forces in the theater. Schwarzkopf designated General Horner as air component commander and Vice Adm. Henry Mauz, Jr. as sea component commander. Having served as forward commander until Schwarzkopf moved his headquarters to Riyadh in late August, Horner was also responsible for airspace control and air defense coordination. Reminiscent of General MacArthur's dual command in the early days of the Korean War, General Schwarzkopf assumed the additional responsibilities of land component commander, reportedly making this decision in deference to the Marines.[85]

As Schwarzkopf's air component commander, Horner's single manager authority complied with basic Air Force and joint doctrine. This centralized direction proved doctrinally sound and was consistent with the roles and missions assigned to the armed forces after the National Security Act of 1947. Learning from its mistakes in Vietnam, the Air Force placed all aircraft entering the theater, including B–52s, under General Horner's control. The other services, however, did not fully comply with the spirit and intent of joint doctrine.[86]

Among prominent exceptions to the single manager rule was Army retention of control over its helicopter gunships, following a pattern set in Vietnam. Army commanders also opposed Horner's control of air operations to prepare the battlefield and support the ground campaign because it violated airland battle doctrine. Navy and Marine commanders complained bitterly about the air component command arrangements. Similar to arguments heard in Korea and Vietnam, they contended that Horner's authority encompassed only coordination of Navy and Marine air operations, not command and control of them.[87] Despite such interservice conflicts, the success of the air campaign against Iraq underscored the dominance of modern air power and the efficacy of doctrine manifested in the epic use of air forces at St. Mihiel and in the Meuse-Argonne offensive of 1918.

The Desert Storm air offensive achieved tactical surprise from the outset. Opening in the predawn hours of January 17, 1991, with massive strikes against the nerve centers of the Soviet-designed Iraqi air defense system, the first wave of ten F–117 stealth fighters penetrated enemy defenses undetected, jarring Baghdad awake with attacks against targets in and around the Iraqi capital. After delivering their ordnance unchallenged, the F–117s turned to their egress routes before enemy batteries began firing toward the flashes and streaking shadows overhead. Successive waves of coalition aircraft, unmanned cruise missiles launched from B–52s, and salvos of Tomahawk land-attack missiles from warships in the Persian Gulf and Red Sea, slammed into military targets with devastating accuracy. By dawn, thousands of planes and cruise missiles crippled the Iraqi air defense system and key targets, with the loss of only a single aircraft.[88]

Coalition airmen quickly won air supremacy over Iraq, killing the few MIGs rising to challenge them, destroying others in hardened shelters on the ground, and sending the remnants of Saddam's vaunted air force scurrying to the sanctuary of nearby Iranian bases. The war lasted six weeks, with waves of warplanes relentlessly and methodically pounding military targets from Baghdad to Kuwait. By early February, the air campaign shifted to the Kuwaiti theater where uninterrupted torrents of steel rained down on Saddam's forward positions, rendering his army all but helpless when the ground offensive began before daybreak on February 24. Four days later, after achieving its objective of driving the Iraqi Army from Kuwait, the coalition declared a cease-fire.[89]

From the airman's perspective, the application of air in the Desert Storm campaign brought special lessons for joint planners. While the campaign repeated the pattern of participation by air, sea, and land forces, there was a distinct difference between use of these forces in Desert Storm and their employment in the

Korean and Vietnam conflicts. The greater authority of the combatant comman-der provided by the Goldwater-Nichols act ensured greater cohesion and unity in the joint employment of forces than any other time in the past 40 years. This was especially true of the combined use of air power in the war.[90]

For the Air Force, Desert Storm was the first pure application of its core doctrine since World War II and the results spoke for themselves. Centrally planned and executed with near-flawless precision under direction of the air component commander, the campaign to win air supremacy, to destroy the war-making infrastructure of the enemy, to isolate the battle, and to support the ground offensive was classic in its application. Rapid success of the ground cam-paign suggested that air power virtually completed the objective, which General Powell described as "first we will cut off the enemy's head and then we will kill him," before the ground fighting started. Air Force Chief of Staff Gen. Merrill A. McPeak called the air campaign "a remarkable performance by the coalition air forces." It was, he added, "the first time in history that a field army has been defeated by air power."[91]

Desert Storm helped exorcise the ghosts of Vietnam from the halls of the Pentagon where they had wandered for the past 20 years. Although nonpareil in the annals of air warfare, Desert Storm left some vexing questions for joint plan-ners to ponder. No war is without flaw and Desert Storm was no exception. Wielding single manager authority was key to the air component commander's effective melding of forces, yet Navy complaints about underutilization of its air-craft carriers and underrepresentation on the air component staff would require resolution before the next war.[92] As the military began post-Cold War downsiz-ing and as the new threat environment began to crystallize, these and other inter-service differences were magnified in the wake of Desert Storm. Military lead-ers began to grapple with the roles and missions issues that would lead the armed forces into the twenty-first century.

Toward the 21st Century: Roles and Missions at the Crossroads

In early 1995, a Washington journalist wrote that some defense leaders were "championing the notion that the United States is in one of those rare historical periods when revolutions happen to how wars are fought and how branches of the military are organized." These officials argued that "a range of rapidly advancing technologies" involving "more powerful sensors and computers, radar-evading technology, precision-guided munitions and fiber-optic communi-cations systems" were moving modern warfighting away from "relatively large, sluggish and easily detectible land armies and aircraft carrier fleets toward joint task forces of "smaller, more mobile military units."

Army Gen. John M. Shalikashvili, who succeeded General Powell as Chairman of the Joint Chiefs in 1993, called the Gulf War "a snapshot of this revolution in progress." He believed that advanced technology coinciding with the end of the Cold War altered the face of modern battle and would "blur present-day distinctions among the Army, Navy, Air Force, and Marines." This, in turn, promised to transform Defense Department budgeting.[93]

Among those who shared Shalikashvilli's vision were Secretary of Defense William J. Perry, his deputy John M. Deutch, and Joint Chiefs Chairman Adm. William Owens, despite opposition from individual services and their supporters in Congress. Opponents argued that the future threat remained unclear and that the military had to prepare for a wide range of contingencies including "the kinds of messy, conventional threats" the armed forces faced in Bosnia and Haiti. For the time being, at least, the budgets would "remain dominated by traditional systems such as aircraft carriers, destroyers, jet fighters and tanks."[94]

Opposing views formed the roles and missions crossroads that began to emerge in 1989. At that time, the Joint Staff "began re-examining the strategic context in which we plan the structure of our armed forces"-an effort Chairman Powell described as a dynamic process through which succeeding administrations would divest themselves "of Cold War thinking, assumptions and programs." The re-examination resulted in publication of a revised national military strategy in January 1992, articulating the "shift from a global, Soviet-oriented strategy to a strategy focused on regional contingencies and threats."

"We also began restructuring our forces to meet the enduring demands of our strategy and national interests while adjusting to the end of the Soviet threat and to emerging fiscal constraints," the Chairman said.[95] President Bush discussed the new strategy in a speech in Aspen, Colorado, on August 2, 1990, the same day Iraq invaded Kuwait, calling for "not merely reductions, but restructuring" of America's armed forces.[96]

For its part, the Air Force moved boldly to redefine a strategic vision for air power, to refashion its force structure, and to rethink roles and missions. In June 1990, Secretary of the Air Force Donald B. Rice issued a white paper entitled "Global Reach-Global Power," laying out a strategic planning framework to build the future Air Force. Underlying assumptions of the national military strategy were key to the Air Force blueprint envisioning the post-Cold War threat as regional rather than global, a diminished nuclear threat with increased demands on conventional readiness, and replacement of forward deployment with forward presence as keys to projecting U.S. power around the globe. In Secretary Rice's words, the integral Air Force role in the new strategy illuminated "airpower's inherent strengths-speed, range, flexibility, precision, and lethality." While sustaining nuclear deterrence, the post-Cold War Air Force provided a versatile combat force for theater operations and power projection, rapid global mobility with its airlift and tanker forces, and control of space, the high ground of the future.[97]

Plans to restructure major commands took the Air Force back to the simplicity of its pre-1947 organizational roots. Less than a year after becoming Chief of Staff, General McPeak announced that the time had come to unify air power in the Air Force. Since the days of Billy Mitchell, doctrinal purists taught that air power was indivisible and should be treated as a unified whole, a tenet used by critics to accuse the Air Force of violating its own principle by dividing strategic and tactical air power among major commands.

McPeak noted that the line between tactical and strategic air power had become blurred. "Airplanes have both tactical and strategic capability and should not be constrained by artificial distinctions," he said, adding that this often applied to the strategic or tactical value of targets. While such observations were true of the air war in Southeast Asia, the Persian Gulf air campaign made the case with more finality.[98]

"One man's tactical is another man's strategic," McPeak stated, using the example of the capture of Noriega in January 1990 as a strategic action for the Panamanian Dictator, but a tactical operation for the United States. McPeak punctuated his explanation with images of fighters, bombers, and attack aircraft striking a diverse range of targets in both the Vietnam and Gulf Wars. In the Gulf, McPeak pointed out, "F–117s hit key strategic nodes in Baghdad while F–15Es and F–16s attacked biological and nuclear facilities." A variety of planes attacked missile launch facilities, including the Air Force's primary close air support aircraft, the A–10. "Conversely, B–52s were highly effective against Iraqi ground forces in tactical positions," he concluded.[99]

In reshaping the Air Force in the 1990s, General McPeak resurrected the composite wing structure that existed through World War II. As in Vietnam, the air campaign against Iraq required "the integration of a range of assets-bomb droppers, fighter escort, jamming aircraft, defense suppression planes, airborne radar platforms, tankers and the like." General McPeak added that not all wings would be composite, nor would all composite wings be standardized. Wherever it made sense, however, the Air Force restructured its wings "to integrate a variety of assets into a mission-oriented entity."[100]

In June 1992, the Air Force deactivated SAC and TAC, merging their forces into the new Air Combat Command at Langley AFB, Virginia. A new unified command, the Strategic Command, took on SAC's former role of nuclear deterrence. The Air Combat Command would provide nuclear-capable forces to the Strategic Command and supply combat aircraft to five geographic unified commands-the Atlantic, European, Pacific, Southern and Central Commands.

The Air Force deactivated the Military Airlift Command and established an Air Mobility Command as a component of the Transportation Command. A dual-hatted Air Force general commanded the Air Mobility and Transportation Commands. These and other restructuring efforts reduced the number of Air Force major commands from 13 to 10. A paramount consideration of the reorganization was to prepare Air Force and combatant commanders "to employ air power as an integrated whole to support national objectives."[101]

The Navy and Marine Corps responded to the emerging post-Cold War strategy by launching "an extensive, year-long study of future naval roles and capabilities, in terms of their relevance to the 21st century and a joint warfare environment." A white paper from that study recognized the shift in focus from "separate, independent naval operations at sea for indirect support of the land war" to "direct support of ground operations." In mid-1993, Adm. Frank R. Kelso II, Chief of Naval Operations, explained that the Navy's new strategy entailed "a fundamental shift away from emphasis on open-ocean warfighting *on the sea* toward joint operations conducted *from the sea*." Kelso said the Navy and Marine Corps were committed to joint warfighting and could provide "the initial enabling capability for joint operations," as shown in Somalia. The Army also changed its focus, pulling back from overseas to primary bases in the United States. The Army underwent substantial reductions, "inactivating four divisions and one corps along with consolidating fifty-one war reserve stocks to five."[102]

Defense budgets in the early 1990s reflected force downsizing. From 1991 to 1995, budgets for the military departments declined steadily. The Army budget showed the greatest decrease, dropping from $91.8 billion in 1991 to an average of $64.7 billion over the next four fiscal years. The Air Force budget fell from over $91.2 billion to an average of $77.3 billion in the same years. The Navy's $103.4 billion budget was the highest in 1991, and it retained the highest average of $82.2 billion for the next four fiscal years.

Underpinning budgetary trends and analyses of the mid-1990s was a bottom-up review of post-Cold War military forces and programs ordered by President Bill Clinton. The review concluded that "the United States had to maintain forces capable of fighting and winning two nearly simultaneous major regional conflicts." In addition to the threat of regional conflicts, U.S. forces had to be able to deter nuclear attacks to conduct peace enforcement or intervention operations, to counter international terrorism, and to retain an overseas presence.[103]

The bottom-up review complemented an ongoing inquiry into roles and missions. Remaining as Chairman into October of Clinton's first year as President, General Powell had the Joint Staff, in conjunction with the services and commanders in chief, reexamine military strategy to ensure it aligned with policy guidance from the new Administration. Referencing a phrase used by former President Bush to define the post-Cold War strategic environment, Powell noted that the new Secretary of Defense, Les Aspin, liked to say, "The new world order is long on the new world and short on the order." Any change to roles and missions, Powell believed, had to acknowledge the global responsibilities of the United States. As the only superpower, the United States had to forge an international security environment to replace East-West confrontation. "Maintaining strong, capable and flexible armed forces is essential to protecting our interests and fulfilling those responsibilities," Powell said.[104]

Storm clouds over roles and missions began gathering soon after the Gulf War ended. In July 1992, Senator Sam Nunn reopened the debate when he called for "a no-holds-barred, everything-on-the-table review" of roles and missions. In

Roles and Missions

his capacity as Chairman of the Senate Armed Services Committee, Nunn challenged the Pentagon "to eliminate needless duplication and inefficiencies" among the services, listing 11 specific overlapping missions or roles for examination. Nine of these involved duplication of aviation or space capabilities. Nunn's questioning of the need for four air forces recalled the frustrations of General Spaatz and other senior airman during the conferences at Key West and Newport in 1948.[105]

On the eve of his inauguration, Bill Clinton threw his support behind Senator Nunn's call for "a fresh look" at the roles and misisons of the armed forces. Reciting Nunn's list of redundant capabilities, "from the four separate air forces to duplicative medical, chaplain, and legal corps," Clinton said he would order the Pentagon to "hammer out a new understanding about consolidating and coordinating military roles and missions in the 1990s and beyond." While both Congress and the Executive branch looked to General Powell and the Joint Staff for answers, former Joint Chiefs Chairman, retired Air Force Gen. David Jones spoke prophetically, "Because Colin Powell is still dependant on the other service chiefs for support, major changes will have to come from the outside."[106]

General Powell's report on roles, missions, and functions of the armed forces in February 1993 avoided Senator Nunn's tough questions. Powell explained that the report presented his views and was not a consensus document. He did consult with the Joint Chiefs and combatant commanders and was said to have a struck a compromise on objections from the service chiefs. Defense sources said Powell was reluctant to "start a huge interservice battle" just before he left the Chairman's post later in the year. Critics of Powell's report said it showed the nation's top military officers to be opposed to major changes in roles and missions. The Administration and Congress seemed "ready to forge ahead without them." President Clinton pledged to save billions by eliminating duplication, while Nunn and other members of the Senate Armed Services Committee warned that if the services did not eliminate duplication Congress would do it for them.[107]

Responding to the assertion that the nation could not afford four separate air forces, General Powell maintained that all air arms were essential to protecting the United States. "America has only one Air Force, the United States Air Force," Powell said, but "the Army, Navy, and Marine Corps aviation arms are vital to their assigned warfighting roles, and work jointly to project the nation's air power." Powell recommended consolidating initial fixed-wing flight training and suggested that the services transition to a single primary training aircraft.

Powell also recommended creating a new command, adapted from Atlantic Command, to take charge of continental U.S. bases, forces, and joint training. As a result, the United States Atlantic Command was established in October 1993, with all continental United States forces, except those attached to Pacific Command, assigned to it.[108]

General Powell made another concession by agreeing to include Army attack helicopters as close air support assets and with the principle that close air support should be a primary mission for all services. This contradicted Senator Nunn's suggestion for the Navy to provide close air support for the Marines. Powell's conclusion that "a mix of bombers and attack aircraft" were needed in the interdiction role avoided Nunn's claim that the Navy's medium-range attack aircraft duplicated the Air Force capability. Powell's recommendation to improve operational effectiveness, efficiency, and interoperability in "warfighting support from space" called for a review to determine if the space mission should be centralized under the Strategic Command along with elimination of the Space Command.[109]

Finding no grounds to radically alter roles and missions, Powell pointed to adjustments made by the services on their own initiative and to continuing efforts to improve efficiency and cut costs, including creating the unified Strategic Command and eliminating nuclear weapons from the Army and the Marine Corps. Powell noted that consolidating strategic nuclear weapons under the Strategic Command meant that the command of all strategic bombers, missiles, and submarines would alternate between an Air Force general and a Navy admiral, "an arrangement hard to imagine only a few years ago." Powell thought this "perhaps the most dramatic and fundamental change in the assignment of roles and missions...since they were first established by law in 1947."[110]

Describing his roles and missions report as "a snapshot of a continous process of self-evaluation," Powell reassured Congress that the Joint Staff would "continue to examine other areas for possible consolidation or elimination." He pointed out that the 1991 publication of *Joint Warfare of the U.S. Armed Forces* and development of joint doctrine "would help the services to work more closely together in a period of declining budgets and force structure."[111]

The press criticized General Powell's report because it did not face up to some of the more difficult roles and missions issues. One report noted that the Army "fought off a bid by the Air Force to take over theater air defense," and there was "continuing tension between Navy aviation and Air Force aviation over the strike role." Harsher critics accused the report of undercutting President Clinton's campaign pledge to save $100 billion more than projected in the Bush Administration's five year plan. In April 1994, General Powell told the Armed Services Committee that he was aware of these criticisms, but believed the ideas and suggestions in the report would eventually be seen "as sensible and useful steps to take."[112]

When briefing the status of the Administration's bottom-up review, Secretary of Defense Aspin told Congress that a thorough examination of roles and missions was "critical to restructuring DOD to meet its post-Cold War needs." Aspin called the Powell report "an important first step in that process," but doubted that the report's recommendations would be enough. He promised the bottom-up review would evaluate "the contributions of each service to long-term U.S. defense needs," and would "specifically examine service air power roles and requirements, as well as expeditionary ground force roles and requirements." Despite great anticipation, when Secretary Aspin announced the results of the long-awaited bottom-up review in September 1993, it failed "to sort out the existing accreted, cluttered and often overlapping and duplicating" service roles and missions in the eyes of Congress.[113]

An impatient Congress, one observer wrote, "wanted more than economies and postponements that did not alter institutional habits." The fiscal year 1994 Defense Department Authorization Act called for an independent panel to study the problem and in November 1993, Secretary Aspin established a blue-ribbon commission to conduct hearings and complete the study. The seven-member roles and missions commission, chaired by former Assistant Secretary of Defense Dr. John P. White, began its work in May 1994, with one year to complete its report.

Secretary Aspin, who resigned in January 1994, joined the group. Anxiety in the Pentagon over the study was acute, anticipating dramatic changes as expressed in the legislation creating the commission. Lawmakers said, "The current allocation of roles and missions among the armed forces...may no longer be appropriate for the post-Cold War era." The stage was set for one of the most suspenseful roles and missions dramas in recent military history.[114]

Secretary of Defense Wiliam J. Perry, who succeeded Les Aspin, was committed to change. Perry's deputy, John Deutch, conveyed that message to members of the roles and missions commission at their first meeting, reporting that while defense spending would not increase, "the demands put on the military" would. "In addition to the traditional mission of defending the nation, its allies and its interests," Deutch said, "the administration has assigned the military responsibilities in peacekeeping, peace-making, humanitarian operations and other nonwarfare missions." The latter missions increased after the Cold War, manifested by operations in northern Iraq, Somalia, Bosnia, and Haiti. Perry and other defense officials believed that the roles and missions debate had to dominate the commission's thinking to ensure that "the scaled-down military" could perform those responsibilities.[115]

The Air Force Chief of Staff, General McPeak, said he welcomed the congressionally mandated roles and missions review, believing the commission's findings would complement the "radical reorganization" that he and Air Force Secretary Rice had implemented in 1991. He agreed that "rearranging roles and missions" was essential to "consolidate operations and achieve economies of scale-at no cost in terms of weakening our national defense," but was confident that the Air Force's "core competencies" would be preserved. At the same time, McPeak acknowledged that the aviation capabilities of the Army, Navy, and Marine Corps were "indispensable to their other operations on land and sea." While he firmly believed there should be only one air force, if starting anew, McPeak was resigned to the reality, "We start with the history of how we got here."[116]

General McPeak pointed to the redundancy among the four air forces as the area to which he believed the commission should focus its attention. Any contribution made by the commission to ensure "that the aviation capabilities that all the services possess truly complement one another," in his opinion, was paramount. Citing Air Force land-based fighters and Navy carrier-based fighters as prime examples, the General said that missions and operations of the air forces were often complementary. He suggested, however, that the commission might investigate "apparent overlap, duplication, and redundancy" between Navy and Marine Corps aviation, to make the two air forces more complementary. Another roles and missions issue was how to determine the merits of land based, long-range bombers, and carrier-based bombers and how to use them to maximum effect. Not wanting to repeat the history of building four air arms, McPeak argued fervently to make the Air Force responsible for all space operations. Allowing the Army and Navy to operate separate space commands was a redundancy he believed the nation could no longer afford.[117]

Through the early autumn of 1994, controversy swirled around the roles and missions debate as the Army, Navy, and Air Force secretaries replied to a commission request for issues they wanted to air. While the Army and Navy limited their responses to generic functions, the Air Force proposed far-reaching changes that would affect the forces and capabilities of the other services. There was ample room for disagreement, but the measures proposed by the Air Force were bolder, more visionary, and more controversial than the others.[118]

The roles and missions concepts developed by the Air Force included the premise that "modern land warfare" consisted of four distinct battle areas: rear bases and supporting elements; the close battle for terrain; the deep battle beyond the frontline; and the high battle to win air superiority and defend against enemy aircraft and ballistic missile attacks. Using this division of battle space as a starting point to identify redundant missions and capabilities, Air Staff planners concluded that "no more than two services should be responsible for each type of battle." Excessive overlap in all battle areas provided opportunities to eliminate redundancies and reduce costs. From the Air Force's perspective, this base line would reduce excessive overlap and improve combat effectiveness.[119]

Secretary of the Air Force, Sheila Widnall, presented the Air Force position on roles and missions to the commission in a September 1 letter. Nearing retirement, General McPeak presented an extended version of the Air Force proposals to the commission two weeks later. An earlier briefing to the other services had ended with heated dissent. A major prong of the controversy was a proposal to transfer Marine Corps tactical fighters to the Navy and to refocus the Marines and the Army "on close battle operations." As a corollary, the Army and the Marine Corps would be excluded from deep battlefield attack operations, to be shared by the Air Force and the Navy. Furthermore, McPeak believed the primary responsibility for close air support should be divided among the Army and the

Roles and Missions

Marines, with the Air Force and Navy supporting the ground battle as a secondary mission.[120]

The outgoing Air Force Chief implied the armed forces had "overinvested" in tactical air power, with "too many tactical aircraft" performing collateral and redundant roles. Pointing to the redundancy in close air support, a mission shared by all four air arms, McPeak said flying "Air Force A–10s and F–16s, Navy carrier aircraft, Army helicopters and Marine F/A–18 fighters, plus helicopters and Harrier AV–8s" collectively was a costly and unnecessary burden on the defense budget. "Recently, many have questioned whether this redundancy costs us more than we should spend in this mission area," he said.[121]

Similarly, all services were "heavily involved in the deep battle, an area well serviced by the Navy and the Air Force." This was evident in the Gulf War, where the Marines flew "by far the largest part" of their tactical air sorties in the deep battle area, rather than "in close proximity to air ground operations," raising serious questions about the Marine argument for tactical air requirements as an essential part of the air-ground team. This "overlap or duplication of aviation capabilities" introduced "another boundary management problem" into the heat of combat.[122]

"Another contentious topic is theater air defense, where, again, each service is assigned a primary mission," McPeak stated. He pointed to the proliferation of air defense weaponry among the services, making air space control and boundary management more perilous in a combat theater. In the Gulf War, for instance, compartmentalization of air defense created seams which a shrewder and better equipped enemy might have exploited. McPeak noted that joint doctrine required a theater area air defense commander, usually the Air Force component commander, to have operational control of all air defense assets. McPeak recommended integrating theater air defenses under the Air Force component command "for enduring conditions."[123]

General McPeak recommended that the Air Force become the executive agent for space "to provide focused leadership on defense space matters," saying that it mades no sense for other services to maintain separate space commands and operations "while the Air Force accounts for approximately nine-tenths of U.S. military space dollars and personnel." While there were logical arguments for the Army and Navy to manage their own space interests, McPeak said "cost [was] not one of them."

The Air Force Chief proposed to cut costs by reducing the number of combatant commands. He believed some joint commands, including the Central and Special Operations Commands, were superfluous to post-Cold War strategy. McPeak called the Special Operations Command, mandated by Goldwater-Nichols, an extraneous "fifth service" complicating combat command arrangements.[124]

In the final analysis, McPeak told the commission that the Defense Department needed to avoid duplication and reduce costs and that it could "no longer afford to have all the services operate forces across all the roles and functions." In offering a conceptual framework to review roles and missions, McPeak urged the commission to "focus on core competencies" of the services...to "produce maximum efficiencies in both warfighting and procurement." "Each service should retain those assignments that reflect unique strengths, within an overall framework that emphasizes the most efficient and effective way to generate and sustain combat capability," he argued. After determining "what each service's core business" would be, the next step was to decide how the "resulting service-provided capabilities" should "operate jointly on the modern battlefield."[125]

In their presentations, the Army and Navy Secretaries opposed consolidating service space activities, arguing that these capabilities were complementary rather than competitive. Although each service wanted to retain a strong forward military presence, Air Force bombers and Navy carriers competed for the central role to project American military power overseas. Navy Secretary John Dalton asked the commission to consider assigning the Navy and Marine Corps "primary functions in providing forces to deter conflict, for aiding in carrying out joint operations and serving as the initial crisis response force to meet overseas contingencies." Dalton wanted theater ballistic missile defense assigned to the Navy, arguing that sea-based systems could be "more easily and flexibly positioned" to shoot down missiles and asked the commission to determine whether strategic sealift should be elevated to a primary function for the Navy, as strategic airlift was for the Air Force.[126]

The Secretary of the Army, Togo West, also asked for a review of military airlift and sealift capabilities to support strategic mobility. He requested that "specific areas of the battlefield...not be partitioned among the services" because this would have a debilitating effect on "the joint commanders' ability to effectively control the tempo of an operation." West opposed centralizing theater air defenses under the Air Force or assigning missile defense to the Navy, arguing that the Army should "remain the foundation of air defense" and that ground commanders should control missile defenses. When asked about General McPeak's controversial proposals, the Army Secretary said "the issue of the day" was "jointness," not "the question of narrow or exclusive missions for the services." Yet, the Army argued against production of the Air Force's new stealth fighter, the F–22, because "the United States no longer faces a growing threat from manned jet aircraft." Instead, Secretary West urged more "investment in ballistic missile defenses."[127]

On October 24, the *Washington Post* reported that General McPeak's "blunt and unusually public campaign...to limit the functions performed by the other services" had rekindled "a major new debate" over roles and missions. The newspaper stated that the other service chiefs viewed the attacks on their assigned roles and weapons programs "as an outrageous violation of protocol." The Army, Navy and Marine Corps roles and missions teams took the Air Force to task for its impractical "notion of segmenting the battlefield," contending that the debate should center "on improving ways to apply complementary combat capabilities in battle simultaneously," not on "reserving various areas for specific services." Pointing to "the fast tempo of modern battle," the other services argued that dividing functions by battle areas "would only risk limiting the flexibility of combat commanders."[128]

One journalist reported that McPeak's "blunt-spoken" attacks surprised the other services "because they were not directed primarily at the Navy-the Air Force's traditional rival for power projection and deep-attack roles-but at the Army."[129] Another wrote of Army outrage over McPeak's "call for a clean split between Army and Air Force roles to avoid overlap," reporting that a senior Army officer assailed the Air Force chief's "version of the battlefield" as "simplistic and dangerous," while another declared his fundamental strategy "wrong."[130] Brash remarks by another disgruntled ground officer that air power contributed only "at the margins" in battle and that air forces and navies were mere "add-ons" to armies caused as much of a stir as McPeak's comments.[131]

During an October interview Secretary of Defense Perry tried to distance himself from the dispute. When questioned about General McPeak's claim "that the Persian Gulf War was the first time in history that a field army was defeated by air power," Perry conceded "that the [Iraqi] field army was devastated, if not fully defeated by air power," but hastened to add that "it took a joint operation to win the war." Perry also discussed the "enormous" advances that made air power effective in the Gulf War, but noted that the "same improved intelligence, stealthiness, and emphasis on precision-guided munitions" were "being introduced in the ground forces as well." He denied that "enlargement of the Air Force budget in proportion to the other services" was foreseen from the commission's review of roles and missions. Repeating that "joint air-ground-sea operations" were necessary to win wars, Perry concluded, "That is what our forces are being built on, that is what our budget is based on, and that is what our tactics and doctrine are based on."[132]

The furor over roles and missions subsided after General Fogleman became the new Air Force Chief of Staff near the end of October. A warrior-historian who flew F–100s in combat and was shot down in Vietnam, Fogleman made history by being the first Air Force Academy graduate to rise to the highest post in the Air Force. Predictions that the new Chief's prowess in joint positions in Korea and as head of the Transportation Command made him "the ideal person to close some rifts with the Army and Navy over acquisition funding and roles and missions" proved correct. By 1995, reports claimed that General Fogleman had moved quickly to take "the high drama out" of the roles and missions debate and the services "had settled down to a truce of sorts...with occasional shots fired back and forth."[133]

General Fogleman briefed a revised Air Force position to the commission on December 14, easing interservice tensions. While preserving the basic concept and emphasis on Air Force primary roles in high and deep battles, the new chief withdrew the more contentious proposals of General McPeak, particularly those hurting relations with the Army. Fogleman told the commission that Air Force fixed-wing aircraft would continue to fly close air support as a primary mission, but noted their declining use on the modern battlefield. Other thorny issues, such as integration of air defenses, could be worked out "under existing ownership arrangements," Fogleman said.[134] During the remaining months of the commission's deliberations Fogleman's coalescent views on joint warfighting altered the tempo of the debate.

During his first days as Chief of Staff, General Fogleman made known his belief that "Goldwater-Nichols [had] fundamentally changed the American way of war." In an introductory message, he urged the "men and women of the Air Force," to be proud of their "heritage" and "core capabilities," but to remember that they served as "a team within a team." "Thus, one of our first questions...in contemplating any course of action is its impact on the other services and the joint teams led by the commanders-in-chief of our unified commands," he said. The General said this commitment made it imperative that the "very best people" in the Air Force serve on joint staffs so unified commands would "have people there who do understand air power." For emphasis, he added, "I think our nation is not well served if you don't have people on these joint staffs who understand air power."[135]

General Fogleman brought his philosophy of jointness into the roles and missions debate, with an approach that differed from his predecessor's. He relied less on "the abstract" and more on "the art of the possible," but hastened to dispel rumors that he would take the Air Force in a "new direction." He applauded the structural changes made by General McPeak to adapt "a shrinking force to the new security demands," and stated that the Air Force was "on course" with major programs and policies. In sorting out roles and missions, however, Fogleman believed the services had to stop looking at issues "through the eyes of their component commander" and elevate their focus "up to the joint force commander level." There, they would have a sharper view of how "core competencies and capabilities" should be brought "together on the battlefield."[136]

As Fogleman explained, in minor contingencies, such as the Mayaguez incident or the invasion of Grenada, the joint force commander would weigh the circumstances and decide whether to assign the dominant role to the land, air, or maritime component. Larger operations such as the Gulf War, however, unfolded sequentially and required an aggregate response by integrated air, sea, and land components. Air power would probablly dominate in the opening phases, protecting the force buildup, ranging the battlefield, and taking the deep battle to the enemy.

Fogleman emphasized he was not talking just about the Air Force, "but air power"-the full air component of complementary carrier and land-based air forces. The situation would change after land forces arrived, consolidated, and initiated land maneuver warfare. The air component's priorities also changed, in terms of apportionment, determining where to apply the effort to support the joint force commander's objectives. This required that air, land, and maritime components plan and apply their core competencies jointly, and that they view the battle through the joint force commander's eyes.[137]

The storm over roles and missions abated, but some interservice disputes continued to simmer as the commission continued its deliberations. Only an occasional headline pointing to the long-standing Air Force-Navy feud over forward presence broke the lull before completion of the commission report. The Air Force took the position that forward presence was a shared role and that "its bombers and fighters, stationed within the theater or deploying from the United States...could be the first United States forces to reach a crisis area."[138]

The global reach of Air Force long-range bombers was demonstrated in the Gulf War when two B–52s carried out a "forty-seven-hour 20,000-mile trans-global mission from Barksdale AFB, Louisiana, to targets in Kuwait and back."[139] A 1995 Air Force white paper expanded the definition of global presence "to include not only...air, land, and sea forces, but...space forces and information-based capabilities."[140]

Naval strategists embraced a narrower view of forward presence, contending that it meant continually deploying carrier groups and Marine amphibious groups in foreign waters to respond to global crises. A key naval strategist scoffed at the Air Force claim that the response of air power based in the United States to global crises was a form of military presence. "I don't care...how you color that son of a bitch, it is not forward presence," he said.[141]

The Air Force version of forward presence as "a team effort" was consonant with joint policy and doctrine. Since becoming Chairman of the Joint Chiefs, General Shalikashvili worked "to inject more joint flavor into doctrine, manning, exercises, readiness and requirements." The Chairman selected "five critical issues" in what he called the "prolonged march toward jointness." He made joint doctrine "his first order of business" since it underpinned "everything about joint warfighting." Combatant commanders became more involved "in vetting the doctrine" and working other issues.[142]

The Vice Chairman, Adm. William Owens, also worked to fuse "systems and the people...together" to give combatant commanders "the forces they need for any contingencies." Owens called for a new discipline to force the services "to design weapons that will work together, eliminate duplication in their missions and buy equipment that corresponds to the threat."[143]

As the commission neared the end of its work, the *Navy Times* reported that the effort "plowed no new ground." The paper obtained a draft of the commission report which rejected "the argument that the Pentagon needlessly had 'four air forces'." It proposed consolidating "some responsibilities among the services, but not as many as some hoped-and others feared." The commission believed that all services could "play a role in 'forward presence'—showing the flag to help deter crises."

Ruling out "any large-scale consolidation" of roles and missions, the commission advocated building on the improvements legislated by Goldwater-Nichols to strengthen roles and powers of the Chairman of the Joint Chiefs, regional, and combatant commanders and to achieve "better integration of the country's national security bureaucracy." They recommended creating "a new functional 'joint command' whose sole job would be to develop joint doctrine and training for U.S.-based forces." Underpinning the findings was a belief "that all major, and even most minor, operations" in the future would be joint.[144]

This preliminary insight into the commission's thinking seemed to prove the skeptics right about the prospects for meaningful roles and missions reform. General McPeak expressed his doubts in an interview soon after his retirement, stating that real roles and missions reform probably meant having "to rebuild the armed forces," which, in turn, required the firm hand of a determined President. "I'm very skeptical about the chances of making much progress on roles and missions until some later point in history," he said.[145]

At the eleventh hour, reports indicated that the commission had rejected the Air Force view of the 21st-century battle and would "recommend that the Army and the Marines continue to share the ground fighting, that the Navy still sail the oceans, and that all the services maintain their own air power."[146] Regardless of the outcome, air power and the armed forces remained at a crossroads in the evolution of roles and missions as they prepared to defend the nation and to fight the nation's wars into the 21st Century.

EPILOGUE

The 103d Congress set the stage for the epilogue when it called for an independent study of post-Cold War roles and missions in the 1994 defense bill. Key legislators called for a nonpartisan review citing "chronic...problems of overlap, duplication, and parochialism." Democratic Senator Sam Nunn of Georgia, Chairman of the Senate Armed Services Committee, said the Defense Department "must prepare for the future with a fresh look at the roles and missions that characterized the past 40 years." He believed the force structure needed to be reshaped, reconfigured, and modernized-not just pared down, as in previous reform movements. "We must find the best way to provide a fighting force in the future that is not bound by the constraints of the roles and missions outlined in 1948," Nunn stated.

The Senator and his colleagues believed that Gen. Colin Powell's recent valedictory report and earlier roles and mission studies were swayed by parochial service interests. In the spring of 1994, an eleven-member commission appointed by Secretary of Defense Perry began deliberations. A year later, the commission's findings suggested that their work was no less affected by traditional service doctrines, weapons, and rivalries than General Powell's earlier report.[1]

In a report to the Secretary of Defense on May 24, the commission conceded that the Defense Department had to strike balances that could be interpreted as "counter-intuitive" if the armed forces were to continue to wield "the right mix of air, land, and naval capabilities to meet any threat." Chairman Dr. John White explained that a proper balance was needed between "the high value" placed on competition among the services and the need to reduce costs.

The commission concluded that "Army and Marine Corps capabilities [were] complimentary, not redundant," and that "inefficiencies attributed to the so-called 'four air forces' [were] mostly in the infrastructure, not on the battlefield." Repeating a theme of the Powell report, the commission labelled these "non-issues" which the Defense Department should put "into proper perspective-and therefore to rest."[2]

"Our most important finding is that traditional approaches to roles and missions issues are no longer appropriate," White said, recalling that past attempts to allocate roles and missions had produced "institutional quarrels...and unsatisfactory compromises," and failed to achieve Defense Department goals. The revised frame of reference for roles and missions, and therefore a lodestar for the commission's study, was the Goldwater-Nichols Reorganization Act of 1986. White believed that implementing Goldwater-Nichols was a prime objective which would mold "DOD into a cohesive set of institutions that work toward a common purpose-effective unified military operations." He explained:

Roles and Missions

> The question is no longer "who does what," but how do we ensure that the right set of capabilities is identified, developed, and fielded to meet the needs of unified commanders.[3]

Building on the legacy of Goldwater-Nichols, the commission's report became an institutional blueprint to strengthen joint warfighting. Acknowledging the "superb" capabilities demonstrated by each service in the Gulf War, the report stated that the experience also revealed "they do not work well enough together." Topping a list of initiatives to improve "joint capabilities and joint warfighting" was a proposal that the Chairman of the Joint Chiefs develop a unified vision for the 21st Century. While the Air Force *Global Reach, Global Power* and vision papers issued by the other services added "breadth, flexibility, and synergy to military operations," the commission stessed the need for a central vision.[4]

To strengthen joint doctrine, the commission urged support for the year-old Joint Warfighting Center, created in 1994 to assist "in conceptualizing, developing, and assessing current and future joint doctrine." The commission believed it was essential for the Secretary of Defense to provide resources to fulfill the Center's responsibilities. A related issue was joint training, described in the report as a chronic problem. The commission recommended creating a command which would be "responsible for joint training and integration of forces based in the Continental United States" to separate preparation of forces from the operational responsiblities assigned to the Atlantic Command. The commission also asked that the warfighting commanders be given "greater responsibility...in structuring and controlling joint training, theater logistics, and command, control, and intelligence support."[5]

While concentrating on joint warfighting reforms, the report reaffirmed military roles "that have evolved as DOD has matured." The services had "core competencies" fundamental to their roles. As defined by the commission, these were:

> ...*for the Air Force*, air superiority, global strike/deep attack, and air mobility: *for the Army*, mobile armored warfare, airborne operations, and light infantry operations; *for the Navy*, carrier-based air and amphibious power projection, sea-based air and missile defense, and anti-submarine warfare; *for the Marine Corps*, amphibious operations, over-the-beach forced entry operations, and maritime pre-positioning; and *for the Coast Guard*, humanitarian operations, maritime defense, safety, law enforcement, and environmental protection.[6]

The report supported the Air Force position that each service should contribute to a peacetime overseas presence, but concluded that "DOD must look for more efficient and effective ways" to achieve overseas presence and that the warfighting commanders should take the lead by "experimenting with new approaches".

Urging greater Defense Department influence over space-based support and satellite tasking, the commission reaffirmed the responsibility of the Air Force "for acquisition and operation of multi-user space-based systems." The commission also recommended making the Air Force executive agent for combat search and rescue support and proposed reducing "operational support" fleets, transferring most of these aircraft to the Air Force for management by the Transportation Command.[7]

Consistent with its ruling on the "four air forces" issue, the commission deemed it "appropriate" that all services perform close air support. Since aircraft providing close air support were multipurpose weapons flying "a range of critical combat functions," the report found that "no significant savings" would accrue by removing any of the services' air capabilities without weakening overall warfighting capabilities. Similarly, the commission denied there was needless redundancy in deep-attack weapon systems-noting that the "mix of land-based ballistic missiles, sea-based cruise missiles, and a growing inventory of precision-guided munitions and standoff weapons delivered by aircraft" were all useful. It recommended, however, that the services conduct studies to determine the proper mix of weapon systems.[8]

Senator Nunn instructed the commission to conduct its review of "the forces and programs of the individual services" with an eye to "cost-saving recommendations." After reading the report a veteran defense analyst concluded the panel found "a number of ways to save significant amounts of money, but not necessarily where Nunn had anticipated." A forceful critic of "overlap and duplication" in the armed forces, Nunn expressed doubts about "four air forces" and competing ground capabilities between the Army and the Marines.

The commission disagreed on this point, recommending that the Defense Department could achieve substantial savings by relying on the private sector for high-cost support activities, including logistics, health care, training, acquisition management, and installations and facilities. The commission recommended that downsizing continue, with a proposal to reduce the standing Army by 50,000 troops and shift another 60,000 troops from combat to support duty.[9]

Reaction to the commission's report was mixed. One critic complained that it failed "to transcend service rivalries"[10] while another called the report "rambling," "timid," and "vague," adding "how refreshing it would have been if this unencumbered commission had said something bold."[11] The services generally were pleased and Secretary of Defense Perry agreed with most of the findings. In May, Perry announced that he had selected commission chairman John White to be Deputy Secretary of Defense, a decision one senior editor found "extraordinary."[12]

In a letter to key defense congressional committees in late August, Secretary Perry advised that "an overwhelming majority" of commission proposals had been approved. Perry agreed with the central theme of the report and his office began to develop a unified vision for post-Cold War forces. Perry informed Congress that the Defense Department rejected few recommendations and deferred a final decision on others.

Among the outstanding controversial issues was the question of the proper mix of weapons to perform the deep-strike mission.[13] One journalist recalled this as an issue that "only months ago had the Air Force and the Navy at each other's throats over whether enemy targets should be attacked with carrier-based or land based bombers." Perry requested a comprehensive review of the nation's deep-attack military assets.[14]

At a Pentagon briefing that August afternoon, Deputy Secretary White cautioned reporters that the commission's findings should be viewed in the larger context of Defense Department actions with downsizing and "with refashioning a strategy, in terms of the bottom-up review."[15] Transitioning to a post-Cold War "national military strategy of carrying out two simultaneous wars" was underway, already tested in Iraq, Somalia, and Haiti.

An even greater test loomed in Bosnia. Accepting the challenge to reduce costs, the Defense Department agreed with the commission's "endorsement of the basic division of war fighting labors among the services."[16] The *raison d'e-tre*, after all, lay in the application of military power as an instrument of national policy, not in the tight-fisted appropriation of defense budgets.

The press parodied the decision to restudy the commission's most controversial proposals. One article closed with a wry observation that "by the time all the new studies are concluded, perhaps the world will have changed enough to mandate another comprehensive review."[17] Another article reported that some defense experts called for "a dramatic overhaul of the military," citing a source who called the findings "a disappointment."[18] The media onslaught was brief and the anticipated uproar on Capitol Hill never materialized.

By the end of 1995, lingering silence from Capitol Hill implied consent for the path laid out in the commission's report. After Secretary Perry's letter of late August, the congressional oversight committees withdrew roles and missions from the political frontlines. The topic faded under the glare of issues such as balancing the budget and seeking answers to the entangled Bosnian crisis on NATO's doorstep. Adding to uncertainty on Capitol Hill were announcements from several members of Congress that they would not seek reelection. Senator Sam Nunn, who had been at the forefront of roles and missions reform, was among those who planned to step down, making the liklihood of meaningful challenge to the commission's report more remote.

As for its affect on the post-Cold War epilogue, this uncertainty meant that the curtain would begin to descend for this century, not with finality, but falter-ingly-leaving the "Voices from the Central Blue" waiting in the wings to ponder what tomorrow's journey would bring and whether the future of air power hung in the balance.[19]

Notes

Preface

1. Herman S. Wolk, *Planning and Organizing the Postwar Air Force, 1943-1947* (Washington, D.C., 1984), pp 164-171.
2. Orvil A. Anderson, "How Air Power Grew," *The Air Power Historian*, Apr. 1956, pp 134-137.
3. Alfred Goldberg, ed., *A History of the United States Air Force, 1907-1987* (Princeton, N.J., 1987), pp 115-119.
4. Colonel Thomas G. Roe, USMC, et al., *A History of Marine Corps Roles and Missions, 1775-1962* (Washington, D.C., 1962), pp 1-4.
5. Richard I. Wolf, *The United States Air Force: Basic Documents on Roles and Missions* (Washington, D.C., 1987), p 2.
6. Agenda for 1990 Air Force Doctrine Conference, HQ USAF DCS/Plans and Operations, Maxwell AFB, Alabama, Apr. 18-19, 1990, pp 20, 21; Daniel T. Kuehl and Charles E. Miller, "Roles and Missions, and Functions: Terms of Debate," *Joint Forces Quarterly*, Summer 1994, pp 103-105.
7. Memorandum, for the Secretary of Defense by William J. Crowe, Jr, Chairman, Joint Chiefs of Staff, subj: Report on Roles and Missions of the Armed Forces, Sep. 28, 1989.
8. *Ibid.*, Appendix C, Definition of Terms.
9. Report on "Roles, Missions, and Functions of the Armed Forces of the United States," by Colin L. Powell, Chairman of the Joint Chiefs of Staff, Feb. 10, 1993.
10. Kuehl and Miller, "Roles and Missions, and Functions: Terms of Debate," p 103.
11. Dennis M. Drew, "Stormy Clouds Amass Over Roles, Missions," *Air Force Times*, Dec. 18, 1994, p 54.

Chapter I

1. List of Appropriations for Army Aviation, Army, Navy Aviation, Navy, Combined Services, 1890-1939, compiled by the Budget & Fiscal Div., AAF, undated, AFHRA 131.41-2 [hereafter Appropriations, 1890-1939]; Maurice Matloff, *et al.*, *American Military History* (Washington, D.C., 1969), 350,354, [hereafter Matloff, *Military History*]. In 1902, Congress authorized a ceiling of 100,000 men, but according to Matloff, the average strength fell well below that for the decade.
2. Robert Frank Futrell, *Ideas, Concepts, Doctrine: Basic Thinking in the United States Air Force, Vol I, 1907-1960* (Maxwell AFB, Ala., 1989), 15,16 [hereafter Futrell, *Ideas, Concepts, Doctrine, Vol I*]; Alfred Goldberg, *et al.*, *A History of the United States Air Force, 1907-1957* (Princeton, 1957), 2,3, [hereafter Goldberg, *A History*]. Goldberg notes that aviation pioneer Glenn Curtiss successfully flew the Langley plane in 1914 after making structural changes to it.
3. *Ibid.*; Ltr, Wilbur and Orville Wright to Hon. R. M. Nevin, Jan. 12, 1905; Ltr, R. M. Nevin, House of Rep, to Hon. William H. Taft, Sec of War, Jan. 21, 1905; Ltr, Maj. Gen. G. L. Gillespie, The Pres, Board of Ordnance & Fortification, War Dept., to Hon R. M. Nevin, Jan. 24, 1905; Ltr, Wilbur and Orville Wright to Sec War, Oct. 9, 1905, Ltr, Maj. Gen. J. G. Bates, Pres., Board of Ordnance & Fortification, Oct. 16, 1905. All located in papers of E. L. Jones, AFHRA, 168.6501 & 168.6501-5.
4. Ltr, Wilbur and Orville Wright to Lt. Thomas E. Selfridge, Feb. 25, 1907, in Wright papers at Lib of Congress and AFHRA 168.6501-5.
5. Notes, papers of E. L. Jones, entry for Mar. 16, 1907, AFHRA 168.6501; J. Allen, Office Memorandum No. 6, Office of the Chief Signal Officer, War Dept, Aug. 1, 1907, AFHRA 168.6501-5; Notes, papers of E. L. Jones, entry for Feb. 10,1908, AFHRA 168.6501-6; Goldberg, *A History*, 4.
6. Annual Report of the Chief Signal Officer for fiscal year 1910, Brig. Gen. James Allen, Sep. 1, 1910, pp 24-27, AFHRA 168.6501. 6.
7. Ltr, Brig. Gen. James Allen, Chief Signal Officer of the Army, to The Recorder, Board of Ordnance & Fortification, 10 Oct. 1907, AFHRA 168.6501-5.

8. Papers of E. L. Jones, for Dec. 23, 1907, extracted from files of Board of Ordnance & Fortification, National Archives, AFHRA 168.6501-5.

9. Annual Report of the Secretary of War, 3 Dec. 1910. AFHRA 168.6501-5.

10. *Ibid.*

11. Goldberg, *A History*, 6.

12. *Ibid.*, Field Service Regulations, U. S. Army (Washington, D.C., Feb. 21, 1910), LOC Papers of Millard F. Harmon, AFHRA 168.604-2.

13. Papers of E. L. Jones, entry for Oct. 19, 1911, AFHRA 168.6501-10; The Air Officer's Guide, Fourteenth Edition (Harrisburg, PA., 1962), 2; San Francisco *Examiner*, 23 Jan.1911.

14. Report of Lt. T. D. Milling on the W. T. Scott Projectile Dropping Device, undated, AFHRA 168.6501-10; Lee Kennett, *A History of Strategic Bombing* (New York, 1982), 14, 15. Kennett documents that aerial bombing occurred on two other occasions before WWI, during the Balkan wars of 1912-13 and in French Morocco in 1912.

15. Goldberg, *A History*, 4-8; Report by Capt. C. Def. Chandler, OIC of the SCAS, College Park, Jun. 10, 1912, AFHRA 168.6501-11; Report upon test of aeroplane in connection with artillery fire, by 2d Lt. H. H. Arnold to CO Signal Corps Aviation School, Nov. 6, 1912, AFHRA 168.6501-12. Lt Milling, who flew the plane for Chandler's demonstration later recalled that the Signal Corps wanted to purchase the Lewis gun for training and testing, but the Chief of Ordnance refused. Lewis was forced to go to Belgium to manufacture his guns. After entering the war, the Air Service purchased these same guns to equip its planes, *The Air Power Historian*, Jan.1956, 101.

16. Papers of E. L. Jones, added item for 8/24/12, AFHRA 168.6501-12.

17. Paper by R. F. Futrell, "Identification of Airpower Capabilities, 1903-1945," Jul. 2, 1963 [hereafter Futrell, "Airpower Capabilities"]; William J. Armstrong and Clark Van Fleet, *United States Naval Aviation, 1910-1980* (Washington, D.C., 1980), 2, 3 [here-

after Armstrong and Van Fleet, *Naval Aviation*].

18. Futrell, "Airpower Capabilities," 3; Armstrong and Van Fleet, *Naval Aviation*, 3-12; San Francisco *Examiner*, Jan. 19, 1911, and Items for Jan. 21, 1911, Feb. 17, 1911, and added item 1-26-11, in Papers of E. L. Jones, AFHRA 168.6501-9.

19. Appropriations, 1890-1939, AFHRA 131.41-2; Goldberg, *A History*, 8.

20. Armstrong and Van Fleet, *Naval Aviation*, 16; Adrian O. Van Wyen, *The Aeronautical Board, 1916-1947*, (Washington, D.C., Dir of Naval History, 1947), 1-3.

21. Van Wyen, *The Aeronautical Board, 1916-1947*(Washington D.C.:Dir of Naval History 1947), 1-3. Van Wyen, *Aeronautical Board*, 30; Board of Army and Navy Officers' Report relative to development of aeronautical service, to Secretary of the Navy, Mar. 12, 1917, AFHRA 248.211-76F.

22. See note above.

23. See note above; Holley, *Ideas and Weapons*, 40; Futrell, *Ideas, Concept, Doctrine*, Vol. I, 21.

24. Field Service Regulations, U. S. Army, 1914, corrected to Apr. 15, 1917 (Washington, D.C., Mar. 19, 1914), located in Papers of E. L. Jones, AFHRA 168.6504-4.

25. R. Earl McClendon, *The Question of Autonomy for the United States Air Arm, 1907- 1945* (Maxwell AFB, Ala., 1950), 27-37 [hereafter McClendon, *Question of Autonomy*]; Futrell, *Ideas, Concepts, Doctrine, Vol I*, 16, 17.

26. McClendon, *Question of Autonomy*, 38, 39; Goldberg, *A History*, 8; Edwin L. Williams, Jr., "Legislative History of the Air Arm," *Military Affairs*, Summer 1956, 81, 82 [hereafter Williams, "Legislative History"].

27. Papers of E. L. Jones, items for Apr. 13, 1916, and Apr. 19, 1916, AFHRA 168.6501-19; Goldberg, *A History*, 10; Futrell, *Ideas, Concepts, Doctrine, Vol I*, 19.

28. 64 Congress, 1 Session, House of Representatives, *Hearings on Army Appropriation Bill 1917*, 838-40, as cited in McClendon, *Question of Autonomy*, 44-47; Alfred F. Hurley, *Billy Mitchell, Crusader for Air*

Power (New York, 1964), 20-21 [hereafter Hurley, *Billy Mitchell*].

29.   Russell F. Weigley, *History of the United States Army* (New York, 1967), 350.

30.   William Addleman Ganoe, *The History of the United States Army* (New York, 1924), 456; Goldberg, *A History*, 10, 11; Matloff, *Military History*, 366, 367.

31.   Paper by Major Thomas DeWitt Milling, Subj: Air Power in National Defense, 1928, AFHRA 248.211-122.

32.   McClendon, *Question of Autonomy*, 48, 49; Goldberg, *A History*, 15.

33.   Goldberg, *A History*, 8; Lt. Clayton Bissell, *A Brief History of the Air Corps* (Langley Field, VA, 1927), 15-16.

34.   Air Vice Marshal E. J. Kingston McCloughry, RAF, *The Direction of War* (New York, 1955), 64, 74; Irving B. Holley, *Ideas and Weapons* (Washington, D.C.: 1983), 183, 184 [hereafter Holley, *Ideas and Weapons*].

35.   Flt. Lt. E. J. MacKay, RAF, "The Influence in the Future of Aircraft Upon Problems of Imperial Defense," *Journal, R.U.S.I.*, May 1922, AFHRA 248.211-63 (1916-1932) [hereafter MacKay, *Journal, R.U.S.I.*, May 1922]; *Ecole de Guerre* text, (extracts), History of the Employment of Military Aviation during the War, 1914-1918, 1, 19-23, 27 [hereafter *Ecole de Guerre* text]; Edward Homze, "The Continental Experience," *Air Power and Warfare, Proceedings of the Eighth Military History Symposium, USAF Academy, 1978* (Washington, D.C., 1979), 19 [hereafter *Air Power and Warfare*].

36.   Kenneth P. Werrell, *Archie, Flak, AAA, and SAM: A Short Operational History of Ground-Based Air Defense,* (Maxwell AFB, Ala., 1988), 1, 2.

37.   McKay, *Journal, R.U.S.I.*, May 1922; *Ecole de Guerre* text.

38.   *Air Power and Warfare*, 19; Futrell, "Airpower Capabilities," 4.

39.   Brig. Gen. Frank P. Lahm, "Commentary on Mitchell's Memoirs of World War I," *The Airpower Historian*, Jul. 1962, 189.

40.   B. H. Liddell Hart, "Paris or the Future of War," undated, AFHRA 248.211-63

(1916- 1932); Report by Lt. Zettel, "Aerial Bombardment in WWI and Today," 25 May 1928, AFHRA 248.222.⁻., McCloughry, *The Direction of War*, 53, 71; Maj. William C. Sherman, "The Objectives of Bombardment," Air Warfare Paper, AFHRA 248.211-63 (1916-1932); Sir F. H. Sykes, "Aviation in Peace and War," undated, AFHRA 248.211-63, (1916-1932).

41.   USAF Historical Study No. 100, *History of the Air Corps Tactical School, 1920-1940* (Maxwell AFB, Ala., 1955), 3 [hereafter *History of Tactical School*]; Group Capt. R. A. Mason, RAF, "The British Dimension," *Air Power and Warfare*, Brig. Gen. William Mitchell, *Memoirs of World War I* (New York, 1960), 104-119 [hereafter Mitchell, *Memoirs*].

42.   Holley, *Ideas and Weapons*, 46, 47; Hurley, *Billy Mitchell*, 29, 30; Goldberg, *A History*, 22; Futrell, *Ideas, Concepts, Doctrine, Vol I*, 20; Memorandum for the Chief of Staff, U. S. Expeditionary Force, From Major Mitchell, Aviation Section, Signal Corps, Jun. 13, 1917, in Gorrell's History of the Air Service, AEF, A-23; and reprinted in Maurer Maurer, *The U. S. Service in World War I, Vol II* (Washington, D.C., 1978), 107-111 [hereafter Maurer, *Air Service, Vol II*].

43.   Holley, *Ideas and Weapons*, 48.

44.   Entry, Sep. 3, 1917, Papers of E. L. Jones, AFHRA 168.6501-29; Mitchell *Memoirs*, 156.

45.   Futrell, *Ideas, Concepts, Doctrine, Vol I*, 22.

46.   Lt. Col. William Mitchell, "General Principles Underlying the Use of the Air Service in the Zone of the Advance A. E. F.," Bulletin of the Information Section, Air Service, A. E. F., Vol III, No. 132, Apr. 30, 1918, AFHRA 168.65033 (Apr. 10-May 8, 1918).

47.   Mitchell, *Memoirs*, 156, 190; John F. Shiner, *Foulois and the U. S. Army Air Corps, 1931-1935,* (Washington, D.C., 1983), 9-10; Richard O'Connor, *Black Jack Pershing* (Garden City, N.Y., 1961), 266-269 [hereafter O'Connor, *Pershing*]; Aaron Norman, *The Great Air War* (New York-London, 1968), 489 [hereafter Norman, *Air War*].

48. Norman, *Air War*, 497.

49. Maurer, *Air Service, Vol II*, 141, 152; Colonel Edgar S. Gorrell, U. S. Air Service, "An American Proposal for Strategic Bombing in World War I," *The Air Power Historian*, Apr. 1958, 102-117; A Brief History of the Air Corps, ACTS, Langley AFB, VA, Feb. 25, 1927, 69, AFHRA 248.211-612; Maj. Gen. L. S. Kuter, "Air Power - The American Concept," undated, AFHRA 167.6-50. The Gorrell Plan, approved by Pershing on Jan. 5, 1918, concluded that "to affect the armies in the field it is necessary to affect the manufacturing output of the country." Accordingly, "the sources of German military strength were analyzed and were organized in several groups of objectives for strategic air attack."

50. Mitchell, *Memoirs*, 178. Mitchell wrote in his diary that Liggett was one of the few officers "who is taking a distinct personal interest in aviation." [Isaac Don Devine, *Mitchell, Pioneer of Air Power* (New York, 1958), 117].

51. O'Connor, *Pershing*, 269.

52. Final Report of General John J. Pershing, CINC AEF, (Washington, 1920), 38-40, AFHRA 167.601-1c [hereafter Pershing Final Report]; Historical Division, Dept of the Army, *United States Army in the World War, 1917-1919. Organization of the American Expeditionary Forces*(Washington, 1948), 8-16 [hereafter *Organization of the AEF*].

53. Pershing Final Report, 38-40; *Organization of the AEF*, 10-13.

54. *History of the Air Service in A. E. F., Operations of the Air Service*, undated, AFHRA 248.211-61p, 1; *History of Tactical School*, 3; *Organization of the AEF*, 13, 14.

55. *Organization of the AEF*, 39, 42; Pershing Final Report, 38. 39.

56. *History of the Air Service in the A. E. F.*, 1; Final Report of Chief of Air Service, AEF, Maj. Gen. M. M. Patrick, (Washington, 1921), 9, AFHRA 167.404 [hereafter Patrick Final Report].

57. Pershing Final Report, 45.

58. Patrick Final Report, 13.

59. History of the Air Service in A. E. F., *Operations of the Air Service*, undated, AFHRA 248.211-61p, 1; Maurer, *Air Service, Vol I*, 29.

60. Patrick Final Report, 17.

61. *Ibid.*,3.

62. Pershing Final Report, 76.

63. Patrick Final Report, 19.

64. United States Army Aircraft Production Facts (Washington, D.C., GPO, 1919), 4-10, AFHRA 168.6502-5; James J. Hudson, *Hostile Skies: A Combat History of the American Air Service in World War I* (Syracuse, NY: 1968), 17.

65. Edwin L. Williams, Jr., "Legislative History of the Air Arm," *Military Affairs*, Summer 1956, 84; Item for Apr. 25, 1918, in Papers of E. L. Jones, AFHRA 168.6501-34; Annual Report of Sec of War, Newton D. Baker, for 1918, Vol I, p.1, extract in copies E. L. Jones, AFHRA 168.6501-34; U. S. House of Representatives Report No. 637, 66th Congress, *Expenditures in the War Department-Aviation*, Feb. 16, 1920, 8,9, AFHRA 168.65403C.

66. McClendon, *Question of Autonomy*, Part I, 68,69, AFHRA 239.04-5.

67. U. S. House of Representatives Report No. 637, 66th Congress, *Expenditures in the War Department - Aviation*, Feb. 16, 1920, 22, 23, AFHRA 168.65403C.

68. War Dept Special Order 299-0, Dec. 23, 1918, cited in papers of E. L. Jones AFHRA 168.6501-37. Menoher assumed the directorship on Jan. 2, 1919.

69. Hurley, *Billy Mitchell*, 38.

70. Maurer, *Air Service*, Vol IV, 21-27.

71. Futrell, *Ideas, Concepts, Doctrine*, Vol I, 28, 29.

72. U. S. House of Representatives Report No. 637, 66th Congress, *Expenditures* in the War Department - Aviation, Feb. 16, 1920, 70, AFHRA 168.65403c; McClendon, *Question of Autonomy*, 90-92.

73. Report of a Board of Officers Convened to Report Upon the New (S-2693) and Curry (H. R. - 7925) Bills, Oct. 27, 1919, 8, 9, 20, AFHRA 167.404-3.

74. Extract of Annual report by Secretary of War, Newton D. Baker, Nov. 11, 1919, AFHRA 168.6501-38.

75. *Ibid.*

76. McClendon, *Question of Autonomy*, 83, 84, 94, 95; Ltr, General Pershing to General Menoher, Dec. 16, 1919, AFHRA 168.6501-39.

77. Edwin L. Williams, Jr., "Legislative History of the Air Arm," *Military Affairs*, Summer 1956, 84; Futrell, *Ideas, Concepts, Doctrine, Vol I*, McClendon, *Question of Autonomy*, 99; Extracts from the Army Reorganization Act of 1920, Papers of E. L. Jones, AFHRA 168.6501-40.

78. Lecture by Rear Admiral W. A. Moffett, "The Naval Air Service," delivered at the Army War College, Washington, D.C., Nov. 10, 1925, AFHRA 248.211-76A; Paper, "Progress of Naval Aviation," undated, 11, AFHRA 168.65413-15.

79. Minutes of Meeting before House Subcommittee on Aviation, Committee of Military Affairs, presided over by Hon. Fiorello H. LaGuardia, Dec. 20, 1919, on file in Library of Congress, Ms. Div., Mitchell Papers, Box 32; 2d Indorsement to Chief of Air Service, fm Brig. Gen. William Mitchell, Feb. 16, 1925, Library of Congress, Mitchell Papers, Box 37.

80. Item Apr. 3, 1919, in papers of E. L. Jones, AFHRA 168.6501-37.

81. Hurley, *Billy Mitchell*, 41; Extract of Air Service News Letter, Jan. 15, 1920, 5, 168.6501.38.

82. Secretary of the Navy Jarvis Butler, *NAA Review*, Sep. 1925, as cited in Papers of E. L. Jones, AFHRA 168.6501-38.

83. Van Wyen, *Aeronautical Board*, 31; Report of the Director of Air Service, Maj. Gen. Charles T. Menoher, to the Secretary of War, Aug. 25, 1920, 15-16, AFHRA 168.65404-3 [hereafter Menoher, Report to the Secretary of War, 1920].

84. See Note 83 above; Lecture by Rear Admiral W. A. Moffett, "The Naval Air Service," delivered at the Army War College, Washington, D.C., Nov. 10, 1925, AFHRA 248.211-76A.

85. Appropriations, 1890-1939, AFHRA 131.41-2.

86. Shiner, *Foulois*, 17.

87. Annual Report of the Secretary of the Navy for Fiscal Year 1920, 52, AFHRA 168.65413-17.

88. *Ibid.*, 53.

89. Brig. Gen. William Mitchell, "Aviation Over the Water," *The American Review of Reviews*, Vol 57, No. 3, Oct. 1920, AFHRA 248.211-76M.

90. Item for Oct. 28-Nov. 3., 1920, papers of E. L. Jones, AFHRA 168.6501-40; Maurer Maurer, *Aviation in the U. S. Army, 1919-1939* (Washington, D.C., 1987), 115; Hurley, *Billy Mitchell*, 60-61.

91. Van Wyen, Aeronautical Board, 29, 30. AFHRA 168.6502-7.

Chapter II

1. Orvil A. Anderson, "How Air Power Grew," *The Air Power Historian* (Apr. 1956), pp 134-137.

2. Intvw, Lt. Col. Joe B. Green with Gen. Ira C. Eaker, Washington, D.C., Jan. 28, 1972, p 30, located at Army War College, Carlisle Barracks, Pa.

3. Statement of Brigadier General William Mitchell, Assistant Chief of the Air Service, Jan. 4, 1921, AFHRA 167.404-9; McClendon, *Question of Autonomy*, p 92; Shiner, *Foulois*, p 17.

4. Futrell, *Ideas, Concepts, Doctrine*, Vol I, p 168.

5. Shiner, *Foulois*, p 15, 16.

6. Christopher R. Gabel, *The U. S. Army GHQ Maneuvers of 1941* (Washington, D.C., 1991), p 190; Daniel R. Mortensen, *A Pattern for Joint Operations: World War II Close Air Support North Africa* (Washington, D.C., 1987), pp 13-28, 57-62.

7. Intvw, Green with Eaker, pp 32,33.

8. Shiner, *Foulois*, p 17.

9. Maurer Maurer, *Aviation in the U. S. Army, 1919-1939* (Washington, D.C., 1987), p 5; Appropriations, 1890-1939.

10. Memorandum of Recommendations submitted by General Billy Mitchell and not acted upon, Library of Congress, William Mitchell Papers, Box 32, Air Service 1917-1925.

11. Appropriations, 1890-1939, AFHRA 131.41-2.

12. Gen. Carl Spaatz, USAF Ret, "Let's Reorganize Defense," *Newsweek*, Jan. 31, 1955, p 31.

13. Shiner, *Foulois*, p 18; Hurley, *Billy Mitchell*, p 49.

14. Armstrong and Van Fleet, *Naval Aviation*, pp 48,49. An act of Congress created a Bureau of Aeronautics on Jul. 12, 1921. The Navy Department issued a general order establishing the Bureau on Aug. 10, but the bureau did not become operational until Sep. 1.

15. Eugene Emme, "The American Dimension," *Air Power & Warfare: The Proceedings of the Eighth Military History Symposium*, USAF Academy, 1978 (Washington, D.C.: 1979), pp 68,69.

16. *Our Navy*, the Standard Publication of the U. S. Navy (mid-March, 1926); William Moffett, "Aviation Progress in America," *The New York Times Current History*, pp 775-782, located in Nimitz Library, U. S. Naval Academy, Moffett Papers, Part 2, L 1 & 2.

17. Hurley, *Billy Mitchell*, p 41; Maurer, *Aviation in the U. S. Army*, p 64.

18. Memo for General Menoher, fm Lt. Col. O. Westover, Mar. 4, 1919; Memo for Chief of Training & Operations Group, fm Maj. Gen. Charles T. Menoher, Dir of Air Service, Jun. 19, 1919; Memo for General Menoher, fm Col. O. Westover, Jun. 20, 1919. All located in Westover Papers, AFHRA 168.7089-3.

19. Samuel F. Wells, Jr., "William Mitchell and the *Ostfriesland*: A Study in Military Reform," *The Historian* (August, 1964), p 540; Memo for Chief of Training and Operations Group, fm Maj. Gen Charles T. Menoher, Director of Air Service, Sep. 25 1919, AFHRA 168.7089-3.

20. Brig. Gen. William Mitchell, *Our Air Force: The Key to National Defense* (New York, 1921), pp 15, 159, 199.

21. Hurley, *Billy Mitchell*, pp 60, 61; Wells, pp 546-548; Vice Admiral Alfred W. Johnson, Ret., "The Naval Bombing Experiments," paper by the Naval Historical Foundation, May 31, 1959, [hereafter Johnson,

"Naval Bombing Experiments,"] AFHRA K180.058-1; Ltr, Brig. Gen. William Mitchell to Chief of Staff, subj: Bombing of a Battleship and Auxiliary Craft, Feb. 1, 1921, AFHRA 248.222-69, Vol 1, Pt. 1.

22. Wells, pp 547,548; Hurley, *Billy Mitchell*, pp 64,65; Statement of Brig. Gen. William Mitchell, Asst Chief of the Air Service, to the House Appropriations Committee, Jan.4, 1921, AFHRA 167.404-9; Ltr, R. E. Coontz, Senior Member, the Joint Board, to the Secretary of War, subj: Experiments in Bombing Naval Vessels from Aircraft, Feb. 28, 1921, AFHRA 248.222-69, Vol 7, Pt. 1.

23. Hurley, *Billy Mitchell*, pp 64,65; Wells, pp 549,550.

24. Hurley, *Billy Mitchell*, pp 66,67; Ltr, Robert L. Collins, Adjutant General, to the Chief of the Air Service, subj; Avoidance of Publicity in Connection with Bombing Experiments, May 9, 1921, AFHRA 145.91-140.

25. Hurley, *Billy Mitchell*,p 66; Wells, p 552; Maurer, *Aviation in the U. S. Army* p 115; Report of the Operations of the 1st Provisional Air Brigade in Naval Ordnance Tests, Apr-Aug. 1921, AFHRA 248.222-69.

26. Johnson, "Naval Bombing Experiments."

27. Wells, p 553; Maurer, *Aviation in the U. S. Army*, pp 116-118; Johnson, "Naval Bombing Experiments;" Report of the Joint Board on Results of Aviation and Ordnance Tests, Aug. 18, 1921, p 3, AFHRA 248.222-69. Naval gunfire sank other vessels during the series of tests.

28. Maurer, *Aviation in the U. S. Army*, p 120; Report on Operations of the 1st Provisional Air Brigade in Naval Ordnance Tests, Aug. 29, 1921, Vol 2, Chap. 9-14, pp 24,29, AFHRA 248.222-69.

29. Memorandum for Chief of Air Service, subj: [Report on the Operations of the 1st Provisional Air Brigade], fm Brig. Gen. William Mitchell, Aug. 29, 1921, AFHRA 248.222-69, Apr-Aug. 1921, Vol. 1.

30. *Ibid.*

31. Report of the Joint Board on Results of Aviation and Ordnance Tests held during Jun.

and July, 1921 and Conclusions Reached, Aug. 18, 1921, AFHRA 248.222-69, Apr-Aug. 1921, Vol. 7.

32. Wells, pp 558,559; Maurer, *Aviation in the U. S. Army,* pp 120,121; Hurley, *Billy Mitchell,* pp 68,69.

33. Report of the Operations of the 1st Prov. Air Brigade in the Bombing of the USS *Alabama,* undated, AFHRA 248.222-70; A Brief History of the Air Service, 1919-1931, p 10, AFHRA 168.6501-11; Maurer, *Aviation in the U. S. Army,* pp 122-124.

34. Wells, p 557.

35. Wells, p 560; Armstrong and Van Fleet, p 51; Johnson, "The Naval Bombing Experiments," p 18, AFHRA K180.058-1.

36. Wells, pp 560,561; Armstrong and Van Fleet, pp 51,53,65.

37. Intvw, Green with Eaker, Jan. 28, 1972, pp 30-31; Also see Air Service News Letter, Jul. 10, 1923, extract in papers of E. L. Jones, 168.6501-42.

38. Hurley, *Billy Mitchell*, pp 73-81; Maurer, *Aviation in the U. S. Army,* pp 124,126,127; Brig. Gen. William Mitchell, Report of Bombing Maneuvers conducted off Cape Hattaras, Sep. 15, 1923, AFHRA 248.222-71; Lt. Cmdr. H. B. Crow, "Bombing Tests on the 'Virginia' and 'New Jersey,'" reprint fm *U. S. Naval Institute Proceedings*, undated, AFHRA 248.222-69.

39. Army Regulations, No. 95-10, subj: Air Service, Air Service Troops, Nov. 17, 1921, AFHRA 168.7032-12.

40. Annual Report of the Chief of Air Service for the Fiscal Year ending Jun. 1922, by Maj. Gen. Mason M. Patrick, Sep. 9, 1922, pp 8,9, AFHRA 167.4011.

41. Annual Report of the Chief of Air Service for the Fiscal Year ending Jun. 30, 1923, by Maj. Gen. Mason M. Patrick, Sep. 13, 1923, pp 48,49, AFHRA 167.4011; General Statement of Maj. Gen. Mason M. Patrick to the Lassiter Board, Appendix II to the Lassiter Board Report, AFHRA 145.93-102A.

42. Report of a Committee of Officers Appointed by Secretary of War, subj: Proposed Reorganization for the Air Service, by Maj. Gen. William Lassiter, *et al.*, Mar. 22,

1923, p 6, AFHRA 145.93-102A. Also, AFHRA 167.404-8 and 145.91-110.

43. The Air Service, Fundamental Conceptions Paper, prepared under the direction of the Chief of Air Service, May 9, 1923, AFHRA 248.211-65S. Also, 167.404-10.

44. Ltr, Maj. Gen. Mason Patrick to Lt. Col. Roy C. Kirtland, the General Service Schools, Fort Leavenworth, Ks, Mar. 18, 1924, Nat. Archives, RG 18.

45. Ltr, Maj. Gen. Mason Patrick, Chief of Air Service, to the Adjutant GenerAla., subj: Reorganization of Air Forces for National Defense, Dec. 19, 1924, Library of Congress Manuscript Div, Spaatz Papers, Box No. 3.

46. Maj. Gen. Mason M. Patrick, *Military Aircraft and Their Use in Warfare* (Philadelphia, 1924), pp 9,10. See papers of E. L. Jones, 168.6501-40.

47. Maurer, *Aviation in the U. S. Army,* pp 108-110.

48. Ltr, Joint Planning Committee to the Joint Board, subj: Joint Army and Navy Air Program, Serial No. 243, Jan.28, 1925, AFHRA 145.93-101.

49. Ltr, Secretary of the Navy to the Secretary of War, subj: [Military Aviation Appropriations], Feb. 18, 1924, AFHRA 145.93-101.

50. Ltr, Secretary of the Navy to the Secretary of War, subj: [Military Aviation Appropriations], Sep. 28, 1924, AFHRA 145.93-101.

51. Brig. Gen. William Mitchell, "Notes on the Multi-Motored Bombardment Group Day and Night," undated, AFHRA 248.222-57.

52. Hurley, *Billy Mitchell,* pp 86-89.

53. *Ibid.*, Maurer, *Aviation in the U. S. Army*, pp 127,128.

54. See note above.

55. Oral History Interview with General Carl Spaatz, May 19, 1965, AFHRA K239.0512- 755; Biography of the General of the Army Henry Harley Arnold, Oct. 24, 1946, AFHRA biography files.

56. Ltr, Maj. Gen. Mason Patrick to Col. E. S. Gorrell, Vice Pres., Stutz Motor Car Cp., Indianapolis, Ind., Sep. 11, 1925; Ltr, Gen.

Mason Patrick to Lt. Col. C. B. Amorous, Feb. 12, 1926. National Archives, RG 18.

57. Maj. Gen. Benjamin D. Foulois, with Col. C. V. Glines, *From the Wright Brothers to the Astronauts, The Memoirs of Major General Benjamin D. Foulois* (New York, 1960), pp 197, 298.

58. Ltr, J. H. Selfridge to Rear Adm William A. Moffett, Sep. 14, 1925, located in Moffett Papers, AFHRA Microfilm Reel 0008.

59. Report of President's Aircraft Board (GPO: Washington, D.C., 30 Nov. 1925), pp 4,5. AFHRA 167.48-1 and 168.3952-168, and National Archives, RG 18.

60. *Ibid.*, pp 5,10-13.

61. *Ibid.*, pp 15-26.

62. Goldberg, *A History*, p 36; Air Corps Act of 1926, H. R. 10827, 69th Congress, approved Jul. 2, 1926, AFHRA 248.211-61E; Dissertation Abstract, *The Air Corps Act of 1926; A Study of the Legislative Process* by Harry Howe Ransom, PhD, Princeton University, 1954, AFHRA K112.1-3.

63. Armstrong and Van Fleet, *Naval Aviation*, pp 62.

64. Ltr, Maj. Gen. Mason Patrick to Lt. Col. C. B. Amorous, New York, NY, Feb. 24, 1926, National Archives, RG 18.

65. Testimony of Maj. Gen. Mason Patrick, et al., before the President's Aircraft Board, Sep. 21, 1925, AFHRA 248.211-61V.

66. Ltr, Maj. Gen. Mason M. Patrick to Hon. T. Frank James, subj: [H. R. 10827], May 4, 1926, AFHRA 145.91-106.

67. Mason M. Patrick, *The United States in the Air* (New York: 1928), p 184.

68. Goldberg, *A History*, p 36.

69. "Verbatim Report of Morrow Commission of Inquiry," *Army and Navy JournAl*a., Sep. 26, 1925, pp 15,16, AFHRA 168.69-11.

70. *Ibid.*, pp 8,9.

71. *Ibid.*, p 10.

72. Maurer, *Aviation in the U. S. Army*, pp 165-188. For coverage of these postwar operational improvements, see Chapter XI, "Higher, Farther, and Longer."

73. "Verbatim Report of Morrow Commission of Inquiry," *Army and Navy JournAl*a., Sep. 26, 1925, p 8, AFHRA 168.69-11. The term "air force" was used sparingly in Army Regulations 95-5 and 95-10. For example, Army Regulation No. 95-5, dated Nov. 17, 1921, stated one of the functions of the Air Service was "Development and Operation of an Air Force."

74. Army Regulations No. 95-10, subj: Air Corps, Mar. 10, 1928; Ltr, U. S. Army Adjutant General to Chief of the Air Corps, subj: Principles to be followed in assignment of Air Corps Troops to higher tactical organizations, Jan.17, 1929, with endorsements, AFHRA 248.211-32.

75. Ltr, Admiral S. S. Robison, CinC U. S. Fleet, to Secretary of the Navy, subj: Pending Personnel Legislation Relating to the Status of Naval Aviators, Mar. 15, 26, Nimitz Library Special Collections, U. S. Naval Academy, Moffett Papers, Part 2. J.13.

76. Ltr, Rear Admiral William A. Moffett to Lt. Comdr. DeWitt S. Ramsey, Aide on Staff, CinC U. S. Fleet, subj: [Adm Robison's Criticisms], Nov. 13, 1928, AFHRA Moffett Collection, Reel 0007.

77. Maj. Gen. Mason M. Patrick, *The United States in the Air* (New York:1928), pp ix-xi, 191.

78. Armstrong and Van Fleet, *Naval Aviation*, pp 59,62,63,64,65.

79. Lt Col Edward C. Johnson, *Marine Corps Aviation: The Early Years 1912-1940* (Washington, D.C.: 1977), 54-57; Peter B. Mersky, *U. S. Marine Corps Aviation 1912 to the Present* (Annapolis: 1983), pp 20-24; Ltr, Major Delos C. Emmons, Commandant, Air Corps Tactical School, Langley Field, VA, subj: Marine Corps Activities in Nicaragua, Apr. 20, 1928, AFHRA 248.222-68H.

80. The Joint Board, *Joint Action of the Army and the Navy* (Washington, D.C.:Apr. 23, 1927), pp iv,1-3, AFHRA 168.604-17A.

81. *Ibid.*, pp 1,2,4-7. For brief account of Army-Marine Corps relations, see Gordon W. Keiser, *The U. S. Marine Corps and Defense Unification 1944-47* (Washington, D.C.: 1982), pp 3-5.

82. *Ibid.*, pp 7-10.

83. Adrian O. Van Wyen, *The Aeronautical Board, 1916-1947* (Washington, D.C., Director of Naval History: 1947), p 33. AFHRA 168.6502-7.

84. Armstrong and Van Fleet, *Naval Aviation*, p 78; Ltr, Maj. Carl Spaatz to Maj. H. C. Pratt, Materiel Div., Dayton, Ohio, Aug. 23, 1930, LOC Ms Div, Spaatz Papers, Box 5.

85. Ltr, Maj. Carl Spaatz to Hans J. Adamson, Asst Sec of War, Aug. 29, 1930, Library of Congress, Manuscript Div, Spaatz Papers, Box 5.

86. Ltr, Spaatz to Pratt, Aug. 23, 1930, Library of Congress, Manuscript Div, Spaatz Papers, Box 5.

87. Ltr, Maj. Carl Spaatz to Maj. Gen. Benjamin Foulois, Feb. 29, 1932, Library of Congress, Manuscript Div, Spaatz Papers, Box 5.

88. Maurer, *Aviation in the U. S. Army,* p 285; Shiner, *Foulois,* p 54.

89. Ltr, Rear Adm. William A. Moffett, to Capt. E. S. Land, Aide CINC U. S. Fleet, USS *Texas*, Aug. 11, 1930; Ltr, Moffett to Land, Aug. 13, 1930, AFHRA Moffett Papers, Reel 0006.

90. War Department release, "Army and Navy Agree on Spheres of Activities of Their Air Forces," Jan.9, 1931, AFHRA 168.3952-191; Maurer, *Aviation in the U. S. Army,* p 285; Shiner, *Foulois,* p 54.

91. Armstrong and Van Fleet, p 79; Shiner, *Foulois,* p 55-56.

92. Maurer, *Aviation in the U. S. Army,* p 228,238; Shiner, *Foulois,* p 56-59; Ltr Maj. Carl Spaatz to Col. H.H Arnold, Wright Field, OH, Aug. 31, 1931, Library of Congress, Manuscript Div, Spaatz Papers, Box 5.

93. Maurer, *Aviation in the U. S. Army,* p 289; Shiner, *Foulois,* p 72; Ltr, Major Spaatz to Brig. Gen. Foulois, Jan.22, 1931, Library of Congress, Manuscript Div, Spaatz Papers, Box 5; Robert W. Krauskopf, "The Army and the Strategic Bomber 1930-1939," *Military Affairs* (Summer, 1958), p 88.

94. Interview with Brig. Gen. Laurence Kuter by Maj. C. W. Williams, Oct. 21, 1942, p 14, AFHRA 105.158.

95. Biography of Claire Lee Chennault-Advocate of Pursuit Aviation, HQ AFHRA/RI, Apr. 30, 1982.

96. Ltr, 1st Lt. Kenneth Walker to Maj. Carl Spaatz, Jun. 15, 1934, Library of Congress, Manuscript Div, Spaatz Papers, Box 6.

97. Kuter interview by Williams, p 15, AFHRA 105.518.

98. Shiner, *Foulois,* pp 76-79.

99. *Ibid.*, pp. 79,80; Maurer, *Aviation in the U. S. Army,* pp 289.

100. Shiner, *Foulois,* p. 87; Maurer, *Aviation in the U. S. Army,* p 289,290; Memorandum for Chief of the Air Corps fm Lt. Col. J. E. Chaney, Chief, Plans Div, subj: GHQ Air Force Headquarters, Aug. 17, 1933, w/atchs., AFHRA 145.93-81.

101. Shiner, *Foulois,* pp 125-49; Maurer, *Aviation in the U. S. Army,* pp 299-317; Memo, subj: Control of the GHQ Air Force in the GHQ Command Post Exercise, Jun. 10, 1934, AFHRA 145.93-81; Goldberg, *A History*, p 39.

102. Final Report of War Department Special Committee on Army Air Corps, Jul. 18, 1934, pp 1, 2, 11, AFHRA 145.93-94A; Robert W. Krauskopf, "The Army and the Strategic Bomber, 1930-1939," *Military Affairs* (Summer: 1958), pp 88.

103. Final Report of War Department Special Committee on Army Air Corps, Jul. 18, 1934, pp 12, AFHRA 145.93-94A.

104. *Ibid.*, pp 13,14,19.

105. *Ibid.*, pp 18,66,67.

106. Ltr, General Douglas MacArthur, Chief of Staff, to the Commanding Generals of Armies, Corps Areas, Departments, and GHQ Air Force, subj: Doctrines for the Employment of the GHQ Air Force, Oct. 17, 1934.

107. *Ibid.*

Chapter III

1. Lecture by Maj. Gen. Frank M. Andrews to the Army War College, subj: The GHQ Air Force, Oct. 15, 1936, AFHRA 145.93-108.

Roles and Missions

2. Report of the Chief of Staff, U. S. Army, 1934, extract from Annual Report of the Secretary of War, 1934, p 17, AFHRA 168.6009-31.

3. Goldberg, *A History*, p 40.

4. Maj. Gen. Oscar Westover, "The Army is Behind its Air Corps," Sep. 7, 1931, p 1, 13, AFHRA 248.211-71C.

5. Maj. Gen. H. H. Arnold and Col. Ira C. Eaker, *Winged Warfare* (New York:1941), p 91.

6. Training Regulation No. 440-15, "Air Corps. Employment of the Air Force of the Army," War Dept, Oct. 15, 1935, AFHRA 170.108. In Vol I of Craven and Cate, the authors state that TR 440-15 was a compromise "inclined toward the General Staff's point of view" and was, therefore, "a weak instrument for indoctrination." According to the authors, "the manual remained in force until 1940, but a sampling of Air Force opinion during that interval will indicate that its tenets were by no means universally accepted." Nevertheless, the new manual was a radical revision of the old TR 440-15 published in 1926, and it was "bold" in comparison to earlier air power statements approved by the General Staff.

7. Robert T. Finney, *The Development of Tactical Air Doctrine in the U. S. Air Force, 1917-1951* (Maxwell AFB, Ala.: Research Studies Institute, 1954), pp 14, 15, AFHRA K110.7017-1.

8. Lecture, Maj. Gen. Andrews to AWC, Oct. 15, 1936, AFHRA 145.93-108.

9. Haywood S. Hansell, Jr., USAF (Ret), "Baklavia Redeemed," *Air University Review*, Sep-Oct. 1974, pp 92-106.

10. Maurer, *Aviation in the U. S. Army, 1919-1939*, p 355.

11. Lecture by Maj. Gen. Frank M. Andrews to the Army War College, subj: The GHQ Air Force, Oct. 9, 1937, AFHRA 248.211-62G.

12. Goldberg, *A History*, pp 42, 43; Craven and Cate, *AAF in WWII, Vol I, Plans and Early Operations*, p 66; Appropriations, 1890-1939, AFHRA 131.41-2. In 1937, the GHQ Air Force had approximately 100 modern bombers with which to equip 11 squadrons, averaging about 9 airplanes per squadron.

13. First Official Report of the Sec of the Navy by Flt Adm Ernest J. King, CINC US Flt and CNO, Mar. 1, 1944, incorporated in *The War Reports* (New York: 1947), pp 476-77; Flt Adm Ernest J. King and Walter Muir Whitehill, *Fleet Admiral King, A Naval Record* (New York, 1952), p 248.

14. King and Whitehill, *Fleet Admiral King*, pp 187, 248-65.

15. Ltr, Air Chief Marshall Sir John Slessor to Air Marshall Sir Victor Goddard, Mar. 11, 48, located Library of Congress, Carl Spaatz Collection, Box 20. Slessor formed this opinion of King from their association during WWII.

16. King and Whitehill, *Fleet Admiral King*, p 643.

17. Report of the Chief of Staff, U. S. Army, 1934, p 16, AFHRA 168.6009-31.

18. *Ibid.*, p 17.

19. First Report of the Commanding General of the Army Air Forces, by General of the Army H. H. Arnold, Jan.4, 1944, incorporated in *The War Reports* (New York:1947), pp 303, 304.

20. Lecture, Maj. Gen. Andrews to AWC, Oct. 15, 1936, AFHRA 145.93-108; GHQ Air Force Bulletin No. 1, by Col. H. J. Knerr, Chief of Staff, Apr. 24, 1935, AFHRA 168.6501-48; Air Corps News Letter, Office of the Chief of Air Corps, Vol XVIII, No. II, Jun. 15, 1935, AFHRA 168.69-1.

21. Ltr, Maj. Gen. Frank M. Andrews, CG GHQ Air Force, to the Adjutant GenerAla., subj: Report of 1935 Service Test of GHQ Air Force, Feb. 1, 1936, AFHRA 145.93-75; Memo, Brig. Gen. John H. Hughes, Asst CS, to Chief of Staff, subj: Organization of the GHQ Air Force, Apr. 15, 1936, AFHRA 145.93-76; Maurer, *Aviation in the U. S. Army*, pp 340-341.

22. Memorandum for the Deputy Chief of Staff by Maj. Gen. Westover, Chief of the Air Corps, subj: [Reorganization of the Air Corps],Jan.8, 1936, AFHRA 145.93-80; Memorandum for the Chief of Staff by Maj.

Gen. Westover, subj: Reorganization of the Air Corps, Apr. 25, 1936, AFHRA 145.93-80.

23. Maurer, *Aviation in the U. S. Army*, pp 341, 343.

24. Robert W. Krauskopf, "The Army and the Strategic Bomber, 1930-1939, Part II," *Military Affairs* (Winter 1958/59), pp 209-215.

25. *Ibid.*, Goldberg, *A History*, pp 40-44; Craven and Cate, *AAF in WWII, Vol I, Plans and Early Operations*, pp 63-71.

26. *Joint Action of the Army and the Navy*, Revised by the Joint Board. (Washington, D.C.: GPO, 1935), AFHRA 178.2-31, 1927-1941; Report of the Air Corps Board, Supplement to Study No. 31, "Analytical Study of Joint Action of the Army and the Navy," Oct. 29, 1936, AFHRA 167.5-31, Pt. 2. This supplement bears the caveat, "Do not forward. Not to leave the Office, Chief of Air Corps."

27. The Air Corps Board, Study No. 31, "Report on the Functions of the Army Air Forces," Oct. 29, 1936; Ltr, C. W. Christenberry, Adj. Gen., 1st Ind to Study No. 31, Dec. 8, 1936; Memo to Gen. Arnold fm Chief Plans Div, subj: Air Corps Board Study No. 31 - The Functions of the Army Air Forces, Mar. 18, 1938, AFHRA 167.5-31, 1936-38.

28. History of the I Bomber Cmd: Part I, Jan.1, 1939-Dec. 7, 1941, pp 62-74, AFHRA 422.01-1; Charles D. Bright, ed., *Historical Dictionary of the U. S. Air Force*, (New York, 1992), p 631; Goldberg, *A History*, p 42.

29. Ltr, Maj. Gen. Westover, Chief of the Air Corps to the Adjutant GenerAla., subj: Air Corps Program and Directive, Aug. 31, 1938, AFHRA 145.93-23.

30. Ltr, E. R. Householder, Adjutant General, to the Chief of Air Corps, subj: Air Corps Program and Directive, Oct. 5, 1938, AFHRA 145.93-23.

31. Goldberg, *A History*, p 43; Maurer, *Aviation in the U. S. Army*, pp 405-412.

32. Krauskopf, *Military Affairs*, pp 210, 214.

33. Goldberg, *A History*, p 43.

34. Report of the Air Corps Board, Study No. 44, "Air Corps Mission Under the Monroe Doctrine," Maxwell Field, Ala., Oct. 17, 1938, AFHRA 167.5-44.

35. Goldberg, *A History*, pp 43-44.

36. Ltr, Maj. Gen. E. S. Adams, Adjutant General, to Chief of Arms and Services, and Commandants of General and Special Service Schools, subj: Air Board Report, Sep. 15,1939, AFHRA 167.6-9; Goldberg, *A History*, p 42; Krauskopf, *Military Affairs*, p 214.

37. Goldberg, *A History*, pp 36, 44, 45; Maurer, *Aviation in the U. S. Army*, p 412; Dewitt S. Copp, "Frank M. Andrews: Marshall's Airman," in John L. Frisbee, ed., *Makers of the United States Air Force* (Washington, D.C., 1987) pp 60-61.

38. Craven and Cate, Vol I, pp 136-138.

39. *Joint Board Estimate of United States Over-all Production Requirements*, Sep, 1941, AFHRA 145.81-23.

40. *Ibid.*

41. Ltr, Gen. H. H. Arnold to Commanding GenerAla., GHQ Air Force, subj: Pursuit Training and Pursuit Plane and Tactical Development, Nov. 14, 1939, w/atchs, AFHRA 145.91-409.

42. Bernard L. Boylan, "The Search for a Long Range Escort Plane 1919-1945," *Military Affairs* (Summer 1966), pp 60-66.

43. Christopher R. Gabel, *U. S. Army GHQ Maneuvers of 1941* (Washington, D.C.: 1991), p 38; Col John R. Maney, AWC Lecture, "Evaluation of the Air Weapon by World War II," Nov. 13, 53, AFHRA K239.7162-8; Maj. Gen. Orvil A. Anderson, AWC Lecture, "Development of U. S. Strategic Air Doctrine, ETO WW II," Sep. 20, 1951, AFHRA K239.7162-6; Kenneth R. Whiting, "Soviet Air Power in World War II," *Air Power and Warfare*, pp 98, 108-120.

44. Maney, "Evaluation of the Air Weapon by WWII," Nov. 13, 1953, AFHRA K239.7162-8.

45. *Ibid.*, Col. Jack E. Thomas, AWC Lecture, "German and Soviet Tactical Operations in WWII," Sep. 24, 1951, AFHRA K239.7162-147; Maj. Gen. Orvil A. Anderson, AWC Lecture, "Development of U. S.

Strategic Doctrine, ETO WWII," Sep. 20, 1951, AFHRA K239.7162-6.

46. USAF Historical Study No. 102, *Origins of the Eighth Air Force*, Oct. 1944, AFHRA No. 101-102, pp 81-86.

47. *Ibid.*; Edward Homze, "The Continental Experience," *Air Power and Warfare*, Proceedings of the 8th Military History Symposium, USAF Academy, Oct. 18-20, 1978 (Washington, D.C., 1979), pp 45, 46; Horst Boog, "Higher Command and Leadership in the German Luftwaffe, 1935-1945," *Air Power and Warfare*, p 162.

48. Gabel, *U. S. Army GHQ Maneuvers of 1941*, pp 36-41; Daniel R. Mortensen, *A Pattern for Joint Operations: World War II Close Air Support North Africa*," (Washington, D.C., 1987) pp 13-17.

49. *Joint Board Estimate of United States Overall Production Requirements*, Sep. 11, 1941, AFHRA 145.81-23.

50. Craven and Cate, Vol I, *Plans and Early Operations*, pp 522-523: History of the I Bomber Command, Dec. 7, 1941 to Oct. 15, 1942, Vol I, Pt 2, AFHRA 422.01-2.

51. Craven and Cate, pp 519-521.

52. U. S.-U. K. Staff Conferences, Reports by Chiefs of Staff, ARCADIA, Dec. 1941 AFHRA 145.81-26A; Craven and Cate, pp 253, 254, 528.

53. Msg, CINCUSPACFLT TO CINCUS-FLEET, Subj: Airplane Situation, Hawaiian Area, Jan.7, 1942, AFHRA 145.96-146.

54. Msg, CINCUSFLEET, Adm. E. J. King to Chief of Staff, U. S. Army, subj: Airplane Situation, Hawaiian Area, Feb. 2, 1942, AFHRA 145.96-146.

55. Memo for the Chief of Staff, subj: Allocation of 200 B-24s and 900 B-25s to the Navy, AAF/AWPD, unsigned (bears initials O. A. A., believed to be Orvil A. Anderson), Jan.15, 1942, AFHRA 145.96-146.

56. Ltr, Adm. E. J. King to Lt. Gen. H. H. Arnold, Mar. 5, 1942, AFHRA 145.96-147.

57. Memo for Chief of the Army Air Forces, subj: Proposed Division of Army and Navy Responsibility for Aircraft Production, by Rear Adm. J. H. Towers, Chief, Bureau of Aeronautics, AFHRA 145.96-146.

58. Memo for Gen. Marshall from Gen. Arnold, subj: Diversion of Land-based Army Aircraft to the Navy, Feb. 21, 42; Memo for Chief of Staff from Lt. Gen. H. H. Arnold, Dep Chief of Staff for Air, Subj: Diversion of Medium and Heavy Type Bombardment Aircraft to the Navy, Feb. 25, 1942, AFHRA 145.96-146.

59. Ltr, Lt. Gen. H. H. Arnold, CG AAF, to Adm. E. J. King, CINCUSFLEET, Mar. 9, 1942, AFHRA 145.96-147, Bk 2.

60. Ernest J. King and Walter Muir White-hill, *Fleet Admiral King, A Naval Record* (New York, 1976) pp 454-55. Passages from the exchange of letters between King and Arnold are quoted verbatim in the King-Whitehill volume. Copies of correspondence on the subject are available in AFHRA 145.96-146 and 145.96-147.

61. Timothy J. Warnock, *The Battle Against the U-Boat in the American Theater*, p 9.

62. Ltr, Gen. G. C. Marshall, Chief of Staff, U. S. Army, to Adm. E. J. King, CINCUS-FLT, Apr. 2, 1942, AFHRA 145.96-147, Bk 2.

63. Memo for Chief of the Army Air Forces, subj: Proposed Division of Army and Navy Responsibility for Aircraft Production, by Rear Adm. J. H. Towers, Chief, Bureau of Aeronautics, AFHRA 145.96; Craven and Cate, pp 298, 440-441.

64. Craven and Cate, p 551; King and Whitehill, *Fleet Admiral King*, pp 455, 459.

65. Craven and Cate, Vol I, pp 544, 545.

66. King and Whitehill, *Fleet Admiral King*, pp 459-462.

67. Craven and Cate, Vol II, pp 378-379.

68. Craven and Cate, Vol II, pp 388, 389.

69. *Ibid.*, pp 404, 405; Ltr, Secretary of War Henry L. Stimson to Lt. Gen. Joseph T. McNarney, Dep Chief of Staff, subj: [Anti-submarine Campaign], Jun. 25, 1943, AFHRA 145.96-152.

70. Memorandum for CINCUSFET and CNO, subj: Report Recent and Prospective Developments in Anti-Submarine Operations Since Quadrant, pp 81-84 of Sextant and Eureka Minutes, Nov. 8, 1943, AFHRA 119.151-4; King and Whitehill, *Fleet Admi-*

ral King, pp 467-471; Memorandum, Adm. E. J. King to Gen. Marshall, subj: Anti-Submarine Warfare, Apr. 30, 1943, AFHRA 145.96-152.

71. Ltr, Secretary of War Henry L. Stimson to Lt. Gen. Joseph J. McNarney, subj: [Antisubmarine Campaign], Jun. 25, 1943, AFHRA 145.96-152.

72. Craven and Cate, Vol II, p 408.

73. Memorandum for the Commanding GenerAla., Army Air Forces from Maj. Gen. Thomas T. Handy, Asst Chief of Staff, subj: Transfer of Anti-Submarine Airplanes to the Navy, Jul. 10, 1943, AFHRA 145.96-152.

74. Craven and Cate, Vol II, p 410.

75. Craven and Cate, Vol II, pp 46, 47.

76. *Ibid,* pp 14, 15, 28, 29; Goldberg, *A History,* p 58; USAF Historical Study No 108, The AAF in the Middle East, Jun. 1945, p 66, AFHRA 101-108.

77. See note above.

78. Craven and Cate, vol II, p 17; Air Vice Marshal E. J. Kingston McCloughry, RAF, *The Direction of War* (New York, 1955), p 166.

79. Craven and Cate, Vol II, pp 14, 33, 34, 38; Air Chief Marshal Sir Christopher Foxley Norris, "Marshal of the Royal Air Force Lord Tedder," *The War Lords* (Boston, 1976), p 494; Gen. Lawrence Kuter, "Air Power-The American Concept," undated, AFHRA 167.6-50; Ronald Lewin, "Field Marshal The Viscount Montgomery," *The War Lords,* p 500.

80. Craven and Cate, Vol II, pp 50-55, 62; Howe, George F., *U.S. Army in World War II, Mediterranean Theater of Operations, Northwest Africa: Seizing the Initiative in the West* (OCMH, Dept of Army, Washington, D.C.: 1957), pp 16, 33-35; Gen. William W. Momyer, *Air Power in Three Wars* (Washington, D.C.: 1978), p 40.

81. Msg, Gen. Dwight D. Eisenhower to Maj. Gen. Carl Spaatz, Nov. 13, 1942, in Library of Congress, Manuscript Div, Spaatz Papers, Box 9.

82. Gen. Spaatz, Daily Diary Entry, subj: Conference with Gen. Eisenhower, Oct. 21, 1942, in Library of Congress, Manuscript Div, Spaatz Papers, Box 9.

83. *Ibid.*; Gen. Spaatz, Daily Diary Entry, Conference with Gen. Eisenhower, Oct. 25, 1942; Memo for Gen. Spaatz from Gen. Eisenhower, Oct. 13, 1942. All located in Library of Congress, Manuscript Div, Spaatz Papers, Box 9.

84. Ltr, Arnold to Eisenhower, Nov. 15, 1942; Ltr, Eisenhower to Spaatz, Nov. 12, 1942, Library of Congress, Manuscript Div, Spaatz Papers, Box 9.

85. General Carl Spaatz, Daily Diary Entry for Nov. 12, 1942, Library of Congress, Manuscript Div, Spaatz Papers, Box 9.

86. Ltr, Arnold to Eisenhower, Nov. 15, 1942, Library of Congress, Manuscript Div, Spaatz Papers, Box 9.

87. Ltr, Arnold to Spaatz, Nov. 15, 1942, Library of Congress, Manuscript Div, Spaatz Papers, Box 9.

88. Ltr, Spaatz to Arnold, Nov. 23, 1942, Library of Congress, Manuscript Div, Spaatz Papers, Box 9.

89. Roderic Owen, *Tedder* (London: 1952), pp 173, 174; Kuter, "Air Power - The American Concept," AFHRA 167.6-50.

90. Pamphlet, "Some Notes on High Command in War," by Gen. B. L. Montgomery, Jan.1943, exact reproduction in Command Informational Intelligence Series, Office of the Asst Chief of Air Staff, Intelligence, Washington, D.C., No. 43-111, Jun. 25, 1943, AFHRA 142.034-3.

91. Interview with Gen. Spaatz, CG USSAF in Europe by Dr. Bruce C. Hopper, Historian USSTAF, May 20, 1945, AFHRA 519.1612-2; Futrell, *Ideas, Concepts, Doctrine,* p 69; Lecture by Maj. Gen. O. A. Anderson to the Air War College, subj: Development of U. S. Strategic Air Doctrine, ETO WWII, Sep. 20, 1951, AFHRA K239.7162-6.

92. Gen. Carl Spaatz, Daily Diary Entry for Feb. 4, 1943, Library of Congress, Manuscript Div, Spaatz Papers, Box 10.

93. *Ibid.*

94. Gen. Carl Spaatz, Daily Diary Entry for Feb. 6, 1943, Library of Congress, Manuscript Div, Spaatz Papers, Box 10.

95. Goldberg, *A History,* p 60; Interview

with Mr. Robert A. Lovett, Asst Sec of War for Air, by Asst Chief of Air Staff, Intelligence, Jun. 24, 1943, in Library of Congress, Manuscript Div, Spaatz Papers, Box 3; Martin Blumenson, *Kasserine Pass* (Boston: 1967).

96. George F. Howe, *U. S. Army in World War II, Mediterranean Theater of Operations, Northwest Africa: Seizing the Initiative in the West* (Washington, DC: 1957), pp 16, 33-35; Martin Blumenson, *The Patton Papers, 1940-1945* (Boston: 1957), pp 203-211; OMar. H. Bradley, *A Soldier's Story* (New York: 1951), pp 62, 63.

97. Goldberg, *A History*, pp 60, 61; Blumenson, *Kasserine Pass*, p 331; Craven and Cate, Vol II, pp 104, 105.

98. Craven and Cate, Vol II, pp 205, 206; Richard M. Kohn and Joseph P. Harahan, ed., *USAF Warrior Studies: Air Superiority in World War II and Korea*, Appendix FM 100-20 (Washington, D.C.: 1983); Daniel R. Mortensen, *A Pattern for Joint Operations, World War II Close Air Support North Africa* (Washington, D.C.: 1987), pp 78, 79.

99. See note above.

100. Ltr, Maj. Gen. Carl Spaatz to Lt. Gen. Henry H. Arnold, Dec. 27, 1942, Library of Congress, Manuscript Div, Spaatz Papers, Box 9.

101. Goldberg, *A History*, pp 63, 64.

102. Biographical file on Lt. Gen. Frank Maxwell Andrews, located in AFHRA biographies.

103. Memo for the President, subj: High Altitude Bombing in European Theater, Mar. 22, 1943, by Gen. George C. Marshall, Chief of Staff, U. S. Army, Library of Congress, Manuscript Div, Gen. Henry H. Arnold Papers, Box 3.

104. General Spaatz, Daily Diary Entry for Oct. 27, 1942, Library of Congress, Manuscript Div, Spaatz Papers, Box 9.

105. General Spaatz, Daily Diary Entry, Oct. 29, 1942, Library of Congress, Manuscript Div, Spaatz Papers, Box 9.

106. McCloughry, *The Direction of War*, p 90; USAF Historical Study No 102, pp 10, 13, 14, 81-86; Maj. Gen. Orvil Anderson, Air War College Lecture, "Development of U. S. Strategic Air Doctrine," Sep. 20, 1951, p 15, AFHRA K239.7162-6; European Command Battle Studies, WWII, AFHRA 519.042.

107. Papers and Minutes of Meetings, Sextant and Eureka Conferences, Nov-Dec. 1943, CCS 400, Enclosure to US Chiefs of Staff Memo of Nov. 18, 1943, AFHRA 119.151-4; Lt. Col. Albert N. Garland and Howard Smyth, *Sicily and the Surrender of Italy*, OCMH, Dept of the Army (Washington, D.C.: 1969) pp 292, 293, 306, 553.

108. USAF Historical Study No 102, pp 7, 10-12, 84; Daily Journal by Lt. Gen. Carl Spaatz, Dec. 23, 1943, AFHRA 519.1612-2.

109. Casablanca Conference Minutes, JCS Meeting held at Arfa Camp on Jan.17, 1943, Vol II, p 40, AFHRA 119.151-1; Memo by the British Chiefs of Staff, subj: Command of British and U. S. Forces Operating Against Germany, Nov. 26, 1943, pp 230, 231, AFHRA 119.151-4.

110. Ltr, AF 201-AFP, HQ NATOUSA to Lt. Gen. Carl Spaatz, HQ MAAF, subj: Transfer of Officer, Dec. 24, 1943, AFHRA 519.1612-2; Daily Journal by Lt. Gen. Carl Spaatz, Dec. 20, 1943, AFHRA 519.1612-2.

111. Cable AF434, Lt. Gen. Carl Spaatz, CG, NAAF, to Gen. Henry H. Arnold, CG AAF, Dec. 19, 1943, AFHRA 519.1612-2; Spaatz Daily Journal, Dec. 26, 1943; Paper, Lt. Gen. Carl Spaatz, "Principal Points Discussed with Gen. Arnold," Dec. 1943, AFHRA 519.1612-2.

112. Interview with Gen. Carl Spaatz, CG USSAF in Europe, by Dr. Bruce C. Hopper, Historian, USSTAF, May 20, 1945, AFHRA 519.1612-2; Daily Journal, Lt. Gen. Carl Spaatz, Dec. 13, 1943, AFHRA 519.1612. 2.

113. Interview, Hopper with Spaatz, Jun. 27, 1943, AFHRA 519.1612-2; Interview, Goldberg with Spaatz, May 19, 1965, pp 10, 11; H. H. Arnold, *Global Mission* (New York: 1949), pp 376-377; Ltr, Maj. Gen. H. H. Arnold to CG GHQ Air Force, subj: Pursuit Training and Pursuit Plane and Tactical Development, Nov. 14, 1939, AFHRA 145.409.

114. Interview with Gen. Spaatz by Hopper;

Stephen E. Ambrose, *The Supreme Commander; The War Years of General Dwight D. Eisenhower* (New York: 1970); pp 364-376; Spaatz Daily Journal, Jan.3, 1944.

115. Interview with Gen. Spaatz by Hopper; Memo, W. W. Rostow to Mr. E. S. Mason, subj: The Tactical Use of Air Power in Support of the Invasion, Apr. 25, 1944, AFHRA 145.81-155; Momyer, *Air Power in Three Wars*, p 49; McCloughry, *The Direction of War*, pp 124-126.

116. Forrest C. Pogue, *U. S. Army in World War II*, *The European Theater of Operations*, *The Supreme Command* (Washington, D.C., 1954), pp 1, 30-32, 159; Directive Ltr, Lt. Gen. W. B. Smith, USA, Chief of Staff, Supreme HQ AEF, to Allied Naval Commander, et al., subj: Command and Control of Allied Air Forces, Oct. 14, 1944, AFHRA 145.81-155; Ltr, Maj. Gen. Barney M. Giles, Chief of Air Staff to Lt. Gen. Carl Spaatz, CG USSAF in Europe, interim reply to Spaatz letter of Apr. 22, 1944, undated, AFHRA 145.81-155.

117. Ltr, Dr. David Griggs, the Advisory Specialists Group, USSTAF, to Dr. Edward L. Bowles, Aug. 7, 1944, Library of Congress, Manuscript Div, Arnold Papers, Box 3.

118. Special Study, *Relationship between Past and Present Strategic Concepts*, by Air University/RSI, May 10, 1961; H. M. Cole, *U. S. Army in World War II*, *The European Theater of Operations*, *The Loraine Campaign* (Washington, D.C.: 1950), pp 18, 19.

119. Goldberg, *A History*, pp 70-73; Stephen T. Possony, *Strategic Air Power, The Pattern of Dynamic Security* (Washington, DC: 1949), p x.

120. Memo for the Secretary of Defense, subj: Tactical Air Support, by General of the Army Dwight D. Eisenhower, Chief of Staff, U. S. Army, 1947, Library of Congress, Manuscript Div, Spaatz Papers, Box 28, Oct-Dec. 1947 file.

121. King and Whitehill, *Fleet Admiral King,* p 624.

122. Report by the U. S. British Chiefs of Staff, subj: Directive to the Supreme Commander in the ABDA Area, approved by the President and the Prime Minister, Jan.2, 1942, AFHRA 145.26A; Craven and Cate, Vol I, pp 366-428.

123. Arnold, *Global Mission*, p 246.

124. McCloughry, *The Direction of War*, p 187; Pogue, *Air Power and Warfare. Proceedings of the Eighth Military History Symposium*, USAFA 1978, pp 202-203; Craven and Cate, Vol I, pp 418-419.

125. See note above.

126. Goldberg, *A History*, pp 84-87; Craven and Cate, Vol V, pp 739-741; George W. Garand and Truman R. Strobridge, *History of U. S. Marine Corps Operations in World War II, Vol IV, Western Pacific Operations*, (Washington, DC: 1971), p 735.

127. Craven and Cate, Vol I, pp 366-483.

128. *Ibid*; Goldberg, *A History*, pp 78, 79.

129. Ronald H. Spector, *Eagle Against the Sun* (New York: 1985), p 227; George C. Kenney, *General Kenney Reports* (New York: 1949), pp 52, 52; Herman S. Wolk, "A Wartime Leader," *Airman*, Jul. 1985, pp 15-17.

130. SWPA Report No. 36, "Command and Organizational Data in the Southwest Pacific Area, Air Evaluation Board, May 10, 1946, AFHRA 138.8-34; Craven and Cate, Vol IV, pp 646-651.

131. Minutes, fourth meeting of the Air Board, Dec. 3-4, 1946, Maj. Gen. Hugh J. Knerr, Secretary General presiding, p 181. Kenney recalled that two or three times the question arose as to whether or not the ground commander should have anything to do with "running the air show," and MacArthur said, "No, There's only one Air Commander in this theater and there's only one Naval Commander and one Army Commander, and they aren't going to interfere with each other. I'm still on top."

132. USAF Hist Study No. 101, *The AAF in the South Pacific to Oct. 1942*, by ACAS, Intelligence, Hist Div, Dec. 1944, p 26, AFHRA No. 101-101; Memo for the Chief of Staff, by Gen. H. H. Arnold, CG AAF, subj: Operational Control Army Air Forces, South Pacific Area, Sep. 15, 1942, AFHRA 145.81-116; Ltr, Maj. Gen. M. F. Harmon,

HQ USAFISPA, Noumea, New Caledonia to Lt. Gen. H. H. Arnold, CG AAF, Aug. 18, 1943, AFHRA 145.81-116.

133. Ltr, Maj. Gen. M. F. Harmon, HQ USAFISPA, Noumea, New Caledonia, to Lt. Gen. H. H. Arnold, CG AAF, Aug. 18, 1942, AFHRA 145.81-116.

134. Ltr, Maj Gen M. F. Harmon to Lt Gen H. H. Arnold, CG AAF, Oct. 12, 1942, AFHRA 138.8-34

135. *Ibid.*

136. SWPA Report No. 36, May 10, 1946, AFHRA 138.8-34; Craven and Cate, Vol IV, pp 68-69.

137. Craven and Cate, Vol IV, pp 206-210.

138. SWPA Report No. 36, May 10, 1946, AFHRA 138.8-34; Kenney, *General Kenney Reports*, pp 121,213; Spector, *Eagle Against the Sun*, pp 223-225.

139. Craven and Cate, Vol IV, pp 414, 415; Charles F. Romanus and Riley Sunderland, *United States Army in World War II, Stilwell's Command Problems* (Washington, D.C.,: 1956), pp 466-471.

140. See note above.

141. Futrell, *Ideas, Concepts, Doctrine*, p 82.

142. Goldberg, *A History*, pp 84-87; Craven and Cate, Vol V, pp 739-741, 756.

143. See note above; Coox, *Air Power and Warfare*, p 93.

144. Memo for Gen. LeMay, CSAF, from Brig. Gen. E. B. LeBailley, Dep Dir of Information, subj: Summaries of AAF Problem Areas, Mar. 1, 1961; Arnold, *Global Mission*, p 246; Futrell, *Ideas, Concepts, Doctrine*, p 82.

145. Futrell, *Ideas, Concepts, Doctrine*, p 86; Craven and Cate, Vol V, pp 546, 547, 714.

146. John T. Greenwood, "The Emergence of the Postwar Strategic Air Force," *Air Power and Warfare* (Washington, D.C.: 1979), pp 218, 219.

147. Wolk, *Planning and Organizing the Postwar Air Force,* pp 31-44, 81, 82, 97, 98, 129; Futrell, *Ideas, Concepts, Doctrine*, pp 87-89.

148. Goldberg, *A History*, pp 171, 197, 198; David MacIsaac, *Strategic Bombing in World War II; The Story of the United States Bombing Survey* (New York, 1976).

149. Wolk, *Planning and Organizing the Postwar Air Force*, pp 80-82.

Chapter IV

1. Report of the Chief of Staff, United States Air Force to the Secretary of the Air Force, Jun. 30, 1948, pp 7, 10, 13.

2. Wolk, *Planning and Organizing the Postwar Air Force*, pp 89-98; Futrell, *Ideas, Concepts, Doctrine*, pp 87-89; Orvil Anderson, "How Airpower Grew," *The Air Power Historian*, Apr. 1956, p 137.

3. Ltr, Robert A. Lovett, Asst Secretary for Air, to Lt. Gen. Carl Spaatz, USSAFE, Feb. 12, 1944, Library of Congress, Spaatz Papers, Box 14, Apr. 1944 file. For the definitive study of the quest for unification and autonomy, see Herman Wolk's *Planning and Organizing the Postwar Air Force*.

4. Ltr, Lt. Gen. Carl Spaatz to Mr. Robert A. Lovett, Asst. Sec. for Air, Apr. 13, 1944, Library of Congress, Spaatz Papers, Box 14.

5. Steven L. Reardon, *History of the Office of the Secretary of Defense, The Formative Years, 1947-1950*, (Washington, D.C.: 1984), pp 388-393; Wolk, *Planning and Organizing the Postwar Air Force*, pp 87, 89.

6. Wolk, *Planning and Organizing the Postwar Air Force*, pp 171, 178, 179; Goldberg, *History of the United States Air Force*, p 102.

7. Minutes of AAF Major Commanders Conference at HQ AAF, Mar. 14, 1946, in National Archives, Record Group 341, Item 6.

8. Gen. Carl Spaatz, "Strategic Air Power, Fulfillment of a Concept," *Foreign Affairs*, Vol 24, No.3, Apr. 1946, pp 385-396.

9. Wolk, *Planning and Organizing the Postwar Air Force*, pp 93-95.

10. *Ibid*, pp 86-89, 99.

11. Interview, Alfred Goldberg with Gen. Carl Spaatz, May 19, 1965, p 28, AFHRA K239.0512-755.

12. Stephen Jurika, Jr., ed., *From Pearl Harbor to Vietnam, The Memoirs of Admiral Arthur W. Radford* (Stanford, California: 1980), p 82.

13. Interview, Goldberg with Gen. Spaatz, May 19, 1965; Interview with Gen. Carl Spaatz, by USAF Academy Dept of History, Sep. 27, 1968, AFHRA K239.0512-583; Memo for Mr. Symington from Gen. Carl Spaatz, Jan.7, 1948, Library of Congress, Spaatz Papers, Box 28, Jan.1948 file.

14. Wolk, *Planning and Organizing the Postwar Air Force*, pp 164-167.

15. Minutes of Air Staff Meeting, Aug. 21, 1946, in National Archives, Record Group 341, No. 6.

16. Wolk, *Planning and Organizing the Postwar Air Force*, pp 154-155; Goldberg, *A History*, p 102; Minutes of Air Staff Meeting, Feb. 1, 1947, National Archives, Record Group 341, No. 6. The compromises Norstad had to make with Sherman did not stand him in good stead with some fellow officers. Although they made their peace before General Arnold's death in 1950, Norstad recalled in an interview in 1979 (AFHRA K239.0512-1116) that Arnold had accused him of having "sold us down the river."

17. Memorandum for the Secretary of Defense from General of the Army, Dwight D. Eisenhower, subj: Tactical Air Support, 1947, cited verbatim in Semi-annual Report of the Secretary of the Air Force, Jul. 1-Dec. 31, 1949, pp 233-234, AFHRA 168.022; interview with Gen. Carl Spaatz, by Brig. Gen. Noel Parrish and Dr. Alfred Goldberg, Feb. 21, 1962, AFHRA 105.5-1-2.

18. Minutes of Air Board Conference, Dec. 3-4, 1946, pp 178, 179.

19. *Ibid.*, pp 131-133.

20. Orvil A. Anderson, "How Air Power Grew," *The Air Power Historian*, AF History Foundation, Montgomery, Ala., Apr. 1956.

21. *Ibid.*

22. Lecture, "Weapons Systems and Their Influence on Strategy," by Maj. Gen. O. A. Anderson to the Air War College, Aug. 30, 1951, AFHRA K239.7162-6.

23. Wolf, *Basic Documents on Roles and Missions*, pp 33, 54; Wolk, *Planning and Organizing the Postwar Air Force*, pp 158-160.

24. Wolk, *Planning and Organizing the Postwar Air Force*, pp 171, 178, 179; Goldberg, *A History*, p 102.

25. Wolk, *Planning and Organizing the Postwar Air Force*, pp 216-219; Reardon, *The Formative Years, 1947-1950,* p 315; Walter Millis, ed., *The Forrestal Diaries* (New York: 1951), pp 115, 116; R. Earl McClendon, *Unification of the Armed Forces: Administrative and Legislative Developments 1945-1949* (Maxwell AFB, Ala.: 1952), pp 49, 50.

26. Wolk, *Planning and Organizing the Postwar Air Force*, p 64; McClendon, *Unification of the Armed Forces,* pp 42-45; War Department Bulletin No. 11, "National Security Act of 1947," Jul. 31, 1947, AFHRA 170.102; "Text of the Decisions of the Joint Staff on Assignments for Defense," *The New York Times*, Mar. 28, 1948, AFHRA 168.3-39.

27. Goldberg, *A History*, p 103; Wolk, *Planning and Organizing the Postwar Air Force*, pp 170-171; Wolf, *Basic Documents on Roles and Missions*, pp 61-90. Also see work folders on unification history in AFHRA 168.5-22 through 168.5-30.

28. Reardon, *The Formative Years, 1947-1950,* pp 2-11.

29. Futrell, *Ideas, Concepts, Doctrine*, p 122; John T. Greenwood, "The Emergence of the Postwar Strategic Air Force, 1945-1953," *Air Power and Warfare*, (Washington, D.C.: 1979), pp 215, 229, 279.

30. John T. Greenwood, "The Emergence of the Postwar Strategic Air Force, 1945-1953," *Air Power and Warfare*, pp 220-228.

31. Jacob Neufeld, *Ballistic Missiles in the United States Air Force 1945-1960* (Washington, D.C.: 1990), pp 36-37.

32. Michael A. Palmer, *Origins of the Maritime Strategy: American Naval Strategy in the First Postwar Decade* (Washington, D.C.: 1988), pp 21-32; Wolk, *Planning and Organizing the Postwar Air Force*, pp 216-219; Reardon, *The Formative Years, 1947-1950,* pp 313-316.

33. Reardon, *The Formative Years, 1947-1950,* p 315; Report by the President's Air Policy Commission, "Survival in the Air

Age," Jan.1, 1948, AFHRA 168.6005-140; Summary of the Report of the President's Air Policy Commission, Jan.13, 1948, AFHRA 148.04-9.

34. Memo for Mr. Symington from Carl Spaatz, Jan.7, 1948, Library of Congress, Spaatz Papers, Box 28.

35. Report of the Congressional Aviation Policy Board, 80th Congress, 2d Session, U. S. Senate, Mar. 1, 1948, pp 1-4, 6, AFHRA 168.04-10.

36. *Ibid.*, pp 6, 7.

37. Wolk, *Planning and Organizing the Postwar Air Force*, p 220; Goldberg, *A History*, p 116; Reardon, *The Formative Years, 1947-1950*, p 393; "Text of the Decisions of the Joint Staff on Assignments for Defense," *The New York Times*, Mar. 28, 1948, AFHRA 168.3-39; News Release No. 38-48, Office of the Secretary of Defense, "Secretary Forrestal Announces Results of Key West Conference," Mar. 26, 1948, AFHRA 160.951-2.

38. Air Force Bulletin No. 3, Dept. of the Air Force, Aug. 4, 1948, AFHRA 168.7060-3.

39. News Release No. 38-48, Office of the Secretary of Defense, Mar. 26, 1948, AFHRA 160.951-2; Air Force Bulletin No. 1, Dept. of the Air Force, May 21, 1948, AFHRA 168.7060-3.

40. See note above.

41. Wolk, *Planning and Organizing the Postwar Air Force*, p 220; Thomas C. Hone, *Power and Change* (Washington, D.C.: 1989), p 22; Futrell, *Ideas, Concepts, Doctrine*, Vol I, p 199.

42. Ltr, Carl Spaatz to James H. Doolittle, Shell Oil Company, New York, Apr. 24, 1948, Library of Congress, Spaatz Papers, Box 29, Apr-May 1948 file.

43. See note above.

44. Reardon, *The Formative Years, 1947-1950*, pp 398-400; Millis, *The Forrestal Diaries*, pp 466-467.

45. Millis, *The Forrestal Diaries*, p 466.

46. Memo to Gen. Spaatz and Adm. Towers, from Secretary Forrestal, Aug. 9, 1948.

47. Millis, *The Forrestal Diaries*, pp 468, 497.

48. Memo for Secretary Forrestal from Carl Spaatz and John H. Towers, subj: Your Memorandum of Aug. 9, 1948, Aug. 18, 1948, AFHRA 168.7060-3.

49. *Ibid.*

50. Reardon, *The Formative Years, 1947-1950*, p 397; Goldberg, *A History*, p 116: McClendon, *Unification of the Armed Forces*, pp 73-74; "Strategic Problems Discussed by Secretary Forrestal and Joint Chiefs," *Army and Navy Journal*, 29 Aug. 1948, AFHRA 168.3- 40.

51. Reardon, *The Formative Years, 1947-1950*, p 402.

52. Report of the Secretary of the Air Force to the Secretary of Defense for FY 1948, AFHRA 160.04; Paul Y. Hammond, *The Cold War Years: American Foreign Policy Since 1945* (New York: 1949), pp 26, 27; Royce E. Eckwright, United States Air Access to Berlin, 1945-1965, USAFE Monograph, 1966, pp 4, 5, 21-33. See also: Futrell, *Ideas, Concepts, Doctrine, Vol I*, pp 112, 113, 118-121; Goldberg, *A History*, pp 235-241.

53. *Ibid*; Reardon, *The Formative Years, 1947-1950*, p 335.

54. *Ibid.*

55. *Ibid.*, pp 499-512.

56. John Lewis Gaddis, *Strategies of Containment* (New York: 1982), p 57; George F. Lemmer, *The Air Force and the Concept of Deterrence, 1945-1950* (Washington, D.C.: 1953), pp 25, 26; Greenwood, *Air Power and Warfare*, p 236.

57. Millis, *The Forrestal Diaries*, 513; Timothy W. Stanley, *American Defense and National Security* (Washington, D.C.: 1956), pp 90-91; McClendon, *Unification of the Armed Forces*, pp 94-98.

58. Lt. Gen. James H. Doolittle, USAF Ret., "Wasted Defense Billions," *Air Force*, Dec. 1948, pp 13-15.

59. Millis, *The Forrestal Diaries*, pp 467, 537, 538, 544; Reardon, *The Formative Years, 1947-1950*, pp 43, 44, 46, 47.

60. Mark S. Watson, "Two Years of Unification," *Military Affairs*, Winter, p 193; Reardon, *The Formative Years, 1947-1950*, pp 410-412; Goldberg, *A History*, p 116; James

C. Freund, "The Revolt of the Admirals. Part One," *Airpower Historian*, Jan. 1963, p 1; Palmer, *Origins of the Maritime Strategy*, pp 47, 48; Second report of the Secretary of Defense, FY 1949, AFHRA 160.04.

61. Futrell, *Ideas, Concepts, Doctrine*, p 121; Report of the Committee on Armed Services, House of Representatives, Eighty-First Congress, "Investigation of the B-36 Bomber Program," Jan.10, 1950, p 1 AFHRA 146.6202-2; Paul Y. Hammond, "Supercarriers and B-36 Bombers: Appropriations, Strategy and Politics," in Harold Stein, *American Civil-Military Decisions: A Book of Case Studies* (University of Alabama Press, 1963), pp 465-495, 568.

62. Report of the Committee on Armed Services, Jan.10, 1950, pp 1,2, AFHRA 146.6202-2.

63. *Ibid.*, pp 24,25,32,33; Hearings before the Committee on Armed Services, House of Representatives, Eighty-First Congress, First Session, "Investigation of the B-36 Bomber Program," Washington, D.C., 1949, pp 524-528, AFHRA 146.6202-2.

64. Joint Army and Air Force Bulletin No. 22, National Security Act Amendments of 1949, Debts of the Army and the Air Force, Aug. 22, 1949, AFHRA 170.102; Wolf, *Basic Documents on Roles and Missions*, pp 187-200; Semiannual Report of the Secretary of Defense, Jul. 1 to Dec. 31, 1949, AFHRA 160.04.

65. A Report of Investigation by Committee on Armed Services, House of Representatives, on Unification and Strategy, Mar. 1, 1950, pp 7,8, AFHRA 146.6202-3; Semiannual Report of the Secretary of the Air Force, Jul-Dec. 1949, p 230, AFHRA 168.022.

66. "Is U. S. to Have Three Air Forces? Worried Army Wants Own Support Planes," *U. S. News & World Report*, Jun. 10, 1949, pp 20-21.

67. A Report of Investigation by Committee on Armed Services, Mar. 1, 1950, p 9, AFHRA 146.6202-3.

68. Hearings before the Committee on Armed Services, House of Representatives, 81st Congress, 1st Session, "The National Defense Program-Unification and Strategy," Oct. 1949, pp 8-10, AFHRA 168.6005-141.

69. Palmer, *Origins of the Maritime Strategy*, p 51.

70. Hearings before Committee on Armed Services, Oct. 1949, AFHRA 168.6005-141.

71. *Ibid.*, pp 408,409.

72. *Ibid.*, pp 461,462.

73. *Ibid.*, pp 453,454.

74. *Ibid.*, pp 454,455.

75. Statement of Gen. Hoyt S. Vandenberg, in Report of House of Representatives Committee on Armed Services, B-36 Investigation, Oct. 20, 1949, National Archives, Record Group 41, Box No. 5, Folder No. 6.

76. *Ibid.*

77. Statement of Gen. J. Lawton Collins, in Report, House of Representatives Committee on Armed Services, B-36 Investigation, Oct. 20, 1949, Vol 23, pp 2769-2771, National Archives, Record Group 341, Box No. 4, Folder No. 5.

78. Statement of Gen. Omar. N. Bradley, Chairman, JCS, before the Armed Services Committee of the House of Representatives, undated, AFHRA No. 168.7001-113; Futrell, *Ideas, Concepts, Doctrine, Vol I*, pp 132-133.

79. Statement of Hon. Louis Johnson, Secretary of Defense, before the Armed Services Committee of the House of Representatives, Oct. 21, 1949, Hearings, pp 606-622.

80. Futrell, *Ideas, Concepts, Doctrine, Vol I*, pp 133-134; Reardon, *The Formative Years, 1947-1950*, pp 420-421; A Report of Investigation of the Committee on Armed Services, House of Representatives, on Unification and Strategy, Mar. 1, 1950, AFHRA 146.6202-3.

81. A Report of Investigation of the Committee on Armed Services, Mar. 1, 1950, AFHRA 146.6202-3, pp 50-52.

82. *Ibid.*, pp 13-14, 53, 57-59.

83. *Ibid.*, pp 33, 54.

84. *Ibid*, p 55; Semiannual Report of the Secretary of the Air Force, Jul. 1-Dec. 31, 1949, p 232, ARHRC 168.022; Hearings before Committee on Armed Services, Oct. 1949, p 193, AFHRA 168.6005-141.

85. Hearings before Committee on Armed

Services, Oct. 1949, pp 194, 195, AFHRA 168.6005-141.

86. *Ibid,.* pp 197-200.

87. Goldberg, *A History*, pp 139, 140; John Schlight, "Elwood R. Quesada: Tac Air Comes of Age," in John L. Frisbee, ed., *Makers of the United States Air Force* (Washington, D.C.: 1987), pp 199-203; Hearings before Committee on Armed Services, Oct. 1949, p 483.

88. Hearings before Committee on Armed Services, Oct. 1949, pp 483, 484, 544, 545; Semiannual Report of the Secretary of the Air Force, Jul-Dec. 1949, pp 232-234, AFHRA 168.022; Robert F. Futrell, "A Critical Analysis of Army Positions on Aviation in 1961-1963, as compared with Historical Experience," USAF Historical Division, ASI, Oct. 1963, pp 26-27, AFHRA K239.046-34.

89. Hearings before Committee on Armed Service, Oct. 1949, p 527.

90. Futrell, *Ideas, Concepts, Doctrine*, p 133.

91. Mark W. Clark, *Calculated Risk* (New York, 1950) pp 160-161.

92. Paul Y. Hammond, *The Cold War Years: American Foreign Policy Since 1945* (New York, 1969), pp 40-44; Constance C. Coblenz, *et al.*, *United States Foreign Policy, 1945-1955* (Wisconsin, 1956), pp 126,127; Gaddis, *Strategies of Containment*, pp 69, 70; A Report of Investigation of the Committee on Armed Services, On Unification and Strategy, Mar. 1, 1950, p 33.

93. Robert F. Futrell, *The United States Air Force in Korea, 1950-1953*, Revised Edition (Washington, D.C., 1983), pp 22, 23, 39, 44; Lt. Col. Pat Meid, USMCR, and Maj. James M. Yingling, USMC, *U. S. Marine Operations in Korea, 1950-1953, Vol V, Operations in West Korea* (Washington, D.C., 1972), Appendix B, Korean War Chronology, pp 541-548.

94. James F. Schnabel, *The United States Army in the Korean War: Policy and Direction: The First Year* (OCMH, Washington, D.C., 1972), p 47; Futrell, *The United States Air Forces in Korea*, pp 44, 45.

95. Futrell, *Ideas, Concepts, Doctrine, Vol I*, pp 1, 2, 39-45.

96. Futrell, *Ideas, Concepts, Doctrine, Vol I*, pp 379-397; J. C. Hopkins, *The Development of Strategic Air Command, 1946-1981* (Office of the SAC Historian, Jul. 1, 1982), pp 21, 22, 41.

97. Futrell, *Ideas, Concepts, Doctrine, Vol I*, pp 45, 46, 378, 379; Gen. William W. Momyer, *Air Power in Three Wars* (Washington, D.C., 1978), p 54; Hopkins, p 22.

98. Futrell, *Ideas, Concepts, Doctrine, Vol I*, pp 47-51; Lt Gen George E. Stratemeyer, Korean Diary, Vol II., AFHRA 168.7018; Ltr, Lt. Gen. Edward M. Almond, Cmdnt Army War College, to Chief Army Field Forces, Fort Monroe, VA, subj: Report, Conference of Commandants of Army Service Schools, Dec. 18, 1951, AFHRA K168.15-43.

99. Futrell, *Ideas, Concepts, Doctrine, Vol I*, p 49.

100. See note above. Dr. Wayne Thompson, draft chapter, "The Air War in Korea," pp 13, 14; Col. Don Z. Zimmerman, "FEAF: Mission and Command Relationships," *Air University Quarterly Review*, Summer 1951, pp 95-96.

101. Futrell, *Ideas, Concepts, Doctrine, Vol I*, pp 98-103, 289-300, 324, 325; Gen. Mark W. Clark, *From the Danube to the Yalu* (New York, 1954), pp 2-3; Gen. Otto P. Weyland, "The Air Campaign in Korea," *Air University Quarterly Review*, vol VI, No. 3, (Fall 1953), pp 21, 22; Paper, Subj: The Effectiveness of Tactical Air Support in Korea and Plans for Future Improvement," Dept of Army, G-3, undated, AFHRA K168.15-43, vol 11, tab A.

102. See note above.

103. Paper, subj: The Effectiveness of Tactical Air Support in Korea and Plans for Future Improvement," Dept. of Army, G-3, Undated, AFHRA K168.15-43, Vol 11, Tab A; Gen. Otto P. Weyland, "The Air Campaign in Korea," *Air University Quarterly Review*, Vol VI, Fall 1953, No. 3, pp 3-10, AFHRA K239.309.

104. Weyland, "Air Campaign in Korea," pp 10, 11.

105. Proceedings of the Special Subcommittee on Tactical Aviation of the Committee on

Armed Services, House of Representatives, Aug. 11, 14, 1950, Vols 9 and 10, of Ad Hoc Committee on Tactical Employment of Air Power, 19 volumes, AFHRA K168.15-43.

106. Oral History Interview of Gen. O. P. Weyland by Dr. James C. Hasdorff and Brig. Gen. Noel F. Parrish, Nov. 19, 1974; Thompson, "The Air War in Korea," p 14; Office of the Secretary of Defense, "Air War in Korea," *Air University Quarterly Review*, Fall 1950, AFHRA K239.309.

107. Momyer, *Air Power in Three Wars*, pp 59-62.

108. Stratemeyer's Diary, AFHRA 168.7018-16; Dr. Albert F. Simpson, "Tactical Air Doctrine-Tunisia and Korea," *Air University Quarterly Review*, Summer 1951, pp 17-19, AFHRA K239.309.

109. See note above; "Interview with Lt. Gen. E. M. Almond, Mistakes in Air-Support Methods in Korea," *U. S. News and World Report*, Mar. 6, 1953, pp 58-61.

110. Lynn Montross and Capt. Nicholas A. Canzona, *U. S. Marine Operations in Korea, 1950-1953, Vol III, The Chosin Reservoir Campaign*, Washington, D.C., 1957, pp 249-261, 334, 350-351; Simpson, "Tactical Air Doctrine-Tunisia and Korea," pp 17-19; Ltr, Gen. Mark W. Clark, Chief of Army Field Forces to Chief of Staff, U. S. Army, subj: Tactical Air Support of Ground forces, Sep. 13, 1951, AFHRA K168.15-43; Futrell, *Ideas, Concepts, Doctrine, Vol I*, pp 137-146.

111. Oral History Interview of Gen. O. P. Weyland, by James C. Hasdorff and Brig. Gen. Noel F. Parrish, Nov. 19, 1974, pp 107-111; Walter G. Hermes, *Truce Tent and Fighting Front*, (OCMH, Washington, D.C.: 1966), pp 325-328, 362.

112. General Hoyt S. Vandenberg, as told to Stanley Frank, "The Truth About Our Air Power," *Saturday Evening Post*, Feb. 17, 1951, pp 20, 21.

113. *Ibid.*

114. *Ibid.*

115. Stratemeyer's Diary, AFHRA 168.7018-16; Lt. Col. George E. Tormaen, USAF, "Political Air Superiority in the Korean Conflict," *Air University Quarterly Review*, Winter 1953-54, pp 78-84, AFHRA K239.309; Futrell, *Ideas, Concepts, Doctrine, Vol I*, pp 286, 287.

116. Futrell, *Ideas, Concepts, Doctrine, Vol I*, pp 286, 287; Hermes, pp 498-512.

117. Ltr, J. H. Doolittle, Shell Oil Company, New York, NY, to Maj. Gen. E. E. Partridge, Commander Fifth Air Force, Nov. 10, 1950, AFHRA 168.7014-1.

118. *Ibid.*

119. Air War College Study, "Tactical Air Forces and National Security," by the Evaluation Staff, Apr. 1955, pp 19-27, AFHRA K239.0429-3; Richard P. Weinert, *A History of Army Aviation, 1950-1962, Part I: 1950-1954*, (U. S. Continental Army Command, Fort Monroe, VA, Jun. 1971), p 18; Ltr, Maj. Gen. E. M. Almond, CG X Corps, to Maj. Gen. Charles Bolte, AC/S, G-3, subj: Army Tactical Support Requirements, Dec. 25, 1950, in AU Library, as cited in Robert F. Futrell, *Command and Observation Aviation: A Study in Control of Tactical Air Power*, USAF Historical Study No. 24 (USAF Historical Division: 1952), pp 1, 2.

120. See Note Above.

121. Weinert, pp 56, 57, 78, 79; *Lt. Gen. John Tolson, Airmobility, 1961-1971* (Dept. of the Army, Washington, D.C., 1973), pp 4, 5; R. Earl McClendon, *Army Aviation, 1947-1953* (RSI, Air University, Maxwell AFB, Ala.: May 1954), pp 6, 7, AFHRA K239.04-39. Cited regulation is Joint Army and Air Force Adjustment Regulations 5-10-1. *Combat Joint Operations, ETC.: Employment of Aircraft for Performance of Certain Missions*, May 20, 1949.

122. Weinert, pp 17-26.

123. McClendon, *Army Aviation, 1947-1953*, pp 13-15.

124. What Kind of Air Support Does the Army Want?" Interview with Gen. Mark W. Clark, *Air Force Magazine*, Dec. 1950, pp 24, 25, 52: Futrell, *Ideas, Concepts, Doctrine, Vol I*, pp 541, 706.

125. Twenty years later, the USAF developed the A-10 Thunderbolt II which was designed exclusively for close air support.

126. McClendon, *Army Aviation, 1947-*

1953, pp 22-23; Richard P. Weinert, *History of Army Aviation, 1950-1962, Phase II: 1955-1962* (Historical Office, U. S. Army TRADOC, Fort Monroe, VA, Nov. 1976), p 23; Wolf, *Basic Documents on Roles and Missions*, pp 239-241; Alfred Goldberg and Lt. Col. Donald Smith, *Army Air Force Relations: The Close Air Support Issue*, Project RAND Study R-906-PR, Oct. 1971, p 11.

127. Weinert, pp 56, 57, 78, 79; Lt. Gen. John Tolson, *Airmobility, 1961-1971* (Dept of the Army, Washington, D.C.: 1973), pp 4, 5.

Chapter V

1. Ltr, Dwight D. Eisenhower to Bernard Mannes Baruch, Jun. 30, 1952, in Louis Calambos, ed., *The Papers of Dwight D. Eisenhower: NATO and the Campaign of 1952: XIII* (Baltimore and London, 1989), pp 1262-64.

2. Ltr, Dwight D. Eisenhower to Richard Milhous Nixon, Oct. 1, 1952, in Calambos, ed., *The Papers of Dwight D. Eisenhower*, pp 1366-69; Goldberg, *A History of the United States Air Force*, p 117.

3. Ltr, Dwight Eisenhower to Basil Brewer, Oct. 24, 1952 and Ltr, Eisenhower to Syngman Rhee, Dec. 5, 1952, both in *The Papers of Dwight D. Eisenhower*, pp 1396, 1443, 1444.

4. Dwight D. Eisenhower, *Mandate for Change, 1953-1956* (New York, 1963), pp 109, 166-170, 336-342, 354-375.

5. Eisenhower, *Mandate for Change*, pp 143-149, 445-453; Robert J. Watson, *The Joint Chiefs of Staff and National Policy, 1953-1954*, (Washington, D.C., 1986), pp 1, 187-189.

6. Eisenhower, *Mandate for Change*, p 135.

7. Doris M. Condit, *History of the Office of Secretary of Defense, The Test of War, 1950- 1953* (Washington, D.C., 1988), p 530; Futrell, *Ideas, Concepts, Doctrine*, p 423; Wolf, *Basic Documents on Roles and Missions*, p 247.

8. Futrell, *Ideas, Concepts, Doctrine, Vol I*, p 423; Condit, *The Test of War, 1950-1953*, pp 256-530.

9. Reorganization Plan No. 6 of 1953, Msg from the President to 83d Congress, 1st Session, Document No. 136, Apr. 30, 1953, AFHRA K146.6202-21.

10. *Ibid.*; Condit, *The Test of War, 1950-1953*, p 530; Futrell, *Ideas, Concepts, Doctrine*, p 423; Wolf, *Basic Documents on Roles and Missions*, p 247.

11. Gen. Carl Spaatz, USAF, Ret., "Security Without Bankruptcy," *Newsweek*, May 4, 1953, p 32.

12. Eisenhower, *Mandate for Change*, p 447.

13. "The Services: New Men, New Emphasis," *Newsweek*, May 25, 1953, pp 30, 31; "Defense Confirmation," *Time*, Jun. 8, 1953, p 27; "Joint Chiefs' Radford: A Flexible Chairman for Flexible Defense...And Plenty of Big Bombers," *U. S. News and World Report*, Jun. 3, 1953, p 61.

14. See Note Above; Stephen Jurika, Jr., ed., *From Pearl Harbor to Vietnam, The Memoirs of Admiral Arthur W. Radford* (Stanford, CA, 1980), pp 304, 305, 313.

15. Eisenhower, *Mandate for Change*, p 96.

16. Palmer, *Origins of the Maritime Strategy*, pp 70, 72; "The Navy: Dreamboat Again," *Newsweek*, Nov. 13, 1950, pp 28, 29.

17. Louis Calambos, ed., *The Papers of Dwight D. Eisenhower: NATO and the Campaign of 1952*, XIII (Baltimore and London, 1989), pp 1225-1227; Gen. Carl Spaatz, "The New Look in Warfare," *Newsweek*, Sep. 21, 1953, p 34.

18. Marcelle Size Knaack, *Post-World War II Bombers, 1945-1973* (GPO, 1988), pp 78-81, 212; J. C. Hopkins, *The Development of Strategic Air Command, 1946-1981* (HQ SAC, 1982), pp 53, 54, 64; Marcelle Size Knaack, *Post-World War II Fighters, 1945-1973* (GPO, 1978), pp 115, 193.

19. "Defense Confirmation," *Time*, Jun. 8, 1953, p. 27.

20. *Ibid.*; Jurika, *From Pearl Harbor to Vietnam*, p 314; "Joint Chiefs' Radford: A Flexible Chairman for Flexible Defense...And Plenty of Big Bombers," *U. S. News and World Report*, Jun. 3, 1953, p 61.

21. See note above; Interview with Senator

W. Stuart Symington by Hugh Ahmann and Herman Wolk, May 2 and Dec. 12, 1978, p 75.
22. General Matthew B. Ridgway, *Soldier: The Memoirs of Matthew B. Ridgway* (Westport, Conn., 1956), reprint 1974, pp 266, 267.
23. Robert J. Watson, *The Joint Chiefs of Staff and National Policy, 1953-1954* (Washington, D.C., GPO, 1986), pp 9, 10, 16, 17.
24. Jurika, *From Pearl Harbor to Vietnam*, pp 319-322.
25. *Ibid.*, pp 327-329.
26. *Ibid.*, pp 323, 324; Watson, *The Joint Chiefs of Staff and National Policy, 1953-1954*, pp 23, 24; Futrell, *Ideas, Concepts, Doctrine, Vol I*, pp 425, 428. On pp 18-20, Watson quotes generously from the New Look paper, which Adm Radford cited as being in the archives of the Hoover Institution.
27. Ltr, Lt. Gen. E. E. Partridge, DCS/Ops, HQ USAF, to Lt. Gen. Laurence S. Kuter, Cmdr, Air University, subj: [The Air Force and National Security Policy], w/atchs, Nov. 30, 1953, AFHRA K239.214-8.
28. Air Force Manual 1-2, *United States Air Force Basic Doctrine*, Mar. 1953, revised Apr. 1, 1954 and Apr. 1, 1955.
29. Air War College Study, AWC Evaluation Staff, subj: The Air Force and National Security Policy, Dec. 1, 1954, p IV-1, AFHRA K239.0429-2.
30. Watson, *The Joint Chiefs of Staff and National Policy, 1953-1954*, pp 20, 25.
31. Thomas A. Sturm, *USAF Forces and Bases, 1947-1967*, (Washington, D.C., 1969), pp 26-30; Calambos, ed., *The Papers of Dwight David Eisenhower*, pp 1226-1227.
32. Air War College Study, Dec. 1, 1954, pp IV-2, AFHRA K239.0429-2.
33. Eisenhower, *Mandate for Change*, p 453.
34. Wolf, *Basic Documents on Roles and Missions*, pp 207-218; Jacob Neufeld, *Ballistic Missiles in the United States Air Force, 1945-1960* (Washington, D.C., 1990), p 37; Paper, subj: Policy Guidance on Guided Missiles, atch to Partridge Ltr to Kuter, Nov. 30, 1953, AFHRA K239.214-8.
35. Paper, subj: Policy Guidance on Guided Missiles, atch to Partridge Ltr to Kuter,Nov. 30, 1953, AFHRA K233.214-8.
36. *Ibid.*
37. Kenneth Schaffel, *The Emerging Shield: The Air Force and the Evolution of Continental Air Defense, 1945-1960* (Washington, D.C., 1991), pp 108-110, 113-118.
38. *Ibid.*, p 281; Wolf, *Basic Documents on Roles and Missions*, p 219; Knaack, *Post-World War II Fighters*, pp 159-173.
39. Schaffel, *Emerging Shield*, pp 115-119; Wolf, *Basic Documents on Roles and Missions*, pp 219-222.
40. Schaffel, *Emerging Shield*, pp 241-254; Wolf, *Basic Documents on Roles and Missions*, p 275; Goldberg, *A History*, p 137.
41. Schaffel, *Emerging Shield*, pp 244-246.
42. Study, The Air Force and National Security Policy, pp IV-2, AFHRA K239.0429-2.
43. Jurika, ed., *From Pearl Harbor to Vietnam*, pp 324-325; Watson, *The Joint Chiefs of Staff and National Policy, 1953-1954*, pp 80-84.
44. Watson, *The Joint Chiefs of Staff and National Policy, 1953-1954*, p 86; AFHRA Paper, Compilation of Armed Forces Appropriations and Expenditures, 1948-1961, Oct. 1961, AFHRA K110.7140-1; Jurika, p 327.
45. Watson, *The Joint Chiefs of Staff and National Policy, 1953-1954*, pp 18, 178.
46. Reorganization Plan No. 6 of 1953, AFHRA K146.6202-21; Condit, *The Test of War, 1950-1953*, pp 528-531.
47. Watson, *The Joint Chiefs of Staff and National Polict, 1953-1954*, p 179; Wolf, *Basic Documents on Roles and Missions*, pp 251-273.
48. Watson, *The Joint Chiefs of Staff and National Polict, 1953-1954*, pp 178, 179.
49. Jurika, ed., *From Pearl Harbor to Vietnam*, pp 328, 329; "National Defense: How Great a Debate?" *Newsweek*, Jan.30, 1956, pp 24-25.
50. Ridgway, *Soldier: The Memoirs of Matthew B. Ridgway*, p 271.
51. *Ibid.*, pp 289, 290, 296, 298.
52. Futrell, *Ideas, Concepts, Doctrine*, p. 225.

53. Ridgway, *Soldier: The Memoirs of Matthew B. Ridgway*, p 312; Richard P. Weinert, *A History of Army Aviation, 1950-1952, Phase II: 1955-1962*, (HQ US Army TRADOC, Fort Monroe, VA, Nov. 1976), pp 6, 7.

54. Jurika, *From Pearl Harbor to Vietnam*, p 330.

55. Ridgway, *Soldier: The Memoirs of Matthew B. Ridgway*, p 260.

56. Kenneth W. Condit, *History of the Joint Chiefs of Staff, Volume VI, The Joint Chiefs of Staff and National Policy, 1955-1956* (Washington, D.C., 1992), pp 1, 2.

57. "National Defense: How Great a Debate?" *Newsweek*, Jan.30, 1956, pp 24-25.

58. Gen. Carl Spaatz, USAF Ret., "National Defense Without National Bankruptcy...An Answer to Gen Ridgway," *Newsweek*, Jan.30, 1956, pp 24, 25.

59. *Ibid.*

60. John M. Taylor, *General Maxwell Taylor. The Sword and the Pen*, (New York, 1989), p 97.

61. Maxwell D. Taylor, *Swords and Plowshares* (New York, 1972), p 171.

62. *Ibid.*, p 165; Condit, *The Joint Chiefs of Staff and National Policy, 1955-1956*, pp 5-9; Goldberg, *A History of the United States Air Force*, p 143.

63. Condit, *Joint Chiefs of Staff and National Policy, 1955-1956*, pp 18-19.

64. *Ibid.*, pp 47, 50, 57; Katherine Johnsen, "President's Plan for More B-52 Funds Attacked as '"Not Enough,'" *Aviation Week*, Apr. 16, 1956, p 34. Katherine Johnsen, "Senate Subcommittee Begins Probe To Evaluate Soviet-U. S. Air Status," *Aviation Week*, Apr. 23, 1956, p 40.

65. See Note Above; Report of Proceedings, Hearing held before Subcommittee on the Air Force of the Committee on Armed Services, "Present and Planned Strength of the United States Air Force," The United States Senate, Apr. 16-Jul. 3, 1956, Volumes 1-15, AFHRA K146.6201-26.

66. See Note Above; "Air and the Admirals," *Newsweek*, Apr. 30, 1956, p 35.

67. Report of Proceedings, Hearing held before Subcommittee on the Air Force of the Committee on Armed Services, Vol 5, pp 266, 267, AFHRA K146.6201-26; Katherine Johnson, "Gen LeMay Gives Russia Four Years to Outstrip U. S.," *Aviation Week*, May 7, 1956; pp 28, 29; George M. Watson, Jr., *The Office of the Secretary of the Air Force, 1947-1965* (GPO, 1992), p 159.

68. Katherine Johnson, "Soviet Bison Outstrips U. S. Interceptor," *Aviation Week*, Jun. 4, 1956, p 39; Report of Proceedings, Hearing held before Subcommittee on the Air Force of the Committee on Armed Services, Vols 6 & 7, AFHRA K146.6201-26.

69. Claude O. Witze, "Administration Hits Airpower Opponents," *Aviation Week*, May 14, 1956, pp 26, 27.

70. *Ibid.*

71. "U. S. Air Power Today," *Air University Quarterly Review*, Fall 1956, pp 76, 77.

72. Report of Proceedings, Hearing held before Subcommittee on the Air Force of the Committee on Armed Services, Vols 13, 14, 15, pp 1239-1243, 1252, AFHRA K146.6201-22.

73. Ibid., Vol 15, pp 1225, 1261.

74. Robert Holtz "EditoriAla.: The Senate Airpower Report," *Aviation Week*, Feb. 11, 1957.

75. Katherine Johnsen, "Symington Report Urges Airpower Boost," *Aviation Week*, Feb. 4, 1957, pp 32, 33; Watson, *The Office of the Secretary of the Air Force, 1947-1965*, pp 160, 161.

76. See note above.

77. See note above.

78. Robert Holtz, "Editorial: The Senate Airpower Report," *Aviation Week*, Feb. 11, 1957.

79. Dwight D. Eisenhower, *The White House Years: Waging Peace, 1956-1961* (New York, 1965), pp 240, 244-53.

80. Robert Hotz, "Services Battle for IRBM Jurisdiction," *Aviation Week*, May 28, 1956, pp 26, 27.

81. *Ibid.*

82. *Ibid.*

83. "USAF Adopting New Approach to Interservice Rivalry: Ignore It," *Aviation Week*, Jun. 11, 1956, p 31.

84. *Ibid.*

85. *Ibid.*

86. Richard P. Weinert, History of Army Aviation, Phase II: 1955-1962, pp 1-5, 15, 16.

87. Evert Clark, "Army Outlines Aviation Program, See No Conflict With USAF," *Aviation Week*, Jun. 4, 1956, p 14.

88. Weinert, *History of Army Aviation*, p 17.

89. Wolf, *Basic Documents on Roles and Missions*, pp 293, 294; Condit, *Joint Chiefs of Staff and National Policy*, p 60.

90. Wolf, *Basic Documents on Roles and Missions*, pp 295, 296; Condit, *Joint Chiefs of Staff and National Policy*, p 76; Weinert, p 17.

91. Wolf, *Basic Documents on Roles and Missions*, pp 300, 301; Condit, *Joint Chiefs of Staff and National Policy*, pp 71, 72; Evert Clark, "Impact of Wilson's Memo Will Be Known After Budget Hits Congress," *Aviation Week*, Dec. 3, 1956, p 30.

92. Wolf, *Basic Documents on Roles and Missions*, pp 297, 298; Condit, *Joint Chiefs of Staff and National Policy*, p 65; Evert Clark, "Impact of Wilson's Memo Will Be Known After Budget Hits Congress," *Aviation Week*, Dec. 3, 1956, p 30.

93. Wolf, *Basic Documents on Roles and Missions*, pp 297, 303; Evert Clark, "Impact of Wilson's Memo Will Be Known After Budget Hits Congress," *Aviation Week*, Dec. 3, 1956, p 30.

94. Evert Clark, "Impact of Wilson's Memo Will Be Known After Budget Hits Congress," *Aviation Week*, Dec. 3, 1956, p 30; Maxwell D. Taylor, *Swords and Plowshares*, pp 170, 171.

95. See note above.

96. Wolf, *Basic Documents on Roles and Missions*, pp 317, 319, 320.

97. *Ibid.*, pp 321-323.

98. *Ibid.*, p 117; Futrell, *Ideas, Concepts, Doctrine*, p 221.

99. Futrell, *Ideas, Concepts, Doctrine, Vol I*, p 221; Ltr, Brig. Gen. Henry Viccellio to Gen. O. P. Weyland, subj: [Exercise King Cole], 18 Apr. 1957, AFHRA K417.164-1.

100. Futrell, *Ideas, Concepts, Doctrine, Vol I*, p 221; Richard P. Weinert, *History of Army Aviation, Phase II: 1955-1962*, pp 1-5, 13, 16, 16, 17; Lt. Gen. John J. Tolson, *Airmobility, 1961-1971* (GPO: 1973), pp 1-7.

101. Lt. Gen. James M. Gavin, *War and Peace in the Space Age* (New York: 1958), as cited in Robart A. Olsen, "Air Mobility for the Army," *Military Affairs*, Winter 1964-65, p 166. Olsen notes the Army's ability "to progress somewhat independently of Administration policy"; Weinert, *History of Army Aviation, Phase II: 1955-1962*, p 18.

102. Wolf, *Basic Documents on Roles and Missions*, p 235.

103. *Ibid.*; Neufeld, *Ballistic Missiles*, p 169; Gen Carl Spaatz, "Where We Went Wrong-A Plan for the Future," *Newsweek*, Dec. 30, 1957, p 19; Gen. Carl Spaatz, "A Pentagon for the M-Age," *Newsweek*, Aug. 7, 1957, p 60.

104. Spaatz, *Newsweek*, Aug. 7, 1957, p 60.

105. Gen. Carl Spaatz, "A Matter of Life or Death," *Newsweek*, Jun. 4, 1956, pp 24, 25.

106. 0. Ltr, Maj. Gen. James P. Hodges, Commanding General AAF Trng Cmd, Barksdale, LA, to Gen. Carl Spaatz, CG, AAF, Washington, D.C., Feb. 28, 1946.

107. Gen. Carl Spaatz, "Middle Way the Wise Way," *Newsweek*, Apr. 14, 1958, Futrell, *Ideas, Concepts, Doctrine*, Vol I, pp 580,581; Wolf, *Basic Documents on Roles and Missions*, pp 325, 326. For a full account of the 1958 reorganization, see Futrell, *Ideas, Concepts, Doctrine, Vol I*, pp 573-584. A copy of the Defense Reorganization Act is contained in Wolf's volume of *Basic Documents*, pp 329-338.

108. See note above.

109. Wolf, *Basic Documents on Roles and Missions*, pp 339-353.

110. Watson, *The Office of the Secretary of Defense, 1947-1965*, p 176; Interview with Gen. Thomas D. White, by Joseph W. Angell, Jr., and Alfred Goldberg, Jun. 27, 1961, AFHRA K239.0512-606.

111. Futrell, *Ideas, Concepts, Doctrine*, Vol I, pp 611, 612; Roger J. Spiller, *"Not War But Like War": The American Intervention in Lebanon*, (Leavenworth, KS, Jan.1981), p 1.

112. Maxwell D. Taylor, *The Uncertain Trumpet*, (New York, 1959, 1960), pp 4-10.

113. Spiller, *Not War But Like War*, pp 34-36, 44; Bernard C. Nalty, *The Air Force Role in Five Crises*, (Washington, D.C., 1968), pp 5, 16.

114. Ltr, Maj. Gen. Glen W. Martin to Senator Stuart Symington, Dec. 5,1960, AFHRA 168.7048-2.

115. Taylor, *The Uncertain Trumpet*; Eisenhower, *Waging Peace*, p 575; Tolson, *Air Mobility, 1961-1971*, pp 39-40; Futrell, *Ideas, Concepts, Doctrine*, pp 227-231.

116. History of Tactical Air Command, Jan-Jun. 1960, p 30; AF/CHO Study, *Support of UN Operations in the Congo*, pp 28, 29; Futrell, *Ideas, Concepts, Doctrine, Vol I*, pp 328, 329, 394.

117. Taylor, *The Uncertain Trumpet*, pp 168-172.

118. Weinert, *History of Army Aviation, Phase II: 1955-1962*, pp 25-31; Olsen, *Military Affairs*, Winter, 1964-65, p 167; Taylor, *The Uncertain Trumpet*, p 167. Air Force Historian, Robert F. Futrell, said this concept was leading toward what Lt. Gen. Leslie J. McNair, CG GHQ US Army, described in 1942 as "the invariable tendency on the part of unit commanders to make themselves self-sufficient."

119. *Department of Defense Appropriations for 1961, Hearings before the Subcommittee of the Committee on Appropriations*, House of Representatives, 86th Cong., 2d Sess., (GPO, 1960), pt 2, p 530, Jan. 28, 1960.

120. Edgar F. Raines, Jr., and Maj. David R. Campbell, *The Army and the Joint Chiefs of Staff, Evolution of Army ideas on the Command, Control, and Coordination of the U. S. Armed Forces, 1942-1985* (US Army Center of Military History, 1986), pp 85-86; Futrell, *Ideas, Concepts, Doctrine*, Vol. I, p 454.

121. Rear Adm. Chester W. Nimitz and E. B. Potter, ed., *Sea Power, A Naval History* (Englewoods Cliffs, N.J., 1960), p 881; J. C. Hopkins, *The Development of Strategic Air Command,1946-1981* (SAC History Office, Jul. 1, 1982), pp 84-94.

122. Charles K. Hopkins, *Unclassified History of the Joint Strategic Target Planning Staff (JSTPS)*, (SAC, Mar. 15, 1989), pp 1, 2,; Robert F. Futrell, "The Influence of the Air Power Concept on Air Force Planning, 1945-1962," in *Military Planning in the Twentieth Century, Proceedings of the Eleventh Military History Symposium, 10-12 Oct. 1984*, Lt. Col. Harry R. Borowski, ed., (GPO, 1986), pp 257, 258.

123. Hopkins, *Unclassified History of JSTPS*, pp 3, 4.

124. Nimitz and Potter, *Sea Power*, pp 881-2.

125. Futrell, *Ideas, Concepts, Doctrine*, pp 339-341.

126. Oral History Interview with Secretary of the Air Force, Dudley C. Sharp, undated, AFHRA K239.0512-790; Gen. Thomas D. White, Ret., "What's Wrong with Civil-Military Relations," *Newsweek*, May 27, 1963, p 10.

Chapter VI

1.   Robert Frank Futrell, *Ideas, Concepts, Doctrine: Basic Thinking in the United States Air Force, Vol 2, 1961-1984* (Maxwell AFB, Ala.: Air University Press, 1989), pp 1-10. Futrell wrote that President Kennedy was influenced also by Gen. James M. Gavin's writings and Basil H. Liddel Hart's book, *Deterrent or Defense*.

2.   *Ibid.*, pp 22, 23.

3.   *Ibid.*; Watson, *The Office of the Secretary of the Air Force, 1947-1965*, p 205.

4.   Futrell, *Ideas, Concepts, Doctrine, Vol 2*, pp 91-100; Knaack, *Post-World War II Bombers*, pp 568-570.

5.   Futrell, *Ideas, Concepts, Doctrine*, Vol 2, pp 91-100.

6.   Robert F. Futrell, *The Advisory Years to 1965* (GPO, 1981), pp 79-82; Maxwell D. Taylor, *Swords and Plowshares* (New York, 1972), pp 195-197, 227-244; Oral History Interview #501 with Gen. Maxwell D. Taylor, by Maj. Richard B. Clement and Jacob Van Staaveren, Jun. 11, 1972, p 8, AFHRA K239.0512-501.

7.   Futrell, *Ideas, Concepts, Doctrine, Vol I*, pp 22-26.

8.   Futrell, *Ideas, Concepts, Doctrine, Vol I*, pp 91-100.

9.   Taylor, *Swords and Plowshares*, p 253.

10.   Gen. Thomas D. White, "What's Wrong with Civil Military Relations," *Newsweek*, May 27, 1963, p 30.

11.   Watson, *The Office of the Secretary of the Air Force*, p 205.

12.   Gen. Thomas D. White, "The Air Force Getting Down to New Business," *Newsweek*, May 13, 1963, p 37.

13.   *Ibid.*

14.   Wolf, *Basic Documents on Roles and Missions*, pp 361-364; Ford Eastman, "Army, Navy Reluctantly Back Space Edict," *Aviation Week*, Mar. 27, 1961, pp 25, 26.

15.   Interview, with Gen. Thomas D. White by Joseph W. Angell, Jr., and Alfred Goldberg, Jun. 27, 1961, Oral History #606, AFHRA K239.0512-606.

16.   Futrell, *Ideas, Concepts, Doctrine*, Vol 2, pp 91-100; Gen. White, *Newsweek*, May 13, 1963, p 37.

17.   Marcell Size Knaack, *Post-World War II Fighters, 1945-1973* (GPO, 1973), pp 222-260.

18.   Futrell, *Ideas, Concepts, Doctrine, Vol I*, pp 91-100.

19.   Alfred Goldberg and Lt. Col. Donald Smith, *Army-Air Force Relations: The Close Air Support Issue* (Rand Report R-906-PR, Oct. 1971), p 18.

20.   Robert A. Olson, "Air Mobility for the Army," *Military Affairs*, Winter, 1964-65, pp 167-169; Lt. Gen. John Tolson, *Airmobility, 1961-71* (Dept. of the Army, 1973), pp 18, 19. Olson's article says that the Howze Board was a formalization of an unofficial board created earlier by Gen. Lemnitzer. Tolson's book credits analysts in OSD who were critical of the Army's caution with having prepared the memorandum for McNamara's signature. The book also claims that Gen. Howze was unaware of background maneuvering that resulted in his appointment as board chairman and that he would have protested strongly had he known.

21.   Olson, "Air Mobility for the Army," p 169; Tolson, *Airmobility*, pp 22-24; Goldberg and Smith, *Army-Air Force Relations*, pp 20, 21.

22.   Memo for the Record, Col. Richard H. Ellis, Executive to the Chief of Staff, USAF, Aug. 3, 1962, Secret, material cited is unclassified.

23.   Goldberg and Smith, *Army-Air Force Relations*, pp 20, 21; A Study of Aviation Responsibilities, Air Force-Army, Dir. of Plans, HQ USAF, Jun. 1962, p 1, AFHRA K143.043-5; Memo for Mr. Zuckert, undated and unsigned, in the papers of Maj. Gen. Glenn Martin, AFHRA 168.7048-2.

24.   Memo to the Secretary of the Army by Robert S. McNamara, Apr. 19, 1962, as cited in A Study of Aviation Responsibilities, Jun. 1962, p 14; Memo by Col. James F. Kirkendall, subj: Meeting with Gen. Wheeler on Aerial Vehicles, Dec. 11, 1963; Memo by Col. Richard H. Ellis, subj: Army Inroads to the Air Force Mission, Aug. 3, 1962; Goldberg and Smith, *The Close Air Support Issue*, p 26.

25.   Goldberg and Smith, *Army-Air Force Relations*, pp 19, 22-23. In *Air Mobility, 1961- 1971*, Gen. Tolson wrote that McNamara approved the Army's unilateral tests near the end of 1964 (p 57).

26.   A Study of Aviation Responsibilities, HQ USAF, Jun. 1962, pp 7, 8, AFHRA K143.043- 5.

27.   Tolson, *Airmobility, 1961-1971*, pp 25-50.

28.   Olson, *Military Affairs*, Winter, 196-1965, pp 163-175; Ltr, Brig. Gen. Rollen H. Anthis to Gen. Jacob E. Smart, subj: [End of Tour Report], Nov. 25, 1963, AFHRA K526.131.

29.   Robert F. Futrell, *The Advisory Years to 1965* (GPO, 1981), pp 41-47.

30.   Ltr, Anthis to Smart, Nov. 25, 1963, AFHRA K526.131.

31.   *Ibid*; Draft Memo for Gen. Harris by Lt. Gen. Glen W. W. Martin, Dec. 4, 1964, AFHRA 168.7048-2.

32.   Ltr, Anthis to Smart, Nov. 25, 1963, AFHRA K526.131; Ltr, Maj. Gen. Rollen H. Anthis to USAF DCS/Plans and Ops, subj: Debriefing of Officers Returning from Field

Assignments, Dec. 19, 1963, AFHRA K526.131.

33. Tolson, *Airmobility, 1961-1971*, pp 39, 40.

34. Ltr, Anthis to Smart, Nov. 25, 1963; Ltr, Anthis to USAF DCS/Plans and Ops, Dec. 19, 1963.

35. See note above.

36. Ltr, Maj. GeN.J. H. Moore, Cmdr 2d Air Div to Col Oakley W. Baron, AWC, Jan.18, 1965, AFHRA K526.161; Paper, Gen. William W. Momyer, "Observations of the Vietnam War, Jul. 1966-Jul. 1968," Nov. 1970, AFHRA K740.131.

37. Futrell, *The Advisory Years*, p 227.

38. AFM 1-1, *United States Air Force Basic Doctrine*, Aug. 14, 1964, pp 1-1, 1-2, -13; Futrell, *The Advisory Years*, pp 210, 227; Gen. William W. Momyer, *Air Power in Three Wars* (HQ USAF, 1978), pp 17-20, 118.

39. Momyer, *Air Power in Three Wars*, pp 53, 54, 66, 107, 109; John Schlight, "The Impact of the Orient on Airpower," *The American Military and the Far East*, Proceedings of the Ninth Military History Symposium, USAF Academy, 1980, (GPO, 1082), p 168; Col John Schlight, "Civilian Control of the Military in Southeast Asia," *Air University Review*, Nov-Dec. 1980, p 58.

40. Momyer, "Observations of the Vietnam War," Nov. 1970, AFHRA K740.131; John Schlight, *The Years of the Offensive, 1965-1968* (GPO, 1988), p 159.

41. Momyer, "Observations of the Vietnam War," Nov. 1970, AFHRA K740.131.

42. Goldberg and Smith, *The Close Air Support Issue*, Oct. 1971, p 24. The authors wrote that the Army changed its mind in 1963 on the type of aircraft it wanted for close air support, stating a preference for high-performance, multipurpose aircraft rather than demanding specialized ones for close air support.

43. Riley Sutherland, *Evolution of Command and Control Doctrine for Close Air Support* (AFCHO, Mar. 1973), pp 44-46.

44. Goldberg and Smith, *The Close Air Support Issue*, pp 26, 27, 29.

45. Ltr, Gen. J. P. McConnell, CSAF, to Gen. Hunter Harris, Jr., CINCPACAF, subj: Roles and Missions Quarrel, May 29, 1965.

46. Warren A. Trest, *Single Manager for Air in SVN*, Project CHECO Report, Jul. 1, 1968, AFHRA K717.0413-39.

47. *Ibid*; Jack Shulimson, *U. S. Marines in Vietnam, An Expanding War 1966* (GPO, 1982), pp 3-9.

48. Momyer, "Observations of the Vietnam War," Nov. 1970, AFHRA K740.131; ACSC Student Report by Maj. Carl J. Eschmann, "The Role of Tactical Air Support: Linebacker II," 85-0765, pp 106, 107.

49. Momyer, *Air Power in Three Wars*, pp 72-76, 82, 314; Ltr, Gen. William W. Momyer to Maj. Gen. Robert N. Ginsburg, subj: Khe Sanh, May 23, 1972, AFHRA 168.7041-52; Bernard C. Nalty, *Air Power and the Fight for Khe Sanh*, (Washington, D.C., 1973), pp 80, 81.

50. Bernard C. Nalty, *Air Power and the Fight for Khe Sanh*, pp 68-80; Warren A. Trest, *Khe Sanh (Operation Niagara)*, Project CHECO Report, Sep. 13, 1969; Momyer, "Observations of the Vietnam War," AFHRA K740.131.

51. See note above.

52. *Ibid.*

53. Momyer, "Observations of the Vietnam War," AFHRA K740.131.

54. *Ibid*; Momyer, *Air Power in Three Wars*, pp 117, 118.

55. Momyer, *Air Power in Three Wars*, pp 85-99; Col. John Schlight, "Civilian Control of the Military in Southeast Asia," *Air University Review*, Nov-Dec. 1980, pp 58, 62, 63.

56. See note above.

57. Warren A. Trest, *Control of Air Strikes in SEA, 1961-1966*, Project CHECO Report, Mar. 1, 1967: Kenneth Sams, *Command and Control 1965*, Project CHECO Report, Dec. 15, 1966.

58. See note above.

59. J. S. Butz, Jr, "Those Bombing North Vietnam," *Air Force Magazine*, Apr. 1966, pp 43- 54; Wesley Melyan and Lee Bonetti, *Rolling Thunder, Jul. 1965-Dec. 1966*, Project CHECO Report, Jul. 15, 1967; Address

by Gen. George S. Brown to Order of Deadilians, San Antonio, TX, May 17, 1975.

60. Adm. U. S. Grant Sharp, USN (Ret.), "We Could Have Won in Vietnam Long Ago," *Readers Digest*, May 1969, pp 118-123, Momyer, Observations of the Vietnam War: AFHRA K740.131.

61. Momyer, "Observations of the Vietnam War," AFHRA K740.131; Momyer, *Air Power in Three Wars*, pp 91-99.

62. Butz, "Those Bombing North Vietnam," pp 43-54; Brig. Gen. James R. McCarthy and Col. George B. Allison, *Linebacker II: A View From the Rock*, USAF Southeast Asia Monograph Series, Monograph 8, Maxwell AFB, Ala., 1979; M. F. Porter, *Linebacker: Overview of the First 120 Days*, Project CHECO Report, Sep. 27, 1971.

63. Col. Thomas A. Cardwell, III, "The Quest for Unity of Command," *Air University Review*, May-Jun. 1984, pp 25-29.

64. Sharp, "We Could Have Won in Vietnam Long Ago," *Readers Digest*, May 1969, pp 118-123.

65. *Ibid.*

66. Maj. Paul Burbage, et al., *USAF Southeast Asia Monograph Series, Vol I, The Battle for the Skies over North Vietnam, 1964-1972*, pp 108-111m 130-132, 139-145; Momyer, *Air Power in Three Wars*, pp 145-151, 158-159; James N. Eastman, et al., ed., *Aces and Aerial Victories*, (Washington, D.C., 1976), pp 35-41.

67. Tolson, *Airmobility*, pp 113-114.

68. In his article "Civilian Control of the Military in Southeast Asia," printed in the Nov- Dec. 1980 issue of *Air University Review*, Col. John Schlight quotes Secretary of Defense McNamara as saying the primary objective of Rolling Thunder "was to communicate our political resolve," which ironically wavered throughout the war and failed us in the end.

69. Larry Booda, "USAF, Army Air Roles Evolving Slowly," Aviation Week and Space Technology, May 27, 1967, pp 30, 31; Wolf, *Basic Documents on Roles and Missions*, pp 379- 384.

70. Goldberg and Smith, *The Close Air Support Issue*, Oct. 1971, pp 33, 34.

71. *Ibid.*, p 35.

72. *Ibid.*, pp 32, 37. Goldberg and Smith noted that the Army coined the term "direct aerial fire support" to circumvent the restrictions in DOD Directive 5160.22 of Mar. 18, 1957. The OSD cancellation of this directive in 1971 was supported by the Army but opposed by the Air Force.

73. Momyer, *Air Power in Three Wars*, pp 82, 99.

74. Interview of Gen. Creighton Abrams, Jr., by Kenneth Sams and Maj Phillip Caine, Mar. 3, 1970, pp 109, 110, AFHRA K239.0512-373.

75. Interview of Gen. Maxwell D. Taylor by Maj. Richard B. Clement and Jacob Van Staaveren, Jan.11,1972, AFHRA K229.0512, p 44.

76. Futrell, *Ideas, Concepts, Doctrine, Vol 2*, p 603.

77. James W. Canan, "The Ups and Downs of Jointness," *Air Force Magazine*, Oct. 1985, p 47.

78. Martin E. James, Historical Highlights, United States Air Forces in Europe, 1945-1980, Office of History, HQ USAFE, May 1, 1980; Dept. of the Air Force Historical Summary, Jul. 1, 1968 to Jun. 30, 1969, by Office of Air Force History, undated, p 24.

79. Histories, United States Air Forces in Europe, 1966 through the 1970s.

80. Futrell, *Ideas, Concepts, Doctrine, Vol 2*, pp 344-348, 477.

81. Marc Huett, "Seapower Seen as Answer to Cut in Bases," *The Stars and Stripes*, Nov. 25, 1967, p 2.

82. Memo for Maj. Gen. Smith by Lt. Gen. Glenn W. Martin, DCS Plans and Ops, subj: [Posture Statements by Sec Navy and CNO], Apr. 10, 1968.

83. Annual Reports of the Secretary of Defense, FY 1961-FY 1968.

84. Oral History Interview with Gen. David C. Jones, by Lt. Col. Maurice Maryanow, Aug. 5, 1985, Oct. 15-17, 1985, Jan.20-21, 1986, Mar. 13-14, 1987, pp 176-180, AFHRA K239.0512-1664.

Roles and Missions

85. *Ibid.*

86. *Ibid.*. p 161; Wolf, *Basic Documents on Roles and Missions*, pp 393-400.

87. See Note Above.

88. Robert C. Toth, "Joint Chiefs to Resolve Dispute on Air Strategy," *Los Angeles Times*, Dec. 12, 1980, p 1; White Letter No. 1-80. Commandant of the Marine Corps, Robert H. Barrow, subj: Flexibility in MAGTF Operations, Jan.17, 1980; Dr. Stephen J. Cimbala, "War-Fighting Deterrence and Allied Cohesiveness," *Air University Review*, Sep-Oct. 1984, pp 69- 73; End of Tour Report, Gen. David C. Jones, CINCUSAFE, 1971-1974, AFHRA K570.131.

89. Senate, Close Air Support: Hearings before the Special Subcommittee on Close Air Support of the Preparedness Investigating Subcommittee of the Committee on Armed Services, 92d Congress, 1st Session, 1972, pp 209, 281, 292.

90. *Ibid.*, p 442.

91. *Ibid.*, pp 85, 86.

92. *Ibid.*, pp 262, 263.

93. *Ibid.*, pp 12, 13.

94. Interview with Gen. George Brown by Sams and Kott, Mar. 30, 1970, p 123, AFHRA K239.0512-372; Interview with Gen. Brown by Clement and Swenston, Oct. 19-20, 1970, p 68, AFHRA K239.0512-365.

95. See Note Above.

96. Goldberg and Smith, *The Close Air Support Issue*, p 45; Tolson, *Airmobility, 1951- 1971*, pp 198, 199.

97. Ltr, Gen J. P. McConnell, CSAF, and Gen. Harold K. Johnson, CSA, to Gen. T. J. Conway, U. S. Strike Command, subj: [Joint Doctrine], May 12, 1967; Statements on CAS by Secretary of the Army Froehlke and Army Chief of Staff Abrams before the House Armed Services Committee, Apr. 17, 1973, attached to letter, Brig. Gen. James M. Allen, DCS/Plans, HQ TAC to All Staff, subj: Statements on CAS by the Secretary of the Army and the Chief of Staff, U. S. Army, Jun. 22, 1973.

98. See Note Above.

99. Senate, Close Air Support: Hearings before the Special Subcommittee on Close Air Support of the Preparedness Investigating Subcommittee of the Committee on Armed Services, 92d Congress, 1st Session, 1972, pp 187, 188, 189.

100. *Ibid.*, pp 200, 240.

101. *Ibid.*, p 192.

102. Ltr, Lt. Gen. Robert E. Huyser, DCS/Plans, HQ USAF, to Gen. Dixon, Cmdr TAC, subj: Army/Air Force Dialogue on Areas of Mutual Interest, Nov. 9, 1973, AFHRA K417.168-2. For more comprehensive discussion of TAC-TRADOC dialogues, see Futrell, *Ideas, Concepts, Doctrine*, Vol 2, pp 539-546.

103. Memo, Gen. David C. Jones, CSAF and Gen. Fred C. Weyand, CSA, to Hon Melvin Price, Chairman, Committee on Armed Services, House of Representatives, Aug. 7, 1976.

104. John L. Romjue, *From Active Defense to Airland Battle: The Development of Army Doctrine, 1973-1982*, (History Office, US Army TRADOC, Fort Monroe, VA, Jun. 1984), pp 3-11.

105. *Ibid.*, pp 30, 62.

106. *Ibid.*

107. Futrell, *Ideas, Concepts, Doctrine*, pp 677, 678.

108. Wolf, *Basic Documents on Roles and Missions*, pp 361-364; Futrell, *Ideas, Concepts, Doctrine*, p 144, 679.

109. Department of the Air Force Historical Summary, Jul. 1968 to Jun. 1969, Office of Air Force History, p 65.

110. Futrell, *Ideas, Concepts, Doctrine*, pp 144, 682.

111. Wolf, *Basic Documents on Roles and Missions*, pp 385, 387, 388.

112. Futrell, *Ideas, Concepts, Doctrine*, p 685.

113. AFM 1-2, *United States Air Force Basic Doctrine*, Dec. 1, 1959; AFM 1-1, *United States Air Force Basic Doctrine*, Aug. 14, 1964; AFM 1-1, *United States Air Force Basic Doctrine*, Sep. 28, 1971; AFM 1-1, *United States Air Force Basic Doctrine*, Jan. 15, 1975.

114. AFM 1-1, *Functions and Basic Doctrine of the United States Air Force*, Feb. 18, 1979, pp 2-5, 2-8, 2-9.

115. Futrell, *Ideas, Concepts, Doctrine*, p 689.

Chapter VII

1. Oral History Interview of Gen. David C. Jones, by Lt. Col. Maurice Maryanow with Dr. Richard H. Kohn, Washington, D.C., Aug 5 and Oct 15-15, 1994, Jan 20-21 and Mar 13-14, 1986, pp 140, 161, AFHRC K239.0512-1664.

2. *Ibid.*

3. Caspar W. Weinberger, Secretary of Defense, "The Reality of the Soviet Threat," *Defense 83*, Jun 1983, pp 2-7; Richard D. DeLauer, UnderSecretary of Defense for Research and Engineering, "Countering the Soviet Threat," *Defense 83*, Jun 1983, pp 8-15.

4. The Honorable Harold Brown, Secretary of Defense, "The Persian Gulf and Southwest Asia," *Defense 80*, Jun 1980, pp 2-9.

5. Lawrence E. Benson and Jay E. Hines, *The United States Military in North Africa and Southwest Asia Since World War II* (U.S. Central Command History Office: 1988, pp 33, 39; Warren A. Trest, *Military Unity and National Policy* (AU Press, Maxwell AFB, AL: 1991), p 21.

6. Caspar W. Weinberger, "The Rearming of America," *Defense 81*, pp 2-10, and "The Uses of Military Power," *Defense 85*, pp 2-11.

7. *Ibid.*, Caspar W. Weinberger, "What is Our Defense Strategy?" *Defense 85*, Dec 1995, pp 2-10.

8. Robert E. Ropelewski, "Soviet Weapons Gains Spur U.S. Strategic Modernization," *Aviation Week & Space Technology*, Mar 16, 1985, pp 25-31.

9. Compiled from the annual almanac issues of *Defense*, 1981 to 1990.

10. Trest, *Military Unity and National Policy*, pp 14, 17, 18.

11. Ibid., pp 17, 18; Weinberger, "What is Our Defense Strategy?", p 3.

12. Norman Friedman, *The US Maritime Strategy* (New York: 1988), p. 6; Richard Halloran, *New York Times* Writer, "Submarines Dominate U.S. Nuclear Forces," reported in *Montgomery Advertiser*, Nov 27, 1987, p 30.

13. "Weapons and Forces," *Defense 92*, Sep/Oct 1992, p 20.

14. Norman Cigar, "Soviet Aircraft Carriers, Unfortunate Timing for a Long-Held Dream," *Naval War College Review*, Spring 1992, pp 20-34.

15. Evan Thomas, "Bashing Gaddafi has not quieted the Pentagon's Critics," *Time*, Apr 14, 1986, p 25; Evan Thomas, "Nation," *Time*, May 5, 1986, pp 9, 10, 18.

16. See Note above.

17. Thomas A. Keaney, *Strategic Bombers and Conventional Weapons: Air Power Options*, monograph series (Washington, D.C.: National Defense University Press, 1984), pp 35, 36; Donald D. Chipman and Maj. David Lay, "Sea Power and the B-52 Stratofortress," *Air University Review*, Jan-Feb 1986, p 45; George C. Wilson, "Pentagon Maps New Navy-Air Force Cooperation in Sea Warfare," *The Washington Post*, Oct 7, 1982, p A21.

18. Wilson, "Pentagon Maps New Air Force-Navy Cooperation in Sea Warfare," p A21; James W. Canan, "The Ups and Downs of Jointness," *Air Force*, Oct 1985, p 4.

19. Chipman and Lay, "Sea Power and the B-52 Stratofortress," p. 45.

20. Richard G. Davis, *The 31 Initiatives*, (Washington, D.C.: Office of Air Force History, 1987) pp 30-31.

21. *Ibid.*, p 31.

22. Air Force Policy Letter for Commanders, from the Office of the Secretary of the Air Force, May 15, 1983, and May 1, 1984; Maj. Gen. Bobby J. Maddox, "Army Aviation Branch Implementation," *U.S. Army Aviation Digest*, pp 1-8.

23. Air Force Policy Letter for Commanders, 15 June 1984: Eugene Kozicharow, "USAF, Army Agree on Joint Initiatives," *Aviation Week and Space Technology*, May 28, 1984, pp 22-24; Davis, *The 31 Initiatives*, p 35; Wolf, *Basic Documents on Roles and Missions*, pp 413-423.

24. Wolf, *Basic Documents on Roles and Missions,* pp 413, 414; Kozicharow, p 22; Msg, HQ AFSINC to HQ USAF/PA *et al,* subj: Air Force News Service, 052200Z Jun 1984.

25. Thomas Fuller, "DOD in Space: A Historical Perspective," *Defense 88,* Nov/Dec 1988, pp 16-31; Memorandum to SECDEF from William J. Crowe, Jr., Chairman JCS, subj: Report on Roles and Functions of the Armed Forces, Sep 28, 1989; Trest, *Military Unity and National Policy,* p 21.

26. Fuller, "DOD in Space:A Historical Perspective," p 28.

27. Trest, *Military Unity and National Policy,* p 21.

28. Fuller, "DOD in Space:A Historical Perspective," p 28.

29. George C. Wilson, "Shuttle Flight Continues 25-Year Space Contest," *Washington Post,* Dec 21, 1984, p 1.

30. Associated Press, "Umbrella Space Command Authorized for Pentagon," *Washington Post,* Dec 1, 1984, p 10.

31. "USAF's Space Command To Be Established September 1," *Aviation Week & Space Technology,* Jun 28, 1982, p 30.

32. "Sailors in Space," *Aviation Week & Space Technology,* 1983, p 15.

33. Craig Covault, "Army Renewing Space Program Efforts," *Aviation Week & Space Technology,* Jan 28, 1985, p 21; Fuller, "DOD in Space: A Historical Perspective," p 30.

34. Susan Leonard, "U.S. Space Command nears readiness," *Colorado Springs Gazette Telegraph,* Dec 12, 1985, p 1.

35. Wane Biddle, "Military Role in Space," *New York Times,* Dec 21, 1984, p 1.

36. Leonard Famiglietti, "October Space Command Debut Predicted," *Air Force Times,* Dec 24, 1984, p 4.

37. Archie D. Barret, *Reappraising Defense Organization: An Analysis Based on the Defense Organization Study of 1977-1980* (National Defense University, Washington, D.C., 1983), p xvi; Peter W. Chiarelli, "Beyond Goldwater-Nichols," *Joint Force Quarterly,* Autumn 1993, p 71; William H.

Gregory, "Reorganizing the Chiefs," *Aviation Week & Space Technology,* Nov 1, 1982, p 11; Robert C. Toth, "Joint Chiefs to Resolve Dispute on Air Strategy," *Los Angeles Times,* Dec 12, 1980, p 1.

38. Oral History Interview of General Jones, p 296, AFHRC K239. 0512-1664.

39. Drew Middleton, "Army Chief of Staff Urges a Broad Reorganization," *New York Times,* Mar 31, 1982, p 19.

40. Gen. T.R. Milton, USAF (Ret.), Contributing Editor, "The Quest for Unity," *Air Force Magazine,* Jan 1986, p 102.

41. Jeffrey S. McKitrick, "The JCS: Evolutionary or Revolutionary Reform?" *Parameters,* Spring 1986, pp 64, 65.

42. Gen. Edward C. Meyer, "The JCS-How Much Reform is Needed?" *Armed Forces Journal International,* Apr 1982, pp 82-90; Chiarelli, "Beyond Goldwater-Nichols," pp 71, 72, 73; McKitrick, "The JCS: Evolutionary or Revolutionary Reform?" p 63; Barrett, *Reappraising Defense Reorganization,* p xvii.

43. "Washington Roundup," *Aviation Week & Space Technology,* Jun 20, 1983, p 17.

44. Chiarelli, "Beyond Goldwater-Nichols," p 73.

45. Caspar W. Weinberger, "The Challenges of Organizing and Managing DoD's Resources," *Defense 83,* Oct 1983, pp 2, 3.

46. Bill Keller, New York Times Writer, "Military Reforms Proposed," *The Montgomery Advertiser,* Tuesday, Jan 22, 1985, pp 1A, 5A.

47. *Ibid.*

48. Jim Stewart, Cox Washington Bureau, "Study urges reforms in military leadership," *The Atlanta Constitution,* Oct 16, 1985, p 1A, 14A.

49. "Interview with Former JCS Chairman Adm. Thomas H. Moorer," *Sea Power,* Dec 1985, p 21.

50. Bill Keller, "Proposed Revamping of Military Calls for Disbanding Joint Chiefs," *The New York Times,* Oct 17, 1985, p 20.

51. The Associated Press, "Measure to Expand role of Joint Chiefs chairman is approved by House," *The Atlanta Constitu-*

tion, Nov 21, 1985, p 2A; The Associated Press, "Weinberger backs military restructuring," *The Atlanta Constitution*, Dec 5, 1985, p 2A.

52. Evan Thomas, "Questions and Reforms," *Time*, Apr 14, 1986, p 25.

53. Msg, HQ AFSINC to SAF/PA, et al, subj: Air Force News Services, 132200z Nov 86; Eliot Brenner, UPI, "Senate Says: Remodel Pentagon, *San Antonio Light*, May 8, 1986, p 1; Colonel Donald R. Baucum, "Military Reform: An Idea Whose Time Has Come," *Air University Review*, Jan-Mar 1987, p 79; Sam Nunn, "Military reform paved way for gulf triumph," *Atlanta Constitution*, Mar 31, 1991, p G5.

54. Msg, HQ AFSINC to SAF/PA, et al, subj: Air Force News Service, 132200Z Nov 86; Goldwater-Nichols Department of Defense Reorganization Act of 1986, Public Law 99-433, 99th U.S. Congress, Oct 1, 1986.

55. Nunn, "Military reform paved way for gulf triumph," p G5.

56. Goldwater-Nichols Department of Defense Reorganization Act of 1986, Public Law 99-433, 99th U.S. Congress, Oct 1, 1986.

57. Ibid., Chiarelli, "Beyond Goldwater-Nichols," p 77.

58. Gen. Robert T. Herres, USAF, "Making Interoperability & Jointness a Way of Life," *Defense 88*, Jan/Feb 1988, pp 19-25.

59. Nunn, "Military reform paved way for gulf triumph," p G5.

60. *Ibid.*

61. Memo for the Secretary of Defense from William J. Crowe, Jr., Chairman Joint Chiefs of Staff, subj: Report on Roles and Functions of the Armed Forces, Sep 26, 1989.

62. *Ibid.*, "Cheney Receives Plan to Reshuffle Space Authority at Pentagon," *Defense News*, Nov 13, 1989, p 10.

63. See note above.

64. Memo for the Secretary of Defense from Colin L. Powell, Chairman Joint Chiefs of Staff, subj: Report on Roles and Functions of the Armed Forces, Nov 2, 1989.

65. Barbara Amouyal, "Powell Taps Air Force for Close Air Support Mission," *Defense News*, Nov 13, 1989, p 1.

66. Memo for the Secretary of Defense from Powell, Chairman Joint Chiefs of Staff, Nov 2, 1989.

67. *Ibid.*

68. Barbara Amouyal, "Powell Taps Air Force for Close Air Mission," *Defense News*, Nov 13, 1989, pp 1, 4.

69. Nunn, "Military reform paved way for gulf triumph," p G5.

70. *Ibid.*

71. *Ibid.*, Larry R. Bensen and Jay E. Hines, *The United States Military in North Africa and Southeast Asia Since World War II* (MacDill AFB, FL: USCENTCOM History Office, 1988), pp 39-5.

72. Gen. Duane H. Cassidy, CINCUS-TRANSCOM, "The Development of USTRANSCOM," *Defense Transportation Journal*, Dec 1987, pp 18, 19; John F. Slinkman, "Joint Deployment System for Land, Sea and Air," *The Officer*, Nov 1988, pp 14-16; Nunn, "Military reform paved way for gulf triumph," p G5.

73. Chiarelli, "Beyond Goldwater-Nichols," p 77.

74. Transcript, Gen. Ronald R. Fogleman, Chief of Staff, Air Force, with Defense Writers Group, Feb 15, 1995, p 6.

75. Compiled from the annual almanac issues of Defense, 1989 to 1992.

76. Susan H.H. Young, "Gallery of Air Force Weapons," *Air Force Magazine*, May 1994, pp 118, 120; "B-2 Bomber runs into a wall in the budget-conscious House," *Columbus Ledger-Inquirer*, Jul 13, 1989, p A-4; Tim Weiser, Stealth fighter revived," *Philadelphia Inquirer*, Apr 1, 1991, p 1.

77. Gen. John R. Galvin, USA, CONCEUR, "Flexible Response & Forward Defense," *Defense 88*, Jul/Aug 1988, p 65.

78. Secretary of Defense Dick Cheney, "A New Defense Strategy," *Defense 91*, Mar/Apr 1991, p 9.

79. Gen. P.X. Kelley, Commandant of the Marine Corps, "Marines...Ready Now...Preparing for Tomorrow," *Defense 85*, pp 6, 7;

Roles and Missions

Bensen and Hines, *The United States Military in North Africa and Southwest Asia Since World War II*, pp 44-51.

80. Richard P. Hallion, *Storm Over Iraq; Air Power and the Gulf War* (Washington & London, 1992), pp 156-161; Thomas A. Keaney and Eliot A. Cohen, *Gulf War Air Power Survey Summary Report* (Washington, D.C., 1993), p 1-3, 27.

81. See note above.

82. Colonel Richard T. Reynolds, *Heart of the Storm: The Genesis of the Air Campaign against Iraq* (AU Press, Maxwell AFB, AL, 1995), pp 22-27; Diane T. Putney, "From Instant Thunder to Desert Storm: Developing the Gulf War Air Campaign Phases," *Air Power History*, Fall 1994, p 40.

83. Hallion, *Storm Over Iraq* pp 150-156; Putney, "From Instant Thunder to Desert Storm," pp 40-46; Reynolds, *Heart of the Storm*, pp 24, 51-59; Keaney and Cohen, *Gulf War Air Power Survey Summary Report*, pp 6, 27-53.

84. Nunn, "Military reform paved way for gulf triumph," p G5.

85. Keaney and Cohen, *Gulf War Air Power Survey Summary Report*, pp 3, 5; Col. Edward C. Mann III, Draft Copy of *Thunder and Lightning: Desert Storm and the Airpower Debates* (AU Press, Maxwell AFB, AL, 1995), pp 79-81, AFHRC K239.0472-118.

86. Mann, *Thunder and Lightning: Desert Storm and the Airpower Debates,* p 84; Keaney and Cohen, *Gulf War Air Power Survey Summary Report,* p 145.

87. Mann, *Thunder and Lightning: Desert Storm and the Airpower Debates,* pp 81-84; Keaney and Cohen, *Gulf War Air Power Survey Summary Report,* pp 150, 153-157.

88. Hallion, *Storm Over Iraq,* pp 166-176; Mann, pp 171, 172; Patrick E. Tyler, "U.S. Says Early Air Attack Caught Iraq Off Guard," *New York Times*, Jan 18, 1991, p 10.

89. Hallion, *Storm Over Iraq,* pp 193, 194, 231-38; Keaney and Cohen, *Gulf War Air Power Survey Summary Report,* pp 13, 23, 24.

90. Warren A. Trest, *Military Unity and National Policy: Some Past Effects and Future Implications* (Air University Press, 1991), pp 25, 26.

91. *Ibid.*, p 26.

92. Hallion, *Storm Over Iraq,* pp 241-268; Mann, *Thunder and Lightning: Desert Storm and the Airpower Debates,* pp 81-84.

93. Bradley Graham, "Battle Plans for a New Century," *Washington Post*, Feb 21, 1995, p 1.

94. *Ibid.*

95. Gen. Colin L. Powell, Chairman the Joint Chiefs of Staff, "Budget for a World Turned Upside Down," *Defense 93*, Issue 2, pp 8-11.

96. Interview with Gen. Merrill A. McPeak, Chief of Staff, Air Force, by Col. Charles D. Cooper, *The Retired Officer Magazine*, Jun 1991, p 29.

97. Ike Skelton, "Taking Stock of the New Joint Era," *Joint Forces Quarterly*, Winter 1993-94, p 17; Donald B. Rice, Secretary of the Air Force, "A White Paper Global Reach-Global Power," Jun 1990.

98. Interview with Gen. McPeak, Jun 1991, pp 28, 29; White Paper, "Air Force Restructure," Sep 1991, p 5.

99. See note above.

100. Interview with Gen. McPeak, Jun 1991, p 29.

101. Jack Dorsey, "Building a Better Air Force," *Norfolk Virginian Pilot*, May 31, 1992, p C-1; Robert Goodrich, "Air Mobility Command Activated at Scott Base," *St. Louis Post-Dispatch*, Jun 2, 1992, p 3; White Paper, "Air Force Restructure," Sep 1991, pp 5-7.

102. Frank B. Kelso II, "The Wave of the Future," *Joint Forces Quarterly*, Summer 1993, pp 13-16; Skelton, p 17.

103. Report of the Secretary of Defense to the President and the Congress, by Les Aspin, Secretary of Defense, Jan 1974, pp 11, B-2.

104. Gen. Colin L. Powell, Chairman of the Joint Chiefs of Staff, "Budget for a World Turned Upside Down," *Defense 93*, Mar-Apr 1993, p 9.

105. Mackubin Thomas Owens, "Accountants Vs. Strategists: The New Roles and Missions Debate," *Strategic Review*, Fall

1992, pp 7, 8; David S. Steigman, "Past battles...Future Fights?", *Navy Times*, Jul 20, 1992, p 12.

106. James Kitfeld, "Deconstructing Defense," *Government Executive*, Jan 1993, pp 10, 12.

107. Gen. Colin Powell, Chairman Joint Chiefs, Report on Roles, Missions, and Functions of the Armed Forces of the United States, Feb 1993; William Matthews, "Powell again reworking roles, missions report," *Air Force Times*, Feb 15, 1993, p 22.

108. Msg, Air Force News Kelly AFB, TX, to AIG 9333, subj: Air Force News Service, 162200Z Feb 1993; Skelton, "Taking Stock of the New Joint Era," *Joint Forces Quarterly*, Winter 1993-94, p 19.

109. Powell, Report on Roles, Missions, and Functions, Feb 1993; "The Price of Protecting Pentagon Turf," *New York Times*, Feb 22, 1993, p 16.

110. Skelton, "Taking Stock of the New Joint Era," pp 18, 19; Powell, Report on Roles, Missions, and Functions, Feb 1993, p II-3.

111. Skelton, "Taking Stock of the New Joint Era," pp 18, 19.

112. Margo MacFarland, "OSD Eyes Crowe, Odeen, Carlucci, others for Roles and Missions Panel," *Washington Times*, Feb 3, 1994, p 1; Hearings before the Senate Armed Services Committee, 103d Congress, "Department of Defense Authorization for Appropriations for Fiscal Year 1994 and the Future Year Defense Programs," Apr-Jun 1993, GPO 1994, pp 5, 43; "The Price of Protecting Pentagon Turf," *New York Times*, Feb 22, 1993, p 16.

113. Hearings before the Senate Armed Services Committee on DOD Appropriations for 1994, pp 36, 37; Skelton, "Taking Stock of the New Joint Era," p 19; Stephen S. Rosenfeld, "Scramble Over Roles and Missions," *Washington Post*, Oct 14, 1994, p 27.

114. Rosenfeld, p 27; MacFarland, p 1; William Matthews, "Is Change in Roles Now More Possible?" *Air Force Times*, Jun 6, 1994, p 32.

115. Matthews, "Is Change in Roles Now More Possible?" p 32.

116. James W. Canan, "McPeak Sums It Up," *Air Force Magazine*, Aug 1994, pp 30-33.

117. *Ibid.*

118. Jason Clashow and Robert Holzer, "USAF aggressively Guns for Roles," *Defense News*, Sep 12-18, 1994, p 1; Rowan Scarborough, "Armed Forces battle each other for roles," *Washington Times*, Sep 15, 1994, p 1.

119. Bradley Graham, "Air Force Chief on Attack," *Washington Post*, Oct 24, 1994, p 1.

120. See note above; Steven Watkins, "McPeak: Remove Marines' F/A-18s" Air Force Times, Sep 26, 1994, p 8; Presentation to the Commission on Roles and Missions of the Armed Forces by Gen. Merrill A. McPeak, Sep 14, 1994, copy at AFHRA.

121. Clashow and Holzer, "USAF aggressively Guns for Roles," p 1; McPeak Presentation, Sep 14, 1994.

122. McPeak Presentation, Sep 14, 1994.

123. *Ibid.*

124. *Ibid.*, Canan, "McPeak Sums It Up," p 34; Scarborough, "Armed Forces battle each other for roles," p 1; Bradley Graham, "Air Force Chief on Attack," *Washington Post*, Oct 24, 1994, p 1.

125. McPeak Presentation, Sep 14, 1994.

126. Clashow and Holzer, "USAF aggressively Guns for Roles," p 1; Scarborough, "Armed Forces battle each other for roles," p 1.

127. See note above.

128. Graham, "Air Force Chief on Attack," p 1.

129. John T. Correll, "Roles and Missions Ride Again," *Air Force Magazine*, Feb 1995, p 10.

130. Vince Crawley, Army disputed McPeak war strategy," *European Stars & Stripes*, Nov 6, 1994, p 3.

131. Correll, "Roles and Missions Ride Again," p 10.

132. Interview with William Perry by Johan Benson, *Aerospace America*, Oct 1994, p 11.

133. Julie Bird and Vago Muradian, "Oh Lord, its' hard to be humble...," *Air Force Times*, Sep 12, 1994, p 13; Correll, p 10.

134. Correll, "Roles and Missions Ride Again," pp 10, 11.

135. Msg, Chief of Staff, Air Force, to All Major Commands, subj: [Personal Message for All the Men and Women in the Air Force], 272100Z Oct 1994; Transcript, Chief of Staff Editorial Board with Defense Writers Group, Feb 14, 1995, p 6.

136. Transcript, Chief of Staff Editorial Board with Defense Writers Group, Feb 14, 1995, p 12; David J. Lynch, "The Air Force Takes Stock," *Air Force Magazine*, Feb 1995, p 24.

137. Transcript, Chief of Staff Editorial Board with Defense Writers Group, Feb 14, 1995, pp 12, 13.

138. Correll, "Roles and Missions Ride Again," p 12.

139. Lynch, "The Air Force Takes Stock," p 28.

140. Air Force White Paper, "Global Presence," 1995.

141. Correll, "Roles and Missions Ride Again," p 12.

142. "The Jane's Interview," *Jane's Defense Weekly*, Dec 10, 1994, p 32.

143. William Matthews, "A new era of jointness?"*Air Force Times*, Sep 5, 1994, p 34.

144. Patrick Pexton, Roles & Missions draft offers a peek into future," *Navy Times*, Apr 24, 1995, p 8.

145. Oral History Interview with Gen. Merrill A. McPeak, by the Office of Air Force History, undated.

146. Steven Watkins, "Service could get new roles," *Air Force Times* May 8, 1995, p 26; Gilbert A. Lewthwaite, "Armed Services battle to standstill over roles," *Baltimore Sun* May 15, 1995, p 1.

Epilogue

1. John M. Collins, *Military Roles and Missions: A Framework for Review* (The Library of Congress, Washington, D.C.: May 1, 1995), pp. 16, 17; L. Edgar Prina, "Roles and Missions Debate Enters Final Stages," *Sea Power*, Aug. 1995, p. 29.

2. *Directions for Defense*, Report of the commission on Roles and Missions of the Armed Forces, May 24, 1995, Preface by John P. White, Chairman and p. ES 5.

3. *Ibid*: Memorandum for Chairman, Senate Armed Services Committee, et al., by John P. White, subj: Report of the Commission on Roles and Missions of the Armed Forces, May 24, 1995.

4. *Directions for Defense*, pp. 2-1, 2-2, 2-3.

5. *Ibid*, pp 2-3, 2-11.

6. *Ibid*, pp 2-20.

7. *Ibid*, pp 2-21, 2-22..

8. *Ibid*, pp 2-26, 2-27, 2-28, 2-30.

9. Prina, *Sea Power*, Aug. 1995; Sean D. Naylor, "Roles Panel Seeks Cut of Total Army by 50,000," *Army Times*, Jun. 5, 1995, p 3.

10. Patrick Pexton, "Roles Unit: Jointness is the Way to Go," *Army Times*, Jun. 5, 1995, p 62.

11. George C. Wilson, "Roles Report is Timid, Vague," *Air Force Times*, Jun. 12, 1995, p 62.

12. John T Correll, "Surprise Package on Roles and Missions," *Air Force Magazine*, Aug. 1995, p 15.

13. John Robinson, "Pentagon to Carry Out Most of Commission's Proposals," *Defense Daily*, Aug. 28, 1995, p 288; DOD Looks to Implement Selected Roles and Missions Recommendations," *Defense Daily*, Aug. 31, 1995, p 13.

14. William Matthews, "DOD Review Rolls on," *Defense News*, Aug. 28-Sep. 3, 1995, p. 4.

15. "The Department of Defense: Special Defense Department Briefing," Supplement to the *Federal News Service*, Aug. 28, 1995.

16. Matthews, *Defense News*, p. 4.

17. "End the Roles and Missions Debate," *Defense News*, Sep. 4-10, 1995, p. 22.

18. Matthews, *Defense News*, p. 4.

19. See David MacIsaac's "Voices from the Central Blue: The Air Power Theorists "in Peter Paret, ed., *Makers of Modern Strategy* (Princeton: 1986), pp 624-647, for the genesis of this concluding image.

BIBLIOGRAPHY

Governmental Sources

Prior to the resurgent roles and missions scrutiny of recent years, the primary sources essential to this study were available, but not readily accessible. Finding aids to Air Force historical collections and other government repositories provided few references on the subject. Most relevant documents were catalogued under other subject headings-a fact of life which literally transformed roles and missions research into a refresher course in modern military history.

The lack of adequate finding aids steered the search for primary documentation to other leads such as those in published works. An essential companion to this study is a compilation of 37 basic documents on roles and missions prepared by Richard I. Wolf and published by the Office of Air Force History in 1987. The Wolf volume is a directional compass and anchor linking the chain of roles and missions developments through the first four decades of armed forces unification under the National Security Act of 1947.

Numerous expository official histories are guides to other pockets of primary source material. Particularly useful are contemporary volumes published by the Office of Air Force History and other government agencies. These not only contain coverage of specific roles and missions issues, but carry valuable leads within the indices and footnotes. Three such volumes pointed to primary sources on the roots of military aviation and its experiences in World War I: Juliette A. Hennesy's *The United States Army Air Arm, April 1861 to April 1917*; Thomas R. Greer's *The Development of Air Doctrine in the Army Air Arm, 1917-1941*; and Maurer Maurer's four volumes of edited material on *The U.S. Air Service in World War I*. Another volume which contains useful coverage of the early years of military flight is *A History of the United States Air Force, 1907-1957*, edited by Alfred Goldberg. The Goldberg volume serves as a compass through the evolution of Air Force roles and missions before 1957.

For identifying documentation on the interwar years, Maurer's *Aviation in the U.S. Army, 1919-1939* and John F. Shiner's *Foulois and the U.S. Army Air Corps, 1931-1935* are handy references. Goldberg's general history and Greer's monograph contain other useful material on the years between the wars, as does *Ideas, Concepts, Doctrine: Basic Thinking in the United States Air Force, 1907-1960, Volume I*, by Robert Frank Futrell.

The basic reference for the Air Force's experience in World War II is the seven-volume history, *The Army Air Forces in World War II*, edited by Wesley F. Craven and James Lea Cate. The previously cited volumes by Goldberg, Greer, and Futrell also are valuable leads to World War II sources. Other useful official references are Daniel R. Mortensen's 1987 study of World War II air-ground issues, *A Pattern for Joint Operations: World War II Close Air Support, North Africa* and Richard G. Davis' *Carl Spaatz and the Air War in Europe* published in 1993. The official Army, Navy, and Marine histories of World War II operations also were consulted.

Roles and Missions

Two indispensable official sources of information on roles and missions during the post-World War II period are *Planning and Organizing the Postwar Air Force, 1943-1947*, by Herman S. Wolk, and *History of the Office of the Secretary of Defense: The Formative Years, 1947-1950*, by Steven L. Reardon. George M. Watson Jr.'s *The Office of the Secretary of the Air Force, 1947-1965*, published by the Center for Air Force History in 1993, contains vital information, including a definitive chapter on "The Battle over the B-36." The Navy's insights into the postwar roles and missions struggle are contained in Jeffrey G. Barlow's *Revolt of the Admirals*, published by the Naval Historical Center in 1994. Researchers should also consult an important volume entitled *Air Power and Warfare: The Proceedings of the Eighth Military History Symposium, 1978* for fresh insights into interservice relations during this and earlier period. Goldberg's general history and Futrell's *Ideas, Concepts, Doctrine* are equally helpful.

Futrell's *The United States Air Force in Korea, 1950-1953* is the authoritative reference to the USAF's role and experience in the Korean conflict. Futrell's work was consulted frequently for information about the Korean War period, as was his chapter on the war appearing in the Goldberg history. Two recently published Air Force anthologies *Case Studies in the Development of Close Air Support* (1990) and *Case Studies in the Achievement of Air Superiority* (1994), both edited by Benjamin Franklin Cooling, add to the lore of these particular air missions in Korea and other wars. Another recent addition to the official literature about the war is a second volume in the History of the Office of the Secretary of Defense series entitled, *The Test of War, 1950-1953*, by Doris M. Condit. The five Marine Corps volumes on operations in Korea provided useful information on the Marine's differences with the Air Force. The Navy and Army histories of operations in Korea are also relevant to the study of interservice cooperation.

Eisenhower's eight years in the White House were a critical juncture in the evolution of roles and missions. Bedrock official sources for the period include two JCS histories: *The Joint Chiefs of Staff and National Policy, 1953-1954*, by Robert J. Watson, and *The Joint Chiefs of Staff and National Policy, 1955-1956*, by Kenneth W. Condit. Two official Air Force volumes containing useful references about the policy and direction of the Air Force during the Eisenhower years are Jacob Neufeld's *The Development of Air Force Ballistic Missiles, 1945-1960* (1990), and Kenneth Schaffel's *The Emerging Shield: The Air Force and the Evolution of Continental Air Defense, 1945-1960* (1991). An Army monograph, Roger J. Spiller's *"Not War But Like War": The American Intervention in Lebanon* is an excellent source of information on joint problems encountered during the emergency deployment of U.S. forces. Another useful Army study is *A History of Army Aviation, 1950-1962 (Phase II): 1955-1962)* by Richard P. Weinert, who documents the rise of organic Army aviation between Korea and Vietnam. Futrell's *Ideas, Concepts, Doctrine* must be consulted for commentary on interservice issues relating to this period.

The information explosion that accompanied the employment of American forces in Southeast Asia is reflected in the vast amount of published and unpublished material about the war. Of the officially published works, one in particular must be referenced as a source about the evolution of airmobility in the U.S. Army: *Airmobility, 1961-1971*, by Lt. Gen. John J. Tolson. Aside from this single Army volume, books about the war published by the Office of Air Force History have been most relevant to the study of roles and mission in the Vietnam era. Among the most useful: *The Advisory Years to 1965*, by Robert F. Futrell; *South Vietnam 1965-1968*, by John L. Schlight; *Tactical Airlift*, by Ray L. Bowers, and *Interdiction in Southern Laos, 1960-1968*, by Jacob Van Staaveren. General William W. Momyer's *Air Power in Three Wars* contains useful insights to the study of roles and missions in World War II and Korea, but is consulted most often for its commentary on air power in Vietnam. Another valuable source is *Command Structure for Theater Warfare: The Quest for Unity of Command*, by Colonel Thomas A. Cardwell, III.

Published sources offer little about roles and missions developments between the Vietnam War and the Gulf War. One relevant study exists on Army-Air Force cooperation after Vietnam: *The 31 Initiatives*, by Richard G. Davis, published by the Office of Air Force History in 1987. Another contemporary work provides a good overview of Air Force and Navy cooperation in recent years, especially as it pertains to the collateral responsibilities of the Air Force for sea warfare. This study, entitled *Strategic Bombers and Conventional Weapons: Air Power Options*, was authored by Thomas A. Keaney and published by the National Defense University in 1984.

The basic tools for researching primary source documents showed improvement after the Goldwater-Nichols Reorganization Act of 1986 and the end of the Cold War. Roles and missions terminology appeared more frequently in the titles and contents of primary source documents, and therefore were referenced more often in appropriate finding aids. Most of the new documentation revolved around three primary sources: two formal reports on roles and missions by successive JCS Chairmen (Admiral William J. Crowe, Jr. and General Colin L. Powell) in 1989 and 1993, and another report by the Commission on Roles and Missions of the Armed Forces in 1995. Two special bibliographies prepared at the Air University, Maxwell AFB, Alabama, exemplify the improvement in finding aids. These are the Airpower Research Institute's *Annotated Bibliography for Roles and Missions*, edited by Dr. Jim Titus and Major Jim Forsyth in May 1994, and the Air University Library's *Roles and Missions of the Armed Forces: Selected References*, compiled by Melrose M. Bryant in October 1994. The Air University Library's *Index to Military Periodicals*, dating from 1949, has long been the premier guide to published articles on military topics, including roles and missions. The outstanding collection of books and bound periodicals at the Air University Library were used extensively in research for this study.

Most of the primary sources used to write this study are housed at the USAF Historical Research Agency at Maxwell AFB. The Agency has the complete collection of Air Force organizational histories, along with other relevant holdings such as the personal papers of former Air Force leaders and pioneers, the files of the Air Corps Tactical School, and more than 2,000 oral histories. The E. L. Jones papers were indispensable in researching the foundational years of military aviation history. The Agency is the repository for thousands of studies and documents preserved by Projects CHECO and Corona Harvest, two special Air Force activities to document and evaluate Air Force operations in Southeast Asia. In recent years, the Agency's holdings have been enriched by the Gulf War collection, which includes extensive source materials used to write the Gulf War Air Power Survey.

Various other government repositories provided primary source documents for the study of roles and missions. Research performed at the Office of the Air Force History, the Library of Congress, and the National Archives was most helpful. The personal papers of Air Force leaders in the Manuscript Division at the Library of Congress hold a treasure of information relating to Air Force roles and missions. Congressional hearings on roles and missions issues are a valuable source of information. Documents also were obtained from the Presidential libraries, the Army War College, Carlisle Barracks, Pennsylvania; and the various service history offices in Washington, D.C.

Histories and Studies

Air University Special Study. *Relationships Between Past and Present Strategic Concepts.* Maxwell AFB, AL: Research Studies Institute, 1961.

Armstrong, William J. and Clark Van Fleet. *United States Naval Aviation, 1910-1980.* Washington, D.C.: Dept of the Navy, 1980.

Barlow, Jeffrey G. *Revolt of the Admirals: The Fight for Naval Aviation, 1945-1950.* Washington, D.C.: Naval Historical Center, 1994.

Benson, Lawrence E. and Jay E. Hines. *The United States Military in North Africa and Southeast Asia Since World War II.* MacDill AFB, FL: US CENTCOM History Office, 1988.

Bissell, Clayton. *A Brief History of the Air Corps.* Langley Field, VA: Air Corps Tactical School, 1927.

Borowski, Harry R., ed. *Military Planning in the Twentieth Century: Proceedings of the Eleventh Military History Symposium, USAF Academy, 1984.* Washington, D.C.: Office of Air Force History, 1986.

Burbage, Paul, *et al. USAF Southeast Asia Monograph Series: The Battle for the Skies Over North Vietnam, 1964-1972.* Washington, D.C.: GPO, 1976.

Cardwell, Thomas A. *Command Structure for Theater Warfare. The Quest for Unity of Command.* Maxwell AFB, AL: Air University Press, 1984.

Cole, H.M. *US Army in World War II: The European Theater of Operations, the Lorraine Campaign.* Washington, D.C.: Army Center of Military History, 1950.

Collins, James Lawton, Jr. *The Development and Training of the South Vietnamese Army, 1950-1972.* Washington, D.C.: Department of the Army, 1975.

Condit, Doris M. *History of the Office of Secretary of Defense, The Test of War, 1950-1953,* Washington, D.C.: Historical Office, Office of the Secretary of Defense, 1988.

Condit, Kenneth W. *The Joint Chiefs of Staff and National Policy*, 1955-1956. Washington, D.C.: JCS Historical Division, 1992.

Cooling, Benjamin Franklin, ed., *Case Studies in the Achievement of Air Superiority*. Washington, D.C.: Center for Air Force History, 1994.

Cooling, Benjamin Franklin, ed., *Case Studies in the Development of Close Air Support*. Washington, D.C.: Office of Air Force History, 1990.

Craven, Wesley F., and Cate, James L., eds. *The Army Air Forces in World War II*. 7 Vols. Chicago: University of Chicago Press, 1948-58.

Davis, Richard G., *The 31 Initiatives: A Study in Air Force - Army Cooperation*. Washington, D.C.: Office of Air Force History, 1987.

Dixon, Joe C., ed. *The American Military and the Far East: Proceedings of the Ninth Military History Symposium, USAF Academy, 1980*. Washington, D.C.: Office of Air Force History, 1980.

Field, James A., Jr. *History of the United States Naval Operations, Korea*. Washington, D.C.: Naval Historical Center, 1962.

Finney, Robert T. *The Development of Air Doctrine in the U.S. Air Force, 1917-1951*. Maxwell AFB, AL; Research Studies Institute, 1954.

Frisbee, John L., ed. *Makers of the United States Air Force*. Washington, D.C.: Office of Air Force History, 1987.

Futrell, Robert F., *et al. Aces and Aerial Victories: The United States Air Force in Southeast Asia, 1965-1973*. Washington, D.C.: Office of Air Force History, 1976.

Futrell, Robert F. *Command of Observation Aviation: A Study in Control of Tactical Air Power*. USAF Historical Study No. 24. Maxwell AFB, AL: USAF Historical Division, Air University 1952.

Futrell, Robert F. *Ideas, Concepts, Doctrine: A History of Basic Thinking in the United States Air Force, Vol. I, 1907-1960; Vol II, 1961-1984*. Maxwell AFB, AL: Air University Press 1989.

Futrell, Robert F. *The United States Air Force in Korea, 1950-1953*. Revised edition. Washington, D.C.: Office of Air Force History, 1983.

Futrell, Robert F. *The United States Air Force in Southeast Asia: The Advisory Years to 1965*. Washington, D.C.: Office of Air Force History, 1981.

Gabel, Christopher R. *The U.S. Army GHQ Manuevers of 1941*. Washington, D.C.: Center of Military History, 1991.

Garand, George W., and Strobridge, Truman R. *History of US Marine Corps in World War II.Vol IV*. Washington, D.C.: Marine Corps Historical Center, 1971.

Garland, Albert N., and Smith, Howard M. *Sicily and the Surrender of Italy*. Washington, D.C.: Army Center of Military History, 1965.

Geffen, William, ed. *Command & Commanders in Modern Military History: Proceedings of the Second Military History Symposium, USAF Academy, 1968*. Washington, D.C.: Office of Air Force History, 1971.

Goldberg, Alfred, and Smith, Donald. *Army-Air Force Relations: The Close Air Support Issue*. RAND Report R-906-PR, 1971.

Roles and Missions

Greer, Thomas H., *The Development of Air Doctrine in the Army Air Arm, 1917-1941*. Revised edition. Washington, D.C.: Office of Air Force History, 1985.

Hansell, Haywood S., Jr. *The Strategic Air War Against Germany and Japan*. Washington, D.C.: Army Center of Military History 1986.

Hermes, Walter G. *Truce Tent and Fighting Front*. Washington, D.C.: Army Center of Military History, 1966.

Hone, Thomas C. *Power and Change*. Washington, D.C.: Naval Historical Center, 1989.

Hopkins, Charles K. *Unclassified History of the Joint Strategic Target Planning Staff (JSTPS)*. Offutt AFB, NE: HQ Strategic Air Command, Office of History, 1989.

Howe, George F. *US Army in World War II: Mediterranean Theater of Operations, Northwest Africa, Seizing the Initiative in the West*. Washington, D.C.: Army Center of Military History, 1957.

Hurley, Alfred F., and Ehrhart, Robert C., ed. *Air Power and Warfare: Proceedings of the Eighth Military History Symposium, USAF Academy, 1978*. Washington, D.C.: Office of Air Force History, 1979.

Johnson Edward C. *Marines Corps Aviation: The Early Years, 1912-1940*. Washington, D.C.: USMC History and Museums Division, 1977.

Keaney, Thomas A. and Eliot A. Cohen. *Gulf War Air Power Summary Report*. Washington, D.C.: GPO, 1993.

Keaney, Thomas A. *Strategic Bombers and Conventional Weapons: Airpower Options*. Washington, D.C.: National Defense University, 1984.

Keiser, Gordon W. *The U.S. Marine Corps and Defense Unification, 1994-47*. Washington, D.C.: National Defense University, 1982.

Knaack, Marcelle Size. *Post-World War II Bombers*. Washington, D.C.: Office of Air Force History, 1988.

Knaack, Marcelle Size. *Post-World War II Fighters*. Washington, D.C.: Office of Air Force History, 1978.

Kohn, Richard H., and Harahan, Joseph P., ed. *Air Superiority in World War II and Korea*. Washington, D.C.: Office of Air Force History, 1983.

Lemmer, George F. *The Air Force and the Concept of Deterrence, 1945-1950*. Washington, D.C.: Office of Air Force History, 1963.

Mann, Edward C. *Thunder and Lightning: Desert Storm and The Airpower Debates*. Maxwell AFB: AU Press, 1995.

Maurer, Maurer. *Aviation in the U.S. Army, 1919-1939*. Washington, D.C.: Office of Air Force History, 1978.

Maurer, Maurer, ed. *The US Air Service in World War I*. 4 Vols. Washington, D.C.: Office of Air Force History, 1987.

McCarthy, James R., and Allison, George B. *USAF Southeast Asia Monograph Series: Linebacker II, A View From the Rock*. Washington, D.C.: GPO, 1979.

McClendon, R. Earl. *Army Aviation, 1947-1953*. Maxwell AFB, AL: USAF Historical Division, Air University, 1954.

McClendon, R. Earl. *The Question of Autonomy for the United States Air Arm, 1907-1945*. Maxwell AFB, AL: USAF Historical Division, Air University, 1950.

Meid, Pat, and Yingling, James M. *US Marine Operations in Korea, 1950-1953*. Vol. V. Washington, D.C.: Marine Corps Historical Center, 1972.

Momyer, William W. *Air Power in Three Wars (WWII, Korea, Vietnam)*. Washington, D.C.: GPO, 1978.

Montross, Lynn, and Canzona, Nicholas A. *US Marine Operations in Korea, 1950-1953: The Chosin Reservoir Campaign*. Vol. III. Washington: Marine Corps Historical Center, 1957.

Mortensen, Daniel R. *A Pattern for Joint Operations: World War II Close Air Support, North Africa*. Washington, D.C.: Office of Air Force History & Army Center of Military History, 1987.

Nalty, Bernard C. *Air Power and the Fight for the Khe Sanh*. Washington, D.C.: Office of Air Force History, 1973.

Nalty, Bernard C. *The Air Force Role in Five Crises*. Washington, D.C.: Office of Air Force History, 1968.

Neufeld, Jacob. *Ballistic Missiles in the United States Air Force 1945-1960*. Washington, D.C.: Office of Air Force History, 1990.

Palmer, Michael A. *Origins of the Maritime Strategy: American Naval Strategy in the First Postwar Decade*. Washington, D.C.: Naval Historical Center, 1988.

Pogue, Forrest C. *US Army in World War II: The European Theater of Operations, Supreme Command*. Washington, D.C.: Army Center of Military History, 1954.

Putney, Diane T., ed. *Ultra and the Army Air Forces in World War II*. Washington, D.C.: Office of Air Force History, 1987.

Raines, Edgar F., Jr. and Major David R. Campbell. *The Army and the Joint Chiefs of Staff: Evolution of Army Ideas on the Command, Control, and Coordination of the U.S. Armed Forces, 1942-1985*. Washington, D.C.: Center of Military History, 1986.

Reardon, Steven L. *History of the Office of Secretary of Defense: The Formative Years, 1947-1950*. Washington, D.C.: Historical Office, Office of the Secretary of Defense, 1984.

Reynolds, Richard T. *Heart of the Storm: The Genesis of the Air Campaign Against Iraq*. Maxwell AFB, AL: AU Press, 1995.

Roe, Thomas G., et al. *A History of Marine Corps Roles and Missions, 1775-1962*. Washington, D.C.: Marine Corps Historical Center, 1962.

Romanus, Charles F., and Sunderland, Riley. *Stilwell's Command Problems*. Washington, D.C.: Army Center of Military History, 1956.

Romjue, John L. *From Active Defense to Airland Battle: The Development of Army Doctrine, 1973-1982*. Fort Monroe, VA: Historical Office, US Army Training and Doctrine Command, 1984.

Sams, Kenneth, *et al. Air Operations in Northern Laos, 1 November 1969-1 April 1970*. Project CHECO Report, 1970.

Roles and Missions

Sams, Kenneth, *et al. Air Support of Counterinsurgency in Laos, July 1968-November 1969*. Project CHECO Report 1966.

Sams, Kenneth. *Command and Control 1965*. Project CHECO Report, 1966.

Schnabel, James F. *The United States Army in the Korean War: Policy and Direction, the First Year*. Washington, D.C.: Army Center of Military History, 1972.

Schaffell, Kenneth. *The Emerging Shield: The Air Force and the Evolution of Continental Air Defense, 1945-1960*. Washington, D.C.: Office of Air Force History, 1991.

Schlight, John. *The United States Air Force in Southeast Asia: The Years of the Offensive, 1965-1968*. Washington, D.C.: Office of Air Force History, 1988.

Shaw, Henry I. *et al. History of US Marine Corps Operations in World War II*. Vol. III. Washington, D.C.: Marine Corps Historical Center, 1966.

Shiner, John F. *Foulois and the US Army Air Corps, 1931-1935*. Washington, D.C.: Office of Air Force History, 1983.

Shulimson, Jack. *US Marines in Vietnam: An Expanding War, 1966*. Washington, D.C.: Marine Corps Historical Center, 1982.

Spiller, Roger J. *Not War But Like War: The American Intervention in Lebanon*. Leavenworth Papers No. 3. Fort Leavenworth, KS: Combat Studies Institute, 1981.

Sturm, Thomas A. *USAF Overseas Forces and Bases, 1947-1967*. Washington, D.C.: Office of Air Force History, 1969.

Sunderland, Riley. *Evolution of Command and Control Doctrine for Close Air Support*. Washington, D.C.: Office of Air Force History, 1973.

Tolson, John T. *Airmobility, 1961-1971*. Washington, D.C.: Army Center of Military History, 1973.

Trest, Warren A. *Control of Air Strikes in Southeast Asia, 1961-1966*. Project CHECO Report, 1967.

Trest, Warren A. *Military Unity and National Policy*. Maxwell AFB, AL: AU Press, 1991.

Trest, Warren A. *Single manager for Air in South Vietnam*. Project CHECO Report, 1968.

USAF Historical Study No. 100. *History of the Air Corps Tactical School, 1920-1940*. Maxwell AFB, AL: USAF Historical Division, Air University, 1955.

USAF Historical Study No. 101. *The Army Air Forces in the South Pacific to 1942*. Maxwell AFB, AL: USAF Historical Division, Air University, 1944.

USAF Historical Study No. 102. *Origins of Eighth Air Force*. Maxwell AFB, AL: USAF Historical Division, Air University, 1954.

USAF Historical Study No. 108. *The AAF in the Middle East*. Maxwell AFB, AL: USAF Historical Division, Air University, 1945.

Van Staaveren, Jacob. *Interdiction in Southern Laos, 1960-1968*. Washington, D.C.: Center for Air Force History, 1993.

Van Wyen, Adrien O. *The Aeronautical Board, 1916-1947*. Washington, D.C.: Dir of Naval History, 1947.

Watson, George M., Jr. *The Office of the Secretary of the Air Force, 1947-1965.* Washington, D.C.: Center for Air Force History, 1993.

Weinert, Richard P. *A History of Army Aviation, 1950-1962: Phase I, 1950-1954.* Fort Monroe, VA: Historical Office, Training and Doctrine Command, 1976.

Weinert, Richard P. *A History of Army Aviation, Phase II, 1955-1962.* Fort Monroe, VA: Historical Office, Training and Doctrine Command, 1976.

Werrell, Kenneth P. *Archie, Flak, AAA, and SAM: A Short History of Ground-Based Air Defense.* Maxwell AFB, AL: Air University Press 1988.

Wolf, Richard I. *The United States Air Force Basic Documents on Roles and Missions.* Washington, D.C.: Office of Air Force History, 1987.

Wolk, Herman S. *Planning and Organizing the Postwar Air Force, 1943-1947.* Washington, D.C.: Office of Air Force History, 1984.

Oral Histories

Gen. Creighton Abrams, Jr. Project CHECO: Tan Son Nhut AB, South Vietnam, 1970.

Maj. Gen. Frederick L. Anderson. AAF Historical Office: Washington, D.C., 1947.

Gen. George S. Brown. Project CHECO: Tan Son Nhut AB, Vietnam, 1970.

Lt. Gen. Ira C. Eaker. USAF Historical Division, Liaison Office: Washington, D.C., 1962.

Lt. Gen. Ira C. Eaker. Army War College: Carlisle Barracks, PA, 1972.

Maj. Gen. Benjamin D. Foulois. USAF Historical Division, Liaison Office: Washington, D.C., 1965.

Gen. David C. Jones. USAF Historical Research Center, Maxwell AFB, AL, 1985-86.

Maj. Gen. Laurence Kuter. AAF Historical Office: Washington, D.C., 1942.

Robert A. Lovett. HQ AAF, Intelligence: Washington, D.C. 1943.

Lt. Gen. Glen W. Martin. USAF Historical Division Liaison Office: Washington, D.C., 1966.

Paul H. Nitze. USAF Historical Research Center: Maxwell AFB, AL, 1981.

Dudley C. Sharp. USAF Historical Research Center: Maxwell AFB, AL, undated.

Gen. Carl Spaatz. HQ USSTAF History Office: Europe, 1945.

Gen. Carl Spaatz. USAF Historical Division, Liaison Office: Washington, D.C. 1962.

Gen. Carl Spaatz. USAF Historical Division, Liaison Office: Washington, D.C. 1965.

Gen. Carl Spaatz. Department of History: USAF Academy, CO, 1968.

Senator W. Stuart Symington USAF Historical Research Center, Maxwell AFB, AL, 1978.

Gen. Maxwell D. Taylor. Office of Air Force History: Washington, D.C. 1972.

Gen. Otto P. Weyland. USAF Historical Research Center: Maxwell AFB, AL, 1974.

Gen. Thomas D. White. USAF Historical Division, Liaison Office: Washington, D.C. 1961.

Roles and Missions

Lt. Gen. Kenneth Wolfe. Space Systems Division History Office, 1966.

Reports

Annual Report of the Chief of Air Service for the Fiscal Year Ending June 1922, Sep 9, 1922.

Annual Report of the Chief of Air Service for the Fiscal Year Ending June 30, 1923, Sep 13, 1923.

Annual Report of the Chief Signal Officer of the Army for Fiscal Year 1910, Sep 1, 1910.

Annual Report of the Secretary of the Air Force, for the Fiscal Year 1948.

Annual Report of the Secretary of the Navy for Fiscal Year 1920.

Annual Report of the Secretary of War, Dec 3, 1910.

Annual Report of the Secretary of War for 1918.

Annual Report of the Secretary of War for 1919.

Annual Report of the Secretary of War for 1934.

Arnold, Henry H. *First Report of the Commanding General of the Army Air Forces*, Jan 4, 1944.

Crowe, William J., Jr. *Chairman of the Joint Chiefs of Staff Report on Roles and Functions of the Armed Forces*, Sep 28, 1989.

Final Report of Gen. John J. Pershing, Commander in Chief, American Expeditionary Force. Washington, D.C.: GPO, 1920.

Final Report of the Chief of Air Service, AEF, Maj. Gen. Mason M. Patrick. Washington, D.C.: GPO, 1921.

Final Report of the War Department Special Committee on Army Air Corps, Jul 18, 1934.

Joint Board of the Army and the Navy. *Joint Action of the Army and the Navy*. Washington, D.C.: GPO, Apr 23, 1927.

Joint Board of the Army and the Navy. *Joint Action of the Army and the Navy*. Washington, D.C.: GPO, 1935.

King, Ernest J. *First Official Report of the Secretary of the Navy*, Mar 1, 1944.

Powell, Colin L. *Chairman of the Joint Chiefs of Staff Report on the Roles, Missions, and Functions of the Armed Forces of the United States*, Feb 1993.

Report of President's Aircraft Board. Washington, D.C.: GPO, Nov 30, 1925. Also called the Morrow Board.

Report of the Commission on Roles and Missions of the Armed Forces, May 28, 1995.

Report of the Joint Board on Results of Aviation an Ordnance Tests, Aug 29, 1921.

Report on Operations of the 1st Provisional Air Brigade in Naval Ordnance Tests, Aug 29, 1921.

Report on the Air Corps Mission Under the Monroe Doctrine. Study No. 44. Maxwell AFB, AL: The Air Corps Board, Oct 17, 1938.

Report on the Functions of the Army Air Forces. Study No. 31. Maxwell AFB, AL: The Air Corps Board, Oct 29, 1936.

Rice, Donald B. *A White Paper: Global Reach-Global Power.* Office of the Secretary of the Air Force, Jun 1990.

Semi-Annual Report of the Secretary of the Air Force, Jul-Dec 1949.

Survival in the Air Age: A Report by the President's Air Policy Commission. Washington, D.C.: GPO, 1948. Also called the Finletter Report.

U.S. House of Representatives Report No. 637. *Expenditures in the War Department-Aviation.* 66th Cong. Washington, D.C.: GPO, Feb 16, 1920.

Manuals and Regulations

Air Force Manual 1-1. *Functions and Basic Doctrine of the United States Air Force.* Feb 14, 1979.

Air Force Manual 1-1. *United States Air Force Basic Doctrine.* Aug 14, 1964.

Air Force Manual 1-1. *United States Air Force Basic Doctrine.* Sep 28, 1971.

Air Force Manual 1-1. *United States Air Force Basic Doctrine.* Jan 16, 1975.

Air Force Manual 1-2. *United States Air Force Basic Doctrine.* Mar 1953. Rev. Apr 1954 and Apr 1955.

Air Force Manual 1-2. *United States Air Force Basic Doctrine.* Dec 1, 1959.

Army Field Service Regulations, Feb 21, 1910.

Army Field Service Regulations, 1914, corrected to Apr 15, 1917.

Army Regulation No. 95-10. *Air Service-Air Service Troops.* Nov 17, 1921.

Army Regulation No. 95-10. *Air Corps.* Mar 10, 1928.

Training Regulation No. 440-15. *Air Corps. Employment of the Air Force of the Army.* Washington, D.C.: War Department, Oct 15, 1935.

Congressional Hearings

House. Hearings before the Committee on Armed Services. *Investigation of the B-36 Bomber Program.* 81st Cong., 1st sess. Washington, D.C.: GPO, 1949.

House. Hearings before the Committee on Armed Services. *Roles, Missions, and Functions of the Armed Forces of the United States.* 103d Cong., 1st sess. Washington, D.C.: GPO, 1993.

House. Hearings before the Committee on Armed Services. *The National Defense Program: Unification and Strategy.* 81st Cong., 1st sess. Washington, D.C.: GPO, Oct 1949.

House. Hearings before the Committee on Armed Services. *The Use of Force in the Post-Cold War Era.* 103d Cong., 1st sess. Washington, D.C.: GPO, 1993.

House. Hearings before the Investigative Subcommittee of the Committee on Armed Services. *Roles and Missions of Close Air Support.* 101st Cong., 2d sess. Washington, D.C.: GPO, 1991.

House. Hearings before the Subcommittee of the Committee on Appropriations. *Department of Defense Appropriations for 1961.* 86th Cong., 2d sess. Washington, D.C.: GPO, 1960.

Roles and Missions

Senate. Hearings before the Armed Services Committee. *Department of Defense Authorization for Appropriations for Fiscal Year 1994 and the Future Year Defense Programs, April-June 1993.* 103d Cong., 2d sess. Washington, D.C.: GPO, 1994.

Senate. Hearings before the Committee on Appropriations. *Department of Defense Appropriations for Fiscal Year 1994.* 103d Cong., 1st sess. Washington, D.C.: GPO, 1993.

Senate. Hearings before the Preparedness Investigating Subcommittee of the Committee on Armed Services. *Close Air Support.* 92d Cong., 1st sess. Washington, D.C.: GOP, 1972.

Senate. Hearings before the Subcommittee of the Committee on Armed Services. *A Study of Air Power.* 84th Cong., 2d sess. Washington, D.C.: GPO, 1956.

Non-Governmental Sources

Numerous non-governmental sources were helpful in researching and writing this study. The published memoirs of military leaders who were instrumental in making roles and missions history supplied useful insights. Billy Mitchell's *Memoirs of World War I* is an informative volume about roles and missions growth and other American air experience in the war. Another book which shares unique perspectives of an American air pioneer is Foulois' *From the Wright Brothers to the Astronauts.* George Kenney's *General Kenney Reports* contains useful information about AAF roles and missions in the Pacific during World War II. Tunner's *Over the Hump* does the same for airlift operations in the CBI during World War II. Hap Arnold's *Global Mission* gives the view from the top about some key roles and missions issues faced by the AAF during and after the war.

Some of the views of Navy leaders toward air power, including roles and missions, are contained in the memoirs of Adm. Arthur W. Radford, edited by Stephen Jurika, *From Pearl Harbor to Vietnam*; Ernest King's *Fleet Admiral King: A Naval Record*; and Chester Nimitz's *Sea Power: A Naval History.* Insights into Army views on the use of air power are found in Mark Clark's *Calculated Risk*; Ridgway's *Soldier: The Memoirs of Matthew B. Ridgway*; and Maxwell Taylor's *Swords and Plowshares* and *The Uncertain Trumpet.* Kingston-McCloughry's *The Direction of War* gives an insider's analysis of air warfare from the British perspective. Eisenhower's two volumes entitled *The White House Years* provide larger context for the post-Korean War years.

Biographies on military leaders are a rich source for information about major events and issues relating to roles and missions. Goldberg's portrait of Carl Spaatz in *The War Lords*, edited by Sir Michael Carver, and David Mets' biography of Spaatz, *Master of Airpower*, are essential to an understanding of Spaatz's place in the evolution of Air Force roles and missions. Coffey's *Hap* adds to the wealth of material about General Arnold and his career. Alfred Hurley's study of Billy Mitchell, *Crusader for Air Power*, established the pattern for biographies about America's pioneering airmen. Philip Meilinger's biography of Hoyt S. Vandenberg entitled *The Life of a General* contains important insights into Vandenberg's role before and during his tour as Air Force Chief of Staff.

Some general histories about the Air Force helped anchor the evolution of Air Force roles and missions, and served to verify key developments. Among these are Goldberg's history of the USAF, Dewitt Copp's *A Few Great Captains* and *Forged in Fire*, and David MacIsaac's *Strategic Bombing in World War Two: The Story of the United States Bombing Survey*. MacIsaac's book sheds needed light on the role of Major General Orvil Anderson in developing the Strategic Bombing Survey, and related interservice issues. Borowski's *A Hollow Threat: Strategic Air Power and Containment Before Korea* adds both analysis and context to this period in Air Force history. Richard P. Hallion's *Storm Over Iraq* provides timely insights into air power issues in the Gulf War. His book, *The Naval Air War in Korea*, covers the Navy's air role in the Korean War. The study of Air Force Roles and missions would not be complete without reading *The Army and Its Air Corps: A Study of the Evolution of Army Policy Towards Aviation*, a PhD dissertation by James C. Tate.

Relevant articles and essays on air matters are too numerous to treat in detail. Those that are cited in the footnotes to this study are listed below. As a general rule, anyone who plans to perform serious research into Air Force topics should undertake an early survey of such staple professional journals as *Air Power History*, published by the Air Force Historical Foundation, Washington, D.C.; *Air Power Journal*, the professional journal of the United States Air Force; *Military Review*, published by the U.S. Army Command and General Staff College, Fort Levenworth, KS; *Naval War College Review*, Newport, R.I.; and *U.S. Naval Institute Proceedings*, by the Naval Institute Press, Annapolis, MD. Formerly published as the *Air University Review*, the premier issue of the *Air Power Journal* was released by the Air University Press in the summer of 1987. *Air Power History*, which premiered in 1989, was published formerly as *Aerospace Historian*. Particularly relevant to this study was the inaugural of a new professional military journal, *Joint Forces Quarterly*, in the summer of 1993.

Books

Ambrose, Stephen E. *The Supreme Commander: The War Years of General Dwight D. Eisenhower*. Garden City, NY: Doubleday, 1970.

Arnold, H.H. *Global Mission*. New York: Harper, 1949.

Blumenson, Martin. *Kasserine Pass*. Boston: Houghton Miffin, 1967.

Blumenson, Martin. *The Patton Papers, 1940-1945*. Boston: Houghton Miffin, 1957.

Borowski, Harry R. *A Hollow Threat: Strategic Air Power and Containment Before Korea*. Westport, CT: Greenwood Press, 1982.

Bradley, Omar H. *A Soldier's Story*. New York: Holt, 1951.

Calambos, Louis, ed. *The Papers of Dwight D. Eisenhower: NATO and the Campaign of 1952: Vol XIII*. Baltimore and London: Johns Hopkins University Press, 1989.

Carver, Sir Michael, ed. *The War Lords: Military Commanders of the Twentieth Century*. Boston: Little Brown, 1976.

Roles and Missions

Clark, Mark W. *Calculated Risk*. New York: Harper & Brothers, 1950.

Clark, Mark W. *From the Danube to the Yalu*. New York: Harper & Brothers, 1954.

Coblenz, Constance C., *et al. United States Foreign Policy, 1945-1955*. Washington, D.C.: Brookings Institute, 1956.

Coffey, Thomas M. *Hap: The Story of the US Air Force and the Man Who Built It, General Henry H. "Hap" Arnold*. New York: Viking Press, 1982.

Copp, Dewitt S. *A Few Great Captains*. Garden City, NY: Doubleday, 1980.

Eisenhower, Dwight D. *The White House Years, 1953-1956: Mandate for Change*. Garden City, NY: Doubleday, 1963.

Eisenhower, Dwight D. *The White House Years, 1956-1961: Waging Peace*. Garden City, NY: Doubleday, 1965.

Foulois, Benjamin D., with Glines, C. V. *From the Wright Brothers to the Astronauts: The Memoirs of Major General Benjamin D. Foulois*. New York: McGraw-Hill, 1960.

Friedman, Norman. *The US Maritime Strategy*. New York: Jane's, 1988.

Gaddis, John Lewis. *Strategies of Containment*. New York: Oxford University Press, 1982.

Gavin, James M. *War and Peace in the Space Age*. New York: Harper, 1958.

George, James L., ed. *The U.S. Navy, The View From the 1980s*. Boulder, CO: Westview Press, 1985.

Goldberg, Alfred, ed. *A History of the United States Air Force, 1907-1957*. Princeton: D. Van Nostrand Co., 1957.

Greenfield, Kent Roberts. *American Strategy in World War II: A Reconsideration*. Baltimore: Johns Hopkins Press, 1963.

Greenfield, Kent Roberts. *The Historian and the Army*. New Brunswick, NJ: Rutgers University Press, 1954.

Hallion, Richard P. *Storm Over Iraq: Air Power and the Gulf War*. Washington, D.C.: Smithsonian Institute Press, 1992.

Hallion, Richard P. *The Naval Air War in Korea*. Baltimore: Nautical and Aviation Publishing Co. of America, 1986.

Hammond, Paul Y. *The Cold War Years: American Foreign Policy Since 1945*. New York: Harcourt, Brace & World, 1969.

Hurley, Alfred F. *Billy Mitchell: Crusader for Air Power*. New York: Franklin Watts, 1964.

Jurika, Stephen, Jr., ed. *From Pearl Harbor to Vietnam: The Memoirs of Admiral Arthur W. Radford*. Stanford, CA: Hoover Institution Press, 1980.

Kenney, George C. *General Kenney Reports*. New York: Duell, Sloan and Pearce, 1949.

King, Ernest J. and Whitehill, Walter M. *Fleet Admiral King: A Naval Record*. New York: DaCapo Press, 1976.

Kingston-McCloughry, Edgar James. *The Direction of War*. New York: F.A. Praeger, 1955.

Kissinger, Henry A. *Nuclear Weapons and Foreign Policy*. New York: Harper & Brothers, 1957.

Larrabee, Eric. *Commander in Chief*. New York: Harper & Row, 1987.

MacIsaac, David. *Strategic Bombing in World War Two: The Story of the United States Bombing Survey*. New York & London: Garland, 1976.

Meilinger, Philip S. *Hoyt S. Vandenburg: The Life of a General*. Bloomington: Indiana University Press, 1989.

Mersky, Peter B. *U.S. Marine Corps Aviation 1912 to the Present*. Annapolis: Nautical and Aviation Publishers, Inc., 1983.

Mets, David. *Master of Airpower: General Carl A. Spaatz*. Novato, CA: Presido Press, 1988.

Millis, Walter, ed. *The Forrestal Diaries*. New York: Viking Press, 1951.

Mingo, Howard. *American Heroes of the War in the Air*. Vol. I. New York: Lanciar Publishers, 1943.

Mitchell, William. *Memoirs of World War I*. New York: Random House, 1960.

Mitchell, William. *Our Air Force. The Key to National Defense*. New York: E.P. Dutton, 1921.

Nimitz, Chester W., and Potter, E.B., ed. *Sea Power: A Naval History*. Englewoods Cliffs, NJ: Prentice-Hall, 1960.

Oroln, Roderic. *Tedder*. London: Collins, 1952.

Paret, Peter, ed. *Makers of Modern Strategy*. Princeton, NJ: Princeton University Press, 1986.

Patrick, Mason M. *Military Aircraft and Their Use in Warfare*. Philidelphia: The Franklin Institute, 1924.

Patrick, Mason M. *The United States in the Air*. Garden City: Doubleday, 1928.

Possony, Stephen T. *Strategic Air Power: The Pattern of Dynamic Security*. Washington, D.C.: Infantry Journal Press, 1949.

Ridgway, Matthew B. *Soldier: The Memoirs of Matthew B. Ridgway*. New York: Harper & Brothers, 1956.

Schilling, Warner R., et al. *Strategy, Politics, and Defense Budgets*. New York: Columbia University Press, 1962.

Spector, Ronald H. *Eagle Against the Sun*. New York: Free Press, 1985.

Spiller, Roger J., ed. *Dictionary of American Bibliography, Volume III*. Westport, CT: Greenwood Press, 1984.

Stanley, Timothy W. *American Defense and National Security*. Washington, D.C.: Public Affairs Press, 1956.

Taylor, John M. *General Maxwell Taylor. The Sword and the Pen*. New York: Doubleday, 1989.

Taylor, Maxwell D. *Swords and Plowshares*. New York: W.W. Norton, 1972.

Taylor, Maxwell D. *The Uncertain Trumpet*. New York: Harper, 1960.

Terraine, John. *To Win a War*. Garden City, NY: Doubleday, 1981.

Tunner, William H. *Over the Hump*. New York: Duell, Sloan and Pearce, 1964.

Roles and Missions

Unpublished PhD Dissertation
Tate, James C. *The Army and Its Air Corps: A Study of the Evolution of Army Policy Towards Aviation*. Indiana University, 1976.

Periodicals

Amouyal, Barbara. "Powell Taps Air Force Close Air Support Mission," *Defense News* (Nov 3, 1989).

Anderson, Orvil A. "How Air Power Grew." *The Air Power Historian* (Apr 1956).

Armitage, M.J. "Air Concepts Today and Tomorrow." *The Hawk* The Independent Journal of the RAF Staff college (Feb 1981).

Baucum, Donald R. "Military Reform: An Idea Whose Time Has Come," *Air University Review* (Jan-Mar 1987).

Booda, Larry. "McNamara Pushing USAF-Army Rivalry." *Aviation Week and Space Technology* (Jan 14, 1963).

Booda, Larry. "USAF Army Roles Evolving Slowly," *Aviation Week and Space Technology* (May 27, 1967).

Brown, Harold. "The Persian Gulf and Southwest Asia," *Defense 80* (Jun 1980).

Butz, J.S. "Those Bombing North Vietnam." *Air Force Magazine* (Apr 1966).

Canan, James W. "The Ups and Downs of Jointness." *Air Force Magazine* (Oct 1985).

Cardwell, Thomas A., III "The Quest for Unity of Command." *Air University Review* (May-Jun 1984).

Chiarelli, Peter W. "Beyond Goldwater-Nichols," *Joint Forces Quarterly* (Autumn 1993).

Chipman, Donald D. and Major David Lay, "Sea Power and the B-52 Stratofortress," *Air University Review* (Jan-Feb 1986).

Cigar, Norman. "Soviet Aircraft Carriers, Unfortunate Timing for a Long-held Dream," *Naval War College Review* (Spring 1992).

Cimbala, Stephen J. "War Fighting, Deterrence, and Allied Cohesiveness." *Air University Review* (Sep-Oct 1984)

Clashow, Jason and Robert Holzer. "USAF Aggressively Guns for Roles," *Defense News* (Sep 12-18, 1994).

Cline, Ray S., and Matloff, Maurice. "Development of War Department Views on Unification." *Military Affairs* (Summer 1949).

Cooper, Charles D. "Interview with General Merrill A. McPeak," *The Retired Officer Magazine* (Jun 1991).

Correll, John T. "Roles and Missions Ride Again," *Air Force Magazine* (Feb 1995).

Dater, Henry M. "Needed-The History of American Aviation." *Military Affairs* (Winter 1953).

DeLauer, Richard D."Countering the Soviet Threat," *Defense 83* (Jun 1983).

Doolittle, James H. "Wasted Defense Billions." *Air Force* (Dec 1948).

Dow, Leonard F. "The Case for Genuine National Military Planning." *Air University Quarterly Review* (Summer 1960).

Eastman, Ford, "Army, Navy Reluctantly Back Space Edict," *Aviation Week* (Mar 27, 1961).

Ford, W.W. "Direct Support Aviation. It's Flying Artillery, So it Ought to be in the Army." *United States Army Combat Forces Journal* (Mar 1951).

Fuller, Thomas. "DoD in Space: A Historical Perspective," *Defense 88* (Dec 1988).

Galvin, John R. "Flexible Response & Forward Defense," *Defense 88* (Jul/Aug 1988).

Geelhoed, Bruce. "Executive at the Pentagon: Reexamining the Role of Charles E. Wilson in the Eisenhower Administration." *Military Affairs* (Feb 1980).

Hansell, Haywood S. "Balaklava Revisited." *Air University Review* (Sep-Oct 1974).

Herres, Robert T. "Making Interoperability & Jointness A Way of Life," *Defense 88* (Jan/Feb 1988).

Holley, I.B., Jr. "Of Saber Chargers, Escort Fighters, and Spacecraft." *Air University Review* (Sep-Oct 1983).

Huett, Marc. "Seapower Seen as Answer to Cut," *The Stars and Stripes* (Nov 24, 1967).

Huie, William Bradford. "A Navy or an Air Force?" *Readers Digest* (Dec 1948).

Huston, John W. "The Wartime Leadership of Hap Arnold." *Air Power and Warfare.* Proceedings of the 8th Military History Symposium, USAF Academy, October 18-20, 1978. Washington, D.C.: Office of Air Force History and the United States Air Force Academy, 1979.

Jones, David C. "Why the Joint Chiefs of Staff Must Change." *Armed Forces Journal International* (Mar 1982).

Kelso, Frank B. II. "The Wave of the Future," *Joint Forces Quarterly* (Summer 1993).

Krauskopf, Robert W. "The Army and the Strategic Bomber 1930-1939," *Military Affairs.*(Summer, 1958).

Kuehl, Daniel T. and Charles E. Miller. Roles, Missions, and Functions: Terms of Debate," *Joint Forces Quarterly* (Summer 1994).

Lahm, Frank P. "Commentary on Mitchell's Memoirs of World War I." *The Airpower Historian* (Jul 1962).

Lind, William S. "JCS Reform: Can Congress Take on a Tough One?" *Air University Review* (Sep-Oct 1985.)

Lynch, David J. "The Air Force Takes Stock." *Air Force Magazine* (Feb 1993).

MacKay, E.J. "The Influence in the Future of Aircraft Upon Problems of Imperial Defense." *Journal, R.U.S.I.* (May 1922).

Mackubin, Thomas Owens. "Accountants vs. Strategists: The New Roles and Missions Debate," *Strategic Review* (Fall 1992).

Maddox, Bobby J. "Army Aviation Branch Implementation." *U.S Army Aviation* (Aug 1993).

McKitrick, Jeffrey S. "The JCS: Evolutionary or Revolutionary Reform? *Parameters* (Spring 1986).

Meyer, Edward C. "The JCS-How Much Reform is Needed?" *Armed Forces Journal International* (Apr 1982).

Roles and Missions

Millett, Alan R. "The U.S. Marine Corps: Adaptation in the Post-Vietnam Era." *Armed Forces and Society* (Spring 1983).

Milton, T.R. "The Quest for Unity," *Air Force Magazine* (Jan 1986).

Mitchell, William. "Aviation Over the Water," *The American Review of Reviews* (Oct 1920).

Mitchell, William. "Our Army's Air Service." *The American Reviews of Reviews* (1920).

Mitchell, William. "The Bombing of the Battleships." *The Air Power Historian* (Apr 1957).

Moody, Walton S. "United States Air Force in Europe and the Beginning of the Cold War." *Aerospace Historian* (Summer-Jun 1976).

Office of the Secretary of Defense. "Air War in Korea." *Air University Quarterly Review* (Fall 1950).

Oslon, Robert A. "Air Mobility for the Army." *Military Affairs* (Winter 1964-1965).

Parrish, Noel F. "Vandenberg: Rebuilding the 'Shoestring Air Force." *Air Force Magazine* (Aug 1981).

Powell, Colin L. "Budget for a World Turned Upside Down," *Defense 93* (Mar/Apr 1993).

Putney, Diane T. "From Instant Thunder to Desert Storm: Developing the Gulf War Air Campaign Phases," *Air Power History* (Fall 1994).

Rees, Ed. "A Tribute to Dutch Kindleberger." *The Airpower Historian* (Oct 1962).

Schlight, John. "Civilian Control of the Military in Southeast Asia." *Air University Review* (Nov 1980).

Sharp, U.S. Grant. "We Could Have Won in Vietnam Long Ago." *Readers Digest* (May 1969).

Simpson, Albert F. "Tactical Air Doctrine: Tunisia and Korea." *A University Quarterly Review* (Summer 1951).

Skelton, Ike. "Taking Stock of a New Era," *Joint Forces Quarterly* (Winter 1993-94).

Spaatz, Carl. "Middle Way the Wise Way." *Newsweek* (Apr 14, 1958).

Spaatz, Carl. "Military Tides 'A Matter of Life or Death.'" *Newsweek* (Jun 4, 1956)

Spaatz, Carl. "National Defense Without National Bankruptcy...An Answer to General Ridgway." *Newsweek* (Jan 30, 1954).

Spaatz, Carl. "Let's Reorganize Defense." *Newsweek* (Jan 30, 1955).

Spaatz, Carl. "Strategic Air Power, Fulfillment of a Concept." *Foreign Affairs* (Apr 1946.)

Spaatz, Carl. "The New Look in Warfare." *Newsweek* (September 21, 1953).

Spaatz, Carl. "Where We Went Wrong-A Plan for the Future." *Newsweek* (Dec 30, 1957).

Thomas Evan. "Bashing Gaddafi has not Quieted the Pentagon's Critics," *Time* (Apr 14, 1986).

Tormaen, George E. "Political Air Superiority in the Korean Conflict." *Air University Quarterly Review* (Winter 1953-1954).

Trest, Warren A. "A View From the Gallery: Laying to Rest the Admiral's Revolt of 1949." *Air Power History* (Spring 1995).

Trest, Warren A. "The Legacy of Halfway Unification." *Air University Review* (Sep-Oct 1986).

Vandenberg, Hoyt S. "The Truth About Our Air Power." *Saturday Evening Post* (Feb 17, 1951).

Weinberger, Caspar W. "The Reality of the Soviet Threat," *Defense 83* (Jun 1983).

Weinberger, Caspar W. "The Rearming of America," *Defense 81* (Dec 1981).

Weinberger, Caspar W. "The Uses of Military Power," *Defense 85* (Jun 1985).

Weinberger, Caspar W. "What is Our Defense Strategy?" *Defense 85* (Dec 1985).

Wells, Samual F., Jr. "William Mitchell and the Ostfriesland: A Study in Military Reform," *The Historian* (Aug 1964).

Weyland, Otto P. "The Air Campaign in Korea." *Air University Quarterly Review* (Fall 1953).

White, Thomas D. "The Air Force Getting Down to New Business." *Newsweek* (May 13, 1963).

White, Thomas D. "What's Wrong With Civil Military Relations." *Newsweek* (May 27, 1963).

Williams, Edwin L. Jr. "Legislative History of the Air Arm," *Military Affairs* (Summer 1956).

Williams, Raymond C. "Skybolts and American Foreign Policy." *Military Affairs* (Fall 1966).

Witze, Claude O. "Administration Hits Airpower Opponents," *Aviation Week* (May 14, 1956).

Wolk, Herman S. "A Wartime Leader." Airman (Jul 1985).

Young, Susan H.H. "Gallery of Air Force Weapons," *Air Force Magazine* (May 1994).

Zimmerman, Don. "FEAF: Mission and Command Relationships." *Air University Quarterly Review* (Summer 1951).

Symposia: Published Proceedings

Borowski, Harry R., ed. *Military Planning in the Twentieth Century: Proceedings of the Eleventh Military History Symposium, USAF Academy, 10-12 Oct 1984*. Washington, D.C.: GPO, 1986.

Dixon, Joe C., ed. *The American Military and the Far East: Proceedings of the Ninth Military History Symposium, USAF Academy, 1-3 Oct 1980*. Washington, D.C.: GPO, 1980.

Hurley, Alfred F. and Robert C. Ehrhart, eds. Air Power and Warfare: Proceedings of the Eighth Military History Symposium, USAF Academy, 18-20 Oct 1978. Washington, D.C.: GPO, 1979.

Index

Roles and Missions

Roles and Missions